In Time's eye

In Time's eye

Essays on Rudyard Kipling

Edited by
JAN MONTEFIORE

Manchester University Press

Copyright © Manchester University Press 2013

While copyright in the volume as a whole is vested in Manchester University Press, copyright in individual chapters belongs to their respective authors, and no chapter may be reproduced wholly or in part without the express permission in writing of both author and publisher.

Published by Manchester University Press
Altrincham Street, Manchester M1 7JA, UK
www.manchesteruniversitypress.co.uk

British Library Cataloguing-in-Publication Data is available

Library of Congress Cataloging-in-Publication Data is available

ISBN 978 1 5261 0693 3 *paperback*

First published by Manchester University Press in hardback 2013

This edition first published 2016

The publisher has no responsibility for the persistence or accuracy of URLs for any external or third-party internet websites referred to in this book, and does not guarantee that any content on such websites is, or will remain, accurate or appropriate.

Printed by Lightning Source

Contents

	List of contributors	*page* vii
	Foreword and acknowledgements	ix
1	Introduction – JAN MONTEFIORE	1
2	Rudyard Kipling (1905) – G.K. CHESTERTON	22
3	Rudyard Kipling (1942) – GEORGE ORWELL	28
4	On preparing to read Kipling (1961) – RANDALL JARRELL	42
5	Kipling in South Africa – DAN JACOBSON	58
6	The Great War and Rudyard Kipling – HUGH BROGAN	73
7	'A Kipling-conditioned world': Kipling among the war poets – HARRY RICKETTS	91
8	*Actions and Reactions*: Kipling's Edwardian summer – DANIEL KARLIN	111
9	Rikki-Tikki-Tavi and Indian history – LISA LEWIS	129
10	The young Kipling's search for God – CHARLES ALLEN	142
11	Vagabondage in Rajasthan: Kipling's North Indian travels – JAN MONTEFIORE	159
12	Kipling's 'vernacular': what he knew of it – and what he made of it – HARISH TRIVEDI	177
13	Quotations and boundaries: *Stalky & Co.* – KAORI NAGAI	207
14	Kipling, 'beastliness' and *Soldatenliebe* – HOWARD J. BOOTH	225
15	'A race to leave alone': Kipling and the Jews – BRYAN CHEYETTE	250
	Select bibliography	285
	Index	292

Contributors

Charles Allen is a writer and historian. His many books include *Plain Tales from the Raj* (1975), *The Buddha and the Sahibs* (2002), *Kipling Sahib: India and the Making of Rudyard Kipling* (2007) and most recently *The Taj at Apollo Bunder* (2011).

Howard J. Booth is Lecturer in English Literature at the University of Manchester. The author of many articles on nineteenth- and twentieth-century literature, he is the co-editor of *Modernism and Empire* (with Nigel Rigby, 2000), and editor of *New D.H. Lawrence* (2009) and *The Cambridge Companion to Rudyard Kipling* (2011).

Hugh Brogan is a Research Professor of History at Essex University. His publications include the *Longman History of the United States* (1985, 1999), *Mowgli's Sons: Kipling and Baden-Powell's Scouts* (1987) and most recently *Alexis de Tocqueville: A Biography* (2006).

Bryan Cheyette is Professor of English Literature at Reading University. His publications include *Constructions of 'the Jew' in English Literature and Society* (1993), *Between 'Race' and Culture: Representations of 'the Jew' in English and American Literature* (ed. 1996) and *Muriel Spark* (2000). His most recent book is *Diasporas of the Mind: British Jews and the Nightmare of History* (forthcoming, 2013).

Dan Jacobson is a novelist and Emeritus Professor at University College, London. His books include *Time of Arrival* (1963), *Beggar My Neighbour* (1964), *The Confessions of Joseph Baisz* (1977) and most recently *All for Love* (2005).

Daniel Karlin, Professor of English Literature at Bristol University, is an authority on Victorian literature. His publications include *Robert Browning* (with John Woolford, 1996) and *Proust's English* (2005); editions of Kipling's *The Jungle Books* (1987), *Rudyard Kipling: Selected Poetry and Prose* (1999) and *The Penguin Book of Victorian Verse* (1997); and numerous essays on Kipling, Browning and other writers, Victorian and modern.

Lisa Lewis, Vice-President of the Kipling Society, is a Kipling scholar and critic. She edited Kipling's *Just-So Stories* (1995) and *Rudyard Kipling: Writings on Writing* (with Sandra Kemp, 1996), and has published numerous essays on Kipling including 'T.S. Eliot and Kipling' (1993), 'The manuscript of *Kim*' (2001), 'Seeing things: repetitions and images in "They"' (2004) and 'The Cat that walked with the Daemon' (2007).

Jan Montefiore is Professor of Twentieth-Century English Literature at Kent University. Her books include *Feminism and Poetry* (1987, 2004), *Men and Women Writers of the 1930s* (1996) and *Rudyard Kipling* (2007). She has edited Kipling's *The Man Who Would Be King and Other Stories* for Penguin Classics (2001) and is general editor of Kipling titles in this series. From 2013 she is editor of the *Kipling Journal*.

Kaori Nagai teaches at Kent University. She is the author of *Empire of Analogies: Kipling, India and Ireland* (2007) and co-editor (with Caroline Rooney) of *Kipling and Beyond: Patriotism, Globalism and Postcolonialism*. She edited Kipling's *Plain Tales from the Hills* (2011) and *The Jungle Books* (2013) for Penguin Classics.

Harry Ricketts is a poet, Professor in the Department of English, Film, Theatre and Media Studies at Victoria University of Wellington, New Zealand, and author of *The Unforgiving Minute: A Life of Rudyard Kipling* (1999). His other books include *99 Ways into New Zealand Poetry* (with Paula Green, 2010), *Strange Meetings: The Poets of the First World War* (2010), and most recently *Just Then* (2011).

Harish Trivedi is former Professor of English, University of Delhi. His publications include *Colonial Transactions: English Literature and India* (1993; reprinted 1995, 2013); *Literature and Nation: Britain and India 1800–1990* (ed. with Richard Allen, 1999); and *Interrogating Post-Colonialism: Theory, Text and Context* (ed. with Meenakshi Mukherjee 1996; reprinted 2000, 2006, 2013). He edited, with an introduction and notes, *Kim* for Penguin Classics (2011) and has contributed a chapter on 'Reading Kipling in India' to *The Cambridge Companion to Kipling* (2011).

Foreword and acknowledgements

This collection of essays on Kipling was inspired by the 2007 conference in Canterbury, sponsored by the Kipling Society, commemorating the centenary of award of the Nobel Prize to Rudyard Kipling in 1907, three of its chapters being based on papers given at that conference. Its overarching theme is Kipling's writing in relation to history, which these essays address in different ways and from different perspectives. Covering a wide range of Kipling's poetry and prose, their themes include:

- the changing perceptions of Kipling's writing in and after his lifetime, represented by the first three essays by G.K. Chesterton (1905), George Orwell (1942) and Randall Jarrell (1961);
- Kipling's response to the historical moment he lived through, including his experience of colonial India, his knowledge of Indian 'vernacular' and his perceptions both of recent colonial history such as the 'Mutiny' or 'First Great Rebellion', still a living memory to many in India when Kipling was writing his first work, and of a remoter Indian past which he glimpsed during his travels in Rajasthan in 1887;
- his response as a writer and a patriot to the South African War and its aftermath;
- his perception of the tensions of Edwardian Britain, looking back at the 'Old England' he loved and forward to its perhaps threatened future;
- his political stance in the First World War; and
- his increasingly embittered and right-wing post-war views and their effect on his writing.

Chapters on the politics of literary quotation in the era of high imperialism and on the relationship between Kipling's ideal of Englishness and the soldier-poets of the First World War locate Kipling's writing in its contemporary political context. Discussion of British and imperial politics shades into cultural history in the chapter on Kipling and homosexuality; so in a different way does the chapter on Kipling and the Jews, since British anti-Semitism was influenced by public events such as the role played by Jewish financiers in supporting Britain in the South African war as well as by inherited prejudice.

George Orwell's essay 'Rudyard Kipling' is reprinted here by kind permission of the Orwell Estate and A.M. Heath & Co.; Randall Jarrell's 'On preparing to read Kipling' is reprinted by kind permission of Carcanet Press. A version of Dan Jacobson's 'Kipling in South Africa' appeared in the *London Review of Books* (1993). A shorter version of Kaori Nagai's 'Quotations and boundaries' was published in Japanese in Kazuhisa Takahashi and Makinori Hashimoto (eds), *Rudyard Kipling: Sakuhin to Hihyou* [Works and Criticisms] (Tokyo: Hakushosha, 2003), pp. 309–28. Earlier versions of the following appeared in the *Kipling Journal*: Hugh Brogan's 'The Great War and Rudyard Kipling' (1997), Lisa Lewis 'Rikki Tikki and Indian history' (as 'Rikki revisited', 2000), Charles Allen 'The young Kipling's search for God' ('Ruddy's search for God', 2007), Daniel Karlin '*Actions and Reactions:* Kipling's Edwardian summer' (2009).

1

Introduction

JAN MONTEFIORE

> Cities and Thrones and Powers
> Stand in Time's eye
> Almost as long as flowers
> Which daily die.[1]

Kipling's brief elegy for the vanity of human deeds brings together three themes of this collection of essays: the subjection of his own work and reputation to those processes of time and change of which his poem warns; his relationship to historical institutions of rule and dominance named as 'Thrones and Powers'; and his many-sided artistry, manifested in this ironic vision of the fall of ancient empires mediated through echoes of Milton and Herrick.[2]

An account of Kipling 'in Time's eye' necessarily begins with the changes in his reception, here represented in capsule form by the first three essays from G.K. Chesterton (1905), George Orwell (1942) and Randall Jarrell (1961). His reputation has been notoriously changeable since he arrived in London in 1890 as the young genius from India who in one year had had 'more said about his work, over a wider extent of the world's surface, than some of the greatest of England's writers in their whole lives',[3] in 1895 was sounded out as a possible successor to Tennyson as Poet Laureate,[4] and whose near-death from pneumonia in 1899 was headline news in three continents. Praise was never undiluted: his 'vulgarity' was mocked by Oscar Wilde and attacked by Robert Buchanan and, more devastatingly, Max Beerbohm;[5] and as Kipling's imperialist opinions became more strident after the Boer War he lost the esteem of British literary intellectuals, whom he in turn despised (his close friends included no fellow writer except Rider Haggard, author of thrillingly mythopoeic imperialist fantasy novels). Though Kipling was awarded the Nobel Prize in 1907 for his contribution to world literature, was immensely popular in Britain and the USA and much admired in France, the beginning of his declining reputation at home can be seen in G.K. Chesterton's brief but telling 1905 critique which, while taking Kipling's importance for granted, finds his vision profoundly flawed by its fascination with the seductive machinery of power and speed. This decline increased after the First World War; Kipling's identification with right-wing patriotism did him no good with the disillusioned ex-soldiers Edmund Blunden and Siegfried Sassoon who, as Harry Ricketts shows here, received both his *History of the Irish Guards* and his war poems less than enthusiastically, while his stories' contribution to the postwar literature of mourning was largely ignored. Although the *Jungle Books*, the *Just-So Stories*, the 'Puck' books and *Kim* continued to be widely read and loved by British middle-class children throughout the twentieth century, Kipling's work for adults was increasingly read in terms of 'plain man' conservatism, and the sermonising or demotic poetry which had made him a national institution in late Victorian England became a standing joke to intellectuals. Virginia Woolf mocked his 'Sowers who sow the Seed, and Men who are alone with their Work, and the Flag';[6] T.S. Eliot's more complex views ranged from mockery and affectionate parody to creative engagement with the numinous stories, and an edited anthology of Kipling's poems with a long preface deliberating on his status as a writer, concluding equivocally that his 'great verse' occasionally rose to poetry.[7] Orwell's response to Eliot's anthology indicates how low Kipling was rated in the early 1940s; arguing that for fifty years 'every enlightened person has despised him, and at the end of that time nine-tenths of those enlightened persons are forgotten and Kipling is in some sense still there', his critical but even-handed discussion of Kipling's politics ends by defining him as a 'good bad poet' whose virtues and faults belong to popular culture rather than literature. (Orwell has little to say about Kipling's fiction apart from criticising its 'crudity').

Kipling's literary reputation began to recover once critics turned their attention to his prose.[8] Reappraisals of Kipling published around the centenary of his birth focus not on his success or failure as an ideologue but on his achievement as a writer of stories. Randall Jarrell's preface to his 1961 selection of Kipling's stories, 'On preparing to read Kipling', praises Kipling's extraordinary imagination and verbal finish, discussing him as an artist comparable with Chekhov and Goya; the same point was made, less flamboyantly, in the title of J.M.S. Tompkins' *The Art of Rudyard Kipling* (1959), and repeated with variations by C.A. Bodelsen (1964), and Andrew Rutherford (1964),[9] who all emphasise Kipling's achievement as a writer of imaginative prose, as does Elliott Gilbert's study of his stories *The Good Kipling* (1972).[10] Jarrell also made a persuasive post-Freudian case for reading Kipling's conscious identification with authority as the effect of a traumatised childhood, an approach followed a generation later in Sandra Kemp's study of his stories (1988) and Zohreh Sullivan's psychoanalytic account of his Indian fiction (1993).[11] The critics of the 1960s all emphasised Kipling's standing as a major literary figure because they couldn't take this for granted. Twenty-first-century readers on the whole do; none of the contributors to this book, whether or not they approve of Kipling's politics, feels it necessary to make a literary case for him. (Hugh Brogan's defence of his poetry in the First World War, the sole apparent exception, is concerned with not with Kipling's literary artistry but with his political intelligence.)

But Kipling's changing reputation is only one aspect of his place in history, the overriding theme of this book. Unlike Caroline Rooney's and Kaori Nagai's 2010 collection of post-colonial readings of Kipling's work which relate the 'imperialist nostalgia' of his work to the politics of globalisation, or the collective overviews of Kipling's *oeuvre* in *The Cambridge Companion to Rudyard Kipling* edited by Howard Booth (2011),[12] the recent and new essays in this book read Kipling's work in terms of his relation to different aspects of history. These include his response to and understanding of colonial and pre-colonial India, addressed in different ways by Lisa Lewis, Harish Trivedi, Charles Allen and me; his views of the South African War, discussed by Dan Jacobson, and of the First World War, by Hugh Brogan; his apprehension of the traditions of rooted Englishness, approached in different terms by Harry Ricketts and Daniel Karlin; the cultural politics of his literary awareness and of his ideal of masculinity analysed respectively by Kaori Nagai and Howard Booth; and Bryan Cheyette's analysis of the relation between the racial prejudice against Jews that appears in his work and the fortunes of British imperial power in his lifetime. All draw in different ways on the previously uncollected and/or unpublished work which has become available since the mid-1980s thanks to the ongoing work of editors, especially Thomas Pinney (whose three-volume edition of Kipling's poetry by Cambridge University Press is about to come out as I write in 2012). Andrew Rutherford's 1985 edition of Kipling's *Early Verse* showed the youthful Kipling as an unexpectedly playful, literary and self-conscious as well as prolific poet; Pinney's editions of his early journalism in *Kipling's India* (1986), of *Something of Myself* (1990) with unpublished autobiographical material, and especially of the six volumes of Kipling's letters (1990–2004),[13] give invaluable new information about Kipling's experiences, relationships and opinions. It is now possible to compare Kipling's own account of his 'Seven years' Hard' in India as a young journalist with contemporary evidence of his opinions and movements. The later letters to Rupert Gwynne, Max Aitken and Lord Milner reveal a great deal about his engagement with public events, notably the Boer War and the First World War, sometimes in ways Kipling's admirers may not welcome; Kipling's bald statement to Max Aitken – quoted here by Bryan Cheyette about 'Gehazi', his allegorical satire on Rufus Isaacs' insider dealing in the Marconi Affair – that 'I wrote it for that Jew-boy on the Bench' nails the poem as incontrovertibly anti-Semitic.[14] These letters, and the increased knowledge of Kipling's historical, family and political context and of his contemporary critical reception made available in recent biographies by Andrew Lycett (1999) and others,[15] have been crucial for historicist and post-colonial readings of Kipling's work and its relationship with contemporary debates and power struggles. To be aware, for instance, that the Indian National Congress first met and named itself in December 1885, which happens to be the month when Kipling published 'The Strange Ride of Morrowbie Jukes', and that the furore aroused three years later by Kipling's intensely hostile report of the Congress' meeting in December 1888 in the *Pioneer* helped to prompt his departure from India in 1889,[16] points up the political anxiety implicit in the characterisations of the sinister Gunga Dass in 'Morrowbie Jukes' and the more subtly comic Hurree Babu of *Kim* (which is not, of course, to say that either is simply reducible to his creator's fear and anger at Indian nationalism).[17] The discussions by Dan Jacobson of Kipling's responses to the Boer War and its implications for the British Empire, by Howard Booth of his conceptions of sexual identity and of masculine friendship, by me of the 'Letters of Marque', and by Bryan Cheyette of the attitudes to Jews in Kipling's fiction throughout his lifetime, all draw on this new evidence, especially that of the letters.

The movement towards historicised readings of Kipling's work is, of course, itself part of much broader changes in biographical writing and literary historiography. The difference between Carrington's fairly reticent authorised biography (1955) and the new accounts of Kipling's life by Lycett, Ricketts and others belong to a general turn by British biographers since 1980 towards detailed, deeply contextualised, sexually candid life-writing, while recent biographies of Kipling's mother and her sisters, his son John and his wife Carrie[18] are part of a widely based move to retrieve the stories of marginalised lives. Kipling has also been the subject of what Max Saunders calls 'biografiction',[19] sympathetically in Jane Gardam's poignant re-working of Kipling's story 'Baa Baa Black Sheep' in her novel *Old Filth* (2004) and, less subtly but probably more influentially, in David Haig's 1997 play *My Boy Jack*,[20] which casts Kipling as an Oedipal stage villain in the form of a jingo father blindly destroying the son in whom he invests his hopes. These are not scholarly works (as Hugh Brogan points out, Haig distorted the facts to suit his own version of the Kiplings' family history), but the play's success on the stage and TV has doubtless influenced popular perceptions. It is a poignant irony that the man who wrote the accusatory couplet for the war dead 'If any question why we died / Tell them, because our fathers lied',[21] should have been known to viewers only as the self-deceiving embodiment of his own epigram.

Another change in the interpretations of Kipling's work is a new emphasis on its relations with modernism, especially in the stories he wrote during the first decades of the twentieth century, which are commonly regarded as the 'moment' of modernist writing. This is not just a matter of the fascination with new technologies of transport and communication noticed by Chesterton, which inspired Kipling to celebrate speed in the poems 'The Secret of the Machines' and 'Deep-Sea Cables'; the abolition of spatial distance by cinema, the motor car, and air transport in the stories 'Mrs Bathurst', '"They"' and 'With the Night Mail'; and the exploration of the uncanny power of radio and of the Fleet Street Press in 'Wireless' and 'The Village that Voted The Earth Was Flat'. The son of a couple whose courtship began by swapping quotations from Browning[22] became from his mid-teens both an accomplished writer of parody, a genre whose self-conscious literariness links Victorian and modernist literature, and a brilliant stylistic magpie who borrowed as easily from music-hall songs or Lewis Carroll as from the King James Bible and Anglican hymns. The quotations in his stories, whose political implications in *Stalky & Co.* Kaori Nagai analyses here, very often 'place' their speakers' taste, as when the would-be writer Charlie in 'The Finest Story in the World' responds to Longfellow's poetry with compelling memories of an earlier life, until he falls in love with a second-rate girl who inspires him to ecstatic sub-Swinburne spoutings (taken from Kipling's own juvenilia).[23] The pared-down, ironic stories narrated by his not-always-reliable

'I', and the multiple voices of his poems which are only rarely to be identified with Rudyard Kipling the author, show an awareness of their own artificiality associated with classic modernist texts. Kipling indeed has much in common with some practitioners of high modernism: his stagy performances of demotic coarse vitality in *Barrack Room Ballads* anticipate the work of his admirer Bertolt Brecht, and his poetry's different voices and brilliant parodies, together with his intimations of a numinous 'horror of great darkness' in the most ordinary of middle-class lives, links his work with that of T.S. Eliot. Moreover, as the term 'modernism' has itself been re-worked and historicised in critical narratives which contest both the dominance of a narrow canon of high modernist literature produced between 1900 and 1930 and the binary opposition 'modernist/realist', preferring to read both Victorian and twentieth-century texts as 'cultural formations' inflected by specific socio-historical conditions,[24] so Kipling's work looks less solidly Victorian and more like 'cross-over' writing. Kipling's connections with modernist literature appear here both in Daniel Karlin's reading of the interlinked short stories of *Actions and Reactions* as an ambivalent celebration of an Englishness associated with 'different forms of inauthenticity', and Harry Ricketts' analysis of Kipling's literary links with the poets of the Great War, tracing his imprint both on the 'Georgian' Siegfried Sassoon and Rupert Brooke and the 'modernist' Ivor Gurney and David Jones. A more historicist emphasis is evident in Bryan Cheyette's analysis of Kipling's post-war representations of Jews as increasingly disturbed and paranoid responses to successive crises in British imperial power.

Cheyette's essay also shows how literary readings of Kipling have become increasingly politicised, as he has become the target of critiques from members of those social, racial or sexual categories which were excluded from power by the imperial hierarchy which he idealised, and which appear in his work as despicable, or sinister, or marginalised – or all three, like the Jews in his late stories. Since the illuminating studies by Sandra Kemp and Nora Crook (1990) of the association of women with numinous forces and with the powerful currents of unconscious desires and fears in Kipling's stories,[25] not much has been written on Kipling's representations of women, probably because his antifeminism is too obvious to invite comment.[26] (Not that Kipling was a misogynist; his stories contain many admirable, tough and likeable female characters, and genuine sympathy is implied in his 'Harp-Song of the Dane Women' and 'My Boy Jack' for the hard lot of their anxious female speakers; while the harrowing chapter 'Memorial Day' in *Captains*

Courageous explicitly insists on the heavy price paid by wives and mothers in loneliness and frequent bereavement for the masculine freedom, skill and camaraderie celebrated in this novel. But sympathy with suffering is not the same thing as allying oneself with the sufferers, and Kipling had little time for women's rights.) The question of masculinity in Kipling's writings, however, has been much discussed; the cult of manliness which he shared with other conservative late Victorian male writers of adventure stories analysed by Lyn Pykett (1995), Joseph Bristow (1991) and Kucich (2007)[27] is raised both in Kaori Nagai's discussion of the formative values of the imperial officers in the making during their schooldays in *Stalky & Co.* and in Howard Booth's analysis of Kipling's fierce repudiation of homosexuality and of the uneasy relationship with contemporary homosexual sub-cultures implied in the nostalgia for army masculinity and male friendship which informs *The Light That Failed*.

Still more influential on the reception of Kipling's writings has been the work of post-colonial critics since Edward Said's dissection of the notion of the 'White Man' in *Orientalism* (1978), and the ideal of timeless, conflict-free India in *Kim*[28] followed by Suleri (1992) and Sullivan analysing the conflicted anxiety and vulnerability underlying these colonial ideals, and Don Randall (2000) and John McBratney (2002) discussing the ambivalence and hybridity of Kipling's imperialist mythologies.[29] These readers, like the Marxist Brecht who admired Kipling for writing directly and unapologetically about power and imperialism, do not agree with Auden that 'Time . . . pardoned Kipling and his views' because he wrote well,[30] arguing conversely that the lasting interest of Kipling's work lies precisely in his imperialist 'views' (which they do not pardon) and in the questions which these raise about identity and representation, power and knowledge – all still issues of debate and violence in our contemporary political world.[31] Post-colonial criticism is most obviously represented here in Kaori Nagai's analysis of knowledge and authority in *Stalky & Co.* and Harish Trivedi's lively scrutiny of Kipling's understanding (or not) of Indian 'vernacular' while an alien and critical eye is brought to bear on Kipling's racism by Dan Jacobson explaining how Kipling's conception of 'racial' divisions between Dutch and English settlers and his total indifference to black Africans ('Kaffirs'), appears to one who grew up in a racially divided South Africa, and by Bryan Cheyette tracing Kipling's representations of Jews, those white men who aren't really white, from early ambivalence through a brief moment of 'philo-Semitism', to outright hatred and contempt.

In structuring this essay collection I have followed Andrew Rutherford's landmark critical anthology *Kipling's Mind and Art*, starting with some key early assessments from G.K. Chesterton contesting Kipling's credentials as a national poet, George Orwell's retrospective assessment of his 'bouncing vulgar vitality' and his one-eyed but real 'sense of responsibility', and Randall Jarrell's case for the artistry of his short stories. These early overviews are followed by a mixture of reprinted essays, some from the 1990s and some more recent, by Dan Jacobson, Hugh Brogan, Lisa Lewis, Daniel Karlin, Charles Allen and Kaori Nagai, and new material written for this book by me, Harish Trivedi, Harry Ricketts, Howard Booth and Bryan Cheyette. These appear in more or less chronological order, with some exceptions to allow for connections of theme, so that Hugh Brogan on Kipling's poetry of the First World War is followed by Harry Ricketts on Kipling and the war poets, Ricketts' discussion of 'Albionism' by Daniel Karlin on Kipling's vision of England in *Actions and Reactions*, and Kaori Nagai's essay on the politics of quotation in the 'Stalky' stories follows Harish Trivedi's account of Kipling's less than scholarly knowledge of Indian vernacular languages.

Chesterton's brief but seminal essay 'Rudyard Kipling', first published in *Heretics* (1905), a book of theologically based cultural criticism (the essay on Kipling appears between an attack on the emptiness of 'modern morality' as compared with the wisdom of the Church and a critique of Shaw's limitations as a secular thinker[32]), shows how Kipling struck an anti-imperialist Christian contemporary. The first to salute the importance of Kipling's 'philosophy of steam and slang' which makes poetry of taken-for-granted ordinariness, Chesterton was also the first to perceive the centrality of discipline in Kipling's thinking (an insight later expanded by C.S. Lewis analysing the significance of work and discipline in the essay 'Kipling's World'):[33] 'What attracts Mr Kipling to militarism is not the idea of courage but the idea of discipline . . . The modern army is not a miracle of courage . . . but it is really a miracle of organisation, and that is the true Kiplingite ideal.' Like Orwell, Chesterton grants Kipling's disciplinarian ethic a certain grip on the realities of life ('We may fling ourselves into a hammock in a fit of divine carelessness. But we are glad the net-maker did not create the hammock in a fit of divine carelessness'), and he anticipates recent critics in locating Kipling among the modernists – but for him this is not a compliment. He calls Kipling a cosmopolitan without roots, a worshipper of the State machine who 'admires England because she is strong, not because she is English', utterly seduced by the modern 'motor-car civilisation going on its triumphant way, outstripping time, consuming space, seeing all and seeing nothing'. The unfairness of this accusation that Kipling has no interest in traditional Englishness is obvious (he was to celebrate the 'Old England' of his corner of Sussex in *Puck of Pook's Hill* only a year after this essay appeared) but also telling. Envisaging Kipling as part of the development of a global modernism superseding everything local and rooted, Chesterton's appeal to 'the real life of man' going on in fields and homes untouched by modernity rests on the conservative ideal, which both men shared, of a richly storied, immemorial England opposed to the rush and hurry of globalised modernity. Chesterton's critique of Kipling's modernity thus obliquely makes an implicit case for the Englishness of the 'Puck' books; he had more in common with his opponent than he realised.

Orwell's 1942 essay answers Chesterton's critique, though not intentionally, by reading Kipling not as a modern power-worshipper but as a conservative whose enduring claim to be taken seriously lies in his understanding of the realities of power and responsibility: 'One may disagree to the middle of one's bones with the political attitude implied in 'The Islanders', but one cannot say that it is a frivolous attitude.' He too reads Kipling as an ideologue, looking for the 'message' of his poems (neither man has much to say about Kipling's prose). Unlike the pro-Boer Chesterton, he has a clear understanding of the economic forces of imperialist expansion, arguing that 'Kipling does not seem to realise, any more than the average soldier or colonial administrator, that an empire is primarily a money-making concern', but also insisting that Kipling's identification with rulers gave him a grip on reality not shared by those who have never 'tried to imagine what action and responsibility are like'. Arguing that Kipling appeals not despite but because of his 'vulgarity' so that enjoying his poems is a guilty pleasure like preserving in adulthood a taste for 'cheap sweets', Orwell's commentary on the demotic language of *Barrack Room Ballads* insists that their emotional power depends on its exploitation of cliché and formula, so that his essay also represents an early reading of Kipling's 'good bad poetry' as part of popular culture.

Randall Jarrell's 'On preparing to read Kipling' focuses on appreciating the qualities of Kipling's prose, while viewing his psychology as a man who 'never got over' the experiences of his childhood and youth. He argues that 'Kipling's world had been torn in two and he himself torn in two: for under the part that extenuated everything, blamed for nothing, there was certainly a part that extenuated nothing, blamed for everything – a part whose existence he never admitted, most certainly not to himself' (a view followed by later post-colonial analysts of the contradictions in Kipling' work). This unconscious internal division, says Jarrell, flaws Kipling's art, which can 'see far down into the infra-red, but is . . . blind to some frequencies normal eyes are sensitive to' (which sounds like a coded version of Orwell's balder 'Kipling was only half civilised'). Yet Jarrell insists on the power of Kipling's art to interrogate readers who would prefer to turn away from knowing the depths of pain and horror in the world and in themselves, with which Kipling was all too familiar: 'To our *Are you telling me the truth, or are you reassuring yourself?* . . . he sometimes can say truthfully, *Reassuring you*'. His essay is the subtlest as well as the liveliest of all twentieth-century defences of Kipling the artist.

Dan Jacobson's 'Kipling in South Africa' discusses Kipling's romanticised view of South Africa, his political affiliations and his relationships with political leaders, including his hero-worship of Rhodes, his hatred of the Boers and indifference to black Africans, and the anxieties about the future of the British Empire which the Boers' resistance had raised. For Jacobson, Kipling's commitment to South Africa made for good verse but poor fiction, because 'poetry lends itself more directly to expressing political passions than fiction ever can' since a poet 'can speak directly to the reader . . . whereas the conflicts at the heart of any successful piece of fiction have to be acted out by seemingly autonomous characters with an interior life of their own'. This Kipling could not concede to Britain's Boer enemies, who appear only in the embittered, oversimplified perspective of the loyalist Sikh narrator of 'A Sahibs' War' as treacherous hypocrites with a contemptible idiot son (a far cry from the sympathetically rendered Sussex 'Bee Boy' who 'is not quite right in his head' but can do anything with bees in 'Dymchurch Flit'[34]). Jacobson's point about the superiority of Kipling's South African poems over his propagandist fictions is borne out in Bryan Cheyette's essay, which shows how as Kipling grew more hostile to Jews after the war, equating them with Germans as threats to civilisation, his stories individualised them much less, to the detriment of his art. Complex and interesting figures like Kadmiel with his cynical wit and his passion for justice in 'The Treasure and the Law', or the shrewd but vulnerable Maxwell M'Leod in 'The House Surgeon' (also discussed by Daniel Karlin), are unsatisfactorily replaced by 'the Jews' as a vaguely menacing presence in the margins of the late stories, whereas the rancorously anti-Semitic poems 'Gehazi', 'The Waster', whose coded refrain ingeniously brackets 'the Jew' with 'the Hun', and 'The Burden of Jerusalem', all possess aesthetic virtues (of a dark kind) in their powerful rhythms and verbal vitality. For Jacobson the lasting value of Kipling's South African writings lies in his poems of nostalgia for its landscape, and the dark post-war prophecy of future menace in 'The Dykes': 'We are surrendered to night and the sea – the gale and the tide behind!'[35]

The historian Hugh Brogan assesses the politics of Kipling's poetry of the First World War – unlike Jacobson, endorsing Kipling's views, though with considerable reservations, in his examination of the attitudes to the German invasion of Belgium and France in 1914 as articulated in Kipling's war poetry. Whereas Harry Ricketts focuses principally on the peacetime vision of 'Englishness' in the 'Puck' books which Kipling shared with the war poets, Brogan addresses those public war poems which some readers might be tempted to dismiss as simple propaganda. Attacking a common view of the First World War according to which 'admirals, generals and air marshals [were] vicious incompetents' and servicemen were 'passive victims like sacrificial sheep', yet those 'sheep were heroes who died nobly for their country', Brogan assesses Kipling's grasp on the issues at stake in 'For All We Have and Are' and later poems. He weighs Kipling's ignorance of the German state, his virulent and undiscriminating hatred of the German people (a point also made by Dan Jacobson), his misprision of Kaiser Wilhelm II, who was 'not the genius of pure Evil Kipling thought him', and his credulous acceptance of 'too many of the tall tales' of atrocity, against his realistic grasp of the strategic and moral case for British belligerence. Conceding that the poems he cites are not those which 'have guaranteed [Kipling's] hold on posterity' he is less concerned to discuss Kipling's war record as a poet than to defend his record as a thinker and a citizen.

Harry Ricketts in 'A Kipling-conditioned world' addresses Kipling's connections with and reception by younger war poets. Beginning with Kipling's response to the First World War and the versions of his war poetry as these have been remembered (or constructed) by editors of anthologies and to a lesser degree by literary critics, Ricketts explores the connections between Kipling and the war poets Sassoon, Thomas, Brooke, Gurney and David Jones (quoted in his title), all conventionally thought of as his opposites. Emphasising Kipling's pervasive presence in literary culture during the formative years of these poets, whose minor peers can sound 'more Kipling than Kipling', Ricketts traces both the effects of a patriotic 'Kiplingesque stance' in some of the war poets and the passion for defending 'English earth' against the invader, which they share with Kipling. (Hugh Brogan, who also notices this trope, remarks on its disconnection from the actual intentions of the German High Command). Ricketts traces the connections between Edward Thomas'

'Albionism' and adoption of a 'Kiplingesque stance' and the Englishness hymned by Kipling in the 'Puck' books, showing how much these influenced Ivor Gurney's poetry of place and David Jones' perception of the presence of England's past within the modern present. He shows also how Rupert Brooke's experience of visiting the colonial Pacific in 1912 moved him from simply mocking the cliché of the 'White Man' to a slightly ironic acceptance of a 'Kiplingesque persona', how distaste at the 'Marconi Affair' disenchanted Brooke with liberalism, and how the famous war sonnet 'If I should die' echoes, consciously or not, Kipling's call to battle 'For All We Have and Are'. He also shows how for all Sassoon's overt disapproval of Kipling as 'terribly tub-thumping', his war poetry bears the imprint of the early ironic *Departmental Ditties* and the demotic *Barrack Room Ballads*.

Daniel Karlin addresses Kipling's notion of Englishness in his close reading of *Actions and Reactions* from the angle of peacetime. Noting the stories' responses to the political tensions of Edwardian England, especially the antagonisms existing within the middle class, he points out how wrong the prophetic elements of the book turned out to be: the global development of air traffic did not produce the peaceful world of 'With the Night Mail', and the political hopes of 'An Habitation Enforced' proved as baseless as the fears of 'The Mother Hive'. But, for Karlin, Kipling is 'not a propagandist but a great artist', and for him *Actions and Reactions* 'as a whole represents one of Kipling's most sustained efforts to understand and represent' the complex, imperilled life of his country, its colonial and imperial themes being 'linked to the great overarching structures that [he] discerned in English history, in English nature, and in the English character'. Karlin unpicks the implications of the book's construction, the placing of its stories and the way they echo or modify one another's themes. Pointing out the repeated motifs of home and homecoming, his close reading of the book's opening and closing stories 'An Habitation Enforced' and 'The House Surgeon' (which unlike Bryan Cheyette he finds humanely free of anti-Semitism) interprets the two stories of the regeneration of two English country houses, a beautiful near-ruin and a modern villa, as a dialogue, the ironies generated by their contrasts and parallels producing not an idealized England but a 'contest . . . between two kinds of inauthenticity'.

Lisa Lewis in 'Rikki-Tikki-Tavi and Indian history', the first of four essays on Kipling's Indian writings, probes the historical subtext of this much-loved children's fable about the mongoose and 'the great war which [he] fought single-handed'.[36] Like the other stories in the *Jungle Books*, 'Rikki-Tikki-Tavi' is an animal fable which is also a realist story, which allows Kipling both to imagine a non-human world in detail and depth, and to dramatise human moral and political types (as he would do more explicitly in the later adult fables of corruption and reform 'Below the Mill Dam' and 'The Mother Hive'). After probing the sources and inspirations of this animal fable in Kipling's own experiences, his childhood reading and the ancient Indian *Panchatantra* cycle of beast-fables, Lisa Lewis probes what she calls the 'deep undercurrent' of historical reference in the story set in a bungalow very like 'Belvedere' in Allahabad where Kipling lived in 1887–88, a city with a bloody history of massacres and reprisals during and after the 1857 Indian rebellion known to the British as the 'Mutiny'. In this political subtext the animals in this fable stand for the 'subject' race of Indians, so that the snakes represent native insurgents hoping to repossess their territory and Rikki the defender of the English family stands for loyalist Indian troops. (It would be entirely characteristic of Kipling's hatred of the enemies of British power to personify them as a poisonous serpent, that ancient European emblem of evil). Showing how each of the *Jungle Books* contains 'Mowgli' stories, animal fables of colonial India and one 'Arctic' story, she argues that 'Rikki' corresponds to another story of the Mutiny in the *Second Jungle Book*: 'The Undertakers' in which the ancient 'Mugger' crocodile reminisces about his long-ago feasting on English corpses in the river below Allahabad during what the narrator calls 'the terrible year of the Mutiny', followed during the reprisals by endless multitudes of Indians when 'every ripple brought more dead', until he is shot by a white child who has escaped him and grown up to become a railway engineer bent on getting rid of this devouring nuisance.[37] In both stories the rebels are represented by reptiles who meet satisfactorily violent ends, the anxiety of the memory of the rebellion being contained in (relatively) cosy children's fables in which 'the heroes triumph and the guilty perish'; although Lisa Lewis stresses that the appeal of the story goes well beyond the colonial moral of its subtext.

Charles Allen's essay focuses on the story of the attraction to Eastern religions which forms an undercurrent to Kipling's overt religious identity as a 'God-fearing Christian atheist'[38] who deified a transcendent 'Law' which holds chaos at bay. As a biographer of the young Kipling, Allen keeps close to the story of his life, unpicking his lifelong attraction to Islam, first articulated in the praise for the muezzin's 'splendid cry' in 'The City of Dreadful Night' (1885), his equally lasting hostility to Hinduism and the idealised version of Buddhism much influenced by Edwin Arnold's long poem *The Light of*

Asia (1879), which pervades *Kim*. Unlike most commentators on *Kim*, Allen argues that its narrative consistently moves away from the 'Law' embodied in patriarchal authority figures like Mahbub Ali and Colonel Creighton towards the domination of the feminine represented by the 'unassertive, compliant Tibetan lama' and the women who 'mother' Kim, and that the boy's awakening after his breakdown at the end of the book points not to a return to the 'Great Game' of spying but to the Buddhist 'acquisition of peace of mind'. He concedes that the enlightened 'flirtation with the Middle Way' represented by *Kim* was transitory, and would be followed by Kipling's return to the Narrow Way of 'Christian atheism'. Yet like Daniel Karlin interpreting 'The House Surgeon' as a story that transcends the anti-Semitic attitudes expressed by Kipling in his letters, Allen reads the ending of *Kim* as the triumph of the wisdom of the lama's 'Most Excellent Law' over the patriarchal Law which Kipling so often preached elsewhere.

My own essay on 'Letters of Marque' also examines Kipling's response to his experience of India – here, the Rajasthan states he visited in late 1887 which inspired some of his liveliest early writing, as a neglected classic work. Unlike Harish Trivedi, who describes Kipling's experience of speaking a halting 'vernacular' to Indians as a brief humiliation which he preferred to forget, I argue that the long-term creative influence of these travels is visible in Kipling's re-workings of these 'Letters', particularly in his greatest and least prejudiced fictions of India, the *Jungle Books* and *Kim*. The well-known rewriting of his appalled encounter with the numinous 'Gau-Mukh' (Cow's Mouth) shrine at Chitor in *The Naulahka*[39] should, I argue, be read as an inter-text for the great, chilling scenes set in 'Cold Lairs' in the *Jungle Books*, which subliminally evoke a horrific past history of sieges and massacres in those romantic ruins. More benignly, the combination of beauty, remoteness and contact with Indians during his trip to Boondi (Bundi) fed his ability to imagine otherness with pleasure instead of anxiety in *Kim*, and I suggest that Kim's experience of healing sleep under a tree at the end of the novel, which Charles Allen reads as a re-working of the legend of the Buddha waking under a pipal tree, drew consciously or not on Kipling's deeply felt if brief moment of 'deep accord and fellowship with all things on earth'.[40] Both readings are readily compatible.

Harish Trivedi's detailed engagement with current scholarly debates about Kipling's knowledge and use of Indian languages in his discussion of 'Kipling's "vernacular"' makes a searching scrutiny of how Kipling's 'showed – or showed off' his knowledge of 'native' tongues. Trivedi's essay is the second longest in this book, but, given the complex linguistic and political relationships of North Indian languages and their unfamiliarity to an English-speaking audience, it needs to be. He clarifies the relationships between 'Urdu' and 'Hindi', closely related languages spoken by different religious and ethnic groups, and 'Hindustani', a colonial patois used by the British to communicate with their subjects, and by servants in their households speaking different mother tongues as a *lingua franca*. He argues that when the six-year-old Kipling left for England, he forgot Hindustani and had to re-learn it from scratch (not, it seems, very well) when he returned to India ten years later. Discussing the current scholarly dialogues about Kipling's 'vernacular' usage, he points out Kipling's frequent mistakes in the Hindustani words and phrases he quotes, usually to comic effect, in his early poems and stories; it is a nice postcolonial irony that the writer who endlessly criticized 'natives' for slackness and in the voice of 'The 'Eathen' claimed they were defeated by British troops 'all along o' sloppiness, all along o' mess, / All along o' doin' things rathermore-or-less'[41] should be shown up as himself prone to linguistic sloppiness. Yet Trivedi finds Kipling's creation of the Hindustani-speaking hero in *Kim* truly successful, for in this novel 'Kipling invented a new language which is . . . subliminally inflected suffused and inflected by Urdu and Hindi, so that even when the words are in English, the syntax . . . [is] unmistakably Indian'. Like Charles Allen and me, Trivedi finds that in *Kim* Kipling goes beyond his prejudices, achieving a true understanding of Indian culture in 'one of the supreme examples of radical multi-lingual transactions in English literature'. That said, Trivedi's indictment of Kipling's multiple errors makes it clear how fallible he was when not inspired by his 'Daemon'.

Kaori Nagai's detailed and closely read account of the imperialist significance of the play of quotations in *Stalky & Co.* complements this dissection of Kipling's vernacular. Although her concern is not with the Indian subjects but their British rulers' private dialect, her unfolding of the politics of the imperial archive clarifies the idealised fantasy of authority underpinning the linguistic practices which Trivedi dissects. Like him she emphasises the connection between knowledge of 'native' language and proverbs and mastery: Stalky managing the tensions between Sikh and Pathan by judiciously citing a 'woman's proverb' that makes both men laugh. She redefines the notion of imperial 'hybridity' as developed in critiques of Kipling by Randall and McBratney, arguing that neither Stalky nor Kim is truly hybrid. Because 'the coloniser, as he learns the syntax of the East, is not allowed to lose his markers as white . . . if he wishes to maintain his privileges as the White

Man', his encounter with non-Western cultures is 'not hybridisation, but ... "quotation" – the sampling of other cultures, while interdicting the effects of cultural hybridity'. Kipling's imperial boys, she argues, are masters of quotation, which they use to control natives (they never get their quotes wrong even if, as Trivedi has shown, Kipling's own practice was another story) and to 'fix the Other as a stereotype', while their certainty about sources establishes their colonial authority. She shows how the remarkably well-read boys of *Stalky & Co.* use their knowledge both of books (not all literary) and of dialects to outwit their masters, benignly watched by the all-seeing 'Head', whose omniscient authority is embodied in his splendid library: 'To be summoned to his Office to be caned is to have a glimpse of his collection, and to have access to his books and, through them, to his power.' Gaining admission to this sanctum, the young Kipling thus becomes the librarian of an imperial archive that guarantees the 'authority and authenticity ... of [the] myriad voices from other cultures and contexts' that will become the trademark of his writing.

A different kind of mastery is at issue in Howard Booth's analysis of Kipling's notion of the ideally masculine 'army man' in relation to contemporary late Victorian discourses and practices of same-sex passion. Pointing out that Kipling's life and career spanned a period 'when "the homosexual" was defined and associated sexual identities emerged', Booth shows how foreign the idea of homosexual identity was to Kipling, who perceived what he called 'beastliness' as a 'wrong choice which all might make', the rhetoric of revulsion that it called forth in his letters suggesting a temptation which needed consciously to be fought off. (Kipling was equally furious against lesbians; Booth quotes a 1926 letter to Joynson-Hicks complaining about a flier for *The Well of Loneliness* being sent to his daughter, which may have helped to trigger the novel's prosecution.) Booth suggests that Kipling retreated from the 'representational spaces' of his army stories when it became clear that his own celebration of close friendships between soldiers coincided with the object-choices of such emerging homosexuals as J.A. Symonds (who once entertained hopes of Kipling as a fellow-spirit). Emphasising the visibility of male prostitutes and soldier pick-ups in the early 1890s in the 'seething miles of vice' around Kipling's haunts in Soho and Piccadilly, Booth shows how Kipling's early soldier stories led Symonds to mistake them for 'coded references to same-sex passion'. Kipling's most prolonged exploration of masculinity in *The Light That Failed*, despite the hero's excitement at Tommies fighting – 'my men, my beautiful men!' – represents masculine friendship as way to stave off loneliness, but this proved unsustainable in the increasingly visible presence of homosexual 'soldier-love'. It was no longer emotionally safe for a heterosexual man to long for the sight of 'an army man / Set up and trimmed and taut',[42] and the close untroubled comradeship of Parnesius and Pertinax in *Puck of Pook's Hill* exists only in an unrecoverable past.

Bryan Cheyette's 'A race to leave alone', the longest essay in this book, addresses the question of Kipling and racism by examining how Jews are represented throughout his *oeuvre* in poems and stories: some famous, others obscure. The starting point for Cheyette's complex and wide-ranging discussion of Kipling's work is Hannah Arendt's *Origins of Totalitarianism*, 'the first and best account of the links between the racism and dehumanisation of empire and of fascism with Kipling'. Discussing Kipling's engagement with 'Semitic racial discourse' deriving from 'a much broader history of differentiating Jews racially from other human beings', from the early ambivalence of *Plain Tales from the Hills* through Edwardian 'philo-Semitic' stories 'The House Surgeon' and 'The Treasure and the Law' to the outright virulence of the late stories and poems, Cheyette argues against a 'teleological' reading of Kipling's anti-Semitism as proto-fascist. Agreeing with Orwell, although for different reasons, that 'Kipling is not a fascist', his fascinating analysis of Jews and the remarks about them made by Gentile characters in his work follows Arendt in emphasising the links between racism and empire, showing how Kipling's antagonism to pro-Boer anti-Semites who attacked '[H]ebrew financiers' for supporting British rule in South Africa led him in 'The Treasure and the Law' to create the noble cynic Kadmiel, who by controlling England's money supply enables the establishment in Magna Charta of 'one Law for Jew or Christian'.[43] Like Daniel Karlin, Cheyette appreciates the sympathetically portrayed Jews in 'The House Surgeon', but reads the story's 'message' as a warning that replacing a 'spiritual covenant with empty materialism' leaves you vulnerable to primitive irrational forces, arguing that the disturbingly ambivalent figure of the Jew represents for Kipling both the modern universalism of Capital and the primitivism of the colonial subject. Cheyette shows Kipling moving from ambivalence to the outright hostility which he frequently expressed in his letters after the Marconi Affair (which, as Harry Ricketts shows, also moved Rupert Brooke towards right-wing politics) and he reads 'The Village That Voted The Earth Was Flat' as a pivotal text in which the blue-eyed Jewish impresario 'Bat' Masquerier promotes popular excitement and unrest which become 'disorder on a global scale'. Embittered by the First World War and the visible decline of British power,

Kipling like other supporters of the radical right came to think of Jews as 'global anarchists and financiers', at which point his racism did become fascist. Although not prepared to 'pardon Kipling and his views', Cheyette shows the richness and complexity of Kipling's treatment of what he would call the 'Unloved Race', in the early stories usually individualising his Jewish characters, which become much more marginal, and stereotypically unpleasant, in the later stories and poems. Cheyette sees Kipling 'in Time's eye' by locating his work in the history of the British Empire without allowing a false 'teleological' perspective to attribute to his *oeuvre* the opinions which affected his late work. In a sense, this move to historicise Kipling's changing worldview in relation to developments in British politics is a return to Chesterton insisting that what matters in Kipling's work is his 'message'.

Notes

1 Rudyard Kipling, *Puck of Pook's Hill* (London: Macmillan, 1906), p. 139. This poem is quoted in full by Daniel Karlin in chapter 8 of this volume, p. 126.
2 See 'Thrones, Dominations, Princedoms, Virtues, Powers' in *Paradise Lost* Book V, line 460, in E. Visiak (ed.) *Milton: Complete Poetry and Selected Prose* (Glasgow: Glasgow University Press, 1964), p. 191, and Robert Herrick's poem 'To Daffodils' in *Hesperides* 1648, in Alastair Fowler (ed.) *New Oxford Book of Seventeenth Century Verse* (Oxford: Oxford University Press, 1991). Kipling uses Herrick's image of the short-lived daffodil in stanza 2 of 'Cities and Thrones'.
3 Lockwood Kipling, quoted in Harry Ricketts, *The Unforgiving Minute: A Life of Rudyard Kipling* (London: Chatto & Windus, 1999), pp. 164–5.
4 Andrew Lycett, *Rudyard Kipling* (London: Weidenfeld & Nicholson 1999), p. 374.
5 Oscar Wilde, 'The critic as artist', *The Complete Works of Oscar Wilde* ed. Josephine M. Guy (Oxford: Oxford University Press, 2007) vol. 4, p. 199; Robert Buchanan 'The voice of the hooligan' (1899) in Roger Lancelyn Green (ed.) *Kipling: The Critical Heritage* (London: Routledge and Kegan Paul, 1971) pp. 247–8; Max Beerbohm, 'P.C.X.36', *A Christmas Garland* (London: Heinemann 1912), pp. 11–20, parodying the Mulvaney stories, and *The Poets' Corner* (1904; London and New York: King Penguin, 1943), plate 24.
6 Virginia Woolf, *A Room of One's Own* (1929; London: Penguin 2004), p. 101.
7 T.S. Eliot (1919), collected in Green, *Kipling*, p. 322; *Old Possum's Book of Practical Cats* (London: Faber & Faber, 1937); *A Choice of Kipling's Verse made by T.S. Eliot with an Introductory Essay* (London: Faber & Faber, 1941), pp. 5–36, which discusses Kipling's 'development of the imperial imagination into the historical imagination', drawing on the 'Puck' books and 'later stories of contemporary Sussex, such as *An Habitation Enforced*, *His Son's Wife* [sic] and *The Wish House*, together with '*They*' (p. 32). For the echoes of 'They' in 'Burnt Norton' and of 'Wireless' in 'The Waste Land', see Martin Scofield, *T.S. Eliot* (Cambridge:

Cambridge University Press, 1988), p. 251n., and Jan Montefiore, *Rudyard Kipling* (Horndon: Northcote House, 2007), p. 141.
8 Edmund Wilson's pioneering reappraisal 'The Kipling that nobody read', *The Wound and the Bow* (1941; London: Methuen 1962), expresses admiration for his 'brilliant short stories' (p. 107).
9 J.M.S. Tompkins, *The Art of Rudyard Kipling* (1959; London: Methuen 1964); C.A. Bodelsen, *Aspects of Kipling's Art* (Manchester: Manchester University Press, 1964); Andrew Rutherford (ed.), *Kipling's Mind and Art* (Edinburgh: Oliver & Boyd, 1964).
10 Elliott L. Gilbert, *The Good Kipling: Studies in the Short Story* (Manchester: Manchester University Press, 1972).
11 Sandra Kemp, *Kipling's Hidden Narratives* (Oxford: Oxford University Press, 1988); Zohreh Sullivan, *Narratives of Empire: The Fictions of Rudyard Kipling* (Cambridge: Cambridge University Press, 1993).
12 Kaori Nagai and Caroline Rooney (eds), *Kipling and Beyond: Patriotism, Globalisation and Postcolonialism* (Basingstoke: Palgrave Macmillan, 2011); Howard J. Booth (ed.), *The Cambridge Companion to Rudyard Kipling* (Cambridge: Cambridge University Press, 2011).
13 Kipling, *Early Verse by Rudyard Kipling 1879–1889: Unpublished, Uncollected and Rarely Collected Poems*, ed. Andrew Rutherford (Oxford: Clarendon Press, 1986); Kipling, *Kipling's India: Uncollected Sketches 1884–6*, ed. Thomas Pinney (London: Macmillan, 1986); *Something of Myself and Other Autobiographical Writings* (Cambridge: Cambridge University Press, 1990); *The Letters of Rudyard Kipling*, 6 vols (Basingstoke: Palgrave Macmillan, 1990–2004). Because Kipling and later his widow Carrie burned most of his letters, Morton Cohen (ed.), *Rudyard Kipling to Rider Haggard: The Record of a Friendship* (London: Hutchinson, 1965) is the nearest thing to a surviving published correspondence.
14 Kipling to Max Aitken, 14 November 1913, *The Letters of Rudyard Kipling, Volume 4: 1911–19*, ed. Thomas Pinney (Basingstoke: Macmillan, 1998), p. 208. See also Bryan Cheyette, chapter 15 in this volume, pp. 250–84.
15 See Lycett, *Rudyard Kipling*; Ricketts, *The Unforgiving Minute*; David Gilmour, *The Long Recessional: The Imperial Life of Rudyard Kipling* (London: John Murray, 2002); Philip Mallett, *Rudyard Kipling: A Literary Life* (London: Macmillan, 2002); Charles Allen, *Kipling Sahib: India and the Making of Rudyard Kipling* (London: Little, Brown, 2007).
16 Allen, *Kipling Sahib*, pp. 202, 286–7.
17 See the discussion of Hurree Babu in Montefiore, *Rudyard Kipling*, pp. 91–5; also Harish Trivedi's introduction to his edition of *Kim* (London: Penguin Classics, 2011), pp. xxxviii–xl.
18 Tonie and Valmai Holt, *My Boy Jack: The Search for Kipling's Only Son* (Barnsley: Leo Cooper, 1998); Adam Nicolson, *The Hated Wife: Carrie Kipling 1862–1939* (London: Faber & Faber, 2001); Judith Flanders, *A Circle of Sisters: Alice Kipling, Georgiana Burne-Jones, Agnes Poynter and Louisa Baldwin* (London: Viking Press, 2001).

19 Max Saunders, *Self Impressions: Life Writing, Autobiografiction and the Forms of Modern Literature* (Oxford: Oxford University Press, 2010), p. 216.
20 David Haig, *My Boy Jack* (London: Nick Hern Books, 1997).
21 Kipling, 'Common Form' from 'Epitaphs of the War', *Works* (Ware: Wordsworth, 1994), p. 390.
22 Lycett, *Rudyard Kipling*, p. 25.
23 Kipling, *Many Inventions* (London: Macmillan, 1893), p. 126; *Wee Willie Winkie and Other Stories* (London: Macmillan, 1895), p. 271; *Early Verse*, p. 138.
24 Lyn Pykett, *Engendering Fiction: The English Novel in the Early Twentieth Century* (London: Edward Arnold, 1995), p. 1; see also David Trotter, *The English Novel in History, 1895–1920* (London: Routledge, 1993) and Trudi Tate, *Modernism, History and the First World War* (Manchester: Manchester University Press, 1998).
25 Kemp, *Kipling's Hidden Narratives*, pp. 100–23; see also Nora Crook, *Kipling's Myths of Love and Death* (London: Macmillan, 1990).
26 For a recent account of women in Kipling, see Kaori Nagai 'Kipling and gender' in Booth (ed.), *The Cambridge Companion to Rudyard Kipling*, pp. 66–79.
27 Pykett, *Engendering Fiction*, pp. 66–8; see also Joseph Bristow, *Empire Boys: Adventures in a Man's World* (London: HarperCollins, 1991), John Kucich, *Imperial Masochism: Fact, Fantasy and Social Class* (Princeton, NJ: Princeton University Press, 2006), and Montefiore, *Rudyard Kipling*, chapter 4, 'Being a Man'.
28 Edward Said, *Orientalism* (London: Routledge, 1978), introduction to *Kim* (London: Penguin Modern Classics, 1987), reprinted in *Culture and Imperialism* (London: Viking, 1992).
29 Sara Suleri, *The Rhetoric of British India* (Chicago: Chicago University Press, 1992); Zohreh Sullivan, *Narratives of Empire*; Don Randall, *Kipling's Imperial Boy* (London: Macmillan, 2000), John McBratney, *Imperial Subjects, Imperial Spaces* (Princeton, NJ: Princeton University Press, 2002). See also the discussions of Kipling by Thomas Richards in *The Imperial Archive: Knowledge and the Fantasy of Empire* (London: Verso, 1993) and more recently by Douglas Kerr in *Eastern Figures: Orient and Empire in British Writing* (Hong Kong: Hong Kong University Press, 2007).
30 W.H. Auden, 'In Memory of W.B. Yeats' (1939), in E. Mendelson (ed.), *The English Auden: Poems, Essays, and Dramatic Writings 1927–1939* (London: Faber & Faber, 1976), p. 242.
31 See Judith Plotz's account of the resurrection of 'The White Man's Burden' by neo-conservative Americans in 'Kipling and the new American empire', in Rooney and Nagai (eds), *Kipling and Beyond*, pp. 37–57.
32 G.K. Chesterton, *Heretics* (London: John Lane, 1905), pp. 31–46.
33 *Ibid.* pp. 38–9; C.S. Lewis 'Kipling's world', in *They Asked for a Paper* (London: Geoffrey Bles, 1962), pp. 72–92.
34 Kipling, 'Dymchurch Flit', *Puck*, p. 258.
35 Kipling, 'The Dykes', *Works*, p. 307, quoted by Jacobson in chapter 5 in this volume, pp. 100–1.
36 Kipling, *The Jungle Book* (London: Macmillan, 1895), p. 163.

37 Kipling, *Second Jungle Book* (London: Macmillan, 1895), pp. 132, 136.
38 Lycett, *Rudyard Kipling*, p. 520.
39 See Montefiore, *Rudyard Kipling*, pp. 28, 30.
40 Kipling, *From Sea to Sea* (London: Macmillan, 1899), vol. 1, Letter XIX, p. 192.
41 Kipling, 'The 'Eathen', *Works*, p. 451.
42 Kipling, *The Light That Failed* (London: Macmillan, 1891), p. 193; 'In Partibus', *Early Verse*, p. 472, quoted by Howard J. Booth in chapter 14 of this volume, pp. 232–4.
43 Kipling, *Puck*, p. 285.

2

Rudyard Kipling (1905)

G.K. CHESTERTON[1]

The first and fairest thing to say about Rudyard Kipling is that he has borne a brilliant part in recovering the lost provinces of poetry. He has not been frightened by that brutal materialistic air which clings only to words; he has pierced through to the romantic, imaginative matter of the things themselves. He has perceived the significance and philosophy of steam and slang. Steam may be, if you like, a dirty by-product of science. Slang may be, if you like, a dirty by-product of language. But at least he has been among the few who saw the divine parentage of these things, and knew that where there is smoke there is fire – that is, that wherever there is the foulest of things, there also is the purest. Above all, he has something to say, a definite view of things to utter, and that always means that a man is fearless and faces everything. For the moment we have a view of the universe, we possess it.

Now the message of Rudyard Kipling, that upon which he has really concentrated, is the only thing worth worrying about in him or in any other man. He has often written bad poetry, like Wordsworth. He has often said silly things, like Plato. He has often given way to mere political hysteria, like Gladstone. But no one can reasonably doubt that he means steadily and sincerely to say something, and the only serious question is, What is that which he has tried to say? Perhaps the best way of stating this fairly will be to begin with that element which has been most insisted by himself and by his opponents – I mean his interest in militarism. But when we are seeking for the real merits of a man it is unwise to go to his enemies, and much more foolish to go to himself.

Now, Mr Kipling is certainly wrong in his worship of militarism, but his opponents are, generally speaking, quite as wrong as he. The evil of militarism is not that it shows certain men to be fierce and haughty and excessively warlike. The evil of militarism is that it shows most men to be tame and timid and excessively peaceable. The professional soldier gains more and more power as the general courage of a community declines. Thus the Pretorian guard became more and more important in Rome as Rome became more and more luxurious and feeble. The military man gains the civil power in proportion as the civilian loses the military virtues. And as it was in ancient Rome so it is in contemporary Europe. There never was a time when nations were more militarist. There never was a time when men were less brave. All ages and all epics have sung of arms and the man; but we have effected simultaneously the deterioration of the man and the fantastic perfection of the arms. Militarism demonstrated the decadence of Rome, and it demonstrates the decadence of Prussia.

And unconsciously, Mr Kipling has proved this, and proved it admirably. For in so far as his work is earnestly understood the military trade does not by any means emerge as the most important or attractive. He has not written so well about soldiers as he has about railway men or bridge builders, or even journalists. The fact is that what attracts Mr Kipling to militarism is not the idea of courage, but the idea of discipline. There was far more courage to the square mile in the Middle Ages, when no king had a standing army, but every man had a bow or sword. But the fascination of the standing army upon Mr Kipling is not courage, which scarcely interests him, but discipline, which is, when all is said and done, his primary theme. The modern army is not a miracle of courage; it has not enough opportunities, owing to the cowardice of everybody else. But it is really a miracle of organization, and that is the truly Kiplingite ideal. Kipling's subject is not that valour which properly belongs to war, but that interdependence and efficiency which belongs quite as much to engineers, or sailors, or mules, or railway engines. And thus it is that when he writes of engineers, or sailors, or mules, or steam-engines, he writes at his best. The real poetry, the 'true romance' which Mr Kipling has taught, is the romance of the division of labour and the discipline of all the trades. He sings the arts of peace much more accurately than the arts of war. And his main contention is vital and valuable. Everything is military in the sense that everything depends upon obedience. There is no perfectly epicurean corner; there is no perfectly irresponsible place. Everywhere men have made the way for us with sweat and submission. We may fling ourselves into a hammock in a fit of divine carelessness. But we are glad that the net-maker did not make the hammock in a fit of divine carelessness. We may jump upon a child's rocking-horse for a joke. But we are glad that the carpenter did not leave the legs of it unglued for a joke. So far from having merely preached that a soldier cleaning his side-arm is to be adored because he is military, Kipling at his best and clearest has preached that the baker baking loaves and the tailor cutting coats is as military as anybody.

Being devoted to this multitudinous vision of duty, Mr Kipling is naturally a cosmopolitan. He happens to find his examples in the British Empire, but almost any other empire would do as well, or, indeed, any other highly civilized country. That which he admires in the British army he would find even more apparent in the German army; that which he desires in the British police he would find flourishing in the French police. The ideal of discipline is not the whole of life, but it is spread over the whole of the world. And the worship of it tends to confirm in Mr Kipling a certain note of worldly wisdom, of the experience of the wanderer, which is one of the genuine charms of his best work.

The great gap in his mind is what may be roughly called the lack of patriotism – that is to say, he lacks altogether the faculty of attaching himself to any cause or community finally and tragically; for all finality must be tragic. He admires England, but he does not love her; for we admire things with reasons, but love them without reasons. He admires England because she is strong, not because she is English. There is no harshness in saying this, for, to do him justice, he avows it with his usual picturesque candour. In a very interesting poem, he says that –

If England was what England seems[2]

– that is, weak and inefficient; if England were not what (as he believes) she is – that is powerful and practical –

How quick we'd chuck 'er! But she ain't![3]

He admits, that is, that his devotion is the result of a criticism, and this is quite enough to put it in another category altogether from the patriotism of the Boers, whom he hounded down in South Africa. In speaking of the really patriotic peoples, such as the Irish, he has some difficulty in keeping a shrill irritation out of his language. The frame of mind which he really describes with beauty and nobility is the frame of mind of the cosmopolitan man who has seen men and cities.

> For to admire and for to see,
> For to be'old this world so wide.[4]

He is a perfect master of that light melancholy with which a man looks back on having been the lover of many women. He is the philanderer of the nations. But a man may have learnt much about women in flirtations, and still be ignorant of first love; a man may have known as many lands as Ulysses, and still be ignorant of patriotism.

Mr Rudyard Kipling has asked in a celebrated epigram[5] what they can know of England who know England only. It is a far deeper and sharper question to ask, 'What can they know of England who know only the world?' for the world does not include England any more than it includes the Church. The moment we care for anything deeply, the world – that is, all the other miscellaneous interests – becomes our enemy. Christians showed it when they talked of keeping one's self 'unspotted from the world'; but lovers talk of it just as much when they talk of the 'world well lost'. Astronomically speaking, I understand that England is situated on the world; similarly, I suppose that the Church was part of the world, and even the lovers inhabitants of that orb. But they all felt a certain truth – the truth that the moment you love anything the world becomes your foe. Thus Mr Kipling does certainly know the world; he is a man of the world, with all the narrowness that belongs to those imprisoned in that planet. He knows England as an intelligent English gentleman knows Venice. He has been to England a great many times; he has stopped there for long visits. But he does not belong to it, or to any place; and the proof of it is this, that he thinks of England as a place. The moment we are rooted in a place, the place vanishes. We live like a tree with the whole strength of the universe.

The globe-trotter lives in a smaller world than the peasant. He is always breathing an air of locality. London is a place, to be compared to Chicago; Chicago is a place, to be compared to Timbuctoo. But Timbuctoo is not a place, since there, at least, live men who regard it as the universe, and breathe, not an air of locality, but the winds of the world. The man in the saloon steamer has seen all the races of men, and he is thinking of the things that divide men – diet, dress, decorum, rings in the nose as in Africa, or in the ears as in Europe, blue paint among the ancients, or red paint among the modern Britons. The man in the cabbage field has seen nothing at all; but he is thinking of the things that unite men – hunger and babies, and the beauty of women, and the promise or menace of the sky. Mr Kipling, with all his merits, is the globe-trotter; he has not the patience to become part of anything. So great and genuine a man is not to be accused of a merely cynical cosmopolitanism; still, his cosmopolitanism is his weakness. That weakness is splendidly expressed in one of his finest poems, *The Sestina of the Tramp Royal*,[6] in which a man declares that he can endure anything in the way of hunger or horror, but not permanent presence in one place. In this there is certainly danger. The more dead and dry and dusty a thing is the more it travels about; dust is like this and the thistle-down and the High Commissioner in South Africa. Fertile things are somewhat heavier, like the heavy fruit trees on the pregnant mud of the Nile. In the heated idleness of youth we were all rather inclined to quarrel with the implication of that proverb which says that a rolling stone gathers no moss. We are inclined to ask, 'Who wants to gather moss, except silly old ladies?' But for all that we begin to perceive that the proverb is right. The rolling stone rolls echoing from rock to rock; but the rolling stone is dead. The moss is silent because the moss is alive.

The truth is that exploration and enlargement made the world smaller. The telegraph and the steamboat make the world smaller. The telescope makes the world smaller; it is only the microscope that makes it larger. Before long the world will be cloven with a war between the telescopists and the microscopists. The first study large things and live in a small world; the second study small things and live in a large world. It is inspiring without doubt to whizz in a motor-car round the earth, to feel Arabia as a whirl of sand or China as a flash of rice-fields. But Arabia is not a whirl of sand and China is not a flash of rice-fields. They are ancient civilizations with strange virtues buried like treasures. If we wish to understand them it must not be as tourists or inquirers, it must be with the loyalty of children and the great patience of poets. To conquer these places is to lose them. The man standing in his own kitchen-garden, with fairyland opening at the gate, is the man with large ideas. His mind creates distance; the motor-car stupidly destroys it. Moderns think of the earth as a globe, as something one can easily get round, the spirit of a schoolmistress. This is shown in the odd mistake perpetually made about Cecil Rhodes. His enemies say that he may have had large ideas, but he was a bad man. His friends say that he may have been a bad man, but he certainly had large ideas. The truth is that he was not a man essentially bad, he was a man of much geniality and many good intentions, but a man with singularly small views. There is nothing large about painting the map red; it is an innocent game for children. It is just as easy to think in continents as to think in cobble-stones. The difficulty comes in when we seek to know the substance of either of them. Rhodes's prophecies about the Boer resistance are an admirable comment on how the 'large ideas' prosper when it is not a question of thinking in continents, but of understanding a few two-legged men. And under all this vast illusion of the cosmopolitan planet, with its empires and its Reuter's agency, the real life of man goes on concerned with this tree or that temple, with this harvest or that drinking-song, totally uncomprehended, totally untouched. And it watches from its splendid parochialism, possibly with a smile of amusement, motor-car civilization going its triumphant way, outstripping time, consuming space, seeing all and seeing nothing, roaring on at last to the capture of the solar system, only to find the sun cockney and the stars suburban.

Notes

1 Abridged from G.K. Chesterton, 'Rudyard Kipling', *Heretics* (London: John Lane, 1905), pp. 42–53.
2 Rudyard Kipling 'The Return', *Rudyard Kipling's Verse: The Definitive Edition* (London: Hodder and Stoughton, 1940), p. 485.
3 Kipling, *ibid.*, p. 486.
4 Kipling, 'For To Admire', *Definitive Verse*, p. 457.
5 Kipling, 'The English Flag', *Definitive Verse*, p. 221.
6 Kipling, *Definitive Verse*, p. 87.

3

Rudyard Kipling (1942)

GEORGE ORWELL[1]

It was a pity that Mr Eliot should be so much on the defensive in the long essay with which he prefaces this selection of Kipling's poetry,[2] but it was not to be avoided, because before one can even speak about Kipling one has to clear away a legend that has been created by two sets of people who have not read his works. Kipling is in the peculiar position of having been a by-word for fifty years. During five literary generations every enlightened person has despised him, and at the end of that time nine tenths of those enlightened persons are forgotten and Kipling is in some sense still there. Mr Eliot never satisfactorily explains this fact, because in answering the shallow and familiar charge that Kipling is a 'Fascist', he falls into the opposite error of defending him where he is not defensible. It is no use pretending that Kipling's view of life, as a whole, can be accepted or even forgiven by any civilized person. It is no use claiming, for instance, that when Kipling describes a British soldier beating a 'nigger' with a cleaning rod in order to get money out of him, he is acting merely as a reporter and does not necessarily approve what he describes. There is not the slightest sign anywhere in Kipling's work that he disapproves of that kind of conduct – on the contrary, there is a definite strain of sadism in him, over and above the brutality which a writer of that type has to have. Kipling *is* a jingo imperialist, he *is* morally insensitive and aesthetically disgusting. It is better to start by admitting that, and then to try to find out why it is that he survives while the refined people who have sniggered at him seem to wear so badly.

And yet the 'Fascist' charge has to be answered, because the first clue to any understanding of Kipling, morally or politically, is that fact that he was *not* a Fascist. He was further from being one than the most humane or the most 'progressive' person is able to be nowadays. An interesting instance of the way in which quotations are parroted to and fro without any attempt to look up their context or discover their meaning is the line from 'Recessional', 'Lesser breeds without the Law'. This line is always good for a snigger in pansy-left circles. It is assumed as a matter of course that the 'lesser breeds' are 'natives', and a mental picture is called up of some pukka sahib in a pith helmet kicking a coolie. In its context the sense of the line is almost the exact opposite of this. The phrase 'lesser breeds' refers almost certainly to the Germans, and especially the pan-German writers, who are 'without the Law' in the sense of being lawless, not in the sense of being powerless. The whole poem, conventionally thought of as an orgy of boasting, is a denunciation of power politics, British as well as German. Two stanzas are worth quoting (I am quoting this as politics, not as poetry):

> If, drunk with sight of power, we loose
> Wild tongues that have not Thee in awe,
> Such boastings as the Gentiles use,
> Or lesser breeds without the Law –
> Lord God of hosts, be with us yet,
> Lest we forget – lest we forget!
>
> For heathen heart that puts her trust
> In reeking tube and iron shard,
> All valiant dust that builds on dust,
> And guarding, calls not Thee to guard,
> For frantic boast and foolish word –
> Thy mercy on Thy People, Lord!³

Much of Kipling's phraseology is taken from the Bible, and no doubt in the second stanza he had in mind the text from Psalm cxxvii: 'Except the Lord build the house, they labour in vain that build it; except the Lord keep the city, the watchman waketh but in vain.' It is not a text that makes much impression on the post-Hitler mind. No one, in our time, believes in any sanction greater than military power; no one believes that it is possible to overcome force except by greater force. There is no 'Law', there is only power. I am not saying that this is a true belief, merely that it is the belief which all modern men do actually hold. Those who pretend otherwise are either intellectual cowards, or power-worshippers under a thin disguise, or have simply not caught up with the age they are living in. Kipling's outlook is pre-Fascist. He still believes that pride comes before a fall and that the gods punish *hubris*. He does not foresee the tank, the bombing place, the radio and the secret police, or their psychological results.

But in saying this, does not one unsay what I said about Kipling's jingoism and brutality? No, one is merely saying that the nineteenth-century imperialist outlook and the modern gangster outlook are two different things. Kipling belongs very definitely to the period 1885–1902. The Great War and its aftermath embittered him, but he shows little sign of having learned anything from any event later than the Boer War. He was the prophet of British imperialism in its expansionist phase (even more than his poems, his solitary novel, *The Light That Failed*, gives you the atmosphere of that time) and also the unofficial historian of the British army, the old mercenary army which began to change its shape in 1914. All his confidence, his bouncing vulgar vitality, sprang out of limitations which no Fascist or near-Fascist shares.

Kipling spent the later part of his life in sulking, and no doubt it was political disappointment rather than literary vanity that accounted for this. Somehow history had not gone according to plan. After the greatest victory she had ever known, Britain was a lesser world power than before, and Kipling was quite acute enough to see this. The virtue had gone out of the classes he idealized, the young were hedonistic or disaffected, the desire to paint the map red had evaporated. He could not understand what was happening, because he had never had any grasp of the economic forces underlying imperial expansion. It is notable that Kipling does not seem to realize, any more than the average soldier or colonial administrator, that an empire is primarily a money-making concern. Imperialism as he sees it is a sort of forcible evangelizing. You turn a Gatling gun on a mob of unarmed 'natives', and then you establish 'the Law', which includes roads, railways and a court-house. He could not foresee, therefore, that the same motives which brought the Empire into existence would end by destroying it. It was the same motive, for example, that caused the Malayan jungles to be cleared for rubber estates, and which now causes those estates to be handed over intact to the Japanese. The modern totalitarians know what they are doing, and the nineteenth-century English did not know what they were doing. Both attitudes have their advantages, but Kipling was never able to move forward from one into the other. His outlook, allowing for the fact that after all he was an artist, was that of the salaried bureaucrat who despises the 'box-wallah' and often lives a lifetime without realizing that the 'box-wallah' calls the tune.

But because he identifies himself with the official class, he does possess one thing which 'enlightened' people seldom or never possess, and that is a sense of responsibility. The middle-class Left hate him for this quite as much as for his cruelty and vulgarity. All left-wing parties in the highly industrialized countries are at bottom a sham, because they make it their business to fight against something which they do not really wish to destroy. They have international aims, and at the same time they struggle to keep up a standard of life with which those aims are incompatible. We all live by robbing Asiatic coolies, and those of us who are 'enlightened' all maintain that those coolies ought to be set free; but our standard of living, and hence our 'enlightenment', demands that the robbery shall continue. A humanitarian is always a hypocrite, and Kipling's understanding of this is perhaps the central secret of his power to create telling phrases. It would be difficult to hit off the one-eyed pacifism of the English in fewer words than in the phrase, 'making mock of uniforms that guard you while you sleep'.[4] It is true that Kipling does not understand the economic aspect of the relationship between the highbrow and the Blimp. He does not see that the map is painted red chiefly in order that the coolie may be exploited. Instead of the coolie he sees the Indian Civil Servant; but even on that plane his grasp of function, of who protects whom, is very sound. He sees clearly that men can only be highly civilized while other men, inevitably less civilized, are there to guard and feed them.

How far does Kipling really identify himself with the administrators, soldiers and engineers whose praises he sings? Not so completely as is sometimes assumed. He had travelled very widely while he was still a young man, he had grown up with a brilliant mind in mainly philistine surroundings, and some streak in him that may have been partly neurotic led him to prefer the active man to the sensitive man. The nineteenth-century Anglo-Indians, to name the least sympathetic of his idols, were at any rate people who did things. It may be that all that they did was evil, but they changed the face of the earth (it is instructive to look at a map of Asia and compare the railway system of India with that of the surrounding countries), whereas they could have achieved nothing, could not have maintained themselves in power for a single week, if the normal Anglo-Indian outlook had been that of, say, E.M. Forster. Tawdry and shallow though it is, Kipling's is the only literary picture that we possess of nineteenth-century Anglo-India, and he could only make it because he was just coarse enough to be able to exist and keep his mouth shut in clubs and regimental messes. But he did not greatly resemble the people he admired. I know from several private sources that many of the

Anglo-Indians who were Kipling's contemporaries did not like or approve of him. They said, no doubt truly, that he knew nothing about India, and on the other hand he was from their point of view too much of a highbrow. While in India he tended to mix with 'the wrong' people, and because of his dark complexion he was wrongly suspected of having a streak of Asiatic blood. Much of his development is traceable to his having been born in India and having left school early. With a slightly different background he might have been a good novelist or a superlative writer of music-hall songs. But how true is it that he was a vulgar flag-waver, a sort of publicity agent for Cecil Rhodes? It is true, but it is not true that he was a yes-man or a time-server. After his early days, if then, he never courted public opinion. Mr Eliot says that what is held against him is that he expressed unpopular views in a popular style. This narrows the issue by assuming that 'unpopular' means unpopular with the intelligentsia, but it is a fact that Kipling's 'message' was one that the big public did not want, and, indeed, has never accepted. The mass of the people, in the nineties as now, were anti-militarist, bored by the Empire, and only unconsciously patriotic. Kipling's official admirers are and were the 'service' middle class, the people who read *Blackwood's*. In the stupid early years of this century, the Blimps, having at last discovered someone who could be called a poet and who was on their side, set Kipling on a pedestal, and some of his more sententious poems, such as 'If',[5] were given almost Biblical status. But it is doubtful whether the Blimps have ever read him with attention, any more than they have read the Bible. Much of what he says they could not possibly approve. Few people who have criticized England from the inside have said bitterer things about her than this gutter patriot. As a rule it is the British working class that he is attacking, but not always. That phrase about 'the flannelled fools at the wicket and the muddied oafs at the goals'[6] sticks like an arrow to this day, and it is aimed at the Eton and Harrow match as well as the Cup-Tie Final. Some of the verses he wrote about the Boer War have a curiously modern ring, so far as their subject-matter goes. 'Stellenbosch', which must have been written about 1902, sums up what every intelligent infantry officer was saying in 1918, or is saying now, for that matter.

Kipling's romantic ideas about England and the Empire might not have mattered if he could have held them without having the class prejudices which at that time went with them. If one examines his best and most representative work, his soldier's poems, especially *Barrack-Room Ballads*, one notices that what more than anything else spoils them is an underlying air of patronage.

Kipling idealizes the army officer, especially the junior officer, and that to an idiotic extent, but the private soldier, though lovable and romantic, has to be a comic. He is always made to speak in a sort of stylized cockney, not very broad but with all the aitches and final 'g's' carefully omitted. Very often the result is as embarrassing as the humorous recitation at a church social. And this accounts for the curious fact that one can often improve Kipling's poems, make them less facetious and less blatant, by simply going through them and transplanting them from cockney into standard speech. This is especially true of his refrains, which often have a truly lyrical quality. Two examples will do (one is about a funeral and the other about a wedding):

> So it's knock out your pipes and follow me!
> And it's finish up your swipes and follow me!
>   Oh, hark to the big drum calling.
>   Follow me – follow me home![7]

and again:

> Cheer for the Sergeant's wedding –
> Give them one cheer more!
> Grey gun-horses in the lando,
> And a rogue is married to a whore![8]

Here I have restored the aitches etc. Kipling ought to have known better. He ought to have seen that the two closing lines of the first of these stanzas are very beautiful lines, and that ought to have overridden his impulse to make fun of a working-man's accent. In the ancient ballads the lord and the peasant speak the same language. This is impossible to Kipling, who is looking down a distorting class perspective, and by a piece of poetic justice one of his best lines is spoiled – for 'follow me 'ome' is much uglier than 'follow me home'. But even where it makes no difference musically the facetiousness of his stage cockney dialect is irritating. However, he is more often quoted aloud than read on the printed page, and most people instinctively make the necessary alterations when they quote him.

Can one imagine any private soldier, in the nineties or now, reading *Barrack-Room Ballads* and feeling that here was a writer who spoke for him? It is very hard to do so. Any soldier capable of reading a book of verse would notice at once that Kipling is almost unconscious of the class war that goes on in an army as much as elsewhere. It is not only that he thinks the soldier comic, but that he thinks him patriotic, feudal, a ready admirer of his officers and proud to be a soldier of the Queen. Of course that is partly true, or battles could not be fought, but 'What have I done for thee, England, my England?'⁹ is essentially a middle-class query. Almost any working man would follow it up immediately with 'What has England done for me?' In so far as Kipling grasps this, he simply sets it down to 'the intense selfishness of the lower classes'¹⁰ (his own phrase). When he is writing not of British but of 'loyal' Indians he carries the 'Salaam, sahib' motif to sometimes disgusting lengths.¹¹ Yet it remains true that he has far more interest in the common soldier, far more anxiety that he shall get a fair deal, than most of the 'liberals' of his day or our own. He sees that the soldier is neglected, meanly underpaid and hypocritically despised by the people whose incomes he safeguards. 'I came to realize,' he says in his posthumous memoirs, 'the bare horrors of the private's life, and the unnecessary torments he endured.'¹² He is accused of glorifying war, and perhaps he does so, but not in the usual manner, by pretending that war is a sort of football match. Like most people capable of writing battle poetry, Kipling had never been in battle, but his vision of war is realistic. He knows that bullets hurt, that under fire everyone is terrified, that the ordinary soldier never knows what the war is about or what is happening except in his own corner of the battlefield, and that British troops, like other troops, frequently run away:

> I 'eard the knives be'hind me but I dursn't face my man,
> Nor I don't know where I went to, 'cause I didn't stop to see,
> Till I 'eard a beggar squealin' out for quarter as 'e ran,
> An' I thought I knew the voice an' – it was me!¹³

Modernize the style of this, and it might have come out of one of the debunking war books of the nineteen-twenties. Or again:

> An' now the hugly bullets come peckin' through the dust,
> An' no one wants to face 'em, but every beggar must;
> So, like a man in irons, which isn't glad to go,
> They moves 'em off by companies uncommon stiff an' slow.¹⁴

Compare this with:

> 'Forward the Light Brigade!'
> Was there a man dismayed?
> No! Though the soldier knew
> Someone had blundered.¹⁵

If anything, Kipling overdoes the horrors, for the wars of his youth were hardly wars at all by our standards. Perhaps that is due to the neurotic strain in him, the hunger for cruelty. But at least he knows that men ordered to attack impossible objectives *are* dismayed, and also that fourpence a day is not a generous pension.

How complete or truthful a picture has Kipling left us of the long-service, mercenary army of the late nineteenth century? One must say of this, as of what Kipling wrote about nineteenth-century Anglo-India, that it is not only the best but almost the only literary picture we have. He has put on record an immense amount of stuff that one could otherwise only gather from verbal tradition or from unreadable regimental histories. Perhaps his picture of army life seems fuller and more accurate than it is because any middle-class English person is likely to know enough to fill up the gaps. At any rate, reading the essay on Kipling that Mr Edmund Wilson has just published or is just about to publish,[16] I was struck by the number of things that are boringly familiar to us and seem to be barely intelligible to an American. But from the body of Kipling's early work there does seem to emerge a vivid and not seriously misleading picture of the old pre-machine-gun army – the sweltering barracks in Gibraltar or Lucknow, the red coats, the pipeclayed belts and the pillbox hats, the beer, the fights, the floggings, hangings and crucifixions, the bugle-calls, the smell of oats and horse-piss, the bellowing sergeants with foot-long moustaches, the bloody skirmishes, invariably mismanaged, the crowded troopships, the cholera-stricken camps, the 'native' concubines, the ultimate death in the workhouse. It is a crude, vulgar picture, in which a patriotic music-hall turn seems to have got mixed up with one of Zola's gorier passages, but from it future generations will be able to gather some idea of what a long-term volunteer army was like. On about the same level they will be able to learn something of British India in the days when motor cars and refrigerators were unheard of. It is an error to imagine that we might have had better books on these subjects if, for example, George Moore, or Gissing, or Thomas Hardy, had had Kipling's opportunities. That is the kind of accident that cannot happen. It was not possible that nineteenth-century England should produce a book like *War and Peace*, or like Tolstoy's minor stories of army life, such as *Sebastopol* or *The Cossacks*, not because the talent was unnecessarily lacking but because no one with sufficient sensitiveness to write such books would ever have made the appropriate contacts. Tolstoy lived in a great military empire in which it seemed natural for almost any young man of family to spend a few years in the army, whereas the British Empire was and still is demilitarized to a degree which continental observers find almost incredible. Civilized men do not readily move away from the centres of civilization, and in most languages there is a great dearth of what one might call colonial literature. It took a very improbable combination of circumstances to produce Kipling's gaudy tableau, in which Private Ortheris and Mrs Hauksbee pose against a background of palm trees to the sound of temple bells, and one necessary circumstance was that Kipling himself was only half civilized.

Kipling is the only English writer of our time who has added phrases to the language. The phrases and neologisms which we take over and use without remembering their origin do not always come from writers we admire. It is strange, for instance, to hear the Nazi broadcasters referring to the Russian soldiers as 'robots', thus unconsciously borrowing a word from a Czech democrat[17] whom they would have killed if they could have laid hands on him. Here are half a dozen phrases coined by Kipling which one sees quoted in leaderettes in the gutter press or overhears in saloon bars from people who have barely heard his name. It will be seen that they all have a certain characteristic in common:

> East is East, and West is West.
> The white man's burden.
> What do they know of England who only England know?
> The female of the species is more deadly than the male.
> Somewhere East of Suez.
> Paying the Dane-geld.[18]

There are various others, including some that have outlived their context by many years. The phrase 'killing Kruger with your mouth',[19] for instance, was current till very recently. It is also possible that it was Kipling who first let loose the use of the word 'Huns' for Germans; at any rate he began using it as soon as the guns opened fire in 1914.[20] But what the phrases I have listed above have in common is that they are all of them phrases which one utters semi-derisively (as it might be 'For I'm to be Queen o' the May, mother, I'm to be Queen o' the May'[21]), but which one is bound to make use of sooner or later. Nothing could exceed the contempt of the *New Statesman*, for instance, for Kipling, but how many times during the Munich period did the *New Statesman* find itself quoting that phrase about paying the Dane-geld? (On the first page of his recent book, *Adam and Eve*, Mr Middleton Murry quotes the well-known lines 'There are nine and sixty ways / Of constructing tribal lays / And every single one of them is right.' He attributes these lines to Thackeray. This is probably what is known as a 'Freudian error'. A civilized person would prefer not to quote Kipling – i.e. would prefer not to feel that it was Kipling who had expressed his thought for him.[22]) The fact is that

Kipling, apart from his snack-bar wisdom and his gift for packing much cheap picturesqueness into a few words ('Palm and Pine' – 'East of Suez' – 'The Road to Mandalay'), is generally talking about things that are of urgent interest. It does not matter, from this point of view, that thinking and decent people generally find themselves on the other side of the fence from him. 'White man's burden' instantly conjures up a real problem, even if one feels that it ought to be altered to 'black man's burden'. One may disagree to the middle of one's bones with the political attitude implied in 'The Islanders',[23] but one cannot say that it is a frivolous attitude. Kipling deals in thoughts which are both vulgar and permanent. This raises the question of his special status as a poet, or verse-writer.

Mr Eliot describes Kipling's metrical work as 'verse' and not 'poetry', but adds that it is '*great* verse', and further qualifies this by saying that a writer can only be described as a 'great-verse-writer' if there is some of his work 'of which we cannot say whether it is verse or poetry'.[24] Apparently Kipling was a versifier who occasionally wrote poems, in which case it was a pity that Mr Eliot did not specify these poems by name. The trouble is that whenever an aesthetic judgement on Kipling's work seems to be called for, Mr Eliot is too much on the defensive to be able to speak plainly. What he does not say, and what I think one ought to start by saying in any discussion of Kipling, is that most of Kipling's verse is so horribly vulgar that it gives one the same sensation as one gets from watching a third-rate music-hall performer recite 'The Pigtail of Wu Fang Fu' with the purple limelight on his face, *and yet* there is much of it that is capable of giving pleasure to people who know what poetry means. At his worst, and also his most vital, in poems like 'Gunga Din' or 'Danny Deever',[25] Kipling is almost a shameful pleasure, like the taste for cheap sweets that some people secretly carry into middle life. But even with his best passages one has the same sense of being seduced by something spurious, and yet unquestionably seduced. Unless one is merely a snob and a liar it is impossible to say that no one who cares for poetry could not get any pleasure out of such lines as:

> For the wind is in the palm trees, and the temple bells they say
> 'Come you back, you British soldier, come you back to Mandalay!',[26]

and yet those lines are not poetry in the same sense as 'Felix Randal' or 'When icicles hang by the wall' are poetry. One can, perhaps, place Kipling more satisfactorily than by juggling with the words 'verse' and 'poetry', if one describes him simply as a good bad poet. He is as a poet what Harriet

Beecher Stowe was as a novelist. And the mere existence of work of this kind, which is perceived by generation after generation to be vulgar and yet goes on being read, tells one something about the age we live in.

There is a great deal of good bad poetry in English, all of it, I should say, subsequent to 1790. Examples of good bad poems – I am deliberately choosing diverse ones – are 'The Bridge of Sighs', 'When all the World is Young, Lad', 'The Charge of the Light Brigade', Bret Harte's 'Dickens in Camp', 'The Burial of Sir John Moore', 'Jenny Kissed Me', 'Keith of Ravelston', 'Casabianca'.[27] All of these reek of sentimentality, and yet – not these particular poems, perhaps, but poems of this kind, are capable of giving true pleasure to people who can see clearly what is wrong with them. One could fill a fair-sized anthology with good bad poems, if it were not for the significant fact that good bad poetry is usually too well known to be worth re-printing. It is no use pretending that in an age like our own, 'good' poetry can have any genuine popularity. It is, and must be, the cult of a very few people, the least tolerated of the arts. Perhaps that statement needs a certain amount of qualification. True poetry can sometimes be acceptable to the mass of the people when it disguises itself as something else. One can see an example of this in the folk-poetry that England still possesses, certain nursery rhymes and mnemonic rhymes, for instance, and the songs that soldiers make up, including the words that go to some of the bugle-calls. But in general ours is a civilization in which the very word 'poetry' evokes a hostile snigger or, at best, the sort of frozen disgust that most people feel when they hear the word 'God'. If you are good at playing the concertina you could probably go into the nearest public bar and get yourself an appreciative audience within five minutes. But what would be the attitude of that same audience if you suggested reading them Shakespeare's sonnets, for instance? Good bad poetry, however, can get across to the most unpromising audiences if the right atmosphere has been worked up before hand. Some months back Churchill produced a great effect by quoting Clough's 'Endeavour'[28] in one of his broadcast speeches. I listened to this speech among people who could certainly not be accused of caring for poetry, and I am convinced that the lapse into verse impressed them and did not embarrass them. But not even Churchill could have got away with it if he had quoted anything much better than this.

In so far as a writer of verse can be popular, Kipling has been and probably still is popular. In his own lifetime some of his poems travelled far beyond the bounds of the reading public, beyond the world of school prize-days, Boy Scout sing-songs, limp-leather editions, poker-work and calendars, and out in the yet vaster world of the music halls. Nevertheless, Mr Eliot thinks it worth-while to edit him, thus confessing to a taste which others share but are not always honest enough to mention. The fact that such a thing as good bad poetry can exist is a sign of the emotional overlap between the intellectual and the ordinary man. The intellectual *is* different from the ordinary man, but only in certain sections of his personality, and even then not all the time. But what is the peculiarity of a good bad poem? A good bad poem is a graceful monument to the obvious. It records in memorable form – for verse is a mnemonic device, among other things – some emotion which very nearly every human being can share. The merit of a poem like 'When all the World is Young, Lad' is that, however sentimental it may be, its sentiment is 'true' sentiment in the sense that you are bound to find yourself thinking the thought it expresses sooner or later; and then, if you happen to know the poem, it will come back into your mind and seem better than it did before. Such poems are a kind of rhyming proverb, and it is a fact that definitely popular poetry is usually gnomic or sententious. One example from Kipling will do:

> White hands cling to the bridle rein
> Slipping the spur from the booted heel;
> Tenderest voices cry 'Turn again!'
> Red lips tarnish the scabbarded steel:
> Down to Gehenna or up to the Throne,
> He travels the fastest who travels alone,[29]

There is a vulgar thought vigorously expressed. It may not be true, but at any rate it is a thought that everyone thinks. Sooner or later you will have occasion to feel that he travels the fastest who travels alone and there the thought is, ready made and, as it were, waiting for you. So the chances are that, having once heard this line, you will remember it.

One reason for Kipling's power as a good bad poet I have already suggested – his sense of responsibility, which made it possible for him to have a world-view, even though it happened to be a false one. Although he had no direct connexion with any political party, Kipling was a Conservative, a thing that does not exist nowadays. Those who now call themselves Conservatives are either Liberals, Fascists or the accomplices of Fascists. He identified himself with the ruling power and not with the opposition. In a gifted writer this seems to us strange and even disgusting, but it did have the advantage of giving Kipling a certain grip on reality. The ruling power is always faced with the question, 'In such and such circumstances, what would you *do*?', whereas the opposition is not obliged to take responsibility or make any real decisions. Where it is a permanent and pensioned opposition, as in England, the quality of its thought deteriorates accordingly. Moreover, anyone who starts out with a pessimistic, reactionary view of life tends to be justified by events, for Utopia never arrives and 'the gods of the copybook headings',[30] as Kipling himself put it, always return. Kipling sold out to the British governing class, not financially but emotionally. This warped his political judgement, for the British ruling class were not what he imagined, and it led him into abysses of folly and snobbery, but he gained a corresponding advantage from having at least tried to imagine what action and responsibility are like. It is a great thing in his favour that he is not witty, not 'daring', has no wish to *épater les bourgeois*. He dealt largely in platitudes, and since we live in a world of platitudes, much of what he said sticks. Even his worst follies seem less shallow and less irritating than the 'enlightened' utterances of the same period, such as Wilde's epigrams or the collection of cracker-mottoes at the end of *Man and Superman*.

Notes

1 George Orwell, 'Rudyard Kipling', first published in *Horizon*, 1945; reprinted in *Critical Essays* (London: Secker & Warburg, 1946), p. 109.
2 T.S. Eliot (ed.), *A Choice of Kipling's Verse Made by T.S. Eliot, with an Essay on Rudyard Kipling* (London: Faber & Faber, 1941).
3 Rudyard Kipling, 'Recessional', *Rudyard Kipling's Verse: The Definitive Edition* (London: Hodder and Stoughton, 1940), p. 328.
4 Kipling, 'Tommy', *Definitive Verse*, p. 399.
5 Kipling, 'If –', *Definitive Verse*, p. 576.
6 Kipling, 'The Islanders', *Definitive Verse*, p. 302.
7 Kipling, 'Follow Me 'Ome' *Definitive Verse*, p. 446.
8 Kipling, 'The Sergeant's Weddin', *ibid.*, p. 447.
9 W.E. Henley, 'Pro rege nostro' (1890), reprinted in A. Quiller-Couch (ed.), *Oxford Book of English Verse* (London: Oxford University Press, 2nd edition, 1939), p. 1029.
10 Kipling, 'The Drums of the Fore and Aft', *Wee Willie Winkie and Other Stories* (London: Macmillan, 1895), p. 329.
11 Orwell probably has in mind 'A Sahib's War' (*Traffics and Discoveries*, 1904), narrated by the devoted Sikh soldier Umr Singh, and the adoring Bhil NCO 'Bukta' in 'The Tomb of his Ancestors', *The Day's Work* (London: Macmillan, 1899).

12 Kipling, *Something of Myself and Other Autobiographical Writings*, ed. Thomas Pinney (Cambridge: Cambridge University Press, 1990), p. 34.
13 Kipling, 'That Day', *Definitive Verse*, p. 437.
14 Kipling, 'The 'Eathen', *Definitive Verse*, p. 452.
15 Tennyson, 'The Charge of the Light Brigade', in Christopher Ricks (ed.), *The Poems of Tennyson* (London: Longmans, 1969), p. 1035.
16 Edmund Wilson, 'The Kipling that nobody read', *The Wound and the Bow* (1941; London: Methuen, 1962).
17 The liberal Czech writer Karel Čapek (1890–1938) coined the word 'robot' in his 1920 play *Rossum's Universal Robots*.
18 Kipling, *Definitive Verse*: 'Ballad of East and West', p. 234; 'The White Man's Burden', p. 323; 'The English Flag' (misquoting 'What should they know of England?'), p. 221; 'The Female of the Species', p. 267; 'Mandalay', p. 420; 'Dane-geld', p. 713.
19 Kipling, 'The Absent-Minded Beggar', *Definitive Verse*, p. 459.
20 Kipling, 'For All We Have and Are' ('The Hun is at the gate!'), *Definitive Verse*, p. 329.
21 Tennyson, 'The May Queen', in Ricks (ed.), *Poems of Tennyson*, p. 418.
22 Kipling, 'In the Neolithic Age', *Definitive Verse*, p. 342, and Middleton Murry, *Adam and Eve: An Essay towards a New and Better Society* (London: Dakers, 1944), p. 1. For technical reasons I have parenthesised this remark, which Orwell inserted as a footnote when he reprinted 'Rudyard Kipling' in *Critical Essays* (see note 1).
23 Kipling, 'The Islanders', *Definitive Verse*, p. 301.
24 Eliot (ed.), *A Choice of Kipling's Verse*, pp. 35–6.
25 Kipling, 'Gunga Din', 'Danny Deever', *Definitive Verse*, pp. 406, 397.
26 Kipling, 'Mandalay', *Definitive Verse*, p. 420.
27 Thomas Hood, 'Bridge of Sighs', in Quiller-Couch (ed.), *Oxford Book of English Verse*, p. 776; Charles Kingsley, 'When All the World is Young', *The Water-Babies: A Fairy Tale for a Land-Baby* (1863; London: Macmillan, 1888), p. 91; Tennyson, 'The Charge of the Light Brigade', in Ricks (ed.), *Poems of Tennyson*, p. 1035; Bret Harte, 'Dickens in Camp', *Complete Poetical Works* (New York: P.F. Collier & Son, 1898), p. 209; Charles Wolfe, 'The Burial of Sir John Moore at Corunna', in Quiller-Couch (ed.), *Oxford Book of English Verse*, p. 712; Leigh Hunt, 'Jenny Kissed Me', in Quiller-Couch (ed.), *Oxford Book of English Verse*, p. 701; Sydney Dobell, 'The Ballad of Keith of Ravelstone', in Quiller-Couch (ed.), *Oxford Book of English Verse*, p. 93; Felicia Hemans, 'Casabianca', *The Works of Mrs Hemans, with a Memoir by her Sister* (Edinburgh: Blackwood; London: Cadell, 1893), vol. 4, p. 157, p. 227.
28 A. Clough, 'Endeavour', in Quiller-Couch (ed.), *Oxford Book of English Verse*, p. 898.
29 Kipling, 'The Winners', *Definitive Verse*, p. 530.
30 Kipling, 'The Gods of the Copybook Headings', *Definitive Verse*, p. 793.

4

On preparing to read Kipling (1961)

RANDALL JARRELL[1]

Mark Twain said that it isn't what they don't know that hurts people, it's what they do know that isn't so.[2] This is true of Kipling. If people don't know about Kipling they can read Kipling, and then they'll know about Kipling: it's ideal. But most people already do know about Kipling – not very much, but too much: they know what isn't so, or what might just as well not be so, it matters so little. They know that, just as Calvin Coolidge's preacher was against sin[3] and the Snake was for it, Kipling was for imperialism; he talked about the white man's burden; he was a crude popular – immensely popular – writer who got popular by writing 'If –' and 'On the Road to Mandalay,' and *The Jungle Book*, and stories about India like Somerset Maugham, and children's stories; he wrote, 'East is East and West is West and never the twain shall meet'; he wrote, 'The female of the species is more deadly than the male'[4] – or was that Pope? *Somebody* wrote it. In short: Kipling was someone people used to think was wonderful, but we know better than that now.

People certainly didn't know better than that then. 'Dear Harry,' William James begins. (It is hard to remember, hard to believe, that anyone ever called Henry James *Harry*, but if it had to be done, William James was the right man to do it.)

> Last Sunday I dined with Howells at the Childs', and was delighted to hear him say that you were both a friend and an admirer of Rudyard Kipling. I am ashamed to say that I have been ashamed to write of that infant phenomenon, not knowing, with your exquisitely refined taste, how you might be affected

by him and fearing to *jar*. [It is wonderful *to have the engineer / Hoist with his own petard.*] The more rejoiced am I at this, but why didn't you say so ere now? He's more of a Shakespeare than anyone yet in this generation of ours, as it strikes me. And seeing the new effects he lately brings in *The Light That Failed*, and that Simla Ball story with Mrs Hauksbee in the *Illustrated London News*, makes one sure now that he is only at the beginning of a rapidly enlarging career, with indefinite growth before him. Much of his present coarseness and jerkiness is youth only, divine youth. But *what* a youth! Distinctly the biggest literary phenomenon of our time. He has such human entrails, and he takes less time to get under the heartstrings of his personages than anyone I know. On the whole, bless him.

All intellectual work is the same, – the artist feeds the public on his own bleeding insides. Kant's *Kritik* is just like a Strauss waltz, and I felt the other day, finishing *The Light That Failed*, and an ethical address to be given at Yale College simultaneously, that there was no *essential* difference between Rudyard Kipling and myself as far as that sacrificial element goes.'[5]

It surprises us to have James take Kipling so seriously, without reservations, with Shakespeare – to treat him as if he were Kant's *Kritik* and not a Strauss waltz. (Even Henry James who could refer to 'the good little Thomas Hardy',[6] – who was capable of applying to the Trinity itself the adjective *poor* – somehow felt that he needed for Kipling that coarse word *genius*, and called him, at worst, 'the great little Kipling.') Similarly, when Goethe and Matthew Arnold write about Byron, as if he were an ocean or a new ice age: 'our soul,' wrote Arnold, 'had *felt* him like a thunder's roll.'[7] It is as though mere common sense, common humanity, required this of them: the existence of a world figure like Byron demands (as the existence of a good or great writer does not) that any inhabitant of the world treat him somehow as the world treats him. Goethe knew that Byron 'is a child when he reflects,'[8] but this did not prevent him from treating Byron exactly as he treated that other world figure Napoleon.

An intelligent man said that the world felt Napoleon as a weight, and that when he died it would give a great *oof* of relief. This is just as true of Byron, or of such Byrons of their days as Kipling and Hemingway: after a generation or two the world is tired of being their pedestal, shakes them off with an *oof*, and then – hoisting onto its back a new world figure – feels the penetrating satisfaction of having made a mistake all its own. Then for a generation or two the Byron lies in the dust where we left him: if the old world did him more than justice, a new one does him less. 'If he was so good as all that, why isn't he still famous?' the new world asks – if it asks anything.

And then when another generation or two are done, we decide that he wasn't altogether a mistake people make in those days, but a real writer after all – that we like *Childe Harold* a good deal less than anyone thought of liking when we like *Don Juan* a good deal more. Byron *was* a writer, people just didn't realise the sort of writer he was. We can feel impatient with Byron's world for liking him for the wrong reasons, and with the succeeding world for disliking him for the wrong reasons, and we are glad that our world, the real world, has at last settled Byron's account.

Kipling's account is still unsettled. Underneath, we still hold it against him that the world quoted him in its sleep, put his in its headlines when he was ill, acted as if he were God; we are glad that we have Hemingway instead, to put in *our* headlines when his plane crashes. Kipling is in the dust, and the dust seems to us a very good place for him. But in twenty or thirty years when Hemingway is there instead, and we have a new Byron-Kipling-Hemingway to put in our news programs when his rocket crashes, our resistance to Hemingway will have taken the place of our resistance to Kipling, and we shall find ourselves will to entertain the possibility that Kipling *was* a writer after all – people just didn't realize the sort of writer he was.

There is a way of travelling into this future – of realizing, now, the sort of writer Kipling was – that is unusually simple, but that people are unusually unwilling to take. The way is: to read Kipling as if one were not prepared to read Kipling; as if one didn't already know about Kipling; as if one were setting out, naked, to see something that is there naked. I don't entirely blame the reader if he answers: 'Thanks very much; if it's just the same to you, I'll keep my clothes on.' It's only human of him – man is the animal that wears clothes. Yet aren't works of art in some sense a way of doing without clothes, a means by which reader, writer, and subject are able for once to accept their own nakedness? the nakedness not merely of the 'naked truth,' but also of the naked wishes that come before and after that truth? To read Kipling, for once, not as the crudely effective, popular writer we know him to be, but as, perhaps, the something else that even crudely effective, popular writers can become, would be to exhibit a magnanimity that might do justice both to Kipling's potentialities and to our own. Kipling did have, at first, the 'coarseness and jerkiness'[9] and mannered vanity of youth, human youth; Kipling did begin as a reporter, did print in newspapers the *Plain Tales from the Hills* which ordinary readers – and, unfortunately, most extraordinary ones – do think typical of his work; but then for half a century he kept writing. Chekhov began by writing jokes for magazines, skits for vaudeville; Shakespeare began by writing *Titus Andronicus* and *The Two Gentlemen of Verona*, some of the crudest plays any crudely effective, popular writer has ever turned out. Kipling is neither a Chekhov nor a Shakespeare, but he is far closer to both than to the clothing-store-dummy-with-the-solar-topee we have agreed to call Kipling. Kipling, like it or not, admit it or not, was a great genius; and a great neurotic; and a great professional, one of the most skillful writers who have ever existed – one of the writers who have used English best, one of the writers who most often have made other writers exclaim, in the queer tone they use for the exclamation: 'Well, I've got to admit it really is *written*.' When he died and was buried in that foreign land England, that only the Anglo-Indians know, I wish that they had put above his grave, there in *their* Westminster Abbey: 'It really was *written*.'

Mies Van Der Rohe said, very beautifully: 'I don't want to be interesting, I want to be good.'[10] Kipling, a great realist but a greater inventor, could have said that he didn't want to be realistic, he wanted to get it right: that he wanted it not the way it did or – statistics show – does happen, but the way it really would happen. You often feel about something in Shakespeare or Dostoevsky that nobody ever said such a thing, but it's just the sort of thing people would say if they could – is more real, in some sense, than what people do say. If you have given your imagination free rein, let things go as far as they want to go, the world they made for themselves while you watched can have, for you and later watchers, a spontaneous finality. Some of Kipling has this spontaneous finality; and because he has written so many different kinds of stories – no writer of fiction of comparable genius has depended so much, for so long, on short stories alone – you end dazzled by his variety of realization: so many plants, and so many of them dewy!

If I had to pick one writer to invent a conversation between an animal, a god, and a machine, it would be Kipling. To discover what, if they ever said, the dumb would say – this takes real imagination; and this imagination of what isn't is the extension of a real knowledge of what is, the knowledge of a consummate observer who took no notes, except of names and dates: 'If a thing didn't stay in my memory I argued it was hardly worth writing out.'[11] Knowing what the peoples, animals, plants, weathers of the world look like, sound like, smell like, was Kipling's *métier*, and so was knowing the words that could make someone else know. You can argue about the judgment he makes of something, but the thing is there. When as a child you first begin to read, what attracts you to a book is illustrations and conversations, and what scares you away is 'long descriptions.' In Kipling illustration and conversation and description (not long description; read, even the longest of his descriptions is short) have merged into a 'toothsome amalgam'[12] which the child reads with a grown-up's ease, and the grown-up with a child's wonder. Often Kipling writes with such grace and command, such a combination of experienced mastery and congenital inspiration, that we repeat with Goethe: 'Seeing someone accomplishing arduous things with ease gives us an impression of witnessing the impossible.'[13] Sometimes the arduous thing Kipling is accomplishing seems to us a queer, even an absurd thing for anyone to wish to accomplish. But don't we have to learn to consent to this, with Kipling as with other good writers? – to consent to the fact that good writers just don't have good sense; that they are going to write it their way, not ours; that they are never going to have the objective, impersonal rightness they should have, but only the subjective, personal wrongness from which we derived the idea of the rightness. The first thing we notice about *War and Peace* and *Madame Bovary* and *Remembrance of Things Past* is how wonderful they are; the second thing we notice is how much they have wrong with them. They are not at all the perfect work of art we want – so perhaps Ruskin was right when he said that the person who wants perfection knows nothing about art.

Kipling says about a lion cub he and his family had on the Cape: 'He dozed on the stoep, I noticed, due north and south, looking with slow eyes up the length of Africa';[14] this, like several thousand such sentences, make you take for granted the truth of his 'I made my own experiments in the weights, colours, perfumes, and attributes of words in relation to other words, either as read aloud so that they may hold the ear, or, scattered over the page, draw the eye'.[15] His words range from gaudy effectiveness to perfection; he is a professional magician but, also, a magician. He says about stories: 'A tale from which pieces have been raked out is like a fire that has been poked. One does not know that the operation has been performed, but everyone feels the effect.'[16] (He then tells you how best to rake out the pieces: with a brush and Chinese ink you grind yourself.) He is a kind of Liszt – so isn't it just empty bravura then? Is Liszt's? Sometimes; but sometimes bravura is surprisingly full, sometimes virtuosos are surprisingly plain: to boil a potato perfectly takes a chef home from the restaurant for the day.

Kipling was just such a potato boiler: a professional knower of professionals, a great trapeze artist, cabinetmaker, prestidigitator, with all the unnumbered details of others' guilds, crafts, mysteries, techniques at the tip of his fingers

– or at least, at the tip of his tongue. The first sentences he could remember saying as a child had been haltingly translated into English 'from the vernacular'[17] (that magical essential phrase for the reader of Kipling!), and just as children feel that it is they and not the grown-ups who see the truth, so Kipling felt about many things that it is the speakers of the vernacular and not the sahibs who tell the truth; that there are many truths that, to be told at all, take the vernacular. From childhood on he learned – to excess or obsession, even – the vernaculars of earth, the worlds inside the world, the many species into which place and language and work divide man. From the species which the division of labour produces it is only a step to the animal species which evolutionary specialization produces, so that Kipling finds it easy to write stories about animals; from the vernaculars or dialects or cants which place or profession produces (Kipling's slogan is, almost, 'The cant *is* the man') it is only a step to those which time itself produces, so that Kipling finds it easy to write stories about all the different provinces of the past, or the future (in 'As Easy as A.B.C.'), or Eternity (if his queer institutional stories of the bureaucracies of Heaven and Hell are located there). Kipling was no Citizen of the World, but like the Wandering Jew he had lived in many places and known many peoples, an uncomfortable stranger repeating to himself the comforts of earth, all its immemorial contradictory ways of being at home.

Goethe, very winningly, wanted to have put on his grave a sentence saying that he had never been a member of any guild, and was an amateur until the day he died. Kipling could have said, 'I never saw the guild I wasn't a member of,' and was a professional from the day he first said to his ayah, in the vernacular – not being a professional myself, I don't know what it was he said, but it was the sort of thing a man would say who, from the day he was sixteen till the day he was twenty-three, was always – 'luxury of which I dream still!'[18] – shaved by his servant before he woke up in the morning.

This fact of his life, I've noticed, always makes hearers give a little shiver; but it is all the mornings when no one shaved Kipling before Kipling woke up, because Kipling had never been to sleep, that make me shiver. 'Such night-wakings' were 'laid upon me through my life,'[19] Kipling writes, and tells you in magical advertising prose how lucky the wind before dawn always was for him. You and I should have such luck! Kipling was a professional, but a professional possessed by both the Daemon he tells you about, who writes some of the stories for him, and the demons he doesn't tell you about, who write some others. Nowadays we've heard to call part of the unconscious *it* or *id*; Kipling had not, but he called this Personal Demon of his *it*. (When he told his father that *Kim* was finished his father asked: ' "Did *it* stop, or you?" ' Kipling told him that it was It.)²⁰ 'When your Daemon is in charge,' Kipling writes, 'do not try to think consciously. Drift, wait, and obey.' He was sure of the books in which 'my Daemon was with me . . . When those books were finished they said so themselves with, almost, the water-hammer click of a tap turned off.' (Yeats said that a poem finishes itself with a click like a closing box.) Kipling speaks of the 'doom of the makers': when their Daemon is missing they are no better than anybody else; but when he is there, and they put down what he dictates, 'the work he gives shall continue, whether in earnest or jest.'²¹ Kipling even 'learned to distinguish between the peremptory motions of my Daemon, and the "carry-over" of induced electricity, which comes of what you might call mere "frictional" writing.'²² We always tend to distrust geniuses about genius, as if what they say didn't arouse much empathy in us, or as if we were waiting till some more reliable source of information came along; still, isn't what Kipling writes a coloured version of part of the plain truth? – there is plenty of supporting evidence. But it is interesting to me to see how thoroughly Kipling manages to avoid any subjective guilt, fallible human responsibility, so that he can say about anything in his stories either: 'Entirely conscious and correct, objectively established, independently corroborated, the experts have testified, the professionals agree, it is the consensus of the authorities at the Club' or else: 'I had nothing to do with it. I know nothing about it. *It* did it. The Daemon did it all.' The reader of Kipling – this reader at least – hates to give all the credit to the Professional or to the Daemon; perhaps the demons had something to do with it too. Let us talk about the demons.

One writer says that we only notice what hurts us – that if you went through the world without hurting anyone, nobody would even know you had been alive. This is quite false, but true, too: if you put it in terms of the derivation of the Principle of Reality from the primary Principle of Pleasure, it does not even sound shocking. But perhaps we only notice a sentence if it sounds shocking – so let me say grotesquely: Kipling was someone who had spent six years in a concentration camp as a child; he never got over it. As a very young man he spent seven years in an India that confirmed his belief in concentration camps; he never got over this either.

As everybody remembers, one of Goya's worst engravings has underneath it: *I saw it*.²³ Some of Kipling has underneath: *It is there*. Since the world is a necessary agreement that it isn't there, the world answered: *It isn't*, and told Kipling what a wonderful imagination he had. Part of the time Kipling answered stubbornly: *I've been there* (*I am there* would have been even truer), and part of the time he showed the world what a wonderful imagination he had. Say *Fairy tales!* enough to a writer and he will write you fairy tales. But to our *Are you telling me the truth or are you reassuring yourself?* – we ask it often of any writer, but particularly often of Kipling – he sometimes can say truthfully: *Reassuring you*; we and Kipling have interests in common. Kipling knew that 'every nation, like every individual, walks in a vain show – else it could not live with itself'; Kipling knew people's capacity not to see: 'through all this shifting, shouting brotheldom the pious British householder and his family bored their way back from the theatres, eyes-front and fixed, as though not seeing.'[24] But he himself had seen, and so believed in, the City of Dreadful Night, and the imperturbable or delirious or dying men who ran the city; this City outside was the duplicate of the City inside; and when the people of Victorian Europe didn't believe in any of it, except as you believe in a ghost story, he knew that this was only because they didn't *know* – he knew. So he was obsessed by – wrote about, dreamed about, and stayed awake so as not to dream about – many concentration camps, of the soul as well as of the body; many tortures, haunting, hallucinations, deliria, diseases, nightmares, practical jokes, revenges, monsters, insanities, neuroses, abysses, forlorn hopes, last chances, extremities of every kind; these and their sweet opposites. He feels the convalescent's gratitude for mere existence, that the world is what the world was: how blue the day is, to the eye that has been blinded! Kipling praises the cessation of pain and its more blessed accession, when the body's anguish blots out for a little 'Life's grinning face ... the trusty Worm that dieth not, the steadfast Fire also.'[25] He praises man's old uses, home and all the ways of home: its Father and Mother, there to run to if you could only wake; and praises all our dreams of waking, our fantasies of return or revenge or insensate endurance. He praises the words he has memorized, that man has made from the silence; the senses that cancel each other out, that man has made from the senselessness; the worlds man has made from the world; but he praises and reproduces the sheer charm of – few writers are so purely charming! – the world that does not need to have anything done to it, that is simply there around us as we are there in it. He knows the joy of finding exactly the right words for what there are no words for; the satisfactions of sentimentality and brutality and love too, the 'exquisite tenderness' that began in cruelty. But in the end he thanks God most for the small drugs that last – is grateful that He has not laid on us 'the yoke of too long Fear and Wonder' but has given us Habit and Work: so that his Seraphs waiting at the Gate praise God

> Not for any miracle of easy Loaves and Fishes
> But for doing, 'gainst our will, work against our wishes,
> Such as finding food to fill daily emptied dishes . . .

praise him

> Not for Prophecies or Powers, Visions, Gifts, or Graces
> But for the unregardful hours that grind us in our places
> With the burden on our backs, the weather in our faces.[26]

'Give me the first six years of a child's life and you can have the rest' are the first words of *Something of Myself*, Kipling's reticent and revealing autobiography. The sentence exactly fits and exactly doesn't fit. For the first six years of his life the child lived in Paradise, the inordinately loved and reasonably spoiled son of the best of parents; after that he lived in the Hell in which the best of parents put him, and paid to have him kept: in 'a dark land, and a darker room full of cold, in one wall of which a white woman made naked fire . . . a woman who took in children whose parents were in India.' The child did not see his parents again for the next six years. He accepted the Hell as 'eternally established . . . I had never heard of Hell, so I was introduced to it in all its terrors . . . I was regularly beaten . . . I have known a certain amount of bullying, but this was calculated torture – religious as well as scientific . . . Deprivation from reading was added to my punishments. . . . I was well beaten and sent to school through the streets of Southsea with the placard 'Liar' between my shoulders . . . Some sort of nervous breakdown followed, for I imagined I saw shadows and things that were not there, and they worried me more than the Woman . . . A man came down to see me as to my eyes and reported that I was half-blind. This, too, was supposed to be "showing-off," and I was segregated from my sister – another punishment – as a sort of moral leper.'

At the end of the six years the best of parents came back for their leper ('She told me afterwards that when she first came up to my room to kiss me goodnight, I flung up an arm to guard off the cuff that I had been trained to expect'[27]), and for the rest of their lives they continued to be the best and most loving of parents, blamed by Kipling for nothing, adored by Kipling for everything: 'I think I can truthfully say that those two made up for me the only public for whom then I had any regard whatever till their deaths, in my forty-fifth year.'[28]

My best of parents cannot help sounding ironic, yet I do not mean it as irony. From the father's bas-reliefs for *Kim* to the mother's 'There's no Mother in Poetry, my dear,'[29] when the son got angry at her criticism of his poems – from beginning to end they are bewitching; you cannot read about them without wanting to live with them; they were the best of parents. It is *this* that made Kipling what he was: if they had been the worst of parents, even fairly bad parents, even ordinary parents, it would all have made sense, Kipling himself could have made sense out of it. As it was, his world had been torn in two and he himself torn in two: for under the part of him that extenuated everything, blamed for nothing, there was certainly a part that extenuated nothing, blamed for everything – a part whose existence he never admitted, most especially not to himself. He says about some of the things that happened to him during those six years: 'In the long run these things and many more of the like drained me of any capacity for real, personal hatred for the rest of my life.'[30] To admit from the unconscious something inadmissible, one can simply deny it, bring it up into the light with a *No*; Kipling has done so here – the capacity for real, personal hatred, real, personal revenge, summary fictional justice, is plain throughout Kipling's work. Listen to him tell how he first began to write. He has just been told about Dante: 'I bought a fat, American-cloth-bound notebook and set to work on an *Inferno*, into which I put, under appropriate tortures, all my friends and most of the masters.' (Why only *most*?) Two were spared, one for the Father and one for the Mother.) Succinct and reticent as *Something of Myself* is, it has room for half a dozen scenes in which the helpless Kipling is remorselessly, systematically, comprehensively humiliated before the inhabitants of his universe. At school, for instance: 'H – then told me off before my delighted companions in his best style, which was acid and contumelious. He wound up with a few general remarks about dying as a "scurrilous journalist" . . . The tone, matter, and setting of his discourse were as brutal as they were meant to be – brutal as the necessary wrench on the curb that fetches up a too-flippant colt.' Oh, necessary, entirely necessary, we do but torture in education! one murmurs to these methodical justifications of brutality as methodical, one of authority's necessary stages. Here is another master: 'Under him I came to feel that words could be used as weapons, for he did me the honor to talk at me plentifully . . . One learns more from a good scholar in a rage than from a score of lucid and laborious drudges; and to be made the butt of one's companions in full form is no bad preparation for later experiences. I think this "approach" is now discouraged for fear of hurting the soul of youth, but in essence it is no more than rattling tins or firing squibs under a colt's nose. I remember nothing save satisfaction or envy when C – broke his precious ointments over my head.'[31] Nothing? Better for Kipling if he had remembered – not remembering gets rid of nothing. Yet who knows? he may even have felt – known that he felt – 'nothing save satisfaction and envy,' the envying satisfaction of identification. As he says, he was learning from a master to use words as weapons, but he had already learned from his life a more difficult lesson: to know that, no matter how the sick heart and raw being rebel, it is all for the best; in the past there were the best of masters and in the future there will be the best of masters, if only we can wait out, bear out, the brutal present – the incomprehensible present that someday we shall comprehend as a lesson.

The scene changes from England to India, school to Club, but the action – passion, rather – is the same: 'As I entered the long, shabby dining-room where we all sat at one table, everybody hissed. I was innocent enough to ask: "What's the joke? Who are they hissing?" "You," said the man at my side. "Your damn rag has ratted over the Bill." It is not pleasant to sit still when one is twenty while all your universe hisses you.'[32] One expects next a sentence about how customary and salutary hissing is for colts, but for once it doesn't come; and when Kipling's syntax suffers as it does in this sentence, he is remembering something that truly is not pleasant. He even manages somewhat to justify, somehow to justify, his six years in Hell: the devils' inquisitions, after all, 'made me give attention to the lies I soon found it necessary to tell; and this, I presume, is the foundation of literary effort . . . Nor was my life an unsuitable preparation for my future, in that it demanded constant wariness, the habit of observation and attendance on moods and tempers; the noting of discrepancies between speech and action; a certain reserve of demeanour; and automatic suspicion of sudden favours.'[33] I have seen writers called God's spies, but Kipling makes it sound as if they were just spies – or spies on God. If only he could have blamed God – his Gods – a little consciously, forgiven them a little unconsciously! could have felt that someone, sometimes, doesn't *mean* something to happen! But inside, and inside stories, everything is meant.

After you have read Kipling's fifty or seventy-five best stories you realize that few men have written this many stories of this much merit, and that very few have written more and better stories. Chekhov and Turgenev are two who immediately come to mind; and when I think of their stories I cannot help thinking of what seems to me the greatest lack in Kipling's.

I don't know exactly what to call it: a lack of dispassionate moral understanding, perhaps – of the ability both to understand things and to understand that there is nothing to do about them. (In a story, after all, there is always something you *can* do, something that a part of you is always trying to make you do.) Kipling is a passionate moralist, with a detailed and occasionally profound knowledge of part of things; but his moral spectrum has shifted, so that he can see far down into the infrared, but is blind for some frequencies normal eyes are sensitive to. His morality is the one-sided, desperately protective, sometimes vindictive morality of someone who has been for some time the occupant of one of God's concentration camps, and has had to spend the rest of his life justifying or explaining out of existence what he cannot forget. Kipling tries so hard to celebrate and justify true authority, the work and habit and wisdom of the world, because he feels so bitterly the abyss of pain and insanity that they overlie, and can do – even will do – nothing to prevent.

Kipling's morality is the morality of someone who has to prove that God is not responsible for part of the world, and that the Devil is. If Father and Mother were not to blame for anything, yet what did happen to you could happen to you – if God is good, and yet the concentration camps exist – then there has to be *someone* to blame, and to punish too, some real, personal source of the world's evil. (He finishes 'At the End of the Passage' by having someone quote: ' "There may be Heaven, there must be Hell. / Meanwhile there is our life here. Well?" '[34] In most of his stories he sees to it that our life here is Heaven and Hell.) But in this world, often, there is nothing to praise but no one to blame, and Kipling can bear to admit this in only a few of his stories. He writes about one source of things in his childhood: 'And somehow or other I came across a tale about a lion-hunter in South Africa who fell among lions who were all Freemasons, and with them entered into a conspiracy against some wicked baboons. I think that, too, lay dormant until the Jungle Books began to be born.'[35] In Chekhov or Turgenev, somehow or other, the lions aren't really Freemasons and the baboons aren't really wicked. In Chekhov and Turgenev, in fact, most of the story has disappeared from the story: there was a lion-hunter in South Africa, and first he shot the lions, and then he shot the baboons, and finally he shot himself; and yet it wasn't *wicked*, exactly, but human – very human.

Kipling had learned too well and too soon that, in William James's words: 'The normal process of life contains moments as bad as any of those which insane melancholy is filled with, moments in which radical evil gets its innings and takes its solid turn. The lunatic's visions of horror are all drawn from the material of daily fact. Our civilization is founded on the shambles, and each individual existence goes out in a lonely spasm of helpless agony. If you protest, my friend, wait till you arrive there yourself!'[36] Kipling had arrived there early and returned there often. One thinks sadly of how deeply congenial to this torturing obsessive knowledge of Kipling's the First World War was: the death and anguish of Europe produced some of his best and most terrible stories, and the death of his own son, his own anguish, produced 'Mary Postgate,' that nightmarish, most human and most real daydream of personal revenge. The world *was* Hell and India underneath, after all; and he could say to the Victorian, Edwardian Europeans who had thought it all just part of his style: 'You wouldn't believe me!'

Svidrigailov says: ' "We are always thinking of eternity as an idea that cannot be understood, something immense. But why must it be? What if, instead of all this, you suddenly find just a little room there, something like a village bath-house, grimy, and spiders in every corner, and that's all eternity is . . . I, you know, would certainly have made it so deliberately." '[37] Part of Kipling would have replied to this with something denunciatory and biblical, but another part would have blurted eagerly, like somebody out of *Kim*: 'Oah yess, that is dam-well likely! Like a dak-bungalow, you know.' It is an idea that would have occurred to him, down to the last *deliberately*.

But still another part of Kipling would suddenly have seen – he might even later have written it down, according to the dictates of his Daemon – a story about a boy who is abandoned in a little room, grimy, with spiders in every corner, and after a while the spiders come a little nearer, and one of them is Father Spider, and one of them is Mother Spider, and the boy is their Baby Spider. To Kipling the world was a dark forest full of families: so that when your father and mother leave you in the forest to die, the wolves that come to eat you are always Father Wolf and Mother Wolf, your real father and real mother, and you are – as not even the little wolves ever quite are – their real son. The family romance, the two families of the Hero, have so predominant a place in no other writer. Kipling never said a word or thought a thought against his parents, 'both so entirely comprehending that except in trivial matters we had hardly need of words';[38] few writers have made authority so tender, beautiful, and final – have had us miserable mortals serve better masters; *but* Kipling's Daemon kept bringing Kipling stories in which wild animals turn out to be the abandoned Mowgli's real father and mother, a heathen Lama turns out to be the orphaned

Kim's real father – and Kipling wrote down the stories and read them aloud to his father and mother.

This is all very absurd, all very pathetic? Oh yes, that's very likely; but, reader, down in the darkness where the wishes sleep, snuggled together like bats, you and I are Baby Spider too. If you think *this* absurd you should read Tolstoy – all of Tolstoy. But I should remark, now, on something that any reader of Kipling will notice: that though he can seem extraordinarily penetrating or intelligent – inspired, even – he can also seem very foolish or very blind. This is a characteristic of the immortals from which only we mortals are free. They oversay everything. It is only ordinary readers and writers who have ordinary common sense, who are able to feel about things what an ordinarily sensible man should. To another age, of course, our ordinary common sense will seem very very common and ordinary, but not sense, exactly: sense never lasts for long; instead of having created our own personal daydream or nightmare as the immortals do, we merely have consented to the general daydream or nightmare which our age accepted as reality – it will seem to posterity only sense to say so, and it will say so, before settling back into a common sense of its own.

In the relations of mortals and immortals, yesterday's and today's posterities, there is a certain pathos or absurdity. There is a certain absurdity in my trying to persuade you to read Kipling sympathetically – who are *we* to read or not read Kipling sympathetically? part of me grunts. Writing about just which writers people are or are not attracted to, these years – who was high in the nineteenth, who's low in the twentieth – all the other stock-market quotations of the centuries, makes me feel how much such things have to do with history, and how little with literature. The stories themselves are literature. While their taste is on my tongue, I can't help feeling that virtue is its own reward, that good writing will take care of itself. It is a feeling I have often had after reading all of an author: that there it is. I can see that if I don't write this about the stories, plenty of other writers will; that if you don't read the stories, plenty of other readers will. The man Kipling, the myth Kipling is over; but the stories themselves – Kipling – have all the time in the world. The stories – some of them – can say to us with the calm of anything that has completely realized its own nature: 'Worry about yourselves, not us. *We're* all right.'

And yet, I'd be sorry to have missed them, I'd be sorry for you to miss them. I have read one more time what I've read so often before, and have picked for you what seem – to a loving and inveterate reader, one ashamed of their faults and exalted by their virtues – fifty of Kipling's best stories.

Notes

1. Randall Jarrell's 'On preparing to read Kipling' was first published as the foreword to *The Best Short Stories of Rudyard Kipling* (New York: Doubleday, 1961). It was reprinted in *Kipling, Auden & Co: Essays and Reviews, 1935–1964* (Manchester: Carcanet, 1981).
2. 'It ain't so much the things we don't know that get us into trouble. It's the things we know that just ain't so.' Popular observation often attributed most to Mark Twain, as well as to his fellow humourists Artemus Ward, Kin Hubbard and Will Rogers: Ralph Keyes, *The Quote Verifier: Who Said What, Where, and When* (New York: St Martin's Griffin, 2006), p. 3.
3. Entry on Calvin Coolidge, *Oxford Dictionary of Quotations* (Oxford: Oxford University Press, 1964), p. 68.
4. Rudyard Kipling, *Rudyard Kipling's Verse: The Definitive Edition* (London: Hodder and Stoughton, 1940), pp. 234, 367.
5. William James, *The Correspondence of William James: III William and Henry 1890–1894* (Charlottesville: University of Virginia, 1999), p. 301.
6. Martin Seymour-Smith, *Hardy* (London: Bloomsbury, 1994), p. 433.
7. Matthew Arnold, 'Memorial Verses', *Poetical Works*, ed. C.B. Tinker and H.F. Lowry (London: Oxford University Press, 1950), p. 270.
8. Joseph Eckerman, *Conversations with Goethe*, trans. John Oxenford (London: Everyman Dent 1930), p. 21.
9. James, *Correspondence*, p. 301.
10. Werner Blaser, *Mies van der Rohe: The Art of Structure* (London: Thames and Hudson, 1965), p. 12.
11. Kipling, *Something of Myself and Other Autobiographical Writings*, ed. Thomas Pinney (Cambridge: Cambridge University Press, 1990), p. 134.
12. Kipling, 'The Village that Voted the Earth was Flat', *A Diversity of Creatures* (London: Macmillan, 1917), p. 170.
13. Eckermann, *Conversations with Goethe*, p. 144.
14. Kipling, *Something of Myself*, p. 100.
15. Kipling, *ibid.*, p. 43.
16. Kipling, *ibid.*, p. 121.
17. Kipling, *ibid.*, p. 4.
18. Kipling, *ibid.*, p. 38.
19. Kipling, *ibid.*, p. 13.
20. Kipling, *ibid.*, p. 83.
21. Kipling, *ibid.*, pp. 121–3.
22. Kipling, *ibid.*, p. 68.
23. Goya, 'Yo lo vi'; 'Les Desastres de la Guerra 1810–1815' no. 44, *Obra gráfica completa* (Madrid: Casarlegio, 2007), p. 151.
24. Kipling, *Something of Myself*, pp. 52–3.
25. Kipling, 'Hymn to Physical Pain', *Definitive Verse*, pp. 787–8.

26 'Not for any miracle . . . Not for Prophecies', Kipling, 'The Supports', *Definitive Verse*, pp. 767–8.
27 Kipling, *Something of Myself*, pp. 3–12.
28 Kipling, *ibid.*, p. 54.
29 Kipling, *ibid.*, p. 120.
30 Kipling, *ibid.*, p. 12.
31 Kipling, *ibid.*, p. 21.
32 Kipling, *ibid.*, pp. 31–2.
33 Kipling, *ibid.*, p. 6.
34 Kipling, 'At the End of the Passage', *Life's Handicap* (London: Macmillan, 1891), p. 184, quoting Browning, 'Time's Revenges', in Ian Jack (ed.), *Browning: Poetical Works 1833–1964* (Oxford: Oxford University Press, 1970), p. 480.
35 Kipling, *Something of Myself*, p. 7.
36 William James, 'The Sick Soul', *The Varieties of Religious Experience* (Cambridge, MA: Harvard University Press 1985), pp. 136–7.
37 Fyodor Dostoyevsky, *Crime and Punishment*, World's Classics, trans. Jessie Coulson (Oxford: Oxford University Press, 1994), part 4, chapter 2, p. 275.
38 Kipling, *Something of Myself*, p. 52.

5

Kipling in South Africa

DAN JACOBSON

To begin with, a reminiscence. The first piece of verse by Rudyard Kipling I committed to memory – without even knowing I was doing so – was incised in large roman capitals on a wall of the Honoured Dead Memorial in Kimberley, South Africa. During the Anglo-Boer War (1899–1902), Kimberley was besieged for some months by forces from the two independent Boer republics, the Transvaal (De Zuid Afrikaansche Republiek) and the Orange Free State. Among those trapped in the city during the siege was the arch-imperialist Cecil John Rhodes, a former Prime Minister of the Cape Colony, the eponymous founder of the British colony of Rhodesia to the north, and the most prominent among the mining magnates drawn to South Africa by the discovery of diamonds in Kimberley and subsequently of gold in Johannesburg. Rhodes had in fact deliberately moved from Cape Town to Kimberley once it became clear to him that war between Britain and the two 'Dutch' or Boer republics was imminent: this he did out of a sense of *noblesse oblige* to the city in which he had made his first and greatest fortune, and which he felt to be peculiarly 'his' thereafter. (Many other people, the Boer leaders among them, felt the same way about it, which was why they had made Kimberley one of their prime targets.) Once the siege was lifted, Rhodes returned to his house and estate just outside Cape Town, and immediately commissioned his favourite architect, Herbert Baker, to find a prominent site in Kimberley and to design for it a memorial to the imperial troops and local militiamen who had lost their lives defending the city.

Built entirely out of ruddy-yellow granite brought down from Rhodesia, and complete with a massive cannon manufactured locally during the siege, the Honoured Dead Memorial is an imposing, flat-topped affair, half-fortress and half-Doric-temple in appearance. It stands in the middle of a grassed-over traffic circle just outside the grounds of the Kimberley Boys' High School, which I attended for a full ten years. So I had ample opportunity to study the memorial and its inscription as I trudged back and forth between school and home. Not until much later did I learn that the incised words stretching across several yards of stonework had been composed by Rudyard Kipling, at Rhodes' request. The names of both these men had been familiar to me almost as far back as I could remember. In Kimberley – then still a 'company town' dominated by the De Beers Consolidated Mines – Rhodes continued to be regarded as a kind of demi-god; Kipling I knew chiefly as the author of 'Rikki Tikki Tavi', a story about a mongoose battling cobras in an Indian garden, which, like an addict, I had read and reread at frequent intervals over many years. But I knew nothing of the close friendship that had sprung up between the author and the empire-builder; nothing of the three brief visits Kipling had made to Kimberley (during one of which he had enjoyed watching the City Hall burn down);[1] nothing of the fact that Rhodes had formally passed over to Kipling a house (also built by Baker) in the exquisite grounds of the estate he had laid out just under Table Mountain. It was in this house – dubbed 'The Woolsack', to which Rhodes had granted Kipling a 'life tenancy' – where the latter resided with his family during all but two of the lengthy annual visits he made to South Africa between 1898 and 1908.[2]

The direct alliance between the two men was to be of brief duration, however, for Rhodes died (of heart-failure, at the age of forty-nine) some months before the surrender of the Boer republics in November 1902. Thus he never had the opportunity to see in its completed state the memorial he had commissioned for Kimberley, though he would almost certainly have read the inscription Kipling composed for it:

THIS FOR A CHARGE TO OUR CHILDREN IN SIGN OF THE PRICE
                                                                    WE PAID
THE PRICE WE PAID FOR FREEDOM THAT COMES UNSOILED TO
                                                                    YOUR HAND
READ REVERE AND UNCOVER FOR HERE ARE THE VICTORS LAID
THEY THAT DIED FOR THE CITY BEING SONS OF THE LAND[3]

These chiselled, unpunctuated words made a great impression on my schoolboy mind: not least because of their obscurity. I did not know what 'a charge' meant here; plainly it did not refer to something that people did on battlefields or in games of rugby. And who exactly were the 'you', 'we' and 'they' that the lines evoked with such confidence? Most mysterious of all, however, was the command to 'read revere and uncover'. *Uncover?* At school the boys sometimes talked in spooky voices about the massive, never-to-be-opened steel door lodged in one of the monument's walls, behind which (it was said) there was a flight of stairs leading down to a place where all the 'Honoured Dead' from the siege were interred. But if that were the case, who would think of going down there to 'uncover' them? To what end? And what gruesome spectacle would meet their eyes if they actually did it?

By the time I left school some of these puzzles had been resolved; but other, more grown-up ones had taken their place. I knew, for instance, that the 'freedom' proclaimed in the inscription had nothing to do with the ambitions of the Nationalist Afrikaners, the defeated 'children' of the Boers, of whom relatively few had been living in Kimberley when I had entered school, but who in the ten years since then had grown to be a significant minority of its white population. And sure enough, just two or three years later in 1948 there were enough of them in Kimberley and elsewhere, countrywide, to vote the Afrikaner Nationalist Party into power – which it exercised zealously for the next half-century, until its notorious policy of *apartheid* collapsed both from its own inner contradictions and from the pressure put on it by the country's ever-more restive black population. I was also aware that neither the English-speaking nor the Afrikaans-speaking whites had the slightest intention (in those days) of extending the 'freedom' they enjoyed to the black-skinned 'sons of the land', who had always greatly outnumbered both white groups put together. Considerations like these had for me already turned the inscription on the monument into a kind of ponderous joke, a warning to all monument-builders never to take for granted anything about the future they would not live to see.

Remarkably enough, it was in South Africa, near an inconsequential place in the Orange Free State by the name of Karree Siding, that Kipling actually found himself under fire for the first time. His readers would have been much surprised had they learned that this was the case, for by then he had won world-wide fame for what he had written about soldiers and soldiering in India, Burma and Afghanistan. In his last book, *Something of Myself,* a 'partial autobiography' published in 1936, he devoted three or four vividly skittish pages to that baptism of fire near Karree Siding,[4] and in so doing produced a more satisfying piece of prose than anything to be found in the formally composed fictions he had set in South Africa. (Some critics have made big claims for a few of the South African stories, especially for 'A Sahib's War' and the famously mysterious 'Mrs Bathurst'[5] – a tale I have never been able to understand, with or without its admirers' helpful notes.) However, the poems he wrote on South African themes are another matter. They vary in merit of course; the two starkly entitled 'South Africa' are hardly more than doggerel; but the best ('Bridge-Guard in the Karroo', say, or 'The Old Issue') are much superior to the comparable prose pieces. The reason for this, I believe, is that poetry actually lends itself more readily to expressing political passions than fiction ever can. A poet is able to speak directly to the reader, even when he adopts a mask to do so; whereas the conflicts at the heart of any successful piece of fiction have to be acted out by seemingly autonomous characters possessing an interior life of their own.

But it is exactly that kind of autonomy which the politically engaged – and enraged – Kipling could grant to none of the characters who appear in his stories about South Africa. With very few exceptions he regarded the Boers as his personal enemies, and particularly sneaky ones at that, irrespective of whether they lived as British subjects in the Cape Colony or had taken up arms in the Transvaal and the Free State. He felt much the same about the vociferous liberals back 'home', whom he accused of flagrant sentimentality about the Boers and a criminal indifference to the fate of the empire as a whole. Even less forgivable, perhaps, were all the complacent, well-bred, games-playing English amateurs occupying high positions in parliament and the colonies, in the civil service and the army – the flannelled fools and muddied oafs, as he famously described them in his poem 'The Islanders' – who imagined that wars could be won and overseas possessions held without the exercise of ruthlessness and professional skill. In the hands of such idlers, he believed, one government after another had succeeded in putting at risk British interests not just in southern Africa but everywhere else too: above all in India. As Umr Singh, the Sikh mouthpiece of 'A Sahib's War', dutifully puts it, in speaking of what he has witnessed during the war: 'It is for Hind [India] that the Sahibs are fighting this war [in South Africa]. Ye cannot rule in one place and in another bear service. Either ye must everywhere rule or everywhere obey.'[6] In this story Umr Singh constantly parrots the official line that the Anglo-Boer war was 'a white man's war', with the local blacks – and Umr Singh himself – wholly excluded from combat because of the colour of their skin. Hence the story's title ('A Sahib's War') and various developments of its story too, including the scene when the English officer's ghost forbids his Indian servants to revenge his death, a job left to the Australian troops. The fact is that throughout the war both sides used large numbers of blacks as spies, scouts, porters and personal servants; and, more to the point here, the British also put significant units of armed blacks into the field. (This the Boers never dared to do, lest the guns they distributed be turned against them.[7])

The 'geo-political' misgivings expressed here by Umr Singh take one back to Rhodes, to Kipling, and to the curious intensity of their relationship with one another. As it happened, the two men became intimate when each was more or less at the height of his fame. True, Rhodes' reputation had been tarnished by his complicity in the Jameson Raid, a failed attempt to overthrow the government of the Transvaal by organising a military coup from outside the country's borders; hence his enforced surrender of the Prime Ministership of the Cape Colony, four years before the outbreak of the war. (In 1897, Mark Twain wrote of him in *Following the Equator*, 'In the opinion of many people Mr Rhodes *is* South Africa; others think he is only a large part of it. These latter consider that South Africa consists of Table Mountain, the diamond mines, the Johannesburg goldfields, and Cecil Rhodes . . . I admire him, I frankly confess it, and when his time comes I shall buy a piece of the rope for a keepsake.'[8]) It was true also that Kipling, the younger of the pair by about a dozen years, still had to write several of what would become his most widely admired books (*Kim* among them, as well as *Puck of Pook's Hill* and *Just So Stories*); yet his work had already secured for him a degree of popular esteem that was almost Dickens-like in its fervour. Each of the two men could therefore take the eminence of the other for granted, as they did also their shared belief that the English or British 'race' was more qualified than any other to rule over peoples and territories which (in their view) were incapable of governing themselves.

To these affinities were added a few mutually supportive differences. For all the success Rhodes had achieved as a financier and politician, he had difficulty in finding the words in which to express his ambitions: he was 'as inarticulate as a schoolboy of fifteen',[9] according to Kipling, whose own fluency (almost from birth, it seems) was phenomenal. Yet Kipling himself remained a schoolboy of a kind, too, not least in his perpetual hunt for heroes to worship – men of action, usually, who set about shaping the world to their own ends, whether as soldiers, sailors, camel-drivers, district commissioners, surgeons, engineers, gardeners, or empire-builders. And here in Cape

Town he found himself the friend and confidant of the greatest empire-builder of all, whom he had admired for many years (long before meeting Rhodes he had written of him as 'one of the adventurers and captains courageous of old'[10]), and who candidly revealed how much he relied on this newfound confidant to become his 'purveyor of words' (the phrase is quoted by Kipling in *Something of Myself*[11]).

Equally significant to their fellowship was their shared conviction that the world could best be understood – and best mastered, therefore – as 'an aggregation of secret and semi-secret societies, a pattern of circles, intersecting indeed, but closed'.[12] These half-ideas – megalomaniac from one aspect and paranoid from another – were to lead each of them in some strange directions, among which their shared, ardent interest in Freemasonry was probably the most innocent. Kipling's hunger always to be in the know, and to make sure that everyone else knew him to be in the know, is manifest almost everywhere in his writings, sometimes to their advantage, often not. (Especially when he over-indulges in his unique capacity for picking up specialised jargons of all kinds.) As for Rhodes, his schemes ranged from the formation of a secret society with the object of 'furthering the British Empire' and thus 'bringing the whole of the uncivilised world under British rule' (in his first will) to the slightly more modest plan (in his seventh will) to 'rejoin' the United States to the Empire and thus to found 'so great a power as to . . . render wars impossible'.[13] By the time he and Kipling got together these ambitions had been greatly scaled down, publicly at any rate, to the establishment of the Rhodes scholarships at Oxford: a scheme of which Kipling duly became a trustee.

Within a week or two of Rhodes' death Kipling wrote to a friend, 'No words could give you any idea of that great spirit's power . . . It seems absurd to speak of one's own petty loss in the face of such a calamity but I feel as though half of the horizon of my life had dropped away.'[14] This outburst is all the more striking when one thinks of the shattered silence with which he had met the death of his adored older daughter Josephine ('my little Maid'[15]) three years before, not to speak of the even grimmer silence he was plunged into by the second great loss of his life: the death of his only son on the Western Front barely a dozen years later. The grief he felt for his daughter eventually found expression – of a deliberately distanced kind – in one of his most touching stories, 'They'; his son John he mourned as openly as he ever did in the poem 'My Boy Jack', written as if the boy had been lost at sea and not in the mud of the trenches. On the death of Rhodes, on the other hand, he immediately wrote two memorial poems, one of them specifically to be read at the funeral in the Matopos Hills outside Bulawayo. Declamatory and prophetic in style (and utterly mistaken, as time was to show, about what lay ahead), the poem contains a touch of unintended pathos in the final verse, with its covert allusion to the exchanges between the poet and the politician:

> There till the vision he foresaw
>   Splendid and whole arise
> And unimagined Empires draw
>   To council 'neath his skies,
> The immense and brooding Spirit still
>   Shall quicken and control.
> Living he was the land, and dead,
>   His soul shall be her soul.[16]

That stanza appears on the wall of the grandiose Rhodes Memorial, designed once again by Herbert Baker, just below Table Mountain. It was Baker who chose to make use of the lines quoted above, rather than the verses initially and tentatively suggested to him by Kipling, which are more dramatic in tone and looser in form and grammar:

> As tho' again – yea, even once again,
>   We should rewelcome to our stewardship
> The rider with the loose-flung bridle-rein,
>   And chance-plucked twig for whip,
>
> The down-turned hat-brim, and the eyes beneath
>   Alert, devouring – and the imperious hand
> Ordaining matters swiftly to bequeath
>   Perfect the work he planned.[17]

Yet another poem, written by Kipling before he and Rhodes had met, and slightly rephrased after the great man's death, was later still pressed into service as the inscription on a seated bronze of Rhodes now overlooking the rugby fields of the University of Cape Town. It too speaks of 'empire to the northward . . . / Ay, one land / from Lion's Head to the Line'.[18] Lion's Head is a peak guarding the western flank of Table Mountain; 'the Line' of course refers to the equator, some two thousand miles to the north. Though he did not revisit South Africa after 1908, in later years Kipling steadfastly declined the requests of the executors of Rhodes' estate to return 'The Woolsack' to them – presumably because he could not bear to make this symbolic break with his friendship with Rhodes and his memories of the time he and his family had spent in the country.[19] After Kipling's death in 1936 'The Woolsack' did finally fall into the hands of the executors, who passed it on to the University of Cape Town. Today it is used as one of the many administrative buildings on the campus.

With Rhodes dead and 'half the horizon of my life ... dropped away', it might have been expected that Kipling's interest in South Africa would diminish sharply. In fact for another seven years he continued to make protracted annual visits to the Cape, during which time he went on publishing, among much else, poems and stories with a South African setting or derived from his experiences there. In many of these poems he excoriated British complacency and softness of mind, which, he insisted, were on display once again in the payments for damages being made to the Boer inhabitants of the two defeated republics, not to speak of the relatively early return to them of a measure of self-government. This last move he described as putting the Boers 'into a position to uphold and expand their primitive lust for racial domination'[20] – a statement seized on by British essayists and biographers including David Gilmour ('After predicting Dr Verwoerd's police state, Kipling anticipated the apartheid regime'[21]) as evidence of how concerned he was about the fate of South Africa's blacks, should they be left to the mercies of the Boers. Unfortunately, these writers have misunderstood what Kipling meant. From beginning to end of his South African sojourns he took remarkably little interest in black Africans (his furious criticisms of the Treaty of Vereeniging did not include or even notice the indefinite postponement of extending the franchise to native Africans, as Gilmour himself points out),[22] and I have no doubt that it was Boer domination of the British in southern Africa that was on his mind when he wrote the words quoted above. During the earlier decades of the twentieth century the term 'race' was habitually used in South Africa to refer to the quarrel between Boer and Briton, and *not* between white and black – however bizarre that exclusion may seem to us today – and it was repeatedly used in this sense by Kipling in his letters and Rhodes in his speeches.[23] Presumably the blacks were simply too far outside the realm of politics, as the term was commonly understood, to be brought into consideration. (More than twenty years after the end of the Anglo-Boer War, Roy Campbell, who remains the finest lyric poet in English that South Africa has yet produced and who was as sensitive to the local idiom as anyone could be, wrote a satire in rhyming couplets about the country's political and intellectual life. Entitled 'A Veld Eclogue', it focuses on two typically South African simpletons, Johnny (the English-speaker) and

Piet (the Afrikaner), commenting 'Think not that I on racial questions touch / For one was Durban-born, the other Dutch': Durban in those days being the most British, the most true-blue-Tory, of all South Africa's cities.)[24] After inspecting the living conditions of the black mineworkers in Kimberley, who were kept in close confinement by the De Beers Corporation in so-called 'compounds' for their entire term of hire (six months at a time), Kipling noted merely that 'Kaffirs like to steal diamonds'.[25] About the Boers he wrote in his letters in even more hostile fashion after the war had been won than he did while it was still being waged. Occasionally he acknowledges an honourable exception among them; more often he refers to them by such terms as 'a semi-civilized people of primitive tastes', 'a backward coloured breed', 'gorilla-type man' and so forth.[26] Outbursts of this kind may properly be compared with his half-mad imprecations against the Germans ('Huns', 'Boche' etc.) during the First World War. '[T]he idea begins to dawn upon the German mind that this is not a war of victories but a war of extermination for their race ... There can only be killing, butchery, and three nations, at least, desire ardently that the Boche be killed – at retail, since he can't be killed wholesale.'[27] Admittedly, the letter containing that passage was written on the last day of 1915, just months after the death of his son in the battle of Loos, and one hesitates to pass judgement on what any bereaved father might say, in private, in such circumstances. But it was not untypical of much else in his correspondence before and after 1918.

In his post-war published writings on South Africa, Kipling did indeed write several reconciliatory poems like 'Half-Ballade of Waterval', 'Piet', 'Chant-Pagan' and 'The Settler'. These and others were clearly intended to promote a process of healing between the two 'races', and the affecting and reverberating passages that appear in them – descriptions of landscape, evocations of states of mind, renderings of poignant details that only an eye as sharp as Kipling's would register – show how genuinely the prospect of reconciliation appealed to his imagination:

> Here, in a large and sunlit land,
>   Where no wrong bites to the bone,
> I will lay my hand in my neighbour's hand
>   And together we will atone
> For the set folly and the red breach
>   And the black waste of it all;
> Giving and taking counsel each
>   Over the cattle-kraal.[28]

What is troubling about these poems, however, is that they are all *victors'* poems: by which I mean that in each case the suppositious speaker of the poem is a Briton speaking either to his fellow-Britons or to one of his defeated enemies; in none are the latter permitted to utter a phrase or even a single word for themselves. They are pitied for their death in battle or their plight in being shipped off as captives to Ceylon or St Helena; they are congratulated in sportsmanlike fashion for having put up a good fight (and no hard feelings, mind!). Yet the imbalance between the speaker and the spoken-to or spoken-about is never rectified; in the following lines, for example, the intention to honour the dead Boer is plain, yet implicitly the poem honours more highly still the rough, patronising generosity of the British soldier mourning him.

> Ah, there, Piet! whose time 'as come to die.
> 'Is carcass past rebellion, but 'is eyes enquirin' why.
> Though dressed in stolen uniform with badge o' rank complete,
> I've known a lot o' fellers go a dam' sight worse than Piet.[29]

As a man and a writer Kipling was by nature both obsessional and protean: two modes of responding to the world that for him were less at odds with one another than one might expect. Intermittently at least, he was a driven, tormented individual, who had been subject to one major nervous breakdown and other, lesser collapses; haunted by fears of madness and cancer; frequently given to dwelling with manifest pleasure on the pain inflicted upon – or suffered by – his invented characters; insistent on hammering moral lessons into other people's heads (though capable at times of doing the job far more effectively with a single witty phrase). He was also a master at dramatising certain localised forms of obsession, as in his extraordinary story 'The Disturber of the Traffic', where a lighthouse-keeper becomes convinced that the waves in the straits he watches over are running lengthways in sinister, parallel 'streaks'; these distress him so much he eventually takes it into his 'pore sick head'[30] that the only way to stop them is to forbid all ships from passing his light. The story is, in effect, a about a man whose thoughts are incessantly driven down narrow channels – straits indeed – from which he cannot escape.

Unlike the single *idée fixe* in the mind of this unfortunate creature, Kipling's obsessions were themselves protean in nature: they moved in many directions at once. His need to show that he knew as much about everything (mechanical, social, linguistic, religious, historical, masonic etc.) as experts knew about anything was in itself an obsession. So was the ferocity with which he attacked those whom he believed to be his country's enemies: first the Boers, then the Germans (whom he had deeply mistrusted long before the outbreak of the First World War), then the Americans (before they entered the war on Britain's side in 1917), then the Irish republicans (of course), then the Jews (about whom he wrote in increasingly paranoid fashion as he grew older – choosing to forget that the collaboration of the Beits and Rothschilds had been indispensable to the success of his great hero, Rhodes). As a result of his South African experiences, an urgency of a related kind also took command of his preoccupation with the future of the British empire. During his startlingly precocious and productive years in India he had been able to regard the empire, by and large, as a given fact, as a demanding yet thoroughly well-deserved piece of good fortune that no one would ever be able to take from his people or himself. But this he could no longer do. Now he was inclined to see the empire as a grandly evolving project that no bounds could contain and at the same time as a besieged enterprise under threat from powerful enemies of many kinds.

All this cohabited in his mind with a late-developed passion for England itself, which he described as 'the most marvellous of all the foreign countries I have ever been in',[31] and which inspired some of his most thrilled and eloquent writing. What Kipling found so glamorous about England overall, and about the landscapes of southern England especially, was that their topography was inseparable from their human history. Unlike the South African veld, which he admired for other reasons, this landscape was coded, reclusive, idiosyncratic; its hills and fields continually spoke to him of unforgotten historical events and social intimacies impenetrable by outsiders, which he wrote of in *Puck of Pook's Hill*, as well as many of the other stories and poems set in the Sussex countryside in which he had finally made his home. (When T.S. Eliot went public with his admiration for Kipling by producing his *A Choice of Kipling's Verse* (1941), readers who regarded Eliot as the high-priest of an austere, highbrow modernism were surprised to learn of his enthusiasm for a poet written off by most intellectuals of the day as little better than a music-hall balladeer. In fact, Kipling's influence on Eliot – himself far more of a deliberately self-made Englishman than Kipling ever was – had by 1941 already shown itself in two of his own 'historical' or 'country-house' poems, 'Burnt Norton' and 'Little Gidding'.[32]) But if an immemorial bonding together of land and people was what Kipling loved most about England, how could that same people in another guise go about claiming for themselves perpetual title to a vast, amorphous empire that had no natural boundaries whatever? How could England be at once 'An Habitation Enforced',[33] to quote the title of one of his most famous stories, while at the same time serving as a springboard to the seizure and occupation of so many distant parts of the world? And what would happen to all those eager Britons whom he urged for empire's sake to turn themselves into Australians and New Zealanders, say, or South Africans and Canadians – or even, as some had done long before, into Americans, like the leading characters of 'An Habitation Enforced'? In such poems as 'A Song of the English' about the ports of empire, 'The Houses (A Song of the Dominions)', 'Our Lady of the Snows' praising Canadian self-assertion ('Daughter am I in my mother's house / But mistress in my own'[34]), 'The Native-Born', and many others, one can see Kipling trying with a certain desperation to resolve the conflict between his simultaneous enthusiasm for the world-straddling greatness of Britain, on the one hand, and, on the other, for everything about England that was distinctive, allusive, unavailable to others. Would 'the Blood' and 'the Race' and 'the Heritage' (his terms – and his capital letters[35]) be enough to keep in place these two poles of his imagined world? Would the ties between motherland and (white) empire which his poems insisted on be strong enough for the task? Could 'The hush of our dread high altar / Where The Abbey makes us We',[36] as he bathetically put it in 'The Native-Born', really sustain as one people the Britons at home and the British 'natives' yet to be born in countries so geographically remote?

The contrary tug of these impulses led him up many political and poetical blind alleys, but he could never have managed without them. They sustained his extraordinarily prolific and various output almost to the end of his life; they drove him restlessly from one self-assumed public duty to another, from one mode of writing to the next, from one stern exhortation to yet another reproachful outburst against those who let him down, as they so often tended to do. Everything he wrote, all his urgings in prose and verse, he put before the public with a seemingly indiscriminate haste, a shamelessness even, that led him in later years to be mocked as well as honoured for the sheer copiousness of his output. He wrote for adults; he wrote for children; he cajoled and bullied young and old alike; he insulted them, flattered them, warned them, made them laugh, spoke up tenderly for the humblest of them, made their flesh creep with intimations of uncanny forms of life and death, and, when nothing else would do, he bewildered them by retreats into taciturnity, blank refusals either to abandon or to explain the mysterious omniscience his writing so often hinted at.

Protean indeed. He was like a figure from a fairy story: at one moment a noisy bullfrog; at the next, a prince. And something of a prophet too. He had never understood, or even tried to understand, some of the bedrock certainties of South African life, the most prominent among them being the sheer weight of numbers that the indigenous inhabitants of the country would eventually bring to bear on every aspect of its political life. (To be fair, the same could be said about almost all other whites, the novelist Anthony Trollope aside,[37] who visited the country after the great diamond and gold rushes of the 1870s and 1880s.) But Kipling never forgot the crushing defeats the Boers had inflicted on British forces during the first few months of hostilities in South Africa: episodes that had left him with the conviction that since Britain's military and moral unpreparedness for a major war had been revealed to all, an 'Armageddon' must now lie ahead.[38] Thus, ironically enough, it was in England that he set the finest of the poems to emerge from his South African experiences; it was out of the Romney Marsh, some miles from his beloved house, Bateman's, in East Sussex, that he drew the poem's imagery; and it was written with a directly political, propagandist, even warlike purpose. As in many Kipling poems, its metre and rhymes draw on Swinburne, transforming the triumphalist liberal political poetry of the latter's *Songs before Sunrise* to the very different ends of his own imperial nationalism.[39] His aim in this long poem, 'The Dykes', was to incite the British government to introduce universal military training – of a kind similar to that which circumstances had always enjoined on the Boers – for the young men of the United Kingdom. From this distance it could be suggested that the programme of wholesale conscription and re-armament he was urging on Britain might not have averted the European war he feared, but merely hastened its onset. Yet, from this distance, again, who can tell?

One thing we can be certain of is that the language he used in 'The Dykes' survives the occasion of its writing and the motives of the writer himself. As these three verses[40] plucked from it go to show:

> Far off, the full tide clambers and slips, mouthing and tasting all,
> Nipping the flanks of the water-gates, baying along the wall,
> Turning the shingle, returning the shingle, changing the set of the sand . . .
> We are too far from the beach, men say, to know how the outworks stand.
>
> So we come down to the beach, uneasy, to look; uneasily pacing the beach.
> These are the dykes our fathers made: we have never known a breach.
> Time and again the gale has blown by and we were not afraid;
> Now we come only to look at the dykes – at the dykes our fathers made.

O'er the marsh where the homesteads cower apart the harried sunlight flies,
Shifts and considers, wanes and recovers, scatters and sickens and dies –
An evil ember bedded in ash – a spark blown west by the wind . . .
We are surrendered to night and the sea – the gale and the tide behind!

Notes

1 Kipling visited Kimberley twice between January and April 1898 during his first visit to South Africa. He wrote to his friend James Conland that on his return to Kimberley 'I watched the town hall burn down and played about the diamond fields once more' (letter to Conland April 1898, Thomas Pinney (ed.), *The Letters of Rudyard Kipling, Volume 2, 1890–1899* (Basingstoke: Macmillan, 1990), pp. 336–7. He visited Kimberley again in 1904 (See Thomas Pinney (ed.), *The Letters of Rudyard Kipling, Volume 3, 1900–1910* (Basingstoke: Macmillan, 1996), p. 237).
2 Andrew Lycett, *Rudyard Kipling* (London: Weidenfeld & Nicholson 1999), pp. 452–4.
3 Kipling, 'This for a charge': this poem was not collected in *Rudyard Kipling's Verse: The Definitive Edition* (London: Hodder and Stoughton, 1940: text reproduced in *The Works of Rudyard Kipling*, Ware: Wordsworth, 1994). It can be viewed online at http://en.wikipedia.org/wiki/Honoured_Dead_Memorial (last visited 10 September 2012).
4 Kipling, *Something of Myself and Other Autobiographical Writings*, ed. Thomas Pinney (Cambridge: Cambridge University Press, 1990), pp. 92–4.
5 J.M.S. Tompkins, *The Art of Rudyard Kipling* (London: Methuen 1964), pp. 89–91 ('Mrs Bathurst') and pp. 144–5 ('A Sahibs' War'); Elliott L. Gilbert, *The Good Kipling: Studies in the Short Story* (Manchester: Manchester University Press, 1972); Craig Raine, *A Choice of Kipling's Prose* (London: Faber & Faber 1987), p. vii; Philip Mason, 'More thoughts on "Mrs Bathurst" ', *Kipling Journal*, no. 261 (March 1992), pp. 11–20.
6 Kipling, 'A Sahibs' War', *Traffics and Discoveries* (London: Macmillan, 1904), p. 81.
7 Bill Nasson, *The South African War 1899–1902* (London: Arnold, 1999), pp. 210 ff.
8 Mark Twain (ed.), Shelley Fisher Fishkin, *Following the Equator: And Anti-Imperialist Essays* (New York: Oxford University Press, 1996), p. 32.
9 Kipling, *Something of Myself*, p. 87.
10 Kipling, 'From Tideway to Tideway' (1892), chapter 7, collected in *Letters of Travel 1892–1913* (London: Macmillan, 1920), p. 87.
11 Kipling, *Something of Myself*, p. 101.
12 W.L. Renwick, 'Re-reading Kipling', *Kipling's Mind and Art*, ed. Andrew Rutherford (Edinburgh: Oliver & Boyd, 1964), pp. 8–9.
13 J.G. Lockhart and C.M. Woodhouse, *Rhodes* (London: Hodder and Stoughton, 1963), pp. 69–70, 77, 416.
14 Kipling, letter to Edmonia Hill, 8 April 1902, in Pinney (ed.), *The Letters of Kipling*, vol. 3, p. 87.
15 Kipling, letter to Edmonia Hill, 30 July 1899, in Pinney (ed.), *The Letters of Kipling*, vol. 2, p. 376.

16 Kipling, 'The Burial', *Works*, p. 210.
17 Kipling, 'Rhodes memorial: Table Mountain', *Works*, p. 210.
18 Kipling, 'Cape Town' in 'A Song of the English', 1893, *Works*, p. 177.
19 Lycett, *Rudyard Kipling*, p. 775.
20 Kipling, *Something of Myself*, p. 97.
21 David Gilmour, *The Long Recessional: The Imperial Life of Rudyard Kipling* (London: John Murray, 2002), p. 145.
22 Lycett, *Rudyard Kipling*, p. 482; Gilmour, *Long Recessional*, p. 157.
23 Writing of Boers' resentment of the English, Kipling remarks 'The [South African] election was fought on pure racial issues and . . . all who were in any way loyal will come up for punishment' (Pinney (ed.), *Letters of Kipling*, vol. 3 p. 205); 'the Progressives go about saying that racialism is dead', *ibid.* p. 312. Rhodes: 'We [English] are the first race in the world': 1877 speech quoted in Lockhart and Woodhouse, *Rhodes*, p. 68.
24 Roy Campbell, 'A Veld Eclogue: The Pioneers', *Collected Poems* (London: Bodley Head, 1949), p. 23.
25 Kipling, 1898 letter to James Conland, quoted in n. 1.
26 Pinney (ed.), *Letters of Kipling*, vol. 3, pp. 299, 308, 322.
27 Pinney (ed.), *Letters of Kipling*, vol. 4, p. 352.
28 Kipling, 'The Settler', *Works*, p. 212.
29 Kipling, 'Piet', *Works*, p. 480.
30 Kipling, 'The Disturber of Traffic', *Many Inventions* (London: Macmillan, 1893), p. 9.
31 Pinney (ed.), *Letters of Kipling*, vol. 3, p. 113.
32 T.S. Eliot 'Burnt Norton' and 'Little Gidding', *Collected Poems* (London: Faber & Faber, 1962), pp. 189–95, 214–23; *A Choice of Kipling's Verse Made by T.S. Eliot with an Essay on Rudyard Kipling* (London: Faber & Faber, 1941). 'Little Gidding', first published in 1942, existed as a 'complete draft' by 7 July 1941: see Helen Gardner, *The Composition of Four Quartets* (London: Faber & Faber 1978), p. 153.
33 Kipling, 'An Habitation Enforced', *Actions and Reactions* (London: Macmillan, 1910).
34 Kipling, 'Our Lady of the Snows', *Works*, p. 182.
35 Kipling, 'A Song of the English', *Works*, pp. 170–8.
36 Kipling, 'The Native-Born', *Works*, p. 194. The reference in the second line of the quotation is to Westminster Abbey.
37 Anthony Trollope, *South Africa* (London: Chapman & Hall, 1878), pp. 471 ff.
38 Cf. the unnamed general in 'The Captive' who describes the Boer War as 'a first-class dress parade for Armageddon', Kipling, *Traffics and Discoveries*, p. 27.
39 Like 'The Islanders', which also calls for conscription, 'The Dykes' speaks its nationalist message through a pastiche of the bouncy six-foot rhyming couplets and democratic prophetic rhetoric of Swinburne's 'Hymn of Man' in *Songs Before Sunrise* (1871): 'The bow of your godhead is broken, the arm of your conquest is stayed, / Though ye call down God to bear token, for fear of you none is afraid.' *The Poems of A.C. Swinburne in Six Volumes* (London: Chatto & Windus, 1904), vol. 2, p. 102.
40 Kipling, 'The Dykes', *Works*, pp. 306–7.

6

The Great War and Rudyard Kipling

HUGH BROGAN

> Hope lies to mortals,
> And most believe her,
> But man's deceiver
> Was never mine.
>
> The thoughts of others
> Were light and fleeting
> Of lovers' meeting
> Or luck or fame.
> Mine were of trouble
> And mine were steady
> So I was ready
> When trouble came
> (A.E. Housman[1])

Many, many years ago, when I was a young academic at Cambridge, I found myself sitting on a sofa having tea with E.M. Forster. It was the season between Bonfire Night and Christmas. He said that, according to his bedmaker, old people hated Remembrance Sunday: it brought back too many painful memories.

I myself have reservations, chiefly about the way Remembrance Sunday is exploited and manipulated nowadays. It is ten or twenty years since I noticed (like everyone else, I watch the television news) that in the week or so before 11 November, Tory MPs have taken to sporting plastic poppies in their lapels (by the way, why are modern Poppy Day poppies so cheap and ugly?) as if they have contracted a rash. When a general election is pending they put the things on a full fortnight beforehand, and so do members of the other parties. Some years ago a group of pacifists tried to popularise the wearing of white poppies, as if the wearers of the red and the men they commemorated were somehow guilty in the shedding of blood, and in 1999 Peter Tatchell led a group of homosexuals to place pink poppies, arranged in a triangular wreath, on the Cenotaph a week before the official ceremonies.[2] Special efforts are made from time to time to whip up patriotic emotion, as the veterans of the world wars die off; this was especially conspicuous in 2010, the seventieth anniversary of the Battle of Britain. But such exercises are likely to become more difficult in future, and not just because there will be no more veterans of 1939–45 to grace the ceremonies. At my branch of the British Legion it has become a weekly ceremony to observe a minute's silence after the names of the latest dead in Afghanistan have been read out. It is moving because sincere and immediate; but how will its emotion transfer to Remembrance Sunday in, say, ten years' time? Commemorating an army of mercenaries (who cannot be said to have saved the sum of things) must be a very different thing from commemorating two generations of the volunteer and conscript dead.

Yet I doubt if public opinion will be ready to face the difficulty. It does not like to reopen old wounds, to debate old issues. There are few signs that the popular imagination is ready to consider and discuss Britain's twentieth-century wars – the two World Wars particularly – dispassionately, honestly, knowledgeably and accurately. When preparing the first version of this paper in the late 1990s I went to hear a lecture by Professor Brian Bond on the First World War[3] in which he told us how he had recently heard a young woman remark during a television discussion that it was thanks to the public schools that Britain had lost the war. Professor Bond wrote in to say that according to his information Britain had won. The BBC replied politely that he was entitled to his view.

Another anecdote: I once had occasion to read a graduate thesis on women writers and the Great War. I was startled to find that the author, writing nearly eighty years after the Armistice, took it for granted that the absolute pacifists of 1914–18 were right. The war, apparently, should never have been fought, and any writers, even women writers, who thought otherwise – who let their attitudes be tainted by patriotism or any other belligerent propensity – were simply written off as militarists. It had not crossed the writer's mind that you could hate the war and the process of waging war and yet believe that it must be fought and won. As Wagner said of Mendelssohn, I seemed to see an abyss of superficiality opening before me. Nor could I dismiss this piece of work as a mere token of one student's personal eccentricity. On the contrary, the writer was a typical victim of two generations of misrepresentation. It is hardly surprising that an age which finds in Britten's *War Requiem* (which ought to be called *An Anti-War Requiem*) its most representative piece of public music should be unaware that it is possible, in all seriousness and decency, to take more than one view of the Great War. Nor is it surprising that the British generally, so far as I can judge, now hold two logically incompatible beliefs: first that all war is pointless and avoidable, that all admirals, generals and air marshals are vicious incompetents, that all servicemen are passive victims like sacrificial sheep; second that the sheep were heroes who died nobly for their country.

As a professional historian I passionately repudiate this inconsistent and irresponsible myth-mongering. Neither the pacifist nor the nationalist presentation of the two world wars – of the First World War in particular – is an adequate interpretation; and there are some things that are too precious to be relinquished to the self-serving posturing of demagogues, whether of the Left or the Right. Furthermore, a nation which wallows in sentimental falsification of its past is likely to misjudge and mishandle its present, with heaven knows what evil results. The time came long ago to cry halt, as I am glad to report that many of my professional colleagues have done and are doing;[4] and members of the Kipling Society have a particular obligation to raise our voices, for among the many burnt offerings lately set before the God of Slovenly Falsehoods has been the reputation of Rudyard Kipling. It grieves me to say that, to judge by what has appeared in the *Kipling Journal*, we have sometimes failed in our duty. The December 1997 issue of the journal, for example, contained eight pages of comment on the then new play *My Boy Jack* by David Haig (a play which has enjoyed much subsequent success, for instance in 2007 when it was televised on Remembrance Day). The comment was intelligent, good-humoured and well-informed, as was to be expected; and the Holts in particular, who wrote the ground-breaking book about John Kipling[5] whose title Haig borrowed, had some important reservations; but except for one paragraph by the editor (who had not seen the play), all the contributors fell into the very trap which, in my opinion, had swallowed up the dramatist. They all accepted that the war was pointless and that the dead died uselessly. They did not notice that the play amounted to an almost total falsification of the beliefs, views and principles of the Kipling family where the Great War was concerned, and simultaneously displayed a shocking ignorance, indeed I must say prejudice, about the war itself.

The tragedy we were shown in the play is not the tragedy which befell the Kiplings; the interpretation of the war laid before us was one which no one at the time would have endorsed except possibly Bertrand Russell and a handful of pacifists (16,500 conscientious objectors, as against 4.9 million men who enlisted). To a historian, the play is a travesty of the past, and a confirmation if one were needed that myth has displaced truth, and that too many of the British have lost touch with their actual past. Ours is a generation which has succumbed to sentimentality and to what, in my profession, is sometimes called 'presentism': the inability to understand that the past is different, that what seems obvious to us, or to some of us, would have seemed contemptible, even incomprehensible, to our recent ancestors. So my business must be to remind readers of certain facts about the Great War, and to clarify Kipling's response to it.

To begin with young John Kipling, who in life was not the sympathetic but neurotic weakling that David Haig makes him. He was an entirely typical specimen of the young men who rushed to arms in 1914 at their country's call. By Christmas over a million of them had volunteered, 'grinning' (as Philip Larkin writes) 'as if it were all / An August Bank Holiday lark ... Never such innocence again'.[6] It was an extraordinary phenomenon: every other belligerent in 1914 relied on conscription; only Britain disdained it (though to go by the bellicose enthusiasm in all the other countries of Europe, even the great military monarchies might have managed without it). It is inconceivable that John would have held back, and we know that he did not. He was not quite seventeen when the war began, and his bad eyesight might have kept him out of uniform, but he would not allow it to do so. Rejected on his first application for a commission, he said he would volunteer to serve as a private. But his father applied to the Field Marshal Lord Roberts, who got John a commission in his own regiment, the Irish Guards.[7]

John was immensely happy at this; what the action cost his father, Rudyard never told anyone except perhaps his wife, who was paying too. Almost at once the parents recognised that their son's commission was just a deferred death warrant; for subalterns, some of whom they knew, were already falling like ninepins; three weeks after John got his own commission, Kipling wrote of a neighbour's agonising uncertainty about the fate of her son that hers 'is but one case of many, many hundreds'.[8] The Kiplings had only love, pride and courage to help them sustain their loss, in prospect and in actuality. Their only consolation was that John died like a man, for a cause in which he and they believed. How much they would have agreed with George Webb that 'it ill becomes anyone today to trivialise John's determination to play his part';[9] yet that is exactly what Haig (who might have thought twice, given the name he bears) did in his play, and what all do who take a glib view of the First World War.

My present concern, however, is not with John, except incidentally, but with Rudyard Kipling and his interpretation of the issues which brought Germany and Britain to war with each other, and with his justification of British belligerency.

Before proceeding I have to register another protest about *My Boy Jack*. Early in Act I, Kipling is made in 1913 or thereabouts to give a jingoistic speech in the course of his agitation to bring in conscription to Britain. This is true enough in principle, but the speech is silly: Kipling warns against Germany because if it comes to war and Germany wins, 'a vile and meddlesome tribe of bureaucrats will slip unnoticed into our midst . . . [who] will teach our bricklayers to lay bricks the German way.' This and other contentions ('they will tell us what to eat and how to eat it')[10] make Kipling sound like the dottiest sort of saloon-bar Euro-sceptic. No doubt this was Haig's intention, but to anyone knowledgeable about Kipling it is offensive, for whatever we think of his politics he was not silly, or even unrepresentative. Like many other Englishmen, he had been watching Germany with increasing apprehension ever since Kaiser Wilhelm II started building his great navy in 1897; and the perception that imperial Germany meant to overthrow British pre-eminence if she could, by war if necessary, was reinforced by a strengthening sense that German civilisation itself was growing sinister, as is indicated in D.H. Lawrence's story 'The Prussian Officer' in which a soldier, whose sexual beauty infuriates the repressed officer he serves into persecuting him, kills his torturer and dies of sunstroke, everyone thereafter maintaining a collusive silence about the dead officer's violence.[11] Kipling knew, as did everyone else of his time, that Britain was dependent on sea-power and sea-trade not merely for the preservation of her empire, but for survival: a point that was true for no other Great Power, and which the Kaiser and his men would have been well advised to consider before they began frivolously to threaten Britain's lifeline:

> 'Then what can I do for you, all you Big Steamers,
> Oh, what can I do for your comfort and good?'
> 'Send out your big warships to watch your big waters,
> That no one may stop us from bringing you food.

> *'For the bread that you eat and the biscuits you nibble,*
> *The sweets that you suck and the joints that you carve,*
> *They are brought to you daily by all us Big Steamers,*
> *And if anyone hinders our coming you'll starve!'*[12]

Kipling was, it seems, obsessionally convinced that the then Liberal government was neglecting or botching Britain's defences; in this he was grossly unfair, and he was unrealistic in brushing aside the extreme political difficulties that would have frustrated any government which tried to introduce conscription in peacetime; but his support for Lord Roberts' National Service League was neither foolish nor unwise nor dishonourable – indeed, knowing how near the British Expeditionary Force came to destruction in 1914 for lack of numbers, we must surely wish that the League had succeeded – and if David Haig had known what he was talking about he would not have suggested otherwise.

The outbreak of war in 1914 seemed to confirm Kipling's worst forebodings. We, posterity, must strive for a larger view. The First World War was such an appalling disaster that there can only be one verdict on the European generation that brought it about: they failed scandalously in an essential duty and must be blamed, but they must also be pitied. For although it can hardly be denied any longer that it was the wanton decisions of Austro-Hungary and Germany which made the great tragedy inevitable, all the other powers had made mistakes in the years before the war and all were to suffer horribly. So although it is still difficult for us, our task is not to take sides, but to understand. Such a cool approach will help us to appraise Kipling better than either retrospective jingoism or retrospective pacifism.

Given the world which had shaped them and in which they had to take decisions, it is no surprise that in 1914, after long hesitation, the British Cabinet felt obliged to go to war. It was clear that German power posed a long-term threat to the British Empire; Grey, Asquith, Haldane, Churchill and Lloyd George believed that it was their duty to defend that empire. A successful defence required that Britain have friends, or rather allies; therefore when Germany attacked France (which of all the main belligerents in 1914 seems to me to have least to apologise for), Britain must support her associate (I doubt very much whether Britain would have gone to war only to aid Russia). It might have been difficult to unite the country behind that proposition, but the German high command spared the Cabinet from having to make the attempt: in quest of a rapid victory in the west it invaded neutral Belgium. Britain was pledged to protect Belgium, and so it became a matter of honour to fight. German brutality showed what all Germany's opponents or rivals might expect if they did not resist her successfully.

It is impossible to exaggerate the effect of the rape of Belgium on British minds. As Lyn MacDonald has remarked, it gave the Allies a Cause.[13] Even Bernard Shaw, who leaned over backwards to see both sides of the question in his *Common Sense* (and reaped years of unpopularity as a result) eventually denounced the Germans as idolaters and pompous noodles for their failure to see the imbecility of their conduct.[14] H.G. Wells denounced 'blood and iron' and, I am sorry to say, 'flag-wagging Teutonic Kiplingism'.[15] The reaction began even before the atrocities: the indefensible action was atrocity enough. There was an explosion of verse, the first flames of a fire that was to burn for more than four years and add a glory to English literature. I suppose the most famous lines of 1914 were Rupert Brooke's:

> Now God be thanked Who has matched us with His hour,
>   And caught our youth, and wakened us from sleeping,
> With hand made sure, clear eye, and sharpened power,
>   To turn, as swimmers into cleanness leaping...[16]

Charles Carrington, a veteran of the First World War, was to comment that though Brooke's words 'have sometimes seemed hard to justify... that indeed was how it seemed'.[17] Equally strange is John Masefield's rather fine 'August, 1914' which embodies a myth, very powerful at the time (it apparently inspired Edward Thomas to enlist) that Germany must be resisted because she threatened the life of the English countryside. (I suppose this was a consequence of the invasion scares which had been a feature of the pre-war years.[18])

> How still this quiet cornfield is tonight!
> By an intenser glow the evening falls,
> Bringing, not darkness, but a deeper light;
> Among the stooks a partridge covey calls.

The poem turns into a plea for Englishmen to go 'as unknown generations of dead men did':

> For some idea but dimly understood
> Of an English city never built by hands
> Which love of England prompted and made good.[19]

Squires, labourers and peasants were to spring to arms to defend the woods, meadows and very soil of England. It is perhaps philistine to remark that the Kaiser never expressed any wish to destroy English agricultural society; we might think better of him if he had. In fact, so far as I know, the Germans of 1914 never planned to invade Britain and would not have succeeded had they tried. So in retrospect, for many reasons, much of the verse of 1914 seems misguided.

This does not apply to Kipling. The poem which he eventually produced was not the spontaneous effusion of a non-political man wakened, as Brooke so aptly put it, from sleep (Thomas Hardy's 'Men Who March Away' was just such an effusion, and little better than doggerel). Rather was Kipling the nation's recognised prophet. For no one's words did the English-speaking world listen so eagerly as his. In preparing this paper I came across a charming illustration of what he then meant to the people. A bandsman in the Rifle Brigade, finding himself and his comrades mobbed by a cheering, singing, flower-throwing crowd as they marched through Felixstowe, and remembering how contemptuously they had been treated in peacetime at their base in Colchester (they had been barred from many pubs), 'couldn't help thinking of [Kipling's] lines *It's Tommy this and Tommy that, and Tommy wait outside, / But it's "Thank you, Mr Atkins" when the troop-ship's on the tide'.*[20] But Kipling was silent for the whole of August. He was waiting, I guess, until he had something precise to say. It was the conquest of Belgium which at length drove him into utterance.

We need reminding of what that conquest entailed. On 4 August 1914, in breach of international law, her own treaty obligations, common sense and common decency, Germany sent her armies across the frontier and laid siege to Liège. The policy of *Schrecklichkeit*, or frightfulness, was immediately activated. The people of Belgium were to be terrorised into offering no resistance, for the German war-plan did not permit any delays for any cause. The Germans persuaded themselves besides that any Belgian resistance, apart from that offered, to their astonishment, by the Belgian army, was illegal and might be punished by the severest penalties.

So hostages were taken to secure good civilian behaviour, and when that did not work, were shot: six at Warsage on the first day of invasion. Simultaneously the village of Battice was burned to the ground 'as an example'.[21] On 5 August some Belgian priests were shot out of hand on the pretext that they had been organising sharpshooters. On 6 August Zeppelins bombed Liège, thus inaugurating a standard twentieth-century practice, as Barbara Tuchman points out. On 16 August Liège fell, after a defence which excited the world's admiration. On 19 August, at a place called Aerschot, 150 civilians were killed. On 20 August Brussels was occupied.

That day and the next, massacres occurred at Ardennes (211 shot), Teille (50) and Tamines (384). The Germans indulged themselves in an orgy of burning and looting. On 23 August Dinant was sacked, and 644 men, women and children were lined up and shot in the public square: included was a baby three weeks old. The roads south and west were by now choked with refugees. Namur fell to the Germans, and there was another massacre at Visé: all those spared fled across the frontier into Holland, except for 700 boys who were rounded up and, in another innovation with a long future, were deported to help with the harvest in Germany. The French fought heroically at the battle of Charleroi, but were nevertheless forced to retreat. The invaders entered Louvain.

Two days later they began their sack of Louvain, which went on for a week and was soon the most notorious of their crimes. The town was looted and burned, the inhabitants driven off or massacred, and the university library, one of the greatest treasures of its kind in Europe, utterly destroyed. All these incidents were faithfully reported by American newspaper reporters and quickly found their way into the British press. The horrified condemnations of the neutral, perhaps even of the Allied, press seem to have startled the German high command; the sack ended suddenly on 30 August.

On Tuesday 1 September, in *The Times*, Kipling spoke:

> For all we have and are,
> For all our children's fate.
> Stand up and take the war.
> The Hun is at the gate!
> Our world has passed away
> In wantonness o'erthrown.
> There is nothing left today
> But steel and fire and stone!
>   Though all we knew depart,
>   The old Commandments stand: –
>   'In courage keep your heart,
>   In strength lift up your hand.'
>
> Once more we hear the word
> That sickened earth of old: –
> 'No law except the Sword'
> Unsheathed and uncontrolled.
> Once more it knits mankind,
> Once more the nations go
> To meet and break and bind
> A crazed and driven foe.[22]

'Poetry makes nothing happen' said Auden,[23] and it is likely that, by the time these verses appeared, few readers needed Kipling to tell them what the war was about; but no doubt writing them helped him to clarify his own understanding,[24] and reading them may now clarify ours. The issue was the same as that of Hitler's war: alongside Dinant and Louvain, we remember Oradour in 1944 where the SS slaughtered 642 people, and Lidice in 1942, where another village was wiped out in retaliation for the assassination of Reinhard Heydrich.

Schrecklichkeit shattered irreparably the faith and hopes which the nineteenth century had bequeathed to the twentieth; we have paid heavily for their loss ever since; nevertheless, Germany had to be resisted. The point is unaffected by the fact that rumour managed to exaggerate even the truth. To do the Germans justice, they seem to have refrained from rape and mere sadism: the stories of ravished, pregnant girls and of children with hands chopped off [25] seem to have started among the thousands of refugees who got away to England, and to have been amplified by British civilians. These exaggerations eventually had a tragic effect, for not only did they come to blur the memories of what the invaders had actually done, their exposure as fraudulent made people very reluctant to believe what they heard twenty years later, when tales of new horrors began to come out of Germany. Kipling swallowed too many of the tall tales. But it was no false rumour which drove him in August 1914.

The date of the poem has another, probably unplanned significance – only 'probably' because Kipling could throw off finished verse with astonishing speed when necessary. On 30 August, the day he sent his poem to *The Times*, a special edition of the paper carried the celebrated 'Amiens despatch', which brought the first news to an appalled country of the retreat from Mons, the heavy losses of the British Expeditionary Force, and the prospect of total defeat which the Allies now faced. It was to a public reeling from the news that Kipling spoke:

> Comfort, content, delight,
> The ages' slow-bought gain,
> They shrivelled in a night.
> Only ourselves remain
> To face the naked days
> In silent fortitude.
> Through perils and dismays
> Renewed and re-renewed.

> Though all we made depart,
> The old Commandments stand: –
> 'In patience keep your heart,
> In strength lift up your hand.'
>
> No easy hope or lies
> Shall bring us to our goal,
> But iron sacrifice
> Of body, will and soul.
> There is one task for all –
> One life for each to give.
> What stands if Freedom fall?
> Who dies if England live?[26]

This was the prophet of 'Recessional' speaking again; there are clear verbal echoes of the earlier poem in the new, and they are printed side by side in the *Definitive Edition* of Rudyard Kipling's verse.[27] George Webb has objected to Kipling's use (here and elsewhere) of the word 'Hun', even though it was the Kaiser himself who, with characteristic folly, first used it of German troops; but apart from that, I think it can be agreed by all that these were astonishingly apt words for the hour, moving even today, and even today showing not only why so many in 1914 believed in the justice of the Allied cause, but that it actually was just. The message need not be summarised: Kipling is his own interpreter. 'Who dies if England live?'

Answer: hundreds of thousands of young Englishmen, among them the prophet's only son; but Kipling never swerved from what he saw as the cruel truth. The 'sickening word' must be silenced again. This was the issue. In 'The Outlaws', a poem of the same year, he elaborated his view of the Huns:

> They traded with the careless earth,
>   And good return it gave:
> They plotted by their neighbour's hearth
>   A means to make him slave.
>
> When all was ready to their hand
>   They loosed their hidden sword,
> And utterly laid waste a land
>   The oath was pledged to guard.
>
> Coldly they went about to raise
>   To life and make more dread
> Abominations of old days
>   That men believed were dead.[28]

He never changed from this attitude. He came perhaps nearest to what he thought was the root of the evil in that really unworthy and shocking poem 'A Death-Bed', when he picked up a tale that the Kaiser was dying of throat cancer like his father before him:

> 'This is the State above the Law.
>   The State exists for the State alone.'
> *There is a gland at the back of the jaw,*
>   *And an answering lump by the collar-bone.*'[29]

And in October 1918, as the Allies and Germany began to negotiate for an armistice, he published the poem 'Justice', which urged the absolute necessity of punishing the enemy before concluding peace with him:

> A People and their King
>   Through ancient sin grown strong,
> Because they feared no reckoning
>   Would set no bound to wrong;
> But now their hour is past,
>   And we who bore it find
> Evil Incarnate held at last
>   To answer to mankind.
>
> For agony and spoil
>   Of nations beat to dust,
> For poisoned air and tortured soil
>   And cold, commanded lust,
> And every secret woe
>   The shuddering waters saw –
> Willed and fulfilled by high and low –
>   Let them relearn the law . . .
>
> That neither schools nor priests
>   Nor Kings may build again
> A people with the heart of beasts
>   Made wise concerning men.
> Whereby our dead shall sleep
>   In honour, unbetrayed,
> And we in faith and honour keep
>   That peace for which they paid.[30]

But he did not by any means let the British off the hook. Everyone knows his rebuke to his own generation in 'Epitaphs of the War: Common Form':

> If any question why we died
> Tell them, because our fathers lied.[31]

Unfortunately the epigram is too terse to be intelligible – it has even been interpreted as a rejection of the Allied cause,[32] which it certainly was not. But in that case, what was the lie? By 1917 and 1918 no doubt many of the survivors regretted the enthusiasm with which they went to the rescue of France and Belgium in 1914, but Kipling cannot have had that in mind. It is likeliest that he was pursuing his ancient feud with the Liberal government, as in the verse 'Progressive' in the comic poem 'Natural Theology':

> Money spent on Army or Fleet
> > Is homicidal lunacy ...
> My son has been killed in the Mons retreat,
> > Why is the Lord afflicting me?
> Why are murder, pillage and arson
> > And rape allowed by the Deity?
> I will write to The Times, deriding our parson
> > Because my God has afflicted me.[33]

In 'The Covenant', where he rebuked the nation for the pride and folly which brought on the war, it seems that he was, yet again, blaming the Liberals particularly:

> We thought we ranked above the chance of ill.
> > Others might fall, not we, for we were wise –
> Merchants in freedom. So, of our free-will
> > We let our servants drug our strength with lies.
> The pleasure and the potion had its way
> > On us as on the meanest, till we learned
> That he who lies will steal, who steals will slay.
> > Neither God's judgment nor man's heart was turned.[34]

He had been saying this sort of thing since the Boer War, for example in 'The Islanders', the 'flannelled fools' poem, and perhaps would have done better to give it a rest; but he was also impressed and pleased with the response of this decadent nation to the challenge. He had no doubt where the real blame for the catastrophe lay, and he saw a stark contrast between the combatants, 'immemorially trained to refer all thought and deed to certain standards of right and wrong which, [the English] held, lay equally on all men, they had to deal with an enemy for whom right and wrong do not exist except as the State decides.'[35]

From first to last, then, the picture is utterly consistent; and until his death in 1936, Kipling never ceased to warn against the danger of a revived German aggression, and to urge the importance of keeping faith with the dead.

What are we to make of all this? We should start by making some concessions to Kipling's critics. All witnesses agree that Britain became hysterical with hatred of the Germans during the First World War, and Kipling (whose genius had a hysterical side) caught the infection, as is shown by some of the poems quoted above, by the story 'Swept and Garnished' about a German *Hausfrau* haunted by the ghosts of murdered Belgian children, and by the poem 'The Beginnings' with its refrain 'When the English began to hate' which accompanies the great, appalling story 'Mary Postgate'.[36] The dehumanizing intensity with which he wrote privately to friends of the desirability of exterminating any German, 'man or woman', is shocking: 'There is no question of hate or anger or excitement in the matter, any more than there is in flushing out sinks or putting oil on water to prevent mosquitoes hatching eggs. As far as we are concerned, the German is typhoid or plague – Pestis teutonicus, if you like.'[37] He believed the worst allegations about German atrocities in Belgium;[38] he demonised the Kaiser relentlessly; and from the British press he picked up the notions of State idolatry which were attributed to Heinrich von Treitschke, although Treitschke, admittedly not a sympathetic figure, seems only to have purveyed notions common to all European countries, with a German colouring: 'The moment that the state proclaims "Your state and the existence of your state are now at stake", selfishness disappears and party hatred is silenced.'[39] Kipling's knowledge and understanding of Germany were so superficial that he did not perceive that the problem was not that its government was so strong, but that it was so badly organised that it could not control its generals or qualify their blinkered military outlook by political common sense. Thus on 1 August 1914, at the very last hour, the Kaiser, visited by a sudden flash of wisdom, told Moltke that there was no need to go to war in the west: they should concentrate on fighting Russia. Moltke, shattered by the idea which would have cast aside twenty years of planning and preparation, absolutely refused to adopt it, although apparently he realised, only six months later, that the assault on Belgium and France had been a mistake.[40]

The curse of Germany was militarism, the militarism of Prussia as it had developed since 1870; most of the country's mistakes and all its crimes during the First World War can be laid at its door; and it was those crimes which created the atmosphere and attitudes which made later, even greater crimes possible. The evidence that militarism was the enemy was available to Kipling from the moment that Belgium was violated; but, obsessed with the Kaiser, he failed to understand it. Wilhelm II was not a competent ruler, but he was not the genius of pure evil that Kipling made him out to be. That description only applies to a later ruler, who was a follower of General Ludendorff.

On the other hand, Kipling grasped perfectly the case for British belligerence. So far as Britain and the British Empire were concerned, Germany was simply not to be trusted, and Britain could not in prudence stand by while her only ally, France, was destroyed; besides, invasion and occupation by Germany were no joke, and in the name of human solidarity it would have been shameful to grant the Prussians a free hand. These points were well understood in England in August and September 1914, and on the whole they continued to be valid throughout the war. Siegfried Sassoon apparently believed that a peace could have been made in 1917. If so, it would have been peace on Germany's terms, and we know, both from the work of Fritz Fischer and the Treaty of Brest-Litovsk, just how cruel those terms would have been.[41] They would also have weighed most heavily on Britain's European allies. Peace in 1917 was not, as it happened, at all likely; Kipling was not alone in thinking that it could not have been honourable. Yet nobody, reading his *History of the Irish Guards in the Great War*, can doubt that he knew exactly what was the price of war.

The aspect of Kipling which I have discussed in this paper is not that which has guaranteed his hold on posterity. There is much more to be said of his writings on the war: his reportage, his verse, his stories: even an examination of such a comparatively minor work as *Sea Warfare* (1915) reveals a human warmth (not to mention a certain charm, and delicacy of observation) which sets it, as literature, above most of the verse which I have quoted. And there is still much for us to discover in that other work – for example, the amazing passage in 'Mary Postgate' when the dead boy's possessions as Mary burns them may perhaps be read as Kipling's prophylactic against grief: or as a rehearsal, for it was written six months before he lost his own boy. And his account of the battle of Loos in *The Irish Guards*, though as carefully restrained in tone as the rest of that remarkable work, does contain some of the few critical comments on the British high command, its tactics and strategy, that he ever allowed himself in the remark that 'it does not seem to have occurred to anyone to suggest that direct Infantry attacks, after ninety-minute bombardments, on works begotten out of a generation of thought and prevision, scientifically built up by immense labour and applied science, and developed against all contingencies through nine months, are not likely to find a fortunate issue. So while the Press was explaining to a puzzled public what a far-reaching success had been achieved... men died.'⁴² It cannot be a coincidence that it was at Loos that John Kipling died.

But this essay has another concern: to rescue Kipling's reputation from ignorant libel, and to contribute, in however small a way, to a better understanding of that great historical tragedy which was not only his, not only his country's, but the world's – and which we still, after all this time, instinctively call the Great War.

Notes

1 A.E. Housman, 'I to my perils', *Collected Poems of A.E. Housman* (London: Jonathan Cape, 1939), p. 165.
2 *Guardian*, 13 November 1999.
3 Brian Bond, 'A victory worse than defeat? British interpretations of the First World War': 17 November 1997, Liddell Hart Centre, King's College, London.
4 See Trevor Wilson, *The Myriad Faces of War: Britain and the Great War 1914–1918* (Cambridge: Polity Press, 1986); Brian Bond, *The Pursuit of Victory: From Napoleon to Saddam Hussein* (Oxford: Oxford University Press, 1996) and the 1997 lecture mentioned above. For a brief, trenchant and convincing summary of the factors and events which led to the war, see Michael Howard, *The First World War: A Very Short Introduction* (Oxford: Oxford University Press, 2002).
5 For criticism of Kipling's attitude to war in the *Kipling Journal*, see the various reviews of 'My Boy Jack', December 1997, no. 284, pp. 37–44; the Revd Harry Potter, 'Kipling and the First World War', no. 296, December 2000, pp. 19–43; and more recently Dorothea Flothow, 'If any question why he died: John Kipling and the myths of the Great War', no. 326, April 2008 (University of Kent 2007 conference supplement), pp. 62–8.
6 Philip Larkin, 'MCMXIV', *Collected Poems*, ed. Anthony Thwaite (London: Faber & Faber, 1988), p. 127.
7 It is typical of David Haig's numerous small falsifications that he suggests at one point that Roberts was dying when Kipling asked his help (David Haig, *My Boy Jack* (London: Nick Hern Books), 1997, Act I, scene 5, p. 31). In fact Roberts seemed perfectly hale until a few weeks later he went to France, where he caught an infection that proved fatal. Contrary to Haig's play, Kipling did not pester a dying man.
8 Kipling, letter to Andrew MacPhail, 5 October 1914, *The Letters of Rudyard Kipling, Volume 4: 1911–19*, ed. Thomas Pinney (Basingstoke: Palgrave Macmillan, 1996), pp. 259–60. The neighbour was Lady Cecil, whose son George had been killed on 1 September. John Kipling was signed up as Second Lieutenant in the Irish Guards and reported for duty on 14 September 1914 (Andrew Lycett, *Rudyard Kipling* (London: Orion Books, 1999), p. 606).
9 George Webb, 'Editorial', *Kipling Journal* 71, no. 284 (December 1997), p. 11.
10 Haig, *My Boy Jack*, Act I, scene 4, p. 26.

11 D.H. Lawrence, *The Prussian Officer and Other Stories* (London: Duckworth, 1914). See also Jerome K. Jerome's disquieting account of the 'Mensur' duel popular at German Universities in *Three Men on the Bummel* (Bristol: Arrowsmith, 1900), pp. 225–32, described as 'a cruel and brutal game' (p. 232).
12 Kipling, 'Big Steamers', *Rudyard Kipling's Verse: The Definitive Edition* (London: Hodder and Stoughton, 1940). The text of this edition is reproduced in *Works of Rudyard Kipling* (Ware: Wordsworth, 1994), p. 729.
13 Lyn MacDonald, *1914: The Days of Hope* (London: Penguin, 1989), p. 43.
14 Bernard Shaw, *What I Really Wrote about the War* (London: Constable, 1931), pp. 159–60.
15 H.G. Wells, quoted in Barbara Tuchman, *The Guns of August* (New York: Dell & Co., 1963), p. 349.
16 Rupert Brooke, 'Peace', *The Poetical Works of Rupert Brooke*, ed. Geoffrey Keynes (London: Faber & Faber 1946), p. 19.
17 Charles Carrington, *Rudyard Kipling* (London: Macmillan, 1955), p. 423.
18 For fictional pre-war expressions of invasion scares, see Erskine Childers' best-seller *The Riddle of the Sands* (London: Smith and Elder, 1903) and 'Saki' (H.H. Munro) *When William Came: A Story of London under the Hohenzollens* (London: Bodley Head, 1914).
19 John Masefield, 'August 1914', in Dominic Hibbert and John Onions (eds), *Poetry of the Great War: An Anthology* (London: Macmillan, 1986), pp. 40–2. It is perhaps worth remarking that the poem's last stanza seems to owe something to Kipling's 'Puck's Song' (1909): 'And silence broods like spirit on the brae / A glimmering moon begins, the moonlight runs / Over the grasses of the ancient way / Rutted this morning by the passing guns.'
20 MacDonald, *1914*, pp. 50–1. The soldier was quoting Kipling's 'Tommy' – presumably from memory as he slightly misquoted the second line, 'It's "Special Train for Atkins" when the troopship's on the tide' (Kipling, *Works*, p. 398).
21 I take these and the following particulars (to be found in many other places) from Barbara Tuchman, *Guns of August*, pp. 198–359, *passim*.
22 Kipling, 'For All We Have and Are', *Works*, pp. 329–30.
23 W.H. Auden, 'In Memory of W.B. Yeats', *Collected Shorter Poems* (London: Faber & Faber, 1966), p. 142.
24 According to Carrington, Kipling's friend Perceval Landon, a journalist, was visiting Bateman's when Kipling was finishing the poem and 'offered some amendments, which Kipling accepted. It was Landon who carried the poem up from Sussex to *The Times*' (Carrington, *Kipling*, p. 428).
25 Dr Anurag Jain of Queen Mary University of London, showed in his doctoral thesis 'English Writers and Propaganda in the First World War' that the stories about children's hands derived, with obscene irony, from Conan Doyle's book *The Crimes of the Congo* (1909), which told from interviews with Roger Casement how Africans who had not produced their quota of rubber did actually have their right hands cut off. The crimes against Belgians of which the Germans were

falsely accused had thus actually been committed by the Belgians themselves. (I owe this information to Professor Montefiore.)

26 Kipling, 'For All We Have and Are', *Works*, p. 330.
27 Kipling, *Works* (reproducing *Definitive Verse*), pp. 328–30.
28 Kipling, 'The Outlaws', *Works*, p. 323.
29 Kipling, 'A Death-Bed', *Works*, p. 286.
30 Kipling, 'Justice', *Works*, pp. 393–4.
31 Kipling, 'Common Form', *Works*, p. 390.
32 See Jay Winter, *Sites of Memory, Sites of Mourning: The Great War in European Cultural History* (Cambridge: Cambridge University Press, 1995), pp. 220–1. In the discussion which followed my presentation of the original version of this paper to the Kipling Society, Dr Michael Brock suggested that since Kipling more or less abandoned his conscription campaign in the twelve months before the war broke out in favour of his involvement with the Ulster agitation against Home Rule led by Edward Carson, this epitaph may be intended to inculpate himself along with the rest of his generation for not seeing that the European crisis was becoming acute.
33 Kipling, 'Natural Theology', *Works*, pp. 344–5: ellipsis in line 2 in the original.
34 Kipling, 'The Covenant', *Works*, p. 320.
35 Kipling, preface to André Chevrillon, *Britain and the War* (London: Hodder and Stoughton, 1917), p. xiv.
36 Kipling, 'The Beginnings', *Works*, p. 678. These stories 'Swept and Garnished' and 'Mary Postgate' come last in *A Diversity of Creatures* (London: Macmillan, 1917), where they are both dated to 1915 and seem to form a diptych, followed by 'The Beginnings' on the last page (442).
37 Kipling, letter to Herbert Baillie, 12 January 1916 in *Letters, Volume 4*, pp. 355–6.
38 Kipling, letters to Frank Doubleday, 11 September 1914, and to Edward Bok, 18 October 1914, in *Letters, Volume 4*, pp. 255, 263–4.
39 See James Joll, *Origins of the First World War* (London: Longman, 1984), pp. 217–19, for this quotation and for an illuminating sketch of the influence of Treitschke and Nietsche. It is evident that Kipling's views of the German ideology were not unusual, and for good reason.
40 Tuchman, *Guns*, pp. 97–100.
41 See Fritz Fischer, *Germany's Aims in the First World War* (London: Chatto & Windus, 1967). By the winter of 1917–18 Germany had finally defeated Russia on the Eastern Front, and the new Bolshevik government felt constrained (with extreme reluctance) to accept the terms imposed by the victor in the treaty of Brest-Litovsk. But the terms were so savage (among other things, legitimising German looting of the Russian countryside), that they were unenforceable except by constant military pressure, which meant that the Germans were unable to shift enough troops from the east to succeed in their final offensive in France. Characteristically, imperial Germany thus defeated itself.
42 Kipling, *The History of the Irish Guards in the Great War Volume II: The Second Battalion* (1923; Staplehurst: Spellmount, 1997), p. 28. For Kipling's criticism of tactical shortcomings in the battle, see pp. 21, 22, 24.

7

'A Kipling-conditioned world': Kipling among the war poets

HARRY RICKETTS

Dominic Hibberd and John Onions allow Kipling eighteen poems in their 2007 anthology *The Winter of the World: Poems of the Great War*. Wilfred Owen, by comparison, is given fourteen, Siegfried Sassoon thirteen, Isaac Rosenberg and Ivor Gurney ten apiece. Admittedly, Kipling's contributions include eight of his brief, epigrammatic 'Epitaphs of the War'; nonetheless, the size of his allocation suggests that he now holds an integral and unarguable position in the poetry of the First World War.

And not just in the last few years. This has been the pattern since the debunking, idealistic, turbulent 1960s created the modern enthusiasm for Great War poetry and established the canon of 'war poets' that, with occasional special pleading, remains more or less accepted: Edmund Blunden, Rupert Brooke, Robert Graves, Gurney, David Jones, Owen, Rosenberg, Sassoon, Charles Sorley and Edward Thomas. Of these, the 1960s enshrined Owen, in Hibberd's phrase, as 'the national poet of pity', a position he still holds.[1] Central to this enshrinement were two anthologies, Brian Gardner's *Up the Line to Death: The War Poets 1914–1918* (1964) and Ian Parsons' *Men Who March Away: Poems of the First World War* (1965).[2] While Gardner included five of Owen's poems, Parsons gave him pride of place with thirteen and paid his work prominent attention in his introduction. It was these same two anthologies, particularly Gardner's, that reinstalled Kipling as a poet of the war and even made a case for him as a 'war poet' – that is, as a poet at least critical of the war, if not positively anti-war.

Gardner included six poems from Kipling's First World War collection *The Years Between* (1919): 'Mesopotamia', 'The Verdicts', 'A Death-Bed' and three of the 'Epitaphs' ('Bombed in London', 'A Dead Statesman' and 'Common Form'). Parsons also put in 'Mesopotamia' and three 'Epitaphs' ('A Drifter off Tarentum', 'Batteries out of Ammunition' and 'The Refined Man'). Neither anthologist included Kipling's first 'war' poem, 'For All We Have and Are' of early September 1914 ('Stand up and take the war. / The Hun is at the gate!'), nor his retribution-seeking 'Justice' of October 1918 ("Before we loose the word / That bids new worlds to birth, / Needs must we loosen first the sword / Of Justice upon earth").[3] Gardner's Kipling was certainly bitter – 'A Death-Bed' is a chillingly detailed revenge-fantasy based on a rumour that the Kaiser had throat cancer – but he was presented more as grieving parent than as bellicose conscription-advocate:

> He wrote with the voice of ordinary people: fearing for their sons, indignant at the faceless men who seemed responsible for some trick that no one quite understood, tired and bewildered by the inability of politicians and generals to conclude the war.[4]

Such reframing, together with Gardner's and Parsons's selections, offered an only partially accurate account. To exclude not only 'For All We Have and Are' and 'Justice', but also other equally outright propagandist poems like 'The Outlaws', 'The Question' (urging the USA to join the Allies) and the 'The Holy War' (invoking the spirit of John Bunyan) gave an decidedly lopsided sense of Kipling's 'war poetry'. However, this massaged version did make it possible to accommodate Kipling within the then new – and even now still potent – myth of the war and its poetry, encapsulated by Hibberd as 'a story of idealism turning to realism, satire, protest and pity'.[5]

The situation looked rather different when *The Years Between* first appeared in April 1919. Kipling himself was still busily encouraging his American publisher Frank Doubleday to promote the book on that side of the Atlantic as part of the war effort. In notes specifically intended for publicity purposes, he commented that 'My Boy Jack', was '[s]ung at concerts, etc. all over England, and next to "*For all we have and are*" [was] the most popular of the war-verses for quotation.' 'For All We Have and Are' was, he observed, '[g]enerally adjudged at the time it was written as "too serious for the needs of the war" but in 1915 it was realised that it was the truth and was generally used, for propaganda.'[6]

This rare glimpse of 'Kipling on Kipling' needs to be set against a post-Gardner and Parsons reading of 'For All We Have and Are', such as Ann Parry's in *The Poetry of Rudyard Kipling: Rousing the Nation* (1992). For Parry, the answer to the poem's final question, 'Who dies if England live?', 'was not hard to seek when the newspapers carried pictures on a daily basis of young men queuing up to enlist'.[7] To take that final question as real not rhetorical – and more generally to claim that the poem embodies a contradictory attitude towards the war – certainly portrays Kipling in a more sympathetic, 'modern' light. And such a reading is theoretically possible. However, it goes entirely against the rhythmic grain of the last line. It under-reads the talismanic uplift on the word 'England' and the way the concluding, affirmatory 'live' redresses the alliterative downbeat of the previous line: 'Who stands if Freedom fall? / Who dies if England live?'[8] One could argue that here Kipling was trying to cheer himself up as well as those he was addressing in his role as tribal bard, but that is rather different from claiming that he felt deeply divided about what he was saying.

All the same, several of the poems written after his son John's death at Loos in late September 1915 are riddled with ambivalence. One is 'Common Form', among the most adhesive of all the 'Epitaphs':

> If any question why we died,
> Tell them, because our fathers lied.[9]

As Jay Winter and others have demonstrated, the couplet can be read in a number of ways: 'The phrase "because our fathers lied" can be seen as an answer to the question in the first line of the couplet. But it is also possible that Kipling is suggesting that the answer to the question "why did they die?" lay in the mind of the reader. Only he or she can do better than the lies told by the fathers.'[10]

In 1919, the British press reviewed *The Years Between* less extensively than might have been expected but did so along predictable lines. Reviewers tended either to adopt the propagandist view or to write off the volume altogether. So 'E.B.O.' (E.B. Osborn) in the right-wing *Morning Post* enthusiastically hailed Kipling as the 'one honest poet-prophet among all the inverted Balaams of this perplexed epoch', while the reviewer in *The Scotsman* signed off with a vacuous flourish: 'England may well rejoice in a poet so worthy of his fame, and so happy as this latest book shows him to be in bringing home what his country has had to go through and how nobly she has comported herself through the great time of trial.'[11] At the other end of the political spectrum, the new literary editor of the left-wing *Daily Herald*, Siegfried Sassoon, merely dismissed the collection in passing in his 'Literary Notes': 'Of Rudyard Kipling's new poems . . . I can say nothing, as I am not a wicked, swearing man. Kipling has written some great books, but this is not one of them.'[12] The only review anyone now remembers of the collection was by 'T.S.E.' in the liberal *Athenaeum*. There, Eliot witheringly, wittily, dubbed Kipling 'a laureate without laurels', 'one of the Minor Prophets', whose poetic 'formula' could be boiled down to a 'touch of the newspapers, of Billy Sunday, and the Revised Version filtered through Rabbi Zeal-of-the-Land Busy'.[13] (Eliot of course later modified his views of Kipling and edited a famous selection of Kipling's poems, *A Choice of Kipling's Verse* (1941), with the equally famous introduction in which he tied himself and his readers in knots, trying to demonstrate that Kipling was not really a poet but a great verse-writer.)

Not surprisingly, perhaps, it is usually assumed that at the beginning of the war those we have come to call the 'war poets' saw Kipling in a similarly negative light. Gardner, for instance, asserts that 'Of all the poets well-established by 1914, the one for whom the war poets themselves probably had least sympathy was Rudyard Kipling'.[14] Forty years later Hibberd and Onions repeat the assertion in more vehement terms: 'Kipling was detested by many younger writers for his political views'.[15] A sampling of the views of the war poets from just before and soon after the outbreak of war seems to lend support to this view.

In May 1914, Owen, tutoring in Bordeaux, told his mother, presumably as an amazed joke: 'I do between 8 and 9 lessons now, and any time between is seized by my student-friends, who want help with translations of Kipling!'[16] In early July, Sassoon, trying to make conversation over breakfast with the glamorous Brooke, dismissed Kipling's poetry as 'terribly tub-thumping stuff'.[17] A month later, soon after England entered the war, the nineteen-year-old Sorley wrote to a friend: 'I'm thankful to see that Kipling hasn't written a poem yet.'[18] In December 1914, Thomas crisply noted in the journal *Poetry and Drama* that so far 'Mr Kipling has hardly done more than speak in echoes of himself.'[19] Such remarks certainly seem to suggest that the war poets did indeed consider Kipling's work and attitudes as in fundamental opposition to their own – that, across a poetic and ideological no man's land, he represented an enemy of a different kind.

However, the connections between Kipling and at least some of these poets, both in 1914 and as the war dragged on, were often more complicated.

It is easy now to overlook that to grow up in England (and its colonies) in the two decades or so preceding the war was – consciously or not, willingly or not – to absorb Kipling. His work, both poetry and prose, was a shared possession, almost as deeply imprinted as the Bible and Shakespeare, and for public schoolboys the classics. Or, as David Jones put it, looking back from 1961 at his turn-of-the-century childhood: 'One lived in a kind of Kipling-conditioned world without knowing it.'[20] This 'conditioning' shows itself quite blatantly in the work of the now mostly forgotten war poet Gilbert Frankau who, in poems like 'The Beasts in Gray' (1918), sounds more Kipling than Kipling:

> Wherefore, O free-born Peoples –
> Though it last for a year and a day –
> This let us vow in the name of our God:
> 'No truce with the Beasts in Gray!'[21]

But the 'conditioning' also manifests itself in less obvious ways, notably in an ambivalence of attitude which pervades the outlook and output of the war poets.

An illuminating example of such an ambivalence is Edward Thomas. On the one hand, he clearly disliked Kipling's work. Reviewing *Actions and Reactions* in 1909, he strongly implied his own antipathy while pretending to be even-handed:

> It is the combination of strength and tenderness that makes Mr Kipling's work remarkable. Or would these virtues of his be more accurately named brutality and sentimentality? It depends on the point of view; and the point of view depends on whether the style ... appears to you vigorous, manly speech, or the ranting and whining of an unpleasantly accented unpleasant voice.[22]

'[T]he ranting and whining of an unpleasantly accented unpleasant voice': that seems plain enough. And yet the concluding lines of Thomas' own 'This is no petty case of right or wrong', written in December 1915 after he had enlisted in the Artists Rifles, flickers quite unironically in and out of a Kiplingesque stance:

> I am one in crying, God save England, lest
> We lose what never slaves and cattle blessed.
> The ages made her that made us from the dust:
> She is all we know and live by, and we trust
> She is good and must endure, loving her so:
> And as we love ourselves we hate her foe.[23]

Thomas' Albionism, his sense of the survival of an ancient, buried, mythic England and the need to preserve it, can also be glimpsed in poems like 'The Manor Farm':

> a season of bliss unchangeable
> Awakened from farm and church where it had lain
> Safe under tile and thatch for ages since
> This England, Old already, was called Merry.[24]

This is a version of the Albionism Kipling had been more explicitly tapping in his 'Puck' stories and poems (and which can be traced back to a thicket of nineteenth-century writers including Arnold, Tennyson, Jefferies and Morris). So a poem like 'The Run of the Downs' in *Rewards and Fairies* with its celebratory list of place-names asserting England's age-old endurance ('Linch Down, Treyford and Sunwood / Knew Old England before the Flood') can be matched by the comparably evocative list of named places that in his 'If I should ever by chance' Thomas wishes he could give to his elder daughter: 'Codham, Cockridden, and Childerditch, / Roses, Pyrgo and Lapwater'.[25] Thomas' well-known gesture when asked by Eleanor Farjeon 'Do you know what you are fighting for?' of picking up 'a pinch of earth' and replying 'Literally, for this' as he crumbled it in his fingers, is pure Albionism in action.[26] Among other antecedents, it echoes the bonding moment in 'Weland's Sword' from *Puck of Pook's Hill* when Puck hands the children a piece of turf as a token of ownership and belonging, as well as the opening lines of 'A Charm' in *Rewards and Fairies*: 'Take of English earth as much / As either hand may rightly clutch.'[27]

Gurney was an avid Kipling reader and in September 1916 told his friend and patron Marion Scott that reading Kipling's pamphlet *The Fringes of the Fleet* had helped him get through heavy bombardment in a shell hole. He was consciously drawn to the 'Albion' aspect of the 'Puck' stories, to Kipling the literary archaeologist, decoder of the palimpsest of the Sussex landscape. As he wrote to Scott in October 1917: 'I admire Kipling as you know. *But* – before *Puck of Pook's Hill*, he was *not* English. Perhaps is not now, but *Puck* showed us that he realised a virtue not his own.'[28] By 'realised a virtue not his own', Gurney means both that Kipling discovered 'Englishness' for himself and made it real for others. The choice of the word 'virtue' in the already old-fashioned sense of 'inherent power' directly evokes Kipling's 'The Recall' from *Actions and Reactions*: 'I am the land of their fathers./In me the virtue stays.'[29] Such 'virtue' is widely apparent in Gurney's own poetry – particularly that written after the war. 'The Square Thing' – about St Mary's

Church with its medieval perpendicular tower, a few miles outside his native Gloucester – offers a salient example, even down to the word 'virtue':

> At Norton Green the tower stands well off road
> And is a squareness meaning many things;
> Nearest to us, the makers had abode
> Beside the Northern road of priests and kings . . .
>
> And so from virtue mixed of sky and land
> They raised a thing to match our equal dreams.
> It was no common infire moved their hand,
> Building so squarely among meadow streams.[30]

Occasionally, perhaps inevitably, Gurney strikes a less felicitous stance that recalls Kipling. For instance, the image of England as the loved but demanding mother in the rather tortuous opening lines of the fifth of his 'Sonnets 1917' – 'We have done our utmost, England, terrible / And dear taskmistress, darling Mother and stern' – is close in attitude (if not in register) to that of the England of Kipling's 'The Sea-Wife' who 'breeds a breed of roving men / And casts them over the sea'.[31]

According to Jones, it was T.S. Eliot who first pointed out to him, soon after the publication of *In Parenthesis* in 1937, that 'there is a decided something where your work converges with something in Kipling'. (Eliot no doubt spotted Jones' feeling for the history and myth in Kipling because he himself was sensitive to this, writing in the preface to his 1941 Kipling anthology that 'Kipling . . . aims I think to give at once a sense of the antiquity of England, of the number of generations and peoples who have laboured the soil and in turn been buried beneath it, and of the contemporaneity of the past').[32] This 'decided something' is another version of the 'Albionism' of the 'Puck' stories, the slow revelation of a historical-mythical 'England of the mind' (to adapt the title of Seamus Heaney's well-known 1976 essay on Ted Hughes, Geoffrey Hill and Philip Larkin).[33] As a child and teenager, Jones was steeped in *Puck of Pook's Hill* and *Rewards and Fairies*, and came to value them for their 'marvellous archaeological and historical insight'.[34] One element of Jones' 'Kipling-conditioning' – minus the Catholicism – is suggested by his statement in 1954 about the subject matter of *The Anathemata*:

> I was explicitly concerned with a re-calling of certain things which I myself had received, things which are part of the complex deposits of this Island, so of course involving Wales and of course involving the central Christian rite and mythological, historical, etc., data of all sorts. These were, so to say, my 'subject matter'.[35]

Another 'conditioning' element displays itself in the complex layering of material in Jones' prose-poems *In Parenthesis* and *The Anathemata* (1952). This is usually attributed to Jones' reading of Eliot and James Joyce but could equally derive from the proto-modernist technique of the admired 'Puck' stories, the use of which Kipling explains in a well-known passage in *Something of Myself*: 'I worked the material in three or four overlaid tints and textures, which might or might not reveal themselves according to the shifting light of sex, youth, and experience.'[36] Examples of equivalent layering might include the way in which Kipling moves between Parnesius describing late fourth-century Roman Britain and Parnesius chatting to the children about catapults in the Edwardian present, and Jones in Part 7 of *In Parenthesis* slipping between the immediate realities of trench warfare and the epic pitch of Sir Launcelot at the Chapel Perilous in book six of Malory's *Morte D'Arthur*:

> When they put up a flare, he saw many men's accoutrements medleyed and strewn up so down and service jackets bearing below the shoulder-numerals the peculiar sign of their battalions.
> And many of these shields he had seen knights bear beforehand.
>
> And the severed head of '72 Morgan,
> its visage grins like the Cheshire cat
> and full grimly.[37]

The effects of a 'Kipling-conditioned world' on Thomas, Gurney and Jones seem palpable, once noticed, and it would be possible to demonstrate equivalent effects on Owen, Graves, Blunden and Sorley – even on Rosenberg, whose Jewish prophetic utterance intersects fascinatingly, and at times dismayingly, with Kipling's Old Testament strain. (I have in mind Kipling's frequent application to the English of Old Testament imagery in lines like 'Thy mercy on Thy People, Lord!' from 'Recessional' or in the contrast between the 'Doorkeepers of Zion' (the English) and the 'Gatekeepers of Baal' (the Germans) in the significantly entitled 'Zion'. Rosenberg's 1918 poem 'The Destruction of Jerusalem by the Babylonian Hordes' draws on similar resources, although the effect of the lines 'They who bowed to the Bull god / Whose wings roofed Babylon, / In endless hosts darkened / The brightheavened Lebanon' from this culturally Jewish poet is markedly different.[38]) But the two war poets who most prominently exhibit 'Kipling-conditioning' are undoubtedly Brooke and Sassoon.

With Brooke, the 'conditioning' reveals itself more in a pose and persona than in his poetics. When Sassoon disparaged Kipling's poetry as 'terribly tub-thumping stuff', he assumed such a view 'would go down well' with Brooke. To his surprise, he found himself being firmly if gently put right. 'But not always, surely', Brooke replied, admitting he had thought much the same until Eddie Marsh had made him read 'Cities and Thrones and Powers' from *Puck of Pook's Hill*, concluding decisively: 'There aren't many better modern poems than that, you know.'[39]

A letter to St John Lucas in autumn 1905 and Brooke's swansong to the school literary society in 1906 both reveal his earlier views on Kipling. In the letter he describes his recent reading and liberal sympathies: 'I see what I take to be the truth in the Bible, Socrates, Wilde and Shaw . . . I enjoy even Kipling.'[40] His talk to the *Eranos* comprised a sweeping survey of modern poetry during which he endorsed Wilde's famous line in 'The True Function and Value of Criticism' that reading Kipling was like being 'seated under a palm-tree reading life by superb flashes of vulgarity'.[41]

In fact what seems to have changed Brooke's mind about Kipling was not so much a quick tutorial from his friend, admirer and self-appointed patron Edward Marsh, but his recent trip to the Pacific. In letters home, he had persistently used the lens of the Kiplingesque to frame, define and make sense of his new experiences. This framing began as a epistolary game. 'I have crossed the Equator, & so am a Man at last', Brooke wrote to Marsh in early November 1913, the capitalisation of 'Man' signalling the Kiplingism. 'The rest of my life is to be spent in bartering cheap coloured handkerchiefs for priceless native tapestries, & gin for pearls.'[42] Here Brooke is clearly having fun, guying the last line of 'If—' ('And — which is more — you'll be a Man, my son!') and such moments as the one in 'The Winged Hats' in *Puck of Pook's Hill* where the Viking chieftain Amal observes of the Emperor Maximus: 'This was in some sort a Man!'[43] A fortnight later the game was gathering momentum, and taking on a Wildean dimension. The white people Brooke had encountered in hotel bars in Honolulu, Suva and Apia, and the smoking-rooms of steamers in between, were, he told Marsh, 'all very self-consciously Kiplingesque'.[44] That plagiarist Life had yet again been discovered imitating Art. In fact, Brooke was a relatively early user of the term 'Kiplingesque'. His casual usage suggests the imperialist dimension of the 'Kipling-conditioned world' and how over the previous twenty years his stories and poems had for an English-speaking readership invented not only the British Empire but also the stereotypical image of the Englishman and Englishwoman 'somewheres east of Suez'.[45]

To see the Pacific and its characters as a scenario from Kipling clearly appealed. Brooke's description of a chance-met beachcomber makes him sound like the double of McIntosh Jellaludin, loafer and former 'Oxford man' who is the equivocally admired hero of Kipling's 1888 story 'To Be Filed for Reference': 'matriculated at Wadham, & was sent down . . . he rode with the Pytchley, quotes you Virgil, & discusses the ins & outs of the Peninsula campaign . . . Mere Kipling, you see,' Brooke added in case Marsh had missed the point: 'but one gets some good stories'.[46] Another friend was told how in Samoa 'the Englishman strikes roots, imagines he's in a story by Kipling, and elects himself perpetual vice-consul. There are lots about here, mostly married to natives.'[47]

By 19 November when Brooke wrote from Fiji, the game had acquired a new twist. It was not just the other white people in the tropics who were Kiplingesque; Brooke had realised that he was too. 'One feels that one's a White Man – ludicrously', he told Edmund Gosse, with the footnote: 'Vide R. Kipling *passim*.'[48] Capitalisation, spoof-reference, ironic tone: these, like Sassoon's 'terribly tub-thumping' put-down, are reminders of how Kipling's reputation had shifted from his greater-than-Dickens days of the early 1890s to that of the toy-trumpet-tooting dwarf of Max Beerbohm's famous 1904 cartoon.[49] But then Brooke continued with a bemused amusement: 'I kept thinking I was in the Sixth at Rugby, again. These dear good people, with their laughter and friendliness and crowns of flowers – one feels that one *must* protect them.'[50]

What Brooke had surprised in himself was a Kiplingesque side. This cast him in a role similar to that of the 'liberal' novelist in Kipling's 'A Conference of the Powers' (1890), who discovers that he is, after all, really 'one of us', part of the Empire in-group. Or, with a little help from Kipling, was Brooke simply reverting to type? After all, at Rugby, he might have played the naughty aesthete to friends but he remained a star pupil, a figure of admiration and authority, and a credit to his Housemaster father. Not only that, but when his father died suddenly in January 1910, Brooke instantly put his Fabian life in Grantchester on hold and returned to his old school for a term to run his father's House.

In the Pacific, Brooke found this new-old role, this Kiplingesque way of seeing the world, congenial. A few days later, he described to Cathleen Nesbitt how Suva was full of 'staid English officials, heavy with the White Man's Burden'.[51] As with the letter to Gosse, there was a flick of calculated caricature, but Brooke went on:

It's so queer, seeing the thin, much clothed, ancient, over-civilized, silver-bangled, subtle Indians, and these jolly, half-naked, savage children of the earth [the indigenous Fijians], working side by side in obedience to the Clifton and Trinity, or Winchester and New College, man, with his 'Doesn't do to be too friendly with these niggahs, you know. You must make 'em respect you!' That is Empire.[52]

Amused, also impressed, he was clearly aware of being himself a Rugby and King's man.

The adoption of this purposeful, Kiplingesque persona may also have played its part in Brooke's decision to give up 'the National Liberal Club' because, as he told Marsh, 'I hate the Liberal party, & the Marconi affair, & the whole mess, & Rufus Isaacs as Lord Chief Justice.[53] (The Jewish lawyer and Liberal MP Rufus Isaacs was thought to have been involved in insider-trading on the London Stock Exchange in 1912. He was made Lord Chief Justice the following year.) By March 1914 in Tahiti, he had decided that toughness was what he had come all that way to acquire. 'I am what I came out here to be – Hard. Quite, quite hard', he informed Marsh. 'I have become merely a minor character in a Kipling story.'[54] Not exactly a minor character, perhaps, but the mask fitted, and he could and did use the new voice, new code, new set of attitudes, and now without any trace of irony. Brooke even used a Kiplingesque phrase where it seems least expected, to voice approval of a writer very unlike Kipling and totally outside Kipling's sphere of influence: D.H. Lawrence, Brooke told Marsh, after reading *Sons and Lovers*, was 'a big man'.[55] By the time he returned to England in June 1914, what one might call 'the Kiplingisation of Brooke' was complete. The new 'hard' Brooke would soon be publicly cutting old Bloomsbury friends like Lytton Strachey and dropping long-time adorers like Lytton's brother James.

There was of course more to Brooke's 'conversion' than the adoption of a imperialist masculinist stance. One point that Brooke was making to Sassoon by his praise of 'Cities and Thrones and Powers' was that Kipling's own work was often much more than merely Kiplingesque. All the same, when war broke out less than a month later, Brooke did see it in distinctly Kipling terms, echoing his apocalyptic rhetoric: 'if Armageddon is *on*', he told J.C. Squire, 'I suppose one should be there'.[56] That attitude helps to explain his eagerness to join up and how within a few months he had written his famous five war sonnets.

Edward Thomas detected traces of this identification with a Kiplinglike, patriotic stance when in June 1915 he described Brooke's sonnets to Robert

Frost as 'probably not very personal but a nervous attempt [by Brooke] to connect with himself the very widespread idea that self-sacrifice is the highest self-indulgence'.[57] Because what the sonnets also 'connected with', consciously or not, was the sacrificial clarion call of Kipling's 'For All We Have and Are'. The fifth sonnet was in effect an expanded gloss on Kipling's opening and concluding lines ('For all we have and are', 'Who dies if England live?'). Brooke's idealised soldier spelt out in suitably uplifting and patriotic terms what he had been and would remain: 'A dust whom England bore... A body of England's... Giv[ing] somewhere back the thoughts by England given.'[58] Where Kipling in his poem lamented that 'Our world has passed away, / In wantonness o'erthrown', Brooke in the first sonnet, 'Peace', claimed to have found psychic release and renewal in turning away from just such a world 'grown old and cold and weary', full of 'sick hearts', 'half-men' and 'all the little emptiness of love'.[59] In their own fashion, each of the sonnets underwrote Kipling's assertion that 'There is but one task for all – / One life for each to give'.[60] And, whatever one finally makes of Brooke, it has to be said that in his remaining months he willingly took up the task and did give the life.

For Sassoon's part, his rejection of Kipling's poetry as 'terribly tub-thumping stuff' might seem to imply a more general dismissal of a 'Kipling-conditioned world'. However, when he came to write up that breakfast exchange many years later, Sassoon took care to present his swipe at Kipling as more a nervous conversational gambit than a reflection of his real views. '[I]f I had been more at my ease,' he commented, 'I might have saved my credit by telling [Brooke] that I knew by heart the first eight lines, which I really loved, of Kipling's "Neither the harps nor the crowns amused, nor the cherubs' dove-winged races".'[61] These are the opening of 'The Return of the Children', the poem immediately preceding '"They"', Kipling's story about a father's briefly licensed reunion with his dead child, in *Traffics and Discoveries* (1904).

Other evidence of Sassoon's awareness and appreciation of Kipling's work is not hard to find. In October 1905 during his first term at Cambridge, he made an anthology of his favourite poems. This contained the Rossettis, Swinburne, Robert Browning, Tennyson, Keats and Kipling, among many others. Kipling, according to one of Sassoon's biographers, Jean Moorcroft Wilson, was represented by 'his romantic as well as his jingoistic verse'.[62] The 'romantic' pieces presumably included the lines from 'The Return of the Children'.

Before the war, Sassoon led a kind of double life: foxhunting man by day, lyric poet by night. Nothing very Kiplingesque about that. Indeed, it places Sassoon firmly among 'the Sons of Mary' who 'smile and are blessèd', while 'the Sons of Martha' are left to do all the work.[63] Sassoon's early poems – apart from an able pastiche of Masefield's *The Everlasting Mercy* – are old-fashioned and over-literary. Those written after he enlisted but before he saw action are full of mornings glimmering 'out of dreams', larks ascending and trees 'blown to music by the ruffling breeze'.[64] The exception is the Brookeish 'Absolution', which ends: 'Now, having claimed this heritage of heart, / What need we more, my comrades and my brothers?'[65] It was not until February 1916, serving with the Royal Welch Fusiliers in France, that he started to write the poems we think of as distinctly Sassoonian. The first, 'In the Pink', imagines the rum-warmed thoughts of Davies, a private soldier, as he awaits the next day's march to the trenches: 'To-night he's in the pink; but soon he'll die. / And still the war goes on – *he* don't know why.'[66]

Sassoon tended, later on, to be dismissive about literary influences on his war poetry:

> I have never been able to ascertain that my method was modelled on any other writer, though the influence of Hardy's *Satires of Circumstance* is faintly perceptible in a few of the longer poems. I merely chanced on the device of composing two or three harsh, peremptory, and colloquial stanzas with a knock-out blow in the last line.[67]

This is a little disingenuous. Hardy's influence is clearly present in both the 'method' and perspective of a poem like 'In the Pink' and its successors, while the demotic style and voice is indebted, in varying degrees, to Masefield, Housman, and Kipling *passim*, as Brooke might have said.

The Kipling of the *Barrack-Room Ballads* is an obvious forerunner. The cockney trooper in 'The Widow at Windsor' grimly points out the human cost involved in gaining and maintaining an Empire: '(Poor beggars! – it's blue with our bones!)'.[68] The less-deceived speaker in 'Tommy' is all too aware of civilian indifference and complacency: 'An' Tommy ain't a bloomin' fool – you bet that Tommy sees!'[69] Files-on-Parade and the Colour-Sergeant share horror-numbed reactions in 'Danny Deever': ' "What makes you look so white, so white?" said Files-on-Parade. / "I'm dreadin' what I've got to watch," the Colour-Sergeant said.'[70] These speakers are the poetic ancestors of the 'boys' in Sassoon's ' "They" ', who give the lie to the bishop sermonising about the spiritually transformative properties of war:

> 'We're none of us the same!' the boys reply.
> 'For George lost both his legs; and Bill's stone blind . . .
> And Bert's gone syphilitic . . .'[71]

In this particular poem, it is not just a question of the 'Tommy' voices answering back: traces of a 'Kipling-conditioned world' even adhere in Sassoon's title. This is borrowed – inverted commas and all – from the Kipling story paired with 'The Return of the Children'.

Both Kipling and Sassoon felt for and expressed the plight of the ordinary soldier, but had different attitudes to officers. Kipling, whatever he sometimes thought in private, seldom presented officers in his poems and stories as dishonourable or incompetent. Sassoon, as Anthony Powell observed when he met him in the early 1960s, still retained the air of 'Captain Sassoon', but as a junior officer in the war he often played the class renegade.[72] Poems like 'Base Details' and 'Lamentations' show old buffers 'speed[ing] glum heroes up the line to death' or young subalterns so dehumanised by their experiences that they can no longer respond to the suffering of others:

> he howled and beat his chest.
> And, all because his brother had gone west,
> Raved at the bleeding war; his rampant grief
> Moaned, shouted, sobbed, and choked, while he was kneeling
> Half-naked on the floor. In my belief
> Such men have lost all patriotic feeling.[73]

However, two of Sassoon's lesser-known war poems, 'The Quarter-Master' and 'A Ballad', plainly display 'Kipling conditioning'. 'The Quarter-Master', written in March 1916, celebrated Sassoon's middle-aged friend Joe Cottrell, who had risen through the ranks to be quartermaster of the First Battalion of the Royal Welch Fusiliers. Sassoon's pen portrait concludes:

> He's chanced his arm with fate and found his glory;
> He's swung the lead with many a roaring lad:
> Good-luck to him; good-luck to all his kindred!
> It's meeting men like him that makes me glad.[74]

Cottrell is an instantly recognisable Kiplingesque army type, like the Colour-Sergeant praised in 'The 'Eathen' as *the backbone of the Army*. So it is apt that Sassoon's poetic commemoration strongly recalls 'If–'.[75] It does so partly through phrases like 'He's chanced his arm with fate' but mostly by its use of a modified form of Kipling's metrics. 'If –' alternates eleven-syllable lines (with feminine endings) and conventional ten-syllable iambic pentameters (with masculine endings), odd-numbered lines rhyming with odd, even-numbered with even. Sassoon maintains this structure with its

Kiplingesque groundswell, but simplifies the rhyme scheme by rhyming only the even-numbered lines.

Less deftly, 'A Ballad', from October the same year, channels the sardonic anecdotes and civil and military misdemeanours of *Departmental Ditties* with their swinging, seven-foot lines ('And Ahasuerus Jenkins is a Power in the State!'; 'So Exeter Battleby Tring consented his claims to resign, / And died, on four thousand a month, in the ninetieth year of his age'.[76]) In Sassoon's poem, a windy captain after a week in the trenches shoots himself in the foot with predictably ironic results:

> Now the Captain's at the Depot, lame, but happy as a lark;
> And in the billets out in France the men who knew him tell the story
> Of 'the bloke that 'ad an accident when walking in the dark' –
> While the Captain teaches raw recruits the way to blood and glory.[77]

More straightforwardly, Sassoon's poem of survivor's guilt 'Can I Forget? . . .', written in August 1918 at Lancaster Gate hospital, reconfigures and personalises the refrain 'Lest we forget – lest we forget!' of Kipling's 'Recessional':

> Can I forget the voice of one who cried
> For me to save him, save him, as he died? . . .
>
> Can I forget the face of one whose eyes
> Could trust me in his utmost agonies?[78]

It is not difficult, then, to detect Kipling's presence in Sassoon's war poetry. Was this merely an unconscious consequence of 'Kipling conditioning'? Probably not. Sassoon might cast himself as unsophisticated, even naive, in his various memoirs but he was considerably cannier than that. Kipling was one of the stations on his poetic radio, and it is unlikely that his excoriating 'To the Warmongers': 'For you our battles shine / With triumph half-divine' was aimed at him.[79] This makes it surprising that he did not warm to *The Years Between*. At least, 'My Boy Jack', 'Gethsemane' and some of the 'Epitaphs' ought, one feels, to have struck a chord. Perhaps he was put off by the fiercely Tory poems like 'Ulster' and 'The Covenant' or the unforgiving 'Justice'. Perhaps, as the new literary editor of a left-wing paper, he felt another breezy dismissal was more appropriate.

Or perhaps Sassoon always felt ambivalent about Kipling – not an unusual reaction. In May 1935, after hearing the broadcast of Kipling's rearmament speech to the Royal Society of St George, he told Max Beerbohm that Kipling spoke 'like a suave precise professor of military law, also like a prophet who has been disregarded for a decade and a half and was taking his chance to get his own back' – an impression he also memorably recreated in his poem 'Silver Jubilee Celebration':

> Suavely severe – not one bleak syllable blurred –
> In dulcet-bitter and prophetic tones
> (Each word full charged with dynamite deferred)
> He disinterred a battlefield of bones . . .
> And then reminded us that our attempt
> To put all war behind us with the last one
> Had been a dream administrators dreamt;
> In fact a virtuous fallacy – and a vast one.[80]

Yet ' "They" ' remained a favourite and much-read story all Sassoon's life.

As an increasing number of critics have argued since 1960, Kipling's work is by no means as simple as was once thought – or as some detractors continue to claim. It should be no surprise, then, that his influence on the war poets is a complex matter: not a conventional scenario of sentimental patriot and imperialist pitted against sufferers, protestors and satirists, but rather a dialogue in which they partake of his world, and he of theirs – especially after the loss of his son John. In short, the responses of the war poets to Kipling's work suggest more generally that Kipling typically inspired – as he still does – ambivalence. Echoes of his work and his world can be found reverberating throughout their poems, while for his part Kipling in 'My Boy Jack', 'Gethsemane', 'Epitaphs' and elsewhere became a fellow-traveller in their world and went far beyond 'speak[ing] in echoes of himself'.

Notes

1 Dominic Hibberd, *Wilfred Owen: A New Biography* (London: Weidenfeld & Nicolson, 2002), p. 114.
2 Brian Gardner (ed.), *Up the Line to Death: The War Poets 1914–1918* (London: Methuen, 1964); Ian Parsons (ed.), *Men Who March Away: Poems of the First World War. An Anthology*, with an Introduction by I.M. Parsons (London: Chatto & Windus, 1965).
3 Rudyard Kipling, *Rudyard Kipling's Verse: The Definitive Edition* (London: Hodder and Stoughton, 1940), pp. 329, 393.
4 Gardner (ed.), *Up the Line to Death*, p. xxiv. Gardner's version of Kipling as a poet of the Great War differs so markedly from A.E. Rodway's cursory dismissal of Kipling's 'notorious stories and poems of World War 1' in Boris Ford (ed.), 'The last phrase', *The Pelican Guide to English Literature: From Dickens to*

Hardy (London: Pelican, 1958), p. 393 that it is surprising that Gardner omits the stoically anguished 'My Boy Jack' and the poignant 'Gethsemane' from his anthology.
5 Dominic Hibberd and John Onions (eds), *The Winter of the World: Poems of the Great War* (London: Constable, 2007), p. xxxiv. For an attack on this 'even now still potent myth', see Hugh Brogan's excellent 1998 essay 'The Great War and Rudyard Kipling', reprinted in this collection.
6 Kipling, *The Letters of Rudyard Kipling, Volume 4: 1911–19*, ed. Thomas Pinney (London: Macmillan, 1999), pp. 543, 541. As Professor Pinney points out, when Doubleday published the notes in 1919 his short preface made Kipling's authorship apparent without actually disclosing it: 'The material may be said to be authoritative and to state clearly Mr Kipling's own ideas in regard to this book, which he considers his most important' (*Letters, Volume 4*, p. 545).
7 Ann Parry, *The Poetry of Rudyard Kipling: Rousing the Nation* (Bristol: Open University Press, 1992), p. 129. This chapter is a significant recasting of a previous article of Parry's, '*The years between*: Rudyard Kipling and the Great War', *Kipling Journal* 245 (March 1988): 42–61. Despite my reservations about some of her readings, Parry's chapter and article remain by far the most sustained and thoughtful accounts of *The Years Between* as a collection.
8 Kipling, *Definitive Verse*, p. 330.
9 *Ibid.* p. 390. This definitive edition entitles the sequence 'Epitaphs of the War 1914–18'.
10 Jay Winter, *Sites of Memory, Sites of Mourning: The Great War in European Cultural History* (Cambridge: Cambridge University Press, 1995), quoted in Jan Montefiore, *Rudyard Kipling* (Tavistock: Northcote House Publishers, 2007), p. 159. Montefiore's discussion subtly extends Winter's point by showing how the epigram 'echoes, aurally and thematically, J.W. Mackail's translation of Simonides' epigram commemorating the last stand of the 300 Spartans against the Persians at Thermopylae in 480 BC.'
11 *The Morning Post*, 10 April 1919; *The Scotsman*, 10 April 1919.
12 Siegfried Sassoon, *The Daily Herald*, 23 April 1919.
13 T.S. Eliot, 'Kipling redivivus', *Athenaeum*, 9 May 1919, reprinted in Roger Lancelyn Green (ed.), *Kipling: The Critical Heritage* (London: Routledge, 1971), pp. 322, 325.
14 Gardner, *Up the Line to Death*, p. xxiv.
15 Hibberd and Onions (eds), *Winter of the World*, p. xiv.
16 Harold Owen and John Bell (eds), *Wilfred Owen: Collected Letters* (Oxford: Oxford University Press, 1967), p. 250.
17 Siegfried Sassoon, *The Weald of Youth* (London: Faber & Faber, 1942), p. 229.
18 Jean Moorcroft Wilson (ed.), *Collected Letters of Charles Hamilton Sorley* (London: Cecil Woolf, 1990), p. 185.
19 Edward Thomas, 'War poetry' (1914), reprinted in Edna Longley (ed.), *A Language Not to Be Betrayed: Selected Prose of Edward Thomas* (Manchester: Carcanet Press in association with the Mid Northumberland Arts Group, 1981), p. 135.

20 René Hague (ed.), *Dai Greatcoat: A Self-Portrait of David Jones in his Letters* (London: Faber & Faber, 1980), p. 184.
21 Gilbert Frankau, 'The Beasts in Gray', *Poetical Works II* (1923), anthologised in Hibberd and Onions (eds), *Winter of the World*, p. 252.
22 Edward Thomas, review of *Actions and Reactions*, *Saturday Review*, 16 October 1909, quoted in *A Language Not to Be Betrayed*, p. v.
23 Edna Longley (ed.), *Edward Thomas: The Annotated Collected Poems* (Tarset: Bloodaxe Books, 2008), pp. 104–5. Longley provides a helpful discussion of the poem, tracing Thomas' convoluted and conflicted thoughts on the war and on enlisting.
24 Longley (ed.), *Edward Thomas: The Annotated Collected Poems*, p. 45.
25 Kipling, *Definitive Verse*, p. 491; Longley (ed.), *Edward Thomas: Collected Poems*, p. 115.
26 Eleanor Farjeon, *Edward Thomas: The Last Four Years* (London: Oxford University Press, 1958), p. 154.
27 Kipling 'Weland's Sword', *Puck of Pook's Hill* (London: Macmillan, 1906), p. 12; 'A Charm', *Definitive Verse*, p. 500.
28 R.K.R. Thornton (ed.), *Ivor Gurney: Collected Letters* (Manchester: The Mid Northumberland Arts Group & Carcanet Press, 1991), p. 353.
29 Kipling, *Definitive Verse*, p. 487.
30 George Walter and R.K.R. Thornton (eds), *Ivor Gurney: 80 Poems or So* (Manchester: The Mid Northumberland Arts Group & Carcanet Press, 1997), p. 124.
31 R.K.R. Thornton (ed.), *Ivor Gurney: Severn & Somme and War's Embers* (Manchester: The Mid Northumberland Arts Group & Carcanet Press, 1997), p. 51; Kipling, *Definitive Verse*, p. 94.
32 William Blissett, *The Long Conversation: A Memoir of David Jones* (Oxford: Oxford University Press, 1981), p. 48; T.S. Eliot (ed.), *A Choice of Kipling's Verse Made by T.S. Eliot with an Essay on Rudyard Kipling* (London: Faber & Faber, 1941), p. 32.
33 Seamus Heaney, 'Englands of the mind', *Preoccupations: Selected Prose 1968–1978* (London: Faber & Faber, 1980), p. 150.
34 Blissett, *The Long Conversation*, p. 110.
35 Harman Grisewood (ed.), *Epoch and Artist: Selected Writings by David Jones* (London: Faber & Faber, 1959), p. 30.
36 Kipling, *Something of Myself and Other Autobiographical Writings*, ed. Thomas Pinney (Cambridge: Cambridge University Press, 1990), p. 111.
37 David Jones, *In Parenthesis* (London: Faber & Faber, 1936), p. 180.
38 Kipling, *Definitive Verse*, pp. 329, 91; Ian Parsons (ed.), *The Collected Works of Isaac Rosenberg* (London: Chatto & Windus, 1979), p. 116.
39 Sassoon, *The Weald of Youth*, p. 229.
40 Geoffrey Keynes (ed.), *The Letters of Rupert Brooke* (London: Faber & Faber, 1968), p. 31.
41 Christopher Hassall, *Rupert Brooke: A Biography* (London: Faber & Faber, 1964), p. 92.

42 Keynes (ed.), *Letters of Rupert Brooke*, p. 524.
43 Kipling *Puck of Pook's Hill*, p. 214; *Definitive Verse*, p. 576.
44 Keynes (ed.), *Letters of Rupert Brooke*, p. 526.
45 Kipling 'Mandalay', *Definitive Verse*, p. 420.
46 Keynes (ed.), *Letters of Rupert Brooke*, p. 526. 'To Be Filed For Reference' is the final story in Kipling's *Plain Tales from the Hills* (London: Macmillan, 1890).
47 Keynes (ed.), *Letters of Rupert Brooke*, p. 529.
48 *Ibid.*, p. 531.
49 Sidney Low, the editor of the *St James's Gazette*, after reading *Soldiers Three*, remarked that 'It may be ... that a greater than Dickens is here.' quoted in Lancelyn Green, *Kipling: The Critical Heritage*, p. 16.
50 Keynes (ed.), *Letters of Rupert Brooke*, p. 531.
51 *Ibid.*, p. 537.
52 *Ibid.*, p. 538.
53 *Ibid.*, p. 527. Although Brooke could not have known this at the time, his revulsion at the Marconi Affair had its parallel in Kipling's contemporary furious poem 'Gehazi', privately circulated but not published until *The Years Between* in 1919.
54 *Ibid.*, p. 568.
55 *Ibid.*, p. 576.
56 Hassall, *Rupert Brooke*, p. 459. Brooke was alluding to Kipling's story 'The Captive', first published in September 1902, in which an English general in South Africa observes that the Boer War will prove 'a first-class dress-parade for Armageddon': Kipling, *Traffics and Discoveries* (London: Macmillan, 1904), p. 27. Kipling had been predicting such a war for years. 'The big smash is coming one of these days, sure enough,' he told J.W. Mackail in July 1897 in the aftermath of Queen Victoria's Diamond Jubilee, adding 'it will be the common people – the 3rd class carriages – that'll save us': Kipling, *The Letters of Rudyard Kipling, Volume 2: 1890–99*, ed. Thomas Pinney (London: Macmillan, 1990), p. 306. His 1911 poem 'Dane-geld', reminding readers that 'if once you have paid him the Dane-geld / You never get rid of the Dane' (Kipling, *Definitive Verse*, p. 713), clearly has German militarism in mind.
57 R. George Thomas (ed.), *Edward Thomas: Selected Letters* (Oxford: Oxford University Press, 1995), p. 111.
58 Rupert Brooke, *1914 & Other Poems* (London: Sidgwick & Jackson, 1915), p. 15.
59 Kipling, 'Cities and Thrones', *Definitive Verse*, p. 329; Brooke, *1914*, p. 11.
60 Kipling, 'The Return of the Children', *Definitive Verse*, p. 330.
61 Sassoon, *Weald of Youth*, p. 230.
62 Jean Moorcroft Wilson, *Siegfried Sassoon, the Making of a War Poet: A Biography 1886–1918* (London: Gerald Duckworth & Co, 1998), p. 116.
63 Kipling, 'The Sons of Martha', *Definitive Verse*, p. 383. The double-sided Georgie in Kipling's story 'The Brushwood Boy' in *Traffics and Discoveries* – soldier by day, dreamer by night – might be the only exception.
64 Siegfried Sassoon, *Collected Poems 1908–1956* (London: Faber & Faber, 1961), pp. 64, 58.

65 Sassoon, *Collected Poems*, p. 11.
66 *Ibid.*, p. 18.
67 Siegfried Sassoon, *Siegfried's Journey, 1916–1920* (London: Faber & Faber, 1945), p. 29.
68 Kipling, 'Widow of Windsor', *Definitive Verse*, p. 414.
69 Kipling, 'Tommy', *Definitive Verse*, p. 399.
70 Kipling, 'Danny Deever', *Definitive Verse*, p. 397.
71 Sassoon, *Collected Poems*, pp. 23–4.
72 Anthony Powell, *The Strangers All Are Gone* (New York: Holt, Rinehart and Winston, 1982), p. 46. Powell's vivid snapshot of the elderly poet concludes that for 'Captain Sassoon . . . the first war was still in progress'.
73 Sassoon, 'Lamentations', *Collected Poems*, pp. 75–6.
74 Sassoon, 'The Quartermaster', *Siegfried Sassoon: Diaries 1915–1918*, ed. Rupert Hart-Davis (London: Faber & Faber, 1983), p. 44.
75 Kipling, 'The 'Eathen', 'If –', *Definitive Verse*, pp. 453, 576.
76 Kipling, 'Army Headquarters', 'Public Waste', *Definitive Verse*, pp. 6, 15.
77 Rupert Hart-Davis (ed.), *War Poems of Siegfried Sassoon* (London: Faber & Faber, 1983), p. 56.
78 Rupert Hart-Davis (ed.), *Siegfried Sassoon: Diaries 1915–1918* (London: Faber & Faber, 1983), p. 278.
79 Hart-Davis (ed.), *War Poems of Sassoon*, p. 77.
80 Rupert Hart-Davis (ed.), *Siegfried Sassoon: Letters to Max Beerbohm & a Few Answers* (London: Faber & Faber, 1986), pp. 24–5; Sassoon, *Collected Poems*, p. 237.

8

Actions and Reactions: Kipling's Edwardian summer

DANIEL KARLIN

Rudyard Kipling's collection of stories and accompanying poems, *Actions and Reactions*, was published in October 1909. It consisted of eight stories, each followed by a poem; the stories had all previously appeared in magazines in both the United States and Britain, with the exception of the first and last, which appeared in American magazines only. (The Addendum to *Actions and Reactions*, reproduced at the end of this chapter, gives the sequence of stories and poems in the published volume, together with the dates of their magazine publication). Most of the stories were written in the period 1905–09, though two of them are of earlier date, one considerably so. The doublet form of the title follows the pattern of Kipling's later career, starting with *Traffics and Discoveries* in 1904, then *Debits and Credits* in 1926 and *Limits and Renewals* in 1932; we might also mention *Rewards and Fairies* of 1910, though the doublet in that title is a quoted phrase. *Actions and Reactions* has always seemed to me a very suggestive title – though Andrew Lycett's biography reveals that until shortly before publication the working title was *Motions and Emotions*.[1]

Since nothing in Kipling is single-minded, this paper has two beginnings, one fanciful and speculative like a staircase that ends in mid-air, and the other orderly and signposted, like a museum guide. We start with an East Sussex landscape, in the first years of the twentieth century:

> They walked toward it through an all-abandoned land. Here they found the ghost of a patch of lucerne that had refused to die; there a harsh fallow surrendered to yard-high thistles; and here a breadth of rampant kelk feigning to

be lawful crop. In the ungrazed pastures swaths of dead stuff caught their feet, and the ground beneath glistened with sweat. At the bottom of the valley a little brook had undermined its footbridge, and frothed in the wreckage. But there stood great woods on the slopes beyond – old, tall, and brilliant, like unfaded tapestries against the walls of a ruined house.[2]

'All-abandoned' means 'completely, utterly abandoned', and 'abandoned by everyone'; in another sense it means 'abandoned to its own devices, wanton', as people used to speak of an 'abandoned woman'. The land is riotous, filled with a perverse energy: 'rampant', 'glistening with sweat', 'frothing'; at the same time it is a place of exhaustion and entrapment, where even refusing to die means that you become no better than a ghost, and where 'swaths of dead stuff' catch the pilgrims' feet. Crossing this wilderness is like an ordeal: there are echoes of the 'harsh swarth leaves', the 'spiteful' little river and the fields with 'blotches . . . coloured gay or grim' in Robert Browning's poem 'Childe Roland to the Dark Tower Came',[3] and our pilgrims, too, will discover at the end of their journey a building that will seal their fate, though this fate is held to be benign. The phrase 'There stood great woods on the slopes beyond' in particular recalls the climax of Browning's poem: 'There they stood, ranged along the hill-sides, met / To view the last of me, a living frame / For one more picture!'[4]

Who are these pilgrims, and where are they headed? The 'it' they are walking 'toward' in the first sentence is the spire of a village church, but their goal is not salvation, or not of the religious kind. At the village is a post office, connected to the telegraph network, and therefore to the modern world, the world of business and money from which our pilgrims – one of them in particular – have been exiled. George Chapin, a ruthless and successful American financier, has had a stroke from overwork, and is threatened with death if he persists in the thing he truly loves. He is forced abroad with his second-choice love – his wife, Sophie – and they come in the course of their wanderings to this apparently desolate bit of southeast England. Its dilapidated and exhausted appearance puzzles them. 'I thought all England was a garden', Sophie says; and to George it seems as though the land was suffering, like himself, from 'nervous prostration'.[5] His principal anxiety is to be within reach of the network of communication that sustains his sense of himself, even if he is not allowed to make use of it. Kipling, however, has other plans for him. Moreover, it turns out that the great woods are worth a lot of money.

I start with this passage because it is so charged with the tensions, the anxieties, the competing energies that went into Kipling's image of England at this point in her history and his own. England is both dead and alive in this symbolic vision, a place of disorder in both moral and social terms – the weeds 'feigning to be lawful crop', the brook that has 'undermined its footbridge' – yet capable of grandeur, of beauty and of renewal. And yet, when you have said this much, there remains something incongruous about the image of the great woods as 'unfaded tapestries against the walls of a ruined house'. The ruined house must, according to the logic of the image, be the surrounding landscape, which has been getting more and more 'abandoned' as the woods have grown; yet Kipling compares the woods to man-made objects that have somehow defied the process of time. Real tapestries would have faded, and indeed dropped to pieces, long before the house that contained them became a ruin. I do not believe that Kipling was being incompetent or inadvertent here. He was, to borrow Thomas Hardy's phrase, a man who noticed such things.[6] Rather I take the image of the woods as unfaded tapestries to express a further paradox about England, or perhaps the idea of England: a product of ancient growth, but also a work of art that defies time, and indeed defies itself, standing *against* the ruin that it outlasts.

I now begin again, with two disclaimers and a definition. As a textual scholar I am naturally interested in the genesis and textual history of literary works, and *Actions and Reactions* has some striking features in this regard. It would be fascinating, for example, to trace the evolution of the story now called 'The Puzzler', whose colonial politics are up-to-date Edwardian and whose setting is somewhere in Kipling's own adoptive county, Sussex, from its origins over a decade earlier, when it was called 'For Men Only' and was, like 'My Sunday at Home', the product of a visit Kipling made in 1894 to his parents' retirement home in Wiltshire.[7] Equally intriguing is the clearly deliberate exclusion of 'An Habitation Enforced' from the British magazine market, a decision all the more striking when you remember that in this period Kipling's commercial interests were in the hands of a very capable agent, A.P. Watt, who was kept up to the mark by the vigilance of Kipling's wife Carrie. This essay, however, is not concerned with the textual history of *Actions and Reactions*, but with the volume as it presents itself, as a completed structure. This essay is linked to my second disclaimer, which relates to biography. I am not against biographical readings of literary works in general, or Kipling's in particular, and I do not avoid them here; but my use of biography is of a peculiar kind. The theme of *returning* is evidently central to this collection, and one of these returns is to the author's own earlier self and work. This form of return is explicitly addressed in two of the stories

('Garm – A Hostage', and 'A Deal in Cotton') where the narrator draws attention to his early career. Biography is therefore built into the fabric of the volume, and does not need to be imported; and it is to these forms of self-scrutiny that I shall be paying attention, as opposed to the kind of biographical reading that takes 'An Habitation Enforced', the opening story of the volume, as a *reflection* of Kipling's own return, with his American wife Carrie, to an England he famously described as 'the most wonderful foreign land [he had] ever been in'.[8] The distinction here is between biographical readings which begin from the work and lead elsewhere – however interesting 'elsewhere' may prove to be – and those which use biography as a way of lighting up the work from within.

I now turn to the 'Edwardian summer' of my title: a phrase intended in part ironically, because the notion of a halcyon period leading up to the First World War has become the kind of historical cliché which refuses to die no matter how many historians drive a stake through its heart. It is obvious from a reading of *Actions and Reactions* that Kipling, for one, did not imagine himself to be living in one of the two states of illusion commonly projected onto Edwardian society: on the one hand, the suspended animation of an achieved social consensus, in which antagonisms of class and ideology had been dissolved in a solution of English decency, tolerance, and good humour; on the other hand, the blind belief that material prosperity, built on economic and financial interdependence, had somehow made the prospect of catastrophic disruption as unlikely as it was unwelcome. We attribute such attitudes to 'conservatives', and Kipling was undoubtedly a conservative; yet we must acknowledge that his work embodies precisely the opposite views of Edwardian England: intense anxiety about the future, violent ideological conflict, a deep yearning for just that stability and ordered collective culture which he could *not* discern around him. In his fine book on *The Edwardians*, J.B. Priestley, who speaks with the irreverent authority of a 'junior Edwardian', as he calls himself, argues strongly and I think convincingly that the predominant social and political tone of the period was set by class antagonism, but that this antagonism was not between the upper class and those beneath them, nor between the middle class and the proletariat, but within the middle class itself.[9] That intra-class conflict helps to explain the acrid edge of much of Kipling's non-fiction writing of this period, especially his letters: it is the characteristic tone of a combatant in a civil war.

At the same time, the direction in which Kipling's probing intelligence took him was, simply and on the grand scale, erroneous. 'With the Night Mail' is a kind of allegory of this mistakenness: it is both a magnificent tour-de-force and a dead end, as indeed is the re-founding of the House of Lashmar by the American couple in 'An Habitation Enforced'. The future would not belong to international trade regulated by a benign air-traffic control system, or to a version of British pastoral backed by American money – both of them, in different ways, fantasies floating on hot air. The apocalyptic intervention of the Bee Keeper which purges the intellectually corrupt, morally degenerate, racially contaminated society of 'The Mother Hive', leaving a purged and purified remnant 'prepared to go on',[10] does not prophesy either the Great War or its aftermath. *Actions and Reactions* is filled with such intimations of a storm which never arrived, or which struck from a different quarter than the one expected.

Yet there is something more to the idea of an 'Edwardian summer' than either fake enchantment or dramatic irony. Kipling's sense of England, like his sense of himself, was made up of elements whose unstable combinations he was better able to record than to analyse. In the first years of the twentieth century, the years to which most of the stories in *Actions and Reactions* belong, his understanding of England and his own place in it as a writer became richer, more complex, more paradoxical than had been the case, say, in the 1890s, when he entered into what he mistakenly thought was his literary inheritance. The result is a kind of density of significance, in which images and allusions overlap and cross each other, yet without spoiling the effect of a fully achieved expression, like the spreading overarching foliage of a great tree on a perfect summer's day.

I now look in detail at two aspects of *Actions and Reactions*: first, the structure or pattern of the volume; and second, Kipling's re-visiting and re-imagining of earlier work through its stories. Finally – because no discussion of Kipling should avoid contradicting itself – I shall suggest that there is something more to be said about the art of Englishness, and that this something sees Kipling's plenitude of meaning as, to borrow his own phrase, an error in the fourth dimension.

Structure and pattern

Actions and Reactions is a form of the 'structured collection' – a term I borrow from John Woolford, who uses it in his book *Browning the Revisionary* to describe Robert Browning's later collections of shorter poems. In volumes such as *Dramatis Personae* or *Dramatic Idylls*, Woolford argues, the relations between individual poems are as important as the poems themselves, and the volume itself is a kind of long poem. In Browning's case the goal is to achieve, or at any rate gesture towards, the unity or integrity of a single work, without having to accept a monolithic subject or point of view. Truth in the modern world can no longer be singular, the product of a definitive insight and delivered by an authoritative voice; but it may be approached by plural and partial voices. Readers who are resistant to godlike proclamation may be open to human suggestion.[11] I don't think that Kipling shares Browning's philosophical aim, or not quite in the same way; he is unconcerned with the loss of a Romantic wholeness in which he seems never to have believed, and his collections do not postulate a deeper unity than their separate elements. But he was a pattern-maker from the beginning, and he was also interested in what I would call functional as opposed to organic unity: that is, the co-operation or co-ordination of parts in a system that enabled that system to work, to do its job. The breakdown of such a system horrified him, as it does in 'The Mother Hive', in which the infiltration of the hive by the Wax-Moth leads to a disintegration which is traced with obsessive precision in the mechanics of the hive's operation (the bees take to 'cadging round sugar-factories and breweries' instead of gathering nectar) and the fabric of its architecture which becomes 'riddled with little tunnels'.[12] Accordingly there is a strong 'constructive' impulse both in individual stories and in their arrangement in collections; the trend is already marked in *The Jungle Book* and *The Second Jungle Book*, and it increases in the volumes that Kipling issued in the new century. Stories similar in theme are told using different narrative modes; the same motifs turn up in different contexts of time or place, and with different values attached to them; characters and relationships resemble but do not repeat each other. Such patterns are too strong and too visible to be wholly the product of critical ingenuity, though I acknowledge that the bias of interpretation is likely to exaggerate the element of authorial design.

Here are some instances of this pattern of likeness and difference in *Actions and Reactions*. The volume includes two 'non-realist' tales, side by side, 'The Mother Hive' and 'With the Night Mail'. The first is an insect fable and the second a science-fiction fantasy; both are forecasts of the future, in one of which democracy brings about the end of civilisation; in the other, civilisation has brought about the end of democracy. The two stories in which Kipling revisits his earlier fiction are differentiated by class: 'Garm – A Hostage' recalls the narrator's friendship with a private soldier, as in *Plain Tales from the*

Hills, while 'A Deal in Cotton' evokes friendships from the same period with men of his own or a higher social class. 'Garm – A Hostage' forms part of another pairing, for it is one of two dog stories in the volume; it deals with the relationship of a single dog to its owner, and with that owner's individual fate as a small cog in the Indian Army's military machine, and it is told by an autobiographical narrator in a spirit of intimate recollection. The other, 'Little Foxes', deals with a pack of fox-hounds, and with large issues of colonial governance; and its narrator is a practised raconteur, with inside knowledge of a scandalous and obscenely funny story (whose climax, incidentally, repeats the key phrase 'the dark places of the earth', from the early 'Man Who Would Be King'[13]). 'Little Foxes', in turn, follows 'A Deal in Cotton' and 'The Puzzler', all three on colonial or imperial themes, and all hinging on a practical joke, though the jokes are of radically different kinds. The one that lies at the heart of 'A Deal in Cotton' in which the keen young colonial administrator Adam Strickland becomes the unwitting beneficiary of the notoriously cruel slave trader Ibn Makarrah, whom his 'Chief [has] smashed'[14] is scarcely recognisable as a joke at all, and is at home in a story filled with the powers of darkness; the one in 'The Puzzler' drives a surreal carnivalesque farce of male regression; and in 'Little Foxes' a merciless hoax exposes a pompous gullible do-gooder to shame and humiliation. 'Little Foxes' is also, alas, one of those mortifying instances of Kipling's capacity for spiteful caricature, an art in which he tried to be Gillray but succeeded only in becoming a debased Beerbohm, without the wit; but next door to it is 'The House Surgeon', in which every assumption about the poisoned rootedness of Kipling's anti-Semitism is confounded.

These are a few of the many possible connections that can be made between the stories; I have not even mentioned the limitations and expansions offered by the accompanying poems, from the magnificent double-voiced elegy 'The Power of the Dog' ('Brothers and sisters, I bid you beware / Of giving your hearts to a dog to tear'),[15] completely in tune with the story it follows, to the riddling myth of 'The Four Angels', also a great poem, but so outside the ken of 'With the Night Mail', the story to which it is attached, that it seems impossible to make one speak to the other. I concentrate here on one example that can be treated in detail: perhaps the most obvious, but also the richest and most suggestive.

Actions and Reactions begins and ends with two stories about houses, 'An Habitation Enforced' and 'The House Surgeon', though the houses, and indeed the stories, are of very different kinds. Indeed, they are designed both to answer and, so to speak, defy each other across the intervening space of the volume, in which a number of other houses also play their part, including a beehive, a wealthy landowner's mansion ('A Deal in Cotton'), and a gloriously vulgar late Victorian villa built of 'blood-coloured brick, cornered and banded with vermiculate stucco . . . [with] cobalt, magenta and purest apple-green window glass on either side of the front door'.[16] All of these might be drawn into the design; but I will concentrate on the two houses that stand at opposite ends of the volume.

The house in 'An Habitation Enforced' is Friars Pardon, an ancestral dwelling, which we may presume dates from the Dissolution of the Monasteries in the sixteenth century, though the current manor house is Georgian. Friars Pardon is the centre of an estate that used to belong to one family, the Lashmars, who lost it around the end of the eighteenth century. Subsequent owners – the Elphicks and the Moones – have died out, and the estate is in the hands of solicitors in London. The five farms that still belong to the estate are on the edge of solvency, and the manor house itself has stood empty for seventeen years. Attempts have been made to sell it off, but no one will buy it: as the old caretaker, Iggulden, explains, it is 'too far away along from any place'.[17] It is not yet a ruin, though well on the way to becoming one: the downstairs rooms are used for storing wool, the roof is open to the weather. On the other hand many of its original period features are intact, and are lovingly detailed: a 'slim-balustered staircase, wide and shallow and once creamy-white'; 'delicately moulded doors'; 'sea-green mantelpieces . . . adorned with nymphs, scrolls, and Cupids in low relief'. On the first floor is the drawing room, 'a long, green-panelled room lighted by three full-length windows, which overlooked the forlorn wreck of a terraced garden, and wooded slopes beyond'. There are 'bedrooms with dressing-rooms and powdering-closets, and steps leading up and down – boxes of rooms, round, square, and octagonal, with enriched ceilings and chased door-locks'. Even the pathos of decline is infused with elegance, with dignity, above all with authenticity. The Adam fireplaces have not been supplied by a modern firm that manufactures imitations of Georgian style: they are 'the originals'.[18]

What of the house that stands at the other end of the volume? It is called 'Holmescroft', and it was built in 1863. It is located somewhere in the Home Counties, an hour and half's drive from London, in 'an exclusive residential district of dustless roads and elegantly designed country villas, each standing in from three to five acres of perfectly appointed land'. This land, we learn, is selling 'at eight hundred pounds the acre'; the 'new golf links', complete with a 'Queen Anne pavilion', 'had cost nearly twenty-four thousand pounds to create'. Holmescroft itself is 'a large, two-storied, low, creeper-covered residence. A verandah at the south side gave on to a garden and two tennis courts, separated by a tasteful iron fence from a most park-like meadow of five or six acres, where two Jersey cows grazed'. The word 'tasteful', which in English almost invariably means its opposite, alerts us to the inauthenticity of this scene, with its make-believe pastoral. Inside, this temple of wealthy Philistinism boasts 'a wide parquet-floored hall furnished in pale lemon, with huge cloisonné vases, an ebonized and gold grand piano, and banks of pot flowers in Benares brass bowls'. The 'pale oak staircase' leads to 'a spacious landing, where there was a green velvet settee trimmed with silver'.[19] The vulgar opulence of the house contrasts pointedly with the exquisite decay of Friars Pardon. One represents a tradition whose integrity persists even in decline; the other a rootless modernity, whose pretensions are based on nothing more than money.

These observations about the two houses cannot be simply applied to the characters who inhabit them, because these characters complicate the simple opposition between the two kinds of social order that the houses in themselves apparently embody. Friars Pardon is bought, in the course of the story, by the American couple George and Sophie Chapin, who come across it by accident and then discover that they have unwittingly returned to the place from which Sophie's family, a branch of the Lashmars, emigrated to America a century ago. The house is saved and restored, and the farms, we assume, will become productive and profitable; most important of all, the social fabric of the community, based on a neo-feudal structure of respect and mutual obligation, will be repaired and renewed for generations to come, and this outcome depends on the fact that dirty new American money is, so to speak, washed clean by the blood of an authentic ancestral claim (a fantasy packed with ironies, which I examine below). Holmescroft too needs to be healed and restored (hence the title of the story). Years before, three sisters lived in the house, and the youngest died by falling from her bedroom window. The fall was a pure accident, but her older sister thought it was suicide, and that the sinner was therefore, according to her narrow morbid Calvinistic doctrine, eternally damned. Two occult forces converge on the house: the survivor's obsessive anguish at her sister's fate, and the dead woman's equally anguished spirit, desperate to communicate the truth about her death. Between them they blight the life of the new owners, and of everyone who comes to stay in the house, with an atmosphere of fathomless depression. These new owners are a rich Jewish family, who enlist the narrator's help in unlocking the secret of the house's affliction, so that the sisters can be at peace and they can actually enjoy the luxury they have paid for.

The name of these Jewish owners is 'M'Leod' – a patently inauthentic name, since they are Greeks, who are attempting to assimilate into English society – and in another context they might find themselves the targets of Kipling's prickly scorn. And this other context is in fact present in 'An Habitation Enforced', for in the neighbourhood of Friars Pardon is another estate, recently bought and renovated by a certain Mr Sangres, who is vaguely thought to be Brazilian, is certainly dark-skinned, and has made his money in trade. Mr Sangres has done with his estate what the Chapins' tenants fear their new American owners will do with theirs – give up farming as a bad job, evict the tenants, and turn the land into a 'park', with a decorative herd of fallow deer – a version of the same kind of fake pastoral as the M'Leods have on their five acres, nouveau-riche vulgarity on the grand scale. Mr Sangres and his family want to be accepted into the local community, but they have no sense of obligation and think they can simply buy their way in. The community, from grandee to peasant, gives them the cold shoulder, and quite right too, we are asked to think; until, perhaps, we realise that Mr Sangres – 'that nigger Sangres',[20] as he is called by one of the locals – is only Mr M'Leod writ large, or indeed Mr Chapin without the saving grace of his wife's pedigree.

Kipling was in his best work a great artist and not a propagandist or a manipulator of received ideas. In his masterfully ironic hands the opposition between Friars Pardon and Holmescroft turns out to be a contest, not between authenticity and inauthenticity, but between two kinds of inauthenticity, one of which is if anything less honest than the other. In 'The House Surgeon' a Jewish family is made happy by having a Christian curse lifted from the house they inhabit, and this happiness is signified by the daughter's approaching marriage with a young man 'who knew everything about every South American railway stock';[21] this young Jew is evidently a financial speculator, and we might see in him another avatar of Mr Sangres, another non-English interloper into the England whose real values are enshrined in the closed community of Friars Pardon. But the marriage is a cause of delight and celebration at the end of 'The House Surgeon', whereas the ending of 'An Habitation Enforced', as the title has all along intimated, is not free of ambiguity. The M'Leods are a blissfully united family, but the Chapins are divided by what happens to them, and not simply because Sophie is a Lashmar and George is not. His money – acquired in the savage arena of modern capitalist competition, as we are reminded by the story's tremendous opening sentence ('It came without warning, as his hand was outstretched to crumple the Holz and Gunsberg Combine'[22]) – does not so much buy him a place in England as enable his entrapment in a plot where his function is not to own but to breed. The culmination of the renewal of Friars Pardon is the birth of a male heir, who is given not his father's but his mother's name. Earlier in the story George observed that the history of the estate could be seen not in terms of possession but sacrifice. 'People don't seem to matter in this country compared to the places they live in', he says, and he concludes that 'Friars Pardon was a sort of Moloch'. He becomes its latest victim; the house devours him for its own ends, and the final words of the story, spoken by George in the full consciousness of their symbolic import, are an expression of frustration and impotence: 'we can't get out of it'.[23]

The physical distance between these two stories, placed at either end of the volume, stands as an emblem of differences which are properly irreconcilable: that is, which it would be a violation of principle to imagine as somehow easily adjustable. Friars Pardon and Holmescroft are each valued on a scale against which the other appears distorted or diminished. As readers we are invited to juxtapose them, but not to mix them up. If Mr M'Leod were to move to Friars Pardon he would metamorphose into Mr Sangres. But it is part of what gives M'Leod his dignity that he has the tact to know just what kind of Englishman he can become.

Literary returns

I spoke earlier of two stories in which Kipling consciously returns to the subject matter and characters of his early work. Here I have chosen to concentrate on 'Garm – A Hostage'.

The story's setting, and its main characters, would have looked familiar to readers who had followed Kipling since the glory days of his Anglo-Indian career, the period of *Plain Tales from the Hills, Soldiers Three, Life's Handicap* and *Many Inventions*. To such readers the story might well have seemed, at least to begin with, a welcome return to a domain where Kipling's mastery was uncontested, that of Britain's imperial frontier in the North-West Province of India in the last years of the nineteenth century. The persona of the narrator belongs nominally to this time and place: he is Kipling as he used to be, the young man learning his trade as a journalist and writer on the staff of the *Civil and Military Gazette* in Lahore. His friendships embrace both the officers and private soldiers of the British regiments who are quartered in the city, notably the 'Soldiers Three' – Privates Mulvaney, Learoyd and Ortheris – who represent the pockmarked heroism of the British Army's imperial countenance, its savagery, wit and human fellowship.

In the plot of the story readers would have recognised Kipling's interest in the ordinary soldier's barrack-room life, his domestic as opposed to military existence. Boredom, drunkenness, heat-stroke, cholera, petty crime, adultery – these had not been the stuff of romance before Kipling came along. Private Stanley Ortheris gets drunk and narrowly escapes a serious disciplinary charge, thanks to the narrator's timely intervention. As a kind of penance, and as a 'hostage' for his good behaviour, he gives the narrator his dog, a bull-terrier whom the narrator calls 'Garm', the name of the dog who, in Norse mythology, guards the gates of hell. Ortheris stubbornly refuses to take the dog back, though both are broken-hearted. Eventually, on a visit to a hill-station in the Himalayas where Ortheris is recovering from fever, the narrator contrives to reunite them. That is all there is by way of plot: the story is more a mood-piece, an evocation of time and place, and a psychological study, if it is not too grand to put it this way, of guilt, self-punishment and redemption. Again, to describe it in these terms is to evoke comparisons with earlier stories, including one about Ortheris, 'The Madness of Private Ortheris', from *Plain Tales from the Hills*. But such comparisons only take you so far.

The scenery and props of the story are deceptive. Kipling the writer is no longer close to the persona of his narrator; he is no longer an ambitious provincial but a cosmopolitan celebrity, and he has left India, never to return. He has access to his earlier self only through memory. In earlier stories, where the narrator himself plays a part in the action, the time of the narration is close to that of the events related. So, for example, the story 'With the Main Guard', published in 1888, begins with Mulvaney saying something to the narrator, who immediately comments: 'It was Mulvaney who was speaking. The time was one o'clock of a stifling June night, and the place was the main gate of Fort Amara, most desolate and least desirable of all fortresses in India.'[24] We do not know when the narrator is writing this down, and in a sense that question is not important, but if we had to guess we would probably say 'shortly afterwards', or 'when he got home'. Here, by contrast, is the opening of 'Garm': 'One night, a very long time ago, I drove to an Indian military cantonment called Mian Mir to see amateur theatricals.'[25] The phrase 'a very long time ago' reminds us that we are in 1909, and that the narrator is looking down a far longer perspective at his youthful self. The tone has distance in it, measurable even in very small differences of phrasing. When the narrator identifies Fort Amara as 'most desolate and least desirable of all fortresses in India', we feel it probable that the writer himself is *in* India; when he calls Mian Mir 'an Indian military cantonment', it is clear that he is not.

The same sense of distance affects the use of names in the story. The narrator addresses Ortheris by his first name, Stanley, something he almost never does in earlier tales, and refers to him using a variety of circumlocutions: 'my friend', 'his [i.e. the dog's] owner' or 'his master', 'my soldier friend',[26] etc. The only time he actually puts down the name 'Ortheris' in black and white it acts as a kind of disclaimer, which may strike the reader as ironic, or disingenuous, or both: 'I never pretended to understand Private Ortheris; and so I did the next best thing – I left him alone.' When Ortheris comes back secretly to see his dog, the narrator keeps his incognito: he is 'a soldier in white uniform'[27] glimpsed scrambling over the garden wall. These effects are small in themselves but very well judged; they mark the story as not fully belonging to the group where we might naturally think of placing it, and they also suggest that Kipling's 'return' to his earlier self and style has something odd about it.

This oddness is easy enough to detect in the 'tone' of the story, but harder to identify at the level of theme or subject matter, where it ought after all to count most: one senses a change of atmosphere in a familiar room, without quite seeing how the furniture has been rearranged. It is not the presence of a dog; Ortheris had always been associated with dogs, admittedly more as a master dog-thief than a devoted owner. Ortheris's characterisation as moody, stubborn, quixotic, has not altered over twenty years; nor has the basis of his friendship with the narrator, who helps him out of the occasional jam without preaching to him or patronising him. But there is a curious lack of mechanism in the plot. There is no event, no moment of recognition or reversal, to motivate the undoing of Ortheris's self-imposed punishment. He gives the narrator his dog, and refuses to take it back, though he cannot resist visiting it on the sly; we are given the clear impression that this refusal is absolute and unalterable; indeed, another of the 'Soldiers Three', Mulvaney, is given a cameo appearance specifically to make this point: 'He won't take the dog, sorr. You can lay your month's pay on that. Ye know his fits.'[28] Indeed we do, and it seems that Kipling will have to exercise considerable narrative ingenuity to get Ortheris out of this psychological impasse. As readers we are entitled to look forward to a spectacular plot-twist. None is forthcoming. Ortheris falls sick and is sent against his will to a hill-station. He and the dog are now, it seems, finally separated, and the implication is that they will both die; however, the narrator determines to pass through the same hill-station on his annual leave, and to bring the dog to Ortheris; he does so, they are reunited, and live happily ever after. That's it. What has become of Ortheris's sublime, absolute refusal? The story simply wishes it away, as though it were too hard a knot to untie. But Kipling had unravelled far more tangled plot-lines than this one. Twenty years earlier he would have come up with some corresponding action on the part of the narrator from which Ortheris might rescue him and thus repay his debt; or he would have brought Ortheris and the dog together in the context of some episode of liberating comedy or violence. What actually happens, the scene in which the narrator sees Ortheris, 'this one little man, crumpled up and thinking, on the great grey hillside',[29] and then witnesses his joyful repossession of his dog and his self, is very beautiful, but it is completely unmotivated. And that is the point, much more like life than like a story: a clear repudiation of romance in favour of mere contingency. Ortheris was determined to die rather than go back on his word, and then Ortheris goes back on his word and lives.

The reversal of expectation at the level of plot is accompanied by another reversal, which is so obvious that it is easy to miss. I have said that Kipling returns in this story to an older autobiographical persona, that of the young journalist who has friends among both officers and common soldiers in Lahore. In the early stories which feature his dealings with Mulvaney, Learoyd and Ortheris, the narrator's occupation, or personality, or domestic circumstances, are only ever part of the background; in 'Garm – A Hostage' they are the centre of attention. Background has become foreground. Much of the story reads more like an episode from a memoir than a work of fiction, and it is done with great plainness, with only occasional touches of the vivid concrete detail that Kipling had applied to the routines and textures of barrack life. The narrator tells us of morning rides before he goes to his newspaper office, of long dull days of sedentary work, of the exact route to the Hills that he took on his annual leave. Most of the colour in the story is given to the dogs, not just Garm but the narrator's own dog, Vixen, who sleeps in his cot with 'her head on the pillow like a Christian'; we see Garm breaking the back of a pariah dog, and terrifying an ignorant Tommy who tries to steal him, but also sitting aloof in the narrator's carriage as it drives down the Mall, indifferent to the bustle of the scene and preoccupied with his lost master: 'His big eyes were on the horizon, and his terrible mouth was shut.'[30] Gradually, as the story unfolds, we discover that we are learning much more about Garm than about Ortheris, whose character is static and who in any case appears in person only a couple of times; and Garm belongs with the narrator for the duration of the story, so that in exploring his predicament the narrator is bound to speak of himself and of his way of life, simply by way of explanation. It is seemingly artless, yet done with quiet art, this autobiographical sketch which Kipling pretends is merely the by-product of a fiction.

There is, of course, an element of nostalgia in Kipling's design, but even nostalgia serves an artistic purpose. By 1909 Kipling had accepted, and to some extent embraced, his identity as a polemical writer. The narrator who surges up from his personal and literary past comes from a simpler time, and is himself a simpler figure. We have only to compare him to the sardonic, politically engaged narrator of 'The Puzzler' who remarks that the Law Lord, the artist and the great engineer are bound by 'Ties of Common Funk'[31] to measure the distance Kipling has travelled. I think that helps to explain the presence of this reflective and tender story in the embattled world of *Actions and Reactions*. It remains the case that the volume as a whole represents one of Kipling's most sustained efforts to understand and represent this world. 'Garm – A Hostage' is all the more poignant for being the only story in *Actions and Reactions* which is not at any point located in England. The others are all stories of home or homecoming, even when they deal with colonial or imperial themes; these themes are 'brought home' to us in a double sense, by being linked to the great overarching structures that Kipling discerned in English history, in English nature, and in the English character (all of these related, of course, to each other). Again, 'Garm' is exceptional in having nothing to say about these grand matters.

I will conclude with a word of warning, and, as I promised, of contradiction. The temptation, in speaking of *Actions and Reactions* is to take the great overarching structures I spoke of as definitive frames of meaning. But Kipling did not, in the end, think of 'England' as a 'master-word' of this kind. We must not mistake his vision of English history, which prizes duration, and which can accommodate cycles of growth and decay, for a vision of transcendent value. There is a power above duration, the power Kipling acknowledges in his story 'The Bridge-Builders', and in one of the greatest of his poems, 'Cities and Thrones and Powers':

> Cities and Thrones and Powers
>   Stand in Time's eye,
> Almost as long as flowers,
>   Which daily die:
> But, as new buds put forth
>   To glad new men,
> Out of the spent and unconsidered Earth,
>   The Cities rise again.
>
> This season's Daffodil,
>   She never hears,
> What change, what chance, what chill,
>   Cut down last year's;
> But with bold countenance,
>   And knowledge small,
> Esteems her seven days' continuance
>   To be perpetual.
>
> So Time that is o'er-kind
>   To all that be,
> Ordains us e'en as blind,
>   As bold as she:
> That in our very death,
>   And burial sure,
> Shadow to shadow, well persuaded, saith,
>   "See how our works endure!"[32]

This poem forms the preface to 'A Centurion of the Thirtieth', a fable of continuity and rupture between the Roman and British Empires in *Puck of Pook's Hill*, the volume which, along with its sequel *Rewards and Fairies*, brackets *Actions and Reactions* – *Puck* in 1906, and *Rewards* in 1910. I agree with Andrew Lycett that we should read *Actions and Reactions* in conjunction with these books,[33] which make up a condition-of-England trilogy; and I would emphasise that the England of *Actions and Reactions* 'stand[s] in Time's eye' as much as that of the other two.

Addendum to *Actions and Reactions* (1909)

Title of story (*followed by title of accompanying poem*)	Date of first magazine publication
An Habitation Enforced *The Recall*	USA: *Century Magazine*, August 1905
Garm – A Hostage *The Power of the Dog*	USA: *Saturday Evening Post*, 23 December 1899 UK: *Pearson's Magazine*, January 1900
The Mother Hive *The Bees and the Flies*	USA: *Collier's Weekly*, 28 November 1908 UK: *Windsor Magazine*, December 1908 (as 'Adventures of Melissa')
With the Night Mail *The Four Angels*	USA: *McClure's Magazine*, November 1905 UK: *Windsor Magazine*, December 1905
A Deal in Cotton *The New Knighthood*	USA: *Collier's Weekly*, 14 December 1907 UK: *Cassell's Magazine*, January 1908
The Puzzler *The Puzzler*	USA: *North American*, January 1906 and *Collier's Weekly*, 17 February 1906 UK: *Tribune*, 15 and 16 January 1906
Little Foxes *Gallio's Song*	USA: *Collier's Weekly*, 27 March 1909 UK: *Nash's Magazine*, April 1909
The House Surgeon *The Rabbi's Song*	USA: *Harper's Magazine*, September and October 1909

Notes

1 Andrew Lycett, *Rudyard Kipling* (London: Weidenfeld & Nicholson, 1999), p. 521.
2 Kipling, 'An Habitation Enforced', *Actions and Reactions* (London: Macmillan, 1909), p. 8.
3 Robert Browning, 'Childe Roland to the Dark Tower Came', D. Karllu (ed.) *Selected Poems* (Harmondsworth, Penguin Books, 1989), pp. 93–9.
4 *Ibid.*, p. 99.
5 Kipling, 'Habitation', *Actions*, p. 8.
6 Thomas Hardy, 'Afterwards', *Complete Poems*, ed. James Gibson (London: Macmillan, 1976), p. 553.

7 Lycett, *Rudyard Kipling*, p. 360.
8 Kipling to Charles Eliot Norton in *Letters of Rudyard Kipling, Volume 3: 1900–10*, ed. Thomas Pinney (Basingstoke: Macmillan, 1996), p. 113.
9 J.B. Priestley, *The Edwardians* (London: Heinemann, 1970), pp. 87, 91, 104–5.
10 Kipling, 'The Mother Hive', *Actions*, p. 106.
11 John Woolford, *Browning the Revisionary* (London: Palgrave Macmillan, 1988), pp. 35–9.
12 Kipling, 'The Mother Hive', *Actions*, pp. 96, 95.
13 When Mr Groombride the foolish liberal exclaims 'The dark places of the earth are full of cruelty' ('Little Foxes', *Actions*, p. 254), he repeats almost word for word the narrator's description of Indian 'Native States' as 'the dark places of the earth, full of unimaginable cruelty' in 'The Man Who Would Be King', *Wee Willie Winkie and Other Stories* (London: Macmillan, 1899), p. 205.
14 Kipling, 'A Deal in Cotton', *Actions*, p. 180.
15 Kipling, 'The Power of the Dog', *Actions*, p. 79.
16 Kipling. 'The Puzzler', *Actions*, p. 206.
17 Kipling, 'Habitation', *Actions*, p. 12.
18 *Ibid.*, pp. 10–11.
19 Kipling, 'The House Surgeon', *Actions*, pp. 266–7.
20 Kipling, 'Habitation', *Actions*, p. 36.
21 Kipling, 'House Surgeon', *Actions*, p. 269.
22 Kipling, 'Habitation', *Actions*, p. 3.
23 *Ibid.*, p. 50.
24 Kipling, 'With the Main Guard', *Soldiers Three and Other Stories* (London: Macmillan, 1895), p. 55.
25 Kipling, 'Garm – A Hostage', *Actions*, p. 53.
26 *Ibid.*, pp. 53 ff.
27 *Ibid.*, pp. 62, 64.
28 *Ibid.*, p. 64.
29 *Ibid.*, p. 77.
30 *Ibid.*, pp. 58, 69.
31 Kipling, 'Puzzler', *Actions*, p. 218.
32 Kipling, 'Cities and Thrones and Powers', *Puck of Pook's Hill* (London: Macmillan, 1955), p. 139.
33 Lycett, *Rudyard Kipling*, p. 521.

9

Rikki-Tikki-Tavi and Indian history

LISA LEWIS

'Rikki-Tikki-Tavi', the story that made me a lifelong Kipling enthusiast, is a story of multi-layered meanings. As an animal fable it is accessible to young children like me as a very small girl suffering from terrifying nightmares, to whom a kind aunt read a wonderful story about a strange little animal called a mongoose, who would sit on a child's bed and keep watch, ready to kill the wicked creatures that lurked in the shadows after the light was turned off. But it is not only a comforting tale of a protecting guardian, as I realised when my father read out the verse heading as well as the story:

> At the hole where he went in
> Red-eye called to Wrinkle-skin.
> Hear what little Red-eye saith:
> 'Nag, come up and dance with death!'
>
> Eye to eye and head to head,
>   (*Keep the measure, Nag.*)
> This shall end when one is dead;
>   (*At thy pleasure, Nag.*)
> Turn for turn and twist for twist –
>   (*Run and hide thee, Nag.*)
> Hah! The hooded death has missed!
>   (*Woe betide thee, Nag!*)[1]

This is not a play fight, or an easy victory; the poem underlines the fact that Rikki-Tikki is risking his own life. The animal realism is exact: although I have never seen a mongoose kill a snake, I once saw a little tropical cat do this, and she did indeed go through a long weaving dance with the creature before she fooled it into passing the wrong way and was able to seize it by the neck. (It was only a harmless tree snake, but a hunter can't be too careful.) As so often with Kipling, an unfamiliar sight was instantly recognisable from something he had written. The formal rhythm in these verses, which is also the rhythm of a minuet, brings an echo of old times and old violence – of sword-play that is also a 'dance with death', as the duellists manoeuvre for an opening. And as I came to see much later, the story also carries clear allusions to more recent historic violence.

But any discussion of 'Rikki-Tikki' has to begin with the story as animal fable, the aspect that is accessible to a child. Here Kipling seems to have been partly drawing on his own knowledge. The spoof preface he wrote for *The Jungle Book* (which claims throughout that he has gleaned the stories by talking to animals, the others being an Indian 'baggage elephant', a monkey on the slopes of Jakko hill, a captive wolf trained to dance at fairs, and a bird that landed on an ocean-going liner), hints at a dead mongoose behind Rikki-Tikki's character: 'The Editor stands indebted to one of the leading herpetologists of Upper India, a fearless and independent investigator who, resolving "not to live but to know", lately sacrificed his life through over-application to the study of our Eastern Thanatophidia.'[2] Certainly the mongoose described in an early poem from *Echoes*, part of a series of "Nursery Idylls" written in imitation of Christina Rossetti, did lose his life:

> Here's a mongoose
> Dead in the sluice
> Of the bathroom drain.
> How was he slain?
> He must have lain
> Days, it is plain . . .
> Stopper your nose,
> Throw him out to the crows.[3]

If Rikki-Tikki had lost his battle with Nag the cobra, he too might have been found dead in the bathroom sluice. But it was not only a dead mongoose that inspired the story. When Kipling compiled the notes on the Jungle Book characters for the Sussex and Burwash editions, he wrote of Rikki-Tikki-Tavi:

> Mongooses are as bold and clever as I have tried to describe, and they often come into a house or even into an office with people going in and out all the time, and make friends with men there. A perfectly wild mongoose used to

come and sit on my shoulder in my office in India, and burn his inquisitive nose on the end of my cigar, just as Rikki did in the tale.⁴

Kipling's father Lockwood wrote of the mongoose in *Beast and Man in India*:

> Few wild animals take so readily to domestic life as the Indian mongoose, who has been known to domesticate himself among friendly people; first coming into the house through the bath-water exit in chase of snake or rat, and ending, with a little encouragement, by stealing into the master's chair and passing a pink inquisitive nose under his arm to examine a cup of tea held in his hand. This is the footing on which pets should be established.⁵

On the subject of mongooses and snakes, Lockwood writes that 'One of the unalterably fixed beliefs in the native mind is that the mongoose knows a remedy for snake-bite, – a plant which nobody has seen or can identify, but which, when eaten, is an antidote so sure that the mere breath of the animal suffices to paralyse the snake', but this is not true: 'The mongoose has only its quickness of attack and its thick fur for safeguard.'⁶ Kipling echoes this passage in the story:

> If you read the old books of natural history, you will find they say that when the mongoose fights the snake and happens to get bitten, he runs off and eats some herb that cures him. That is not true. The victory is only a matter of quickness of eye and quickness of foot, – snake's blow against mongoose's jump, – and as no eye can follow the motion of a snake's head when it strikes, that makes things much more wonderful than any magic herb.⁷

Roger Lancelyn Green suggests that Kipling was alluding to a human herpetologist in 'Rikki-Tikki-Tavi' as well as one or more examples of the species ichneumon. He mentions Sir Joseph Fayrer, author of *The Thanatophidia of India*, a pamphlet describing half a dozen different poisonous snakes (though it does not include cobras). Green cites Fayrer's grand-daughter as authority both for a friendship between her family and the Kiplings and for her grandfather's connection with the story, although she apparently could not remember the details.⁸ It seems likely that Kipling had adopted the intriguing word "Thanatophidia" from the published pamphlet, and had cross-examined Fayrer personally for details about cobras.

An English literary source for the story seems to be a now-forgotten children's poem, 'The Water Rat', which Kipling quotes in the first chapter of *Something of Myself* when he describes the books which he says helped to comfort him during his long exile in the House of Desolation, including 'two books of verse about child-life', in one of which 'a girl was turned into a water rat "as a matter of course".[9] Lancelyn Green[10] identified these books as the work of Menella Bute Smedley and Elizabeth Anna Hart. In 'The Water Rat' from Hart's *Child Nature*, a child has a pet water rat that comes into the house and gets on the table at mealtimes. Previously, the child's sister has fallen in a pond and drowned. One night the water rat gets into bed with the grieving mother, and the following morning the dead child is found alive and sleeping in her own bed:

> Of course, a fairy pond was that
> And she was saved by fairy force,
> And changed into a water rat,
> All these are matters quite of course.[11]

It was these lines that Kipling half-remembered in *Something of Myself*. Rikki-Tikki-Tavi, who also gets on the table at mealtimes and joins a human to bed, can be said to have some of the characteristics of Hart's water rat.

A much grander literary origin for the story is the ancient cycle of Indian beast-fables called *Panchatantra*. One of these, titled variously 'The Faithful Mongoose' or 'The Brahmin and the Mongoose', tells of a Brahmin, whose wife has gone out leaving him in charge of their baby son. He is summoned to perform a religious ceremony which he must not refuse, so he bids the family's pet mongoose take care of the child. During his absence a snake comes into the room, and is killed by the mongoose. On its master's return the animal runs to greet him, but seeing the snake's blood on its muzzle, the Brahmin jumps to a false conclusion, thinks it has killed his son, and beats the faithful creature to death. Only then does he go to look in the cradle, find a healthy child and see the dead snake. In another version of this story the wife, having neglected her baby, blames the mongoose and encourages her husband to kill it, but it was the first version that caught on widely and was retold in many countries round the world. According to the scholar H.W. Thomas, the *Panchatantra* cycle 'found its way in various disguises, through the Pahlavi, Arabic, Hebrew, and Syriac, into all the chief European languages – it was also represented by versions in languages of southern India and the Malay Islands, Further India, and the Far East.'[12] In the same collection of essays, another writer comments:

> That the migration of fables was originally from East to West, and not vice versa, is shown by the fact that the animals who play the leading parts . . . are mostly Indian ones. In the European versions the jackal becomes the fox . . . This change in the species of the animals in the course of the wandering of the

fables is very instructive. Take, for instance, the well-known Welsh story of Llewellyn and Gelert. The father comes home and is greeted by his hound, which he had left to guard his infant daughter. Its jaws are covered with blood, and thinking it has killed the child, he slays it. Then he finds the child asleep in her cradle, safe and sound, a dead wolf by her side. In the original tale in the Panchatantra, a mongoose and a cobra play the part of dog and wolf.[13]

The details of these various transformations, from mongoose to weasel to dog, and from Brahmin to sheikh to knight to Welsh prince, are traced by the scholar Franklin Edgerton in the introduction to his translation of *Panchatantra*, where the two versions of the story are given.[14] Another story in the *Panchatantra* which seems to have contributed to 'Rikki-Tikki-Tavi' concerns a family of birds, who enlist a mongoose to help them against a wicked snake that wants to eat their nestlings, as Darzee the tailor-bird recruits Rikki-Tikki. The mongoose duly kills the snake and then eats the nestlings itself. In using these Indian legends, Kipling has left out their harsher side. Rikki-Tikki-Tavi is not killed but treated as a hero. Darzee's children are safe from him. It is typical of Kipling, however, having sentimentalised his sources, then to introduce a grim subtext of his own.

The garden where Rikki-Tikki-Tavi lives has been identified[15] as the garden of Belvedere, the house in Allahabad where Kipling lodged with Professor and Mrs Hill during his years on *The Pioneer* newspaper. Mrs Hill described it as 'a famous old bungalow, standing since Mutiny days when nearly every other house was destroyed'.[16] Belvedere was also the setting for 'The Return of Imray', a story of an Englishman murdered by his Indian servant, whose ghost haunts the new tenants of the bungalow until his dead body is found.[17] According to Mrs Hill, this story was inspired by the mundane fact that a disgusting smell was caused by a dead squirrel in the roof space. Kipling's version is one of the spookiest stories he ever wrote. Did he perhaps sense ghosts in the bungalow – ghosts of Englishmen killed by Indians they had foolishly taken for granted?

Though Kipling wrote many tales set in Lahore and Simla, few have been positively located at Allahabad. There was no Allahabad equivalent of 'The Gate of the Hundred Sorrows', or 'In the House of Suddhoo', or 'Beyond the Pale'. There are two possible reasons for this. On *The Pioneer* Kipling was not a local reporter, but editor of a weekly supplement, and a roving correspondent who travelled around India, sending in articles about the independent states of Rajputana, or the coalfields, or the railways, or the city of Calcutta. But it is also true that recent history could have made it risky for an inquisitive mongoose of a journalist to 'run and find out'[18] in the back alleys of the city, asking questions of all and sundry. For only thirty years before, during what we used to call the Indian Mutiny of 1857, known nowadays as the Sepoy Rebellion or the First War of Indian Independence, there had been scenes at Allahabad that must have left considerable bitterness on both sides. A sepoy regiment which was stationed there rose and killed its officers. Joined by a crowd from the city, the rebels massacred Christian converts and looted or destroyed European property, while the Europeans themselves took refuge in the fort, protected by some British volunteers and a detachment of Sikhs. When the fort was relieved, revenge was taken, as Christopher Hibbert describes in *The Great Mutiny*:

> European volunteers and Sikhs descended upon the town, burning houses and slaughtering the inhabitants, old men, women and children as well as those more likely to be active rebels who were submitted to the travesty of a trial. 'The gallows and trees adjoining it had each day the fresh fruits of rebellion displayed upon them,' admitted F.A.V. Thorburn who was appointed Deputy Judge Advocate General. 'Hundreds of natives in this manner perished and some on slight proofs of criminality.'[19]

No such terrible massacres and reprisals had happened in Lahore, where Kipling also had the protection of his father's popularity. As founding head of the Mayo School of Art, Lockwood was a well-known figure in the city who encouraged local craftsmen and helped them sell their work.

The story's links to the Mutiny (I am calling it that, as Kipling would have done) were clarified to me by a new reading of 'Rikki-Tikki-Tavi' recorded by the Indian actor Madhav Sharma, one of a series of Kipling recordings.[20] Sharma's version of *Kim* is wonderful, as are his Mowgli stories, with different Indian voices for the different characters. His version of 'Rikki-Tikki' is less successful, but the voices he has chosen provide a remarkable sidelight on the story. The unsuccessful part is the English family, to whom Sharma gives Lancashire, or possibly Yorkshire, accents that do not quite come off: which seems to place them as junior members of the British Raj – the father would perhaps be one of the businessmen known to their more snobbish fellow-countrymen as 'box-wallahs'. The animals naturally speak like Indians. The cobras are distinctly upper-caste (Nag is almost plummy), and when Nagaina urges her husband to kill the human family, because: 'When the house is emptied of people . . . the garden will be our own again', and a moment later says, 'So long as the bungalow is empty, we are king and queen of the garden',[21] it sounds as though the cobras are members of an old Indian or

Mogul ruling family, plotting to kill the English and take over the land again, as the sepoys and their aristocratic leaders hoped to do in 1857.

Nag himself is not the sort of snake normally found in a bungalow garden. He combines aspects of two species. He has the spectacle markings of a common cobra but his size and his family life are those of a hamadryad, not native to north India, which builds a nest and defends its young. This was once seen as a sub-species, but is now considered a separate genus. Nag bears its title too: the hamadryad is also known as 'the king cobra'. Nag, then, is a fabulous creature, his royalty not scientific but symbolic.

There are more apparent anomalies in the story. The English family have only recently moved into the bungalow; we are not told that it is new, so it seems to have been standing empty for some time – which seems unlikely in an ordinary cantonment. Kipling wrote an uncollected article[22] about a Mutiny site, 'The Little House at Arrah', which stresses how ordinary the house and its setting appear to anyone who does not know its history:

> The French would have covered the building in a glass case, keeping intact each scar of musket and artillery fire. The Americans would have run a big fence round it and exhibited it at 5 cents per head – a pensioned veteran in charge. We, because we are English, prefer to sweep it up and keep it clean and use it as an ordinary house in the civil lines, for the benefit of Her Majesty's servants; just as if nothing worth mentioning had ever taken place in that unattractive compound.[23]

It is improbable, then, that Rikki-Tikki-Tavi's bungalow would have lain empty long enough for a five-foot snake (who might well be thirty years old) to see it as normal that he and his wife are rulers of the garden. Belvedere after all was now an ordinary home, despite its history during and after the Mutiny.

Another odd thing is that there are no human Indians in 'Rikki-Tikki-Tavi' – no servants, and no visible tradesmen. Yet quite modest British households of the Raj would have had a cook, a bearer, a gardener and a sweeper, while Teddy and his mother would have had at least one *ayah* between them. There would have been a *dhobi* to do the washing, and a human Darzee to make and mend the family clothes. It is as though animals have taken the servants' place. Something strange is going on here, and it seems to me to refer to the Mutiny.

Prominent among the leaders of the 1857 Mutiny were a number of dispossessed Indian princes, including the Nana Sahib, dethroned Maharajah of Bithor. The rebellious sepoys belonged to the landowning and farming classes, who bitterly resented the curtailment of their ancient rights by the British Government. Many of them came from Oudh, a formerly independent state which had been annexed by the British the previous year. Allahabad is on the borders of Oudh. It was in that general area that some of the most dramatic events took place, firing the British lust for revenge: the siege of Lucknow; the killing of captive women and children who had surrendered to the Nana Sahib at Kanpur. That the Mutiny was still fresh in British minds when *The Jungle Book* was written is shown by Murray's *Handbook to India*, 1894 edition,[24] in which Lucknow is described almost entirely in terms of the siege, with detailed notes on its sites and almost no reference to the earlier history of the city. This was the aspect of Lucknow the publishers apparently thought English-speaking tourists would want to see. Presumably they knew their market.

Kipling was reluctant to write about the Mutiny. In a letter to a publisher who had apparently asked him for a book or a story on the subject, he firmly refused, saying: "57 is the year we don't mention and I know *I* can't.'[25] The subject comes up obliquely in 'On the City Wall', where the beautiful Lalun tricks the British narrator into smuggling an escaped prisoner across Lahore under cover of a religious riot. Lalun evidently expects old Khem Singh to stir up a new revolt, but he is past it and the project comes to nothing:

> He fled to those who knew him in the old days, but many of them were dead and more were changed, and all knew something of the Wrath of the Government. He went to the young men, but the glamour of his name had passed away, and they were entering native regiments or Government offices, and Khem Singh could give them neither pension, decorations, nor influence – nothing but a glorious death with their back to the mouth of a gun.[26]

The British notoriously executed captured mutineers by blowing them from the mouth of a gun.

The Mutiny is spoken of openly in *Kim*, when the boy stays with the old Rissaldar who had supported the British side and spends an evening listening to tales of those times. The old man tells him:

> '. . . I was then in a regiment of cavalry. It broke. Of six hundred and eighty sabres stood fast to their salt – how many, think you? Three. Of whom I was one.'
>
> 'The greater merit.'
>
> 'Merit! We did not consider it merit in those days. My people, my friends, my brothers fell from me. They said, "The time of the English is accomplished.

Let each strike out a little holding for himself." But I had talked with the men of Sobraon, of Chilianwallah, of Moodkee and Ferozeshah. I said: "Abide a little and the wind turns. There is no blessing in this work." In those days I rode seventy miles with an English Memsahib and her babe on my saddle-bow.'[27]

Edward Said's criticism that such a character would be an exception and untypical ('Kipling has eliminated . . . the likelihood that [this man's] compatriots regard him as (at the least) a traitor to his people'[28]) is echoed by Indian critics such as Bhaskar Rao, Sara Suleri and Zohreh Sullivan, who have suggested that Kipling was afraid to confront the possibility of a further rebellion, that he needed to stress the loyalty of such characters as the Rissaldar in order to reassure himself.[29] Kipling did, however, write one story in which the killings of the Mutiny are described, not in their performance but in the aftermath. In 'The Undertakers' in *The Second Jungle Book* (1895), an old crocodile reminisces about long-ago days of easy living when the Ganges was full of dead, plundered bodies drifting down from such places as Kanpur, where before the massacre in the Bibighar members of the British community had been set adrift in boats and shot at as they drifted downstream:

> Yes, by Allahabad one lay still in the slack-water and let twenty go by to pick one; and, above all, the English were not cumbered with jewellery and nose-rings and anklets as my women are nowadays . . . All the muggers of all the rivers grew fat then, but it was my Fate to be fatter than them all. The news was that the English were being hunted into the rivers, and by the Right and Left of Gunga! we believed that it was true. So far as I went south it was believed to be true; and I went down-stream beyond Monghyr and the tombs that look over the river . . . Thereafter I worked up-stream very slowly and lazily, and a little above Monghyr there came down a boatful of white-faces – alive! They were, as I remember, women, lying under a cloth spread over sticks, and crying aloud. There was never a gun fired at us, the watchers of the fords in those days. All the guns were busy elsewhere. We could hear them day and night inland, coming and going as the wind shifted. I rose up full before the boat, because I had never seen white-faces alive, though I knew them well – otherwise.[30]

The Mugger goes on to describe how he snapped at a child's hands over the side of the boat, but the hands were too small and slipped between his teeth. At the end of the story he is shot by that child, now grown up to be a man.

The Jungle Book and *The Second Jungle Book* (as they were originally published) are balanced in several ways: each combines a set of Mowgli stories with tales in which other Indian animals of varying degrees of wildness or tameness interact in different ways with man. Rikki-Tikki, who as a free creature chooses to associate with humans; Toomai's elephant, which has been captured and trained; other animals that assist the army in various capacities in 'Her Majesty's Servants' are balanced by the village scavengers of 'The Undertakers' and the hermit's wild friends in 'The Miracle of Purun Bhagat'. Each book also has one story set in the Arctic: 'The White Seal' and 'Quiquern'. Can it be that each book also has a story with a Mutiny background?

For Mr Sharma's reading of 'Rikki-Tikki-Tavi' can also be heard as a parable of the Mutiny. Teddy and his parents are new occupiers of the bungalow, as the British were the new rulers of Oudh. One could compare the widowed cobra Nagaina to prominent women rebels like the widowed Rani of Jhansi, or the woman nicknamed 'The Begum', who was responsible for looking after the families imprisoned at Kanpur and who led the group that finally killed them. Rikki-Tikki himself, who belongs to a different species from the snakes, might be compared to the Sikh detachment who helped the British defend the fort at Allahabad and who joined in the subsequent slaughter of the mutineers. Kipling had acquired a positive view of Sikhs from his friend Dunsterville, the original of Stalky, who served in a Sikh regiment.

It would, of course, be a mistake to push these parallels too far. If Nagaina is identified with the Rani of Jhansi, then Nag would become the Rajah of Jhansi, who died three years before the rebellion began. Nor do I suggest that Rikki-Tikki-Tavi is in any sense a Sikh. But the Sikhs and the Muslim rulers of India had been old enemies, and Sikh troops fought on the British side in several famous battles of the Mutiny. In killing the cobras Rikki-Tikki saves the English family as the Sikh detachment at Allahabad saved the British community there. In befriending Teddy and his family, the mongoose has not exactly 'eaten their salt' (as the old Rissaldar would have put it) but he has eaten their meat, banana and boiled egg.

This interpretation of the story enters the world of post-colonial criticism, which scrutinises writers like Kipling for signs that they have lost their imperial nerve. Kipling couldn't face the Mutiny, it might be argued, except in terms of loyal Indians and victorious Britons. His account of 'The Little House at Arrah', in which a handful of British soldiers successfully fought off their besiegers, is told in the words of the Indian attendants who show him around. His adult writing ignores the deaths of women and children because such events threatened his memories of India as a paradise for little English boys. He can only confront such things in a children's fable, where the heroes triumph and the guilty perish. The cobras and the crocodiles must die, the mongoose must live and prosper.

To see Kipling as uneasily conscious of his position as one of a privileged minority, loudly asserting its permanence in order to hide from his own fears, is true up to a point, but it raises one important question. Why do people who have never lived under the British Empire, or who have lived to revolt against it, still find something fascinating in his writings? Sifting through old files in the Kipling Society's office, I once found an account by the British Council representative, who was present, of the dedication of a commemorative plaque outside Kipling's old office in Allahabad. The ceremony was performed by the Indian politician Krishna Menon, renowned for his extreme anti-imperialist views, who murmured to the British representative (when the press were not listening) that he was really rather fond of Kipling.

Why should Indians like Mr Menon feel that way? Why did Professor Edward Said, high priest and guru of the post-colonial school of criticism, seem to harbour a soft corner for *Kim*, even as he denounced its author? Did early reading of the novel help an exiled Said to find himself a glittering career as Little Friend of All the World's Literature? Why did Kipling appeal to South Indian writers like T.N. Murari, who wrote two sequels to *Kim* in which the hero becomes a nationalist,[31] or the Booker Prize winner Arundhati Roy, whose novel *The God of Small Things*[32] stayed at the top of the bestseller lists for over a year? In an interview, Roy once named the three books that mattered most to her as '*Ulysses, The Jungle Book* and *Lolita*';[33] and the lone Indian mother in her novel expresses her love for her children by reading them the Mowgli stories, which they quote delightedly to one another. Why, when I listened to the tapes of Madhav Sharma reading *Kim*, Mowgli and Purun Bhagat, did I hear in his voice such relish and understanding?

It may be that 'Rikki-Tikki-Tavi' is less acceptable to Indian readers because Teddy is a British child, whereas Mowgli is not, and Kim only reluctantly so. Or it may be that they are sensitive to an aspect of the story that Western readers tend not to notice. The Mutiny parable is a deep undercurrent in a story that for most non-Indian readers is mainly about childhood fears. This is one more instance of the richness of Kipling's art.

It is impossible to say how far Kipling himself was aware of this subtext. When writing the story, his pen took charge[34] and was busy making magic. He did sometimes load his fiction with extra meanings. According to his foreword to the American Outward Bound edition of 1897, many of his works were 'double and treble-figured, giving a new pattern in a shift of light',[35] and of *Rewards and Fairies* he famously wrote: 'I worked the material in three or four overlaid tints and textures, which might or might not reveal themselves according to the shifting light of youth, sex and experience.'[36] This accurately describes the undercurrent I have been suggesting. Once Mr Sharma's reading had pointed to this undercurrent, the more I thought about it, the more likely it began to seem. The past history of the bungalow and garden at Belvedere seems to support the notion. The parallels are there in the text.

Notes

1. Rudyard Kipling, *The Jungle Book* (London: Macmillan, 1895), p. 163.
2. *Ibid.*, p. vi.
3. Kipling, 'Here's a mongoose' in 'Nursery Idyls' (*sic*), first published in *Echoes* 1884, reprinted in *Early Verse by Rudyard Kipling 1879–1889: Unpublished, Uncollected and Rarely Collected Poems*, ed. Andrew Rutherford (Oxford: Clarendon Press, 1986), p. 239. The ellipsis at the end of line 6 is Kipling's.
4. Kipling, 1937, foreword to Sussex edition of the *Jungle Books*, reprinted in W.W. Robson (ed.), *The Jungle Books* (Oxford: Clarendon Press, 1992), p. 358.
5. John Lockwood Kipling, *Beast and Man in India: A Popular Sketch of Animals in Their Relation to People* (London: Macmillan, 1891), p. 314.
6. *Ibid.*, pp. 313–14.
7. Kipling, *Jungle Book*, p. 174.
8. Roger Lancelyn Green, *Kipling and the Children* (London: Elek Books, 1965), p. 126.
9. Kipling, *Something of Myself and Other Autobiographical Writings*, ed. Thomas Pinney (Cambridge: Cambridge University Press, 1990), p. 7.
10. Lancelyn Green, *Kipling and the Children*, p. 116.
11. Emily Ann Hart, quoted in *ibid.*, p. 126.
12. H.W. Thomas, 'Language and literature', in G.T. Garrett (ed.), *The Legacy of India* (Oxford: Clarendon Press, 1937), p. 201.
13. H.G. Rawlinson, 'India in European literature and thought', in Garrett (ed.), *Legacy of India*, p. 25.
14. Franklin Edgerton, *The Panchatantra: Translated from the Sanskrit* (London: Allen and Unwin, 1965), pp. 16–19, 147–50.
15. Lancelyn Green, *Kipling and the Children*, p. 126. He gives no source for this identification.
16. Harold Orel (ed.), *Rudyard Kipling: Interviews and Recollections*, vol. 1 (London: Macmillan, 1983), p. 94.
17. *Ibid.* 'The Return of Imray' was collected in *Life's Handicap* (London: Macmillan, 1891).
18. Kipling, *Jungle Book*, p. 165.
19. Christopher Hibbert, *The Great Mutiny: India 1857* (London: Penguin Books, 1980), pp. 201–2.
20. Kipling *The Jungle Books; Kim:* audio recording on CD by Madhav Sharma, Naxos Audio Books, 1995.

21 Kipling, *Jungle Book*, pp. 181–2.
22 R.E. Harbord (ed.), *The Readers' Guide to Rudyard Kipling's Work* (Canterbury: privately printed, 1965–66), vol. 4, pp. 1972–8.
23 Kipling, 'The Little House at Arrah', in Harbord, *Readers' Guide*, vol. 4, p. 1972.
24 *A Handbook to India, Burma and Ceylon* (London: John Murray, 1894; no author given).
25 Kipling, letter to Underwood Johnson, 14 December 1895, in Sandra Kemp and Lisa Lewis (eds), *Rudyard Kipling: Writings on Writing* (Cambridge: Cambridge University Press, 1996), p. 114; also *The Letters of Rudyard Kipling, Volume 2, 1890–99*, ed. Thomas Pinney (Basingstoke: Macmillan, 1990), p. 219.
26 Kipling, 'On the City Wall', *Soldiers Three and Other Stories* (London: Macmillan, 1895), p. 352.
27 Kipling, *Kim* (London: Macmillan, 1901), pp. 74–5.
28 Edward Said, *Culture and Imperialism* (London: Chatto & Windus 1992), p. 178.
29 Post-colonial Indian (and American) critics who have read Kipling's Indian fictions in term of their author's colonial anxiety include K. Bhaskara Rao, *Rudyard Kipling's India* (Norman: University of Oklahoma Press, 1967); Salman Rushdie, *Imaginary Homelands: Essays and Criticism 1981–1991* (London: Granta, 1991); Sara Suleri, *The Rhetoric of British India* (Chicago: University of Chicago Press, 1992); and Zohreh Sullivan, *Narratives of Empire: The Fictions of Rudyard Kipling* (Cambridge: Cambridge University Press, 1994). See also the account of *Kim* in Said, *Culture and Imperialism*.
30 Kipling, *Second Jungle Book* (London: Macmillan, 1895), pp. 132–3.
31 Timeri N. Murari, *The Imperial Agent: The Sequel to Rudyard Kipling's 'Kim'* (London: New English Library, 1987), and *The Last Victory* (London: New English Library, 1990).
32 Arundhati Roy, *The God of Small Things* (London: Flamingo 1997).
33 Arundhati Roy in *The Observer Review*, 25 June 1998, interviewed by Kate Kellaway, p. 4.
34 Kipling, *Something of Myself*, p. 68.
35 Kipling, foreword to *Works in Prose and Verse of Rudyard Kipling: Outward Bound Edition* (New York: Scribner, 1897), vol. 7 (*Jungle Books*), p. iii.
36 Kipling, *Something of Myself*, p. 111.

10

The young Kipling's search for God

CHARLES ALLEN

The most direct signposting of Kipling's credo is found in his declaration of faith made at the age of twenty-four in a letter to Miss Caroline Taylor, written not long after his return from India: 'Chiefly I believe in a personal God to whom we are personally responsible for wrong doing... I disbelieve directly in eternal punishment... I disbelieve in eternal reward ... Summarized it comes to *I believe in God the Father Almighty maker of Heaven and Earth and in one filled with His spirit who did voluntarily die in the belief that the human race would be spiritually bettered thereby.*'[1] It may be that this declaration was written either to bring Kipling's uneasy engagement to Miss Caroline Taylor to an end or to rattle Miss Taylor's Methodist principal father, or both, yet the beliefs expressed are what we would expect of one whose parents had rejected the Methodism of their fathers; who as a boy had experienced the 'full vigour' of Mrs Holloway's evangelical Christianity in the 'House of Desolation' at Southsea; and who during his three and a half years in Lahore only went to church once and that was to ogle the pretty daughter of the military chaplain at Mian Mir barracks. *Plain Tales from the Hills* opens with the anti-Christian story 'Lispeth', whose epigraph rejects 'your cold Christ and tangled Trinities'.[2]

Kipling in his twenties was a man who had turned his back on Christianity, but who had no time for atheism – rather like his own Aurelian McGoggin who believes himself too clever to need the crutch of religious belief and is chastened by a mental breakdown.[3] It is no surprise then to find Kipling at forty-two describing himself in a letter to a friend as 'a God-fearing Christian atheist'.[4] He lives in awe of the 'God of our fathers, known of old – / Lord of our far-flung battle line / Beneath whose awful hand we hold / Dominion over palm and pine'.[5] A decade later, having recently lost his son John in the Great War, Kipling confided to his close friend Rider Haggard that he found himself unable to hold 'the mystic sense of communion' with God, believing that God 'doesn't mean that we should get too near to Him – that a glimpse is all that we are allowed . . . because otherwise we should become unfitted for our work in the world'.[6] This idea of an omnipotent deity too terrifying to approach directly forms the basis of 'The Prayer of Miriam Cohen', the last verse of which reads:

> A veil 'twixt us and Thee, Good Lord,
> A veil 'twixt us and Thee –
> Lest we should hear too clear, too clear,
> And unto madness see![7]

Finding no comfort in this remote Lord God of Hosts, Kipling drew spiritual strength from the Law which holds chaos at bay – an abstract, amorphous Law never defined, but containing elements of the Judaeo-Christian tradition, Masonic ideals of brotherhood[8] and craftsmanship,[9] the Wesleyan ideal of a life of service through action and even the Imperial ideal of the British Empire as a positive force for good. Kipling's Law begins to take shape in the early 1890s in the poem *A Song of the English* and the writing of the *Jungle Book* tales, only to be subverted in 1900 in *Kim* and 'the Most Excellent Law', which I discuss below.

Kipling in India

So much for what might be called Kipling's protestations of faith. But there is a less conscious aspect to Kipling's search for God, running in parallel, which first becomes evident some two years after his arrival in Lahore and while he was still a teenager. The notion, propagated by the man himself in his memoir *Something of Myself*, that Kipling was happy to return to the land of his birth is no longer tenable. He was emotionally blackmailed into the post of 'stunt' at the *Civil and Military Gazette*, Lahore, and when he got there he was unhappy, rebellious and deeply resentful of the constraints of the much-vaunted 'Family Square'. (It is no accident that his first two bursts of kicking over the traces to self-publish work that was deliberately shocking both took place while his parents were away in the Hills and unable to exercise their usual censorship.[10]) The paradise years of his Bombay childhood might never have happened: he conformed absolutely to Anglo-Indian type while also being fearful of the unknown, disease- and ghost-ridden India beyond the ordered boundaries of the Station:

> Unkempt, unclean, athwart the mist
> The seething city looms.
> In place of Putney's golden gorse
> The sickly *babul* [thorny mimosa] blooms.

And:

> A stone's throw out on either hand
> From that well ordered road we tread,
> And all the world is wild and strange:
> *Chural* [ghosts] and ghoul and *Djinn* and sprite
> Shall bear us company tonight,
> For we have reached the Oldest Land
> Wherein the Powers of Darkness range.[11]

This is the 'dark' India of which the eighteen-year-old Kipling spoke in a letter to his cousin Margaret, the 'Wop of Albion', when he wrote that 'if you knew in what inconceivable filth of mind the people of India were brought up from their cradle; if you realised the views . . . they hold about women and their absolute incapacity for speaking the truth as we understand it – the immeasurable gulf that lies between the two races in all things . . . Immediately outside of our own English life, is the dark and crooked and fantastic, and wicked, and awe-inspiring life of the "native".' Yet from that same letter and from his first published stories we know that Kipling, for a combination of reasons that included isolation, sexual urges, insomnia, 'infernal opium' and Dr Collis-Browne's Chlorodyne, had now overcome his inhibitions to reach out for that Indian India – in his own words, to 'penetrate into it'.[12]

One consequence of that penetration was Kipling's discovery of Islam. This first found public expression in the verses of 'The Vision of Hamid Ali', written in the spring of 1885 just after he had completed that dark vision of an India without the Law – implicitly a Hindu, *babu* India – contained in 'The Strange Ride of Morrowbie Jukes'.[13] In 'The Vision of Hamid Ali' three Muslims are pot-smoking the night away in the house of Azizun, Pearl of Courtesans, when one of them breaks out of his stupor to describe a terrifying vision in which he foresees the destruction of Islam – and all the other great religions. It is a crude poem, understandably repudiated by its author, but nonetheless represents a first stab at understanding the dominant religion of Lahore. During this same spring of 1885 Kipling was given his first serious journalistic assignment – reporting on the visit to India of the Amir of Afghanistan in March and April 1885 – which began with a series of traumas, including an encounter with hostile tribesmen in the bazaar in Peshawar, which he afterwards likened to scenes from Dante's *Inferno*: 'Faces of dogs, swine, weasels, and goats, all the more hideous for being set on human bodies, and lighted with human intelligence . . . all giving the onlooker the impression of wild beasts held back from murder and violence.'[14] His dislike of Afghans was further reinforced when a boy threw a stone at him – an act expanded by degrees into the sniper's pot shot described in *Something of Myself*[15] – and this hostility persisted in his reports – until he met two Afghans whose strong characters he admired: one of course is Mahbub Ali, the horse-dealer immortalised in *Kim*; but the first was an unnamed *qazi* or Muslim judge encountered on a train journey, probably just after the Amir's departure. Kipling wrote up an account of their meeting for his paper under the title of 'East and West', prefiguring the poem that it would lead to.[16]

Kipling's reward for his exertions was a month's early leave followed by three and a half months as the *Civil and Military Gazette*'s Simla correspondent, but as soon as he was back in Lahore and away from his parents he resumed his night walks, culminating in that 'weary weary night' in early September 1885 which he wrote up as 'The City of Dreadful Night' in which the city of the dead is briefly brought to life again by the *muezzin*'s call to prayer from the *minar* of the mosque of Wazir Khan:

> The cloud drifts by and shows him outlined in black against the sky, hands laid upon his ears, and broad chest heaving with the play of his lungs – 'Allah ho Akbar'; then a pause while another *Muezzin* somewhere in the direction of the Golden Temple takes up the call – 'Allah ho Akbar.' Again and again; four times in all; and from the bedsteads a dozen men have risen up already. – 'I bear witness that there is no God but God.' What a splendid cry it is, the proclamation of a creed that brings men out of their beds by scores at midnight! Once again he thunders through the same phrase, shaking with the vehemence of his own voice; and then, far and near, the night air rings with 'Mohamed is the Prophet of God.' It is as though he were flinging his defiance to the far-off horizon, where the summer lightning plays and leaps like a bared sword.[17]

From then on Kipling wrote with growing sensitivity about Islam and Muslims, as can be seen in his tribute to his father conveyed in 'The Letter of Halim the Potter'[18] and in 'The Story of Muhammad Din'.[19] He took to referring to God as 'Allah' – a habit which stayed with him right to the end of his life: the Outward Bound Edition (1899) of his works begins with the well-known Koranic invocation 'In the name of God the Compassionate, the Merciful',[20] and he opens *Something of Myself* (1937) by 'ascribing all good fortune to Allah the dispenser of Events'.[21] In the latter we also find Kipling comparing Islam favourably with Judaism. It was not, of course, a question of being a Muslim but of admiring the sure purpose, directness and manliness of Islam, which Kipling saw as having had a positive influence on India. He was not alone in this: similar admiration was expressed by other early twentieth-century English writers, such as E.M. Forster writing how 'when . . . I stood on the minaret of the Taj in Agra, and heard the evening call to prayer from the adjacent mosque, I knew at all events *where* I stood and *what* I heard; it was a land that had not only atmosphere but definite lines and horizons'; Conrad in *Lord Jim* sympathetically describing the Muslim passengers bound for Mecca, the 'unconscious pilgrims of an exacting belief' unjustly despised by the contemptible German skipper as 'dese cattle'; or T.E. Lawrence reflecting more ambivalently on 'the faith of the desert' which 'knows only truth and untruth, belief and unbelief, without any hesitating retinue of finer shades'.[22] Kipling's admiration is most vividly expressed in a scrap of poetry, frequently overlooked, which precedes (for no obvious reason other than the title) the short story 'The Captive' in *Traffics and Discoveries*. Although *Traffics and Discoveries* was published in 1904 I have no doubt that the scrap of poetry was written back in the 1880s in India. The poem's title is 'From the Masjid Al-Aqsa of Sayyid Ahmed (Wahabi)' – Sayyid Ahmad being the name of the fundamentalist preacher and revolutionary who in the 1820s introduced Saudi Arabian Wahhabism to India and tried to raise the Sunni faithful in Hindustan in jihad against the *kaffir*.[23] Following Sayyid Ahmad's death in 1831 his followers built up the Wahhabi movement and took on the British directly in numerous uprisings on the North-West Frontier that continued right up to 1898. In the 1860s and 1870s several Wahhabi conspiracies were uncovered, leading to some high-profile trials. The Viceroy Lord Mayo and the Chief Justice were assassinated by suspected Wahhabis, and by the time Kipling arrived in India 'Wahhabi' had become a loaded word akin to 'Al-Qaeda' today.

Why then would Kipling write a poem about the reviled Wahhabis? The answer seems to be that in June 1888 there commenced the third of four Wahhabi-inspired uprisings in the Black Mountains of Hazara, leading to a 'sharp engagement' with a British punitive force in October at which numbers of Wahhabi 'fanatics' were killed. Prisoners were taken and some of these evidently conveyed to Lahore Central Jail, where a group of them were sketched by John Lockwood Kipling. In February 1889 Kipling went to Lahore to say goodbye to his parents and, although I can find no direct evidence for this in his surviving letters, my surmise is that he saw some of these Wahhabi convicts being marched in chains from Lahore railway station to the Jail, their route taking them through the Civil Lines. Another possibility is that prisoners were brought out from the jail in chain-gangs and put to work – along the Mall, let's say – and that Kipling used his clout as a sahib and newspaper man to talk to them before rushing back to Bikaner House to write his eighteen lines, of which I quote the last fourteen:

> Ere the sad dust of the marshalled feet of the chain-gang swallowed him,
> Observing him nobly at ease, I alighted and followed him.
> Thus we had speech by the way, but not touching his sorrow –
> Rather his red Yesterday and his regal To-morrow,
> Wherein he statelily moved to the clink of his chains unregarded,
> Nowise abashed but content to drink of the potion awarded.
> Saluting aloofly his Fate, he made swift with his story;
> And the words of his mouth were as slaves spreading carpets of glory
> Embroidered with names of the Djinns – a miraculous weaving –
> But the cool and perspicuous eye overbore unbelieving.
> So I submitted myself to the limits of rapture –
> Bound by this man we had bound, amid captives his capture –
> Till he returned me to earth and the vision departed;
> But on him be the Peace and the Blessing: for he was great-hearted![24]

Such warm admiration would have appeared profoundly shocking to Kipling's Anglo-Indian readership, to say nothing of his old patron and proprietor George Allen, who had actually been standing next to Lord Mayo when he was assassinated. The poem only appeared in print after Allen's death in 1900.

Kipling's respect for Islam never deserted him: when he visited Egypt in 1913 he thrilled to the sights, sounds and smells of Cairo, which made him 'voluptuously homesick'. Entering a deserted mosque he found himself comparing it unfavourably with a Christian church: 'Islam has but one pulpit and one stark affirmation – living or dying, one only – and where men have repeated that in red-hot belief through centuries, the air still shakes to it.' He went on to write enthusiastically of the great mosque of Al Azhar and its ancient university and, in a passage that has a particular resonance today, writes of the English understanding Islam 'as no one else does'. He goes on: 'Some men are Mohammedan by birth, some by training, and some by fate, but I have never met an Englishman yet who hated Islam and its people as I have met Englishmen who have hated other faiths. *Musalmani awadani*, as the saying goes – where there are Mohammedans, there is a comprehensible civilisation.'[25]

Kipling was a good hater and the other side of the coin is that in India the greater his sense of affinity with Islam and Muslims, the greater his contempt for Hinduism and Hindus, whom he associated with some of the worst shortcomings of Indian society such as caste, the plight of widows, enforced early marriage and infanticide. We find him at his worst after his move to Allahabad and the 'cow belt' in the autumn of 1887. Here he wrote some of his best short stories and his worst polemics, reaching a nadir with 'The Bride's Progress' which first appeared in the *Pioneer Mail* in February 1888 after a month of travelling that took Kipling south to Benares – the 'city of monstrous creeds' – and on to a Calcutta filled with 'the essence of corruption'.[26] Kipling had already expressed his contempt for Hindu culture in a review of an English translation of the *Mahabharata* in which he parroted Macaulay's notorious *Minute on Education*[27] and in his *Letters of Marque* from Rajputana had expressed a deep discomfort with the overt sexuality of Shaivite worship, with its 'loathsome emblem of creation'.[28] Now he gave free rein to his religious prejudices, which cannot be separated from his hostility towards the politicised, English-educated Bengalis and *babu*-types, whom he considered – unlike the Muslims their conquerors – unfit to exercise political power. 'The Bride's Progress' ends with the British honeymoon couple fleeing Benares, where 'the walls dripped filth, the pavements sweated filth, and the contagion of uncleanliness walked among the worshippers ... at every turn lewd gods grinned and mouthed ... disease stood blind and naked'. As they leave the city they hear the reassuring call of the *muezzin*, reasserting the supremacy of monotheism:

> In the silence a voice thundered over their heads: 'I bear witness that there is no God but God.' It was the mullah proclaiming the Oneness of God in the city of the million manifestations. The call rang across the sleeping city and far over the river, and be sure that the mullah abated nothing of the defiance of his cry for that he looked down upon a sea of temples and smelt the incense of a hundred Hindu shrines.[29]

Although Kipling continued to view Hindu Gods as 'malignant',[30] he went on to write more wisely about Hinduism, most notably in 'The Bridge Builders' and 'The Miracle of Purun Bhagat',[31] while remaining essentially hostile. However, both these stories come from a later phase in Kipling's life, long after he had left India and, crucially, after he had come to know the joys of parenthood. With his wife's pregnancy and the birth of his 'best beloved' Josephine in Vermont in 1892, Kipling rediscovered the child in himself and underwent a softening of the heart that allowed him to write his most accessible and least polemical work, contained in the two *Jungle Book* collections. During this same period he also rediscovered his father, who himself seems to have undergone a distinct change of heart in the four lonely years in Lahore between the break-up of the Family Square in 1889 and his final retirement in 1893. When Lockwood Kipling came alone to stay with his son and his new family in Vermont in June 1893 he arrived with a portmanteau stuffed with Indian drawings, books and ideas gathered over twenty years of working side by side with Indian craftsmen.[32] He had become a more tolerant, more humane person in the process and it is no exaggeration to describe John Lockwood Kipling's role in the years that followed as that of guru to his son. We can see this in the surviving letters, in the son's fulsome tributes to his father in *Something of Myself* and, of course, in *Kim*, the finest fruit of their collaboration. Some mention here should be made of a delightful drawing in pencil now among the papers of John Lockwood Kipling at Sussex. Undated but captioned 'The Infant Buddha, LAHORE MUSEUM No 460', it shows a boy Buddha seated cross-legged, and is drawn as if to suggest that it is a bas-relief from the museum's magnificent collection of Buddhist Gandharan sculptures. Yet the boy Buddha is quite clearly not a carving in stone but a living, breathing child – the very prototype of young Kimball O'Hara. Here is a mystery waiting to be resolved.

Father and son mulled over *Kim* in Vermont in 1893 but it failed to grow and was put to one side in favour of Mowgli. Two years later Kipling tried and failed to get *Kim* going again. Then in the autumn of 1898 one disaster followed hard on the heels of another: the death of Edward Burne-Jones (his 'Uncle Ned') and the complete mental breakdown of his sister Trix. Father and son found solace in working together on *Kim*, which served, in Kipling's words, as his 'Eastern sunlight'.[33] The book was going well when in January 1899 the Kiplings made the fateful decision to visit America, resulting in Josephine's death and her father's near-fatal pneumonia. From then on Kipling lived, as his niece put it, behind a 'barrier'.[34] It was under this dark shadow but also against the background of the start of the Boer War, with Kipling gripped by war-fever, that a first draft of *Kim* was written. Four months later he returned from South Africa deeply frustrated by his government's failure to adequately defend its hard-won empire and determined to put out the message that Britain's imperial mission was under threat. That is what makes

Kipling's achievement so paradoxical, for when he sat down in April 1900 to revise and complete *Kim* what he wrote was a novel that begins as a political allegory about the defence of British India – 'the Great Game that never ceases day and night' – constructed around a boy's search for identity, but then transforms itself into a spiritual journey. *Kim* is a profoundly religious book, set in a sacred landscape 'full of holy men stammering gospels in strange tongues, shaken and consumed by their own zeal; dreamers, babblers and visionaries'.[35] It begins with Kim assertive and aggressive astride that supreme symbol of patriarchal potency the great gun *zam-zammah*, and ends with him resting under a banyan tree all passion spent, awaiting a Buddhist Lama's call to follow him. Kim does not – and could not – become the *chela* of a Hindu guru. In Kipling's eyes Hinduism existed in a moral vacuum – he had seen it in action and had found it wanting – whereas Buddhism in India was non-existent, despite its Indian origins, and could be admired in the abstract for its moral values. The Buddhism represented in *Kim* is a sanitised, idealised, Protestantised Buddhism as propagated by Edwin Arnold in his epic poem *The Light of Asia* (1879).

The Light of Asia was published the year before Ruddy began at United Services College. It was a huge best-seller and we know from George Beresford that Kipling flirted with this Arnoldian Buddhism at school for a term: 'Gigger was the apostle of Buddha or Arnold for a span at Westward Ho! and used to declaim very finely certain portions about "om pani padmi Hum" or words to that effect'.[36] Although Kipling preached reincarnation to his room-mates this seems to have been no more than a passing flirtation – to be renewed only when he was afflicted by his tribulations in the autumn of 1898. Those tribulations coincided with a revival of Western interest in Buddhism, which had suffered a setback in the wake of the Theosophy scandals involving Madame Blavatsky and her so-called 'esoteric Buddhism' – scandals in which John Lockwood Kipling and the *Pioneer* newspaper for which he wrote had been deeply involved.[37] Spurring on this revival in the late 1890s were a series of archaeological discoveries in India: digs by Lockwood Kipling's colleague Aurel Stein in Swat in the wake of the Malakand Campaign of 1898 which greatly enhanced the already unrivalled collection of Graeco-Buddhist statuary at Lahore Museum; and more digs on the Nepal border which led to the discovery of Buddha's birthplace at Lumbini and the ruins of Kapilavastu, the city where the Buddha had been raised as Prince Siddhartha, and from which he had fired the arrow which gave rise to the Spring of the Arrow – the object of the Lama's quest in *Kim*.

Over this same period the Arnoldian perception of Buddhism as a moral philosophy free of gods and rituals received a boost with the translation of Buddhist texts by such Pali scholars as Max Müller,[38] Henry Clarke Warren and T.W. Rhys Davids, all of whom drew on the canon of texts in Pali preserved by the Theravadin Buddhists of Ceylon and Burma. Davids' best-selling *Buddhism* (first published in 1877) and *Dialogues of the Buddha* (1899), along with Warren's *Buddhism in Translations* (1896)[39] are the most obvious sources for Kipling's coverage in *Kim* of such fundamental Buddhist concepts as Deliverance from the Wheel of Life, the Eightfold Path, the Chain of Causation, even the practice of meditation. However, Davids is at pains to explain that the core Buddhist term *Dhammacakka* (in Sanskrit *Dharmacakra*) should not be translated as 'the wheel of Law' – as it is by Arnold and others – and that a more accurate reading would be 'the royal chariot-wheel of a universal empire of truth and righteousness'.[40] Kipling, of course, stuck with Arnold and with Arnold's highlighting in his poem of positive action in obedience of the Law. Indeed, it is impossible to read the closing lines of Kipling's poem 'The Law of the Jungle' – 'Now these are the Laws of the Jungle, and many and mighty are they; / But the head and the hoof of the Law and the haunch and the hump is – Obey!'[41] – without being reminded of similar (if much gentler) invocations in *The Light of Asia*, such as:

> Such is the Law which moves to righteousness,
> Which none at last can turn aside or stay;
> The heart of it is Love, the end of it
> Is Peace and Consummation sweet. Obey![42]

However, in 1897 this Western interpretation of Buddhism received a nasty jolt with the publication of Dr L.A. Waddell's *The Buddhism of Tibet or Lamaism*, which presented Tibet's highly ritualised Vajrayana Buddhism as a 'a priestly mixture of Sivate mysticism, magic and Indo-Tibetan idolatry, overlaid by a thin varnish of Mahayana Buddhism . . . a cloak to the worst forms of devil-worship, by which the poor Tibetan was placed in constant fear of his life from the attacks of malignant devils both in this life and in the world to come'.[43] Waddell's hostile interpretation was supported by the studies of a rival student of Tibet Buddhism, the translator and part-time agent of the Survey of India Sarat Chandra Das, who wrote three influential books on Tibet and Tibetan Buddhism between 1881 and 1899.[44] The headstrong Sarat Chandra Das was subsequently 'dropped' by his British handlers and some trace of this dispute may be detected in the character and actions of the *babu*-spy Hurree Chunder Mookherjee in *Kim*, who turns out to be less Anglicised than he first appeared to be. Perhaps more significantly, Kipling chose to reject Waddell and Das by sanitising his Tibetan lama. He strikes one of the few false notes in *Kim* when he has him protest about some of the practices in Buddhism in Tibet 'being overlaid, as thou knowest, with devildom, charms and idolatry'. He also describes the Lama somewhat misleadingly as a 'Red Hat',[45] a term first used by the Mongol rulers of China to differentiate between the reformed Gelug 'Yellow Hats' order, whom they supported, and the unreformed Sakya, Kagya and Kadam schools, who represented the old Tibetan order.

A striking feature of *Kim* is the steady progression through the novel away from all the characteristics we associate with Kipling as devotee of the Law as imperial order keeping chaos at bay. In the first half of the book he offers us all the conventional set certainties represented by such patriarchal authority figures as Mahbub Ali and Colonel Creighton, the belief system represented by the Revd Bennett and Fr Victor, the priests of the Christian religion, and institutions such as St Xavier's public school, the Indian railways and the British Raj itself – which he then proceeds to subvert in the second half, beginning with Kim's exposure to Lurgan Sahib, who is neither sahib nor Indian nor notably masculine, but nevertheless has the power to reveal to Kim the illusory nature of all things. Kim then abandons the set framework of the British railway system for the disorder of the Grand Trunk Road, 'the backbone of all Hind', before turning his back on the male-dominated world of the plains by entering the matriarchal, natural world of the mountains, which Kipling himself signals by quoting the Indian proverb 'Who goes to the hills goes to his mother'.[46] Now it is the feminine that dominates, represented by the unassertive, compliant Tibetan lama and the two *ayah* or surrogate mother figures of the *Sahiba* and the Woman from Shamleh who – as Kipling goes out of his way to tell us – has transformed herself from the victim of male oppression she was in 'Lispeth'[47] to superwoman. Even the effeminate, giggly Bengali *babu*, Hurrree Chunder, sitting at the feet of the lama, sloughs off his Westernisation to reveal his true self: 'The Hurree Babu of his knowledge – oily, effusive, and nervous – was gone . . . There remained – polished, polite, attentive – a sober, learned son of experience and adversity, gathering wisdom from the lama's lips.'[48]

What is most curious about what might be entitled the historiography of *Kim* literary scholarship is the way in which the novel's ending has consistently been misinterpreted. 'Though it is not expressly stated,' writes Charles

Carrington, 'the reader is left with the assurance that Kim, like Mowgli, and like the Brushwood Boy, will find reality in action, not in contemplation.'[49] After a spell as the Lama's *chela* Kim will return to the real world to serve the British cause as a player of the Great Game. This is the usual reading and one that has led a number of critics, ranging from Edmund Wilson to Edward Said,[50] to take offence at the novel as an imperialist tract. The key passage in this reading is where Kim wakes from the drugged sleep which has followed his physical and mental breakdown. He feels that his soul is 'out of gear with its surroundings' and asks himself 'What is Kim?' – at which point 'easy, stupid tears' run down his nose and with an 'almost audible click' he feels 'the wheels of his being lock up anew with the world without. Things that rode meaningless on the eyeball an instant before slid into proper proportion. Roads were meant to be walked upon, houses to be lived in, cattle to be walked, fields to be tilled, and men and women to be talked to. They were real and true.'[51]

This moment of Arnoldian enlightenment is usually read as Kim moving back into the real world of action – but a genuine Buddhist would interpret it as Kipling's attempt to show Kim's acquisition of peace of mind, having banished all the conflicting thoughts that had provoked his breakdown, very much as described in the *Dhammapada*, as, for example:

> It is good to tame the mind,
> Difficult to hold in, and flighty;
> Rushing where'er it listeth;
> A tamed mind is the bringer of bliss.[52]

Following Kim's enlightenment the Sahiba relinquishes her care, declaring that 'Mother Earth must do the rest'. Kim then goes out to lie upon the earth under a young banyan tree, both of which nourish him as he sleeps: 'Mother Earth ... breathed through him to restore the poise he had lost lying so long on a cot cut off from her good currents. His head lay powerless upon her breast, and his opened hands surrendered to her strength.'[53] Again, to a Buddhist the imagery and sentiments are unmistakable, and are those associated with the Awakening of the Buddha Sakyamuni under the pipal tree at Bodhgaya and with the Buddha's action of the placing his right hand in contact with the earth in the gesture known as *bhumisparsa mudra* – 'calling the earth to witness'.

To a Buddhist there is no ambiguity over what path Kim then follows. While he sleeps Mahbub Ali reappears to claim the boy for the Great Game and disputes with the Lama over who shall have him. 'It is his right to be cleansed from sin – with me', argues the Lama. Mahbub Ali accepts that Kim needs cleansing but explains that afterwards he is 'somewhat urgently needed as a scribe by the State'. To the Lama what happens to Kim afterwards is irrelevant: 'Let him be a teacher, let him be a scribe – what matter? He will have attained Freedom at the end. The rest is illusion.' This irritates Mahbub Ali, who grumbles to himself in Pushtu but then concedes that boy can stay with the Lama for the time being: 'Now I understand that the boy, sure of Paradise, can yet enter Government service, my mind is easier.' He concedes to the Lama that Kim is his disciple, accepting that 'our Friend of all the World put his hand in thine at the first. Use him well, and suffer him to return to the world as a teacher, when thou hast – bathed his legs, if that be the proper medicine for the colt.'

Mahbub Ali, then, is convinced that Kim will return to his world in due course – and most readers seem happy to share his interpretation. But the exchange is not yet over. The Lama does not defer to Mahbub Ali. Instead he responds by suggesting that the Afghan might even convert to Buddhism himself: 'Why not follow the Way thyself, and so accompany the boy?' At first angered and then amused by the Tibetan's insolence Mahbub Ali backs off with the closing remark 'Thy strength is stronger still. Keep it – I think thou wilt. If the boy be not a good servant, pull his ears off'.[54] He then hitches up his belt and swaggers off into the gloaming.

Kim himself has played no part in this dispute over him, but a Buddhist would argue that it represents a struggle between the Middle Way and what Kipling himself called the 'Narrow Way' of hellfire monotheism guided 'by Tophet flares to Judgment Day'[55] – a struggle that ends with victory for the Lama. Like a Bodhisattva or Buddhist saint who returns from the Threshold of Nibbana in order to free others from sin, the Lama has come back to free Kim. 'Certain is our deliverance!' he tells Kim. 'Come!'[56]

Kipling's journey in *Kim* is as remarkable as that undertaken by his hero, and it is no wonder that he also wrote at this time those striking verses about having two sides to his head:

> Something I owe to the soil that grew –
> More to the life that fed –
> But most to Allah Who gave me two
> Separate sides to my head.[57]

After this second flirtation with the Middle Way[58] Kipling reverted to the Narrow Way and his God-fearing Christian atheism. But that he did not entirely abandon Buddhist thinking and, in particular, its doctrine of the causes of suffering, can be seen from a speech he made seven years after the completion of *Kim* when he addressed the students of McGill University, Montreal:

> Some of you here know – and I remember – that youth can be a season of great depression, despondencies, doubts, waverings, the worse because they seem to be peculiar to ourselves and incommunicable to our fellows. There is a certain darkness into which the soul of the young man sometimes descends – a horror of desolation, abandonment, and realised worthlessness, which is one of the most real of the hells in which we are compelled to walk . . . This is due to a variety of causes, the chief of which is the egotism of the human animal itself.

The solution, Kipling went on to suggest, was to lose oneself 'in some issue not personal to yourself . . . But if the dark hour does not vanish, as sometimes it doesn't; if the black cloud will not lift, as sometimes it will not; let me tell you again for your comfort that there are many liars in the world, but there are no liars like our own sensations. The despair and horror mean nothing, because there is for you nothing irremediable, nothing ineffaceable, nothing irrevocable in anything you may have said or thought or done . . . take anything and everything seriously except yourselves.'[59]

Notes

1. Rudyard Kipling to Caroline Taylor, 9 December 1889, University of Sussex, collected in *The Letters of Rudyard Kipling, Volume 1: 1872–89* (Basingstoke: Macmillan, 1990), pp. 378–9.
2. Kipling, 'Lispeth', first published in the *Civil and Military Gazette* 29 November 1886, collected in *Plain Tales from the Hills* (1888; London: Penguin Classics, 2011), p. 5.
3. Kipling, 'The Conversion of Aurelian McGoggin', first published in the *Civil and Military Gazette*, 28 April 1887, afterwards collected in *Plain Tales from the Hills*.
4. Kipling to Lady Edward Cecil, 2 December 1908, quoted in Andrew Lycett, *Rudyard Kipling* (London: Orion Books 1999), p. 520.
5. Kipling, 'Recessional' (1897), *Rudyard Kipling's Verse: The Definitive Edition* (London: Hodder and Stoughton, 1940; text reproduced as *Works of Rudyard Kipling*, Ware: Wordsworth, 1994), p. 328.
6. Kipling, quoted in Rider Haggard's diary of 23 May 1918, in Morton Cohen (ed.), *Rudyard Kipling to Rider Haggard: The Record of a Friendship* (London: Hutchinson, 1997), p. 103.
7. Kipling, 'The Prayer of Miriam Cohen', *Works*, p. 314. This poem was first published as the epigraph to 'The Disturber of Traffic', *Many Inventions* (London: Macmillan, 1893).

8 Marganita Laski states that Kipling 'once said that Freemasonry was the nearest thing to a religion that he knew' but without naming the occasion: M. Laski, *From Palm to Pine: Rudyard Kipling Abroad and at Home* (London: Sidgwick and Jackson, 1987), p. 8.
9 In the poem 'My New-cut Ashlar' (also known as 'L'Envoi') which closes *Life's Handicap* (London: Macmillan, 1891), Kipling deliberately addresses his deity in such Masonic craft terms as 'Great Overseer' and 'Master' and declares 'If there be good in that I wrote, / Thy hand compelled it, Master, Thine' (*Works*, p. 511).
10 Kipling, 'Nursery Rhymes for Little Anglo-Indians', *Echoes*, June 1884, reprinted in *Early Verse by Rudyard Kipling 1879–1889: Unpublished, Uncollected and Rarely Collected Poems*, ed. Andrew Rutherford (Oxford: Clarendon Press, 1986); 'The Gate of the Hundred Sorrows', *Civil and Military Gazette*, 29 September 1884.
11 Kipling, 'The Moon of Other Days', first published in the *Pioneer*, 16 December 1884, collected in *Departmental Ditties* (1886), reprinted in *Works*, p. 63; verse heading to 'In the House of Suddhoo', first published in the *Civil and Military Gazette*, 30 April 1886, collected in *Plain Tales from the Hills*, reprinted in *Works* pp. 64, 501.
12 Kipling to Margaret Burne-Jones, Lahore late November and early December 1885. Kipling Papers, Sussex; printed in *Letters, Volume 1*, p. 99.
13 Kipling, 'The Vision of Hamid Ali' (*Early Verse*, pp. 272–3), was published in the *Calcutta Review* in October 1885, but its acceptance is referred to in a letter to Edith Macdonald dated 30 July 1885. The evolution of 'The Strange Ride of Morrowbie Jukes', first published in *Quartette* (Lahore, *Civil and Military Gazette Annual Supplement*, 1885), collected in *Wee Willie Winkie* (Allahabad: Wheeler, 1888) is set out in Kipling's *Diary 1884–5*, Houghton Library, University of Harvard, reproduced in Kipling, *Something of Myself and Other Autobiographical Writing*, ed. Thomas Pinney (Cambridge: Cambridge University Press, 1990), pp. 199–205.
14 Kipling, 'The City of Evil Countenances', *Civil and Military Gazette*, 1 April 1885.
15 Kipling, *Something of Myself*, p. 28.
16 Kipling, 'East and West', *Civil and Military Gazette*, 14 November 1885; see also 'The Ballad of East and West', first published in *Macmillan's Magazine* in November 1889, *Works*, p. 234.
17 Kipling, 'The City of Dreadful Night', *Civil and Military Gazette*, 10 September 1885, reprinted in *Life's Handicap*, pp. 326–7.
18 Kipling, 'The Letter of Halim the Potter', *Early Verse* pp. 269–72. This poem was written in the form of a Browningesque verse letter to John Lockwood Kipling on his birthday, most probably in June 1885.
19 Kipling, 'The Story of Muhammad Din', *Civil and Military Gazette*, 8 September 1886, collected in *Plain Tales from the Hills*.
20 Kipling, *Works in Prose and Verse of Rudyard Kipling: Outward Bound Edition*, vol. 1 (New York: Scribner, 1897), p. 1.
21 Kipling, *Something of Myself*, p. 3.
22 E.M. Forster, letter to Aunt Laura, 6 November 1921, quoted in P.N. Furbank, *E.M. Forster: A Life*: Vol. 2, *Polycrates' Ring 1914–1970* (London: Secker and

Warburg, 1979), p. 99; Joseph Conrad, *Lord Jim* (1900; London: Penguin Classics, 2007), p. 17; T.E. Lawrence *Seven Pillars of Wisdom* (1935; Ware: Wordsworth Editions, 1997), pp. 20–1.
23 Charles Allen, *God's Terrorists: The Wahhabi Cult and the Roots of Modern Jihad* (London: Little, Brown, 2006), pp. 30 ff.
24 Kipling, *Traffics and Discoveries* (London: Macmillan, 1904), p. 2; *Works* p. 532.
25 Kipling, 'A Serpent of Old Nile', *Egypt of the Magicians*, *Nash's Magazine*, 1913, collected in *Letters of Travel* (London: Macmillan, 1920), p. 149.
26 Kipling, 'A real live city', the first of seven articles published in the *Pioneer* March–April 1888, collected as 'The City of Dreadful Night: Jan–Feb 1888', *From Sea to Sea and Other Sketches: Letters of Travel vol. II* (London: Macmillan, 1900), p. 204.
27 Kipling, 'The Epics of India', *Civil and Military Gazette*, 24 August 1886, collected in *Kipling's India: Uncollected Sketches 1884–88*, ed. Thomas Pinney (London: Macmillan, 1986), pp. 175–8.
28 Kipling, 'Letters of Marque' no. xi, *From Sea to Sea* (London: Macmillan, 1900), vol. 1, p. 100. 'Letters of Marque' were first published in the *Pioneer* between 14 December 1887 and 28 February 1888.
29 Kipling, 'The Bride's Progress' (1888), the twelfth of fifteen articles published in the *Pioneer*, 1887–88, collected as 'The Smith Administration', *From Sea to Sea*, vol. 2, pp. 412–14.
30 Kipling, *Kim* (London: Macmillan, 1901): 'Their Gods are many-armed and malignant', p. 71.
31 Kipling, 'The Bridge-Builders', *The Day's Work* (London: Macmillan, 1898); 'The Miracle of Purun Bhagat', *The Second Jungle Book* (London: Macmillan, 1895).
32 Particularly important for Lockwood Kipling was his association with the master-carver Bhai Ram Singh, who accompanied him to England on his royal contracts. See Charles Allen, *Kipling Sahib: India and the Making of Rudyard Kipling* (London: Abacus 2007), p. 327.
33 Kipling, *Something of Myself*, p. 83.
34 Angela Thirkell, *Three Houses* (Oxford: Oxford University Press, 1931), p. 86.
35 Kipling, *Kim*, pp. 250, 45–6.
36 George Beresford, *Schooldays with Kipling* (London: Gollancz, 1936), p. 247.
37 Kipling, *Something of Myself*, pp. 35–6; Charles Allen, *Kipling Sahib: India and the Making of Rudyard Kipling* (London: Little, Brown, 2007), pp. 143–4.
38 Translations of the *Dhammapada* and the *Sutta Nipata* were first published as *The Dhammada: A Collection of Verses, Being One of the Canonical Books of the Buddhists*, trans. F. Max Muller, and *The Sutta-Nipata* trans. V. Fausböll, vol. 10 of the series *Sacred Books of the East* (Oxford: Clarendon Press, 1881).
39 T.W. Rhys Davids, *Buddhism: Being a Sketch of the Life and Teachings of Gautama, the Buddha* (London: SPCK, 1877; 6 editions and 18,000 copies by 1899), and *Dialogues of the Buddha: Translated from the Pali* (London: Henry Frowde, 1899); Henry Clarke Warren, *Buddhism in Translations* (Boston, MA: Harvard University Press, 1896).

40 Davids, *Buddhism*, p. 38.
41 Kipling, 'The Law of the Jungle', *Works*, p. 560. This poem was written before June 1895 when the last *Second Jungle Book* story was completed, and thus falls into the period when Kipling was beginning to construct *Kim* with his father.
42 Edwin Arnold, *The Light of Asia or: The Great Renunciation Being the Life of Gautama Told in Verse* (London: Trubner, 1879), p. 180.
43 L.A. Waddell *The Buddhism of Tibet or Lamaism* (London: Allen & Co, 1895), p. 30.
44 Sarat Chandra Das, *Religion and History of Tibet* (Calcutta: Baptist Mission Press, 1881); *Indian Pandits in the Land of Snow* (Calcutta: Baptist Mission Press, 1893); *Journey to Lhasa and Central Tibet* (London and New York: John Murray, 1902).
45 Kipling, *Kim*, pp. 12, 247.
46 *Ibid.*, p. 328.
47 Kipling, 'Lispeth'.
48 Kipling, *Kim*, pp. 323–4.
49 Charles Carrington, *Rudyard Kipling: His Life and Work* (London: Macmillan, 1955), p. 362.
50 See Edmund Wilson, 'The Kipling that nobody read' (1941), reprinted in A. Rutherford, *Kipling's Mind and Art* (Edinburgh: Oliver & Boyd, 1986), p. 30; Edward Said, *Culture and Imperialism* (London: Chatto & Windus, 1992), pp. 164–72.
51 Kipling, *Kim*, p. 403.
52 One of a number of sayings from the *Dhammapada* quoted by T.W. Rhys Davids in *Buddhism*, p. 129.
53 Kipling, *Kim*, p. 404.
54 *Ibid.*, pp. 406–8.
55 Kipling, 'Buddha at Kamakura' (1892): *Works*, p. 92; see *Kim* p. 1. 'Tophet' means 'hell'.
56 Kipling, *Kim*, p. 413.
57 *Ibid.*, p. 186: epigraph to Chapter 8. His later revised and enlarged version of 'The Two-Sided Man' begins 'Much I owe to the Lands that grew': *Works*, p. 587.
58 When I read this paper at a meeting of the Buddhist Society in London, a member of the audience declared that I had left out Kipling's most important Buddhist work. 'Oh,' I said, 'you mean his poem *The Buddha at Kamakura*.' 'I mean "If–",' she replied. 'It's a series of Buddhist injunctions. Of course, you have to change the last line, so that it reads "You'll be a *Buddhist*, my son"!' 'If–' was first published in 1910 but appears to have been written much earlier, inspired by the misfortunes that befell Dr Jameson in the wake of the bungled Jameson Raid in 1896 against the Boer Republic of the Transvaal, for which he was tried and imprisoned.
59 Kipling 'Values in Life': address to McGill University 1907, *A Book of Words: Selections from Speeches and Addresses Delivered between 1906 and 1927* (London: Macmillan, 1928), pp. 19–20.

11

Vagabondage in Rajasthan: Kipling's North Indian travels

JAN MONTEFIORE

'Since November last I have been a vagabond on the face of the earth. But such a vagabondage!' (Kipling to Margaret Mackail, 1888)[1]

From late November to late December 1887, Rudyard Kipling travelled in the 'Native States' of North India, enjoying his longest Indian experience of footloose travel. For six of his 'Seven Years Hard' as cub reporter on the *Civil and Military Gazette* in Lahore, he lived with his parents and was kept close to his office by his work apart from the annual family holiday in the 'Hills' and a few short trips. But in November 1887, he was moved by his employers 900 miles south to their principal newspaper the *Pioneer* in Allahabad (Prayag), and shortly afterwards sent to travel through 'Rajputana' (Rajasthan). He zig-zagged from Agra eastwards by rail to Jaipur, then southwest by tonga-carriage to Udaipur, east by tonga and elephant to Chitor and on to Chitor Station, northwest by rail to Ajmir, west to Jodhpur by rail and horseback, east by rail to Ajmir again, southeast by tonga-carriage to Boondi (Bundi), and back to Ajmir and Jodhpur. His weekly 'Letters of Marque' in the *Pioneer* newspaper from 14 December 1887 to 28 February 1888 (the name is a naval joke, referring to a ship's official government licence to operate as a privateer) have been increasingly noticed by critics.[2] They include some of his liveliest early writing, and the experience proved an inspiration for his fictions of India: the short story 'Bubbling Well Road' and the much longer 'The Man Who Would Be King' (both published 1888), the adventure story *The Naulahka* (1892), co-authored with Wolcott Balestier, and later, as I argue here, for important scenes in the *Jungle Books* (1894, 1895) and *Kim* (1901).

Kipling's 'Letters of Marque' would deserve attention for their own sake as a record of India in the late 1880s as observed by a brilliant, prejudiced but highly sensitive observer. The writer was not quite twenty-two and off the leash of his family's authority (his self-description quoted above as a 'vagabond on the face of the earth' lightly aligns him with Cain the outlaw), and he evidently felt liberated by writing for an anonymous, far-off readership, quite unlike the 'picked men at their definite work'[3] he was used to meeting at Lahore's Punjab Club. The *brio* of the Letters noticeably increases as Kipling travels away from familiar territory, as when in Letter XV he describes travelling the bumpy road to Boondi in a tonga (light carriage):

> The road struck boldly into hills with all their teeth on edge, that is to say, their strata breaking across the road in little ripples. The effect of this was amazing. The tonga skipped merrily as a young fawn, from ridge to ridge. It shivered, it palpitated, it shook, it slid, it hopped, it waltzed, it ricocheted, it bounded like a kangaroo, it blundered like a sledge, it swayed like a top-heavy coach on a down-grade, it 'kicked' like a badly coupled railway-carriage, it squelched like a country-cart, it squeaked in its torment, and lastly it essayed to plough up the ground with its nose.[4]

This virtuoso verbal performance matches the balancing act needed to stay in a tonga behaving like an Australian kangaroo, a North American sledge, and an English coach, railway-carriage and country-cart, whose actions – 'it shook, it slid, it hopped, it waltzed, it ricocheted, it bounded like a kangaroo' – anticipate the Mariner in the *Just-So Stories* swallowed by the Whale: 'he banged and he clanged, and he hit and he bit, and he prowled and he howled . . . and he stepped and he lepped, and he danced hornpipes where he shouldn't.'[5] Much of the Letters' charm lies in their narrator's obvious pleasure in his own versatile recounting of the comic bouncing carriage, the tragic history of Chitor, the shuddering 'otherness' of the 'Gau-Mukh' shrine, or the casually elegant list of 'two growling, fluffy little panther-cubs, a black panther who is the Prince of Darkness and a gentleman, and a terrace-full of tigers, bears and Guzerat lions brought from the King of Oudh's sale'.[6]

The self-consciousness of this performance is emphasised by Kipling's use of the third person. Throughout the Letters, he calls himself 'the Englishman', displaying his habitual reticence by emphasising his own racial identity, even in places where 'with a great sinking of his heart, he began to realise that his caste was of no value'.[7] Although 'the Englishman' distances himself from the 'insolent Globe-trotter' content with a quick visit to famous places, he remains apart from what he sees:

> There were butterflies in the tobacco-[field] – six different kinds, and a little rat came out and drank at the ford. To him succeeded the Flight into Egypt. The white banks of the ford framed the picture perfectly – the Mother in blue, on a great white donkey, holding the Child in her arms, and Joseph walking alongside, his hand on the horse's withers. By all the laws of the East, Joseph should have been riding and the Mother walking. This was an exception decreed for the Englishman's special benefit.[8]

That ironic 'decreed' meaning its opposite (Kipling knows that his presence is just a lucky chance) is unconsciously apt; this scene is indeed 'framed' by the Englishman's appreciation. His gaze turns the Indian mother, father and child into a pre-Raphaelite painting of the Holy Family, the actual Indians being completely effaced both by the biblical roles assigned to them and by the knowing rhetoric which reminds readers that unchivalrous 'native' men don't let their women ride, even when one actually does so.

These prejudiced attitudes do not make 'the Englishman' into a crude colonial bully. During the night journey to Udaipur across seventy miles of scrub-land, he plays a distinctly unheroic role when after the breakdown of the mail-tonga in which he is travelling, he has to hitch a lift from a reluctant and heavily armed *Thakur* ('squire') and his retinue who, he fears, may take the mail and leave him behind:

> Seating himself upon the parcels-bag, the Englishman cried in what was intended to be a very terrible voice, but the silence soaked it up and left only a thin trickle of sound, that anyone who touched the bags would be hit with a stick, several times, over the head. The bags were the only link between him and the civilisation which he had so rashly foregone. And there was a pause.

Admitted to the tonga whose interior 'seemed as full as the railway carriage which held Alice in *Through the Looking-Glass*', he is disrespectfully addressed, prodded, bumped and squashed by 'burly Rajputs' for eight hours, with a revolver (which would in British-ruled territory have been an illegal possession for a 'native') 'printing every diamond in the chequer-work of its handle on his right hip'.[9] As David Sergeant has pointed out,[10] Kipling's performance in the 'Letters' is aimed at a conservative Anglo-Indian audience; and his rhetoric, not to mention his very English literary allusion here to Lewis Carroll, emphasises the knowledge and values which he shares with his implied readers. These are likewise evident in Kipling's letter of January 1888 to his cousin Margaret Mackail describing the trip:

> Ach Himmel. Was there ever anything like that dissolute tramp through some of the loveliest and oldest places on the earth . . . I railed and rode and drove and tramped and slept in Kings' palaces or under the stars themselves and saw panthers killed and heard tigers roar in the hills, and for six days had no white face with me, and explored dead cities desolate these three hundred years, and came to stately Residences where I feasted on fine linen and came to desolate way stations where I slept with natives upon the cotton bales and clean forgot that there was a newspapery telegraphic world without. Oh it was a good and clean life and I saw and heard all sorts and conditions of men and they told me the stories of their lives, black and brown and white alike, and I filled three notebooks and walked 'with death and morning on the silver horns' and knew what it was to endure hunger and thirst.[11]

The cousins' shared literary and social background is implied in the phrases 'feasted on fine linen' from the King James Bible, 'all sorts and conditions of men' from the Book of Common Prayer, and the quotation from Tennyson's *Princess*;[12] Kipling's 'good and clean life' of adventure does not so much depart from as knowingly transgress the norms of their common culture. Kipling would shortly recycle these words in 'The Man Who Would Be King', whose frame-story is based an incident related in the same letter to Margaret. An unknown Freemason, 'a brother of mine', entrusted him with a message to be delivered to another unknown Mason, at a remote junction 'on the edge of a desert at five o'clock on a bitterly cold winter morning with all the stars blazing overhead . . . I didn't know the name of the man who gave me the message. He didn't know mine. I didn't know the man who received it and he didn't know me. Wasn't it odd and out of the world?'[13] The narrator of 'The Man Who Would Be King' uses similarly semi-biblical language, boasting how 'I did business with divers Kings . . . Sometimes I wore dress-clothes and consorted with Princes and Politicals, drinking from crystal and eating with silver. Sometimes I lay out upon the ground and devoured what I could get . . . and slept under the same rug as my servant.'[14] And the adventurers in the story clearly owe something to the loafer in the last 'Letter', whose dream of raising 'hundreds of millions' from India if the British Government would only behave like the Rajahs instead of 'peckin'an' fiddlin' over its tuppenny-ha'penny little taxes', sounds like the inspiration for Dravot's boast that he could increase India's revenue from seventy millions to 'seven hundred millions'.[15] That said, 'The Man Who Would Be King' departs from 'Letters of Marque' in its famous description of the 'Native States' as 'the dark places of the earth, full of unimaginable cruelty, touching the Railways and the Telegraph on the one side, and on the other, the days of Haroun al Raschid'.[16] This sounds very like the imaginary kingdom 'Rhatore' in *The Naulahka*, but very unlike Jeypore (Jaipur), Udaipur, Jodhpur and Boondi (Bundi) as described in the 'Letters of Marque'. True, 'the Englishman' constantly complains about the bad roads and the sloppy native drivers repairing harness with bits of string, shudders at the 'plot and counter-plot, league and intrigue' of Indian court life and chortles at a misspelt hospital record-listing cases of 'Numonia' and 'loin-bite' ('it was lion-bite – or tiger, if you insist upon zoological accuracy' – a joke re-cycled in *The Naulahka*). But he mentions no cruelty, unless you count (as Kipling, who tells it as a comic anecdote, clearly does not) the incident when he is left in charge of an elephant who munches house-thatch, and fails to stop her until told by a 'a little breechless boy' to 'Hit her on the feet'.[17] All the states Kipling visits, as Bart Moore-Gilbert has pointed out, have well-built, well-run public provision of waterworks, hospitals and parks, thanks to efficient administrators blessed with abundant funds and no red tape. In 'Jeypore' Kipling admires the 'pure water, sound pipes and well-kept engines of the public water-works with their thronged standpipes', the well-attended hospital which would be the envy of 'ground-down and mutinous practitioners all India over' and the splendid museum whose excellence represents 'a rebuke to all other Museums in India from Calcutta downwards'. Even remote 'Boondi' has a public school 'entirely free and open' and a 'Charitable Dispensary' which serves its patients well despite the doctor's shaky English spelling.

Kipling is careful to emphasise that the men responsible for Jeypore's splendour are Dr Henderson the Curator and Colonel Jacob the engineer, whose 'native' beneficiaries vaguely attribute their blessing to the providential 'Yakub Sahib'.[18] Similarly, in Jodhpur, he admires the administration of finance, the hospitals and waterworks, and marvels at the efficiency with which they are run for the uncomprehending natives, but barely mentions the enlightened and generous prince and efficient prime minister who have commissioned these works. He does note that in Jodhpur 'the Maharaj's right hand in the work of State is Maharaj Sir Pertab Singh, Prime Minister' who is also 'Colonel of a newly raised crack cavalry corps';[19] just as in Jeypore the 'driving power' for the dispensary and waterworks is 'in the hands of a Bengali who has everything but the name of Minister'.[20] But he is much more interested in the 'Hat-Marked Caste' of English officials (i.e. sunburnt, wearing hats not turbans): 'tough, bronzed men, with wrinkles at the corners of the eyes, gotten by looking across much sun-glare' who 'see the works of their hands and the promptings of their brain grow to actual and beneficent life, bringing good to thousands',[21] thanks to the munificence of Rajahs as invisible as the workmen who do the actual building.

All this is very different from Rhatore in *The Naulahka*, where everyone is corrupt and nothing works properly from the moment when the hero arrives there and finds the 'telegraph operator and postmaster-general of the state'[22] asleep. Rhatore's sporting Rajah is plainly modelled on the Maharajah of Jodhpur, described to the 'Englishman' as 'like an English country gentleman',[23] who indeed turns out to be a crack shot with a passion for hunting and shooting, his manners combining courtesy with easy informality. The Maharajah of Rhatore, however, is a drunk and an opium addict whose face 'was bloated and sodden, and his eyes stared wearily above deep, rugged pouches',[24] totally under the thumb of his latest wife who is plotting to murder the Crown Prince to make her own son heir. Her villainy is thwarted by the American heroine Kate, a medical missionary ministering to Rhatore's women, and the buccaneering hero Tarvin, who between them save the Prince from poisoning and get him sent to an English-run public school. The only thing that works efficiently in Rhatore is the army 'drilled exclusively on English model' by its 'burly Rajput captain' Pertab Singh-Ji,[25] who speaks perfect English, like his real-life original Sir Pertab Singh the Prime Minister of Jodhpur. Otherwise the fictional Rhatore is indeed a 'dark place' whose principal dispensary (hospital) is a chaotic mess: a naked lunatic shouts at the patients in its 'filthy central courtyard', women give birth in a suffocating windowless box presided over by 'clay and cow-dung images', instruments are dirty, and everyone is addicted to opium, including the doctors and nurses.[26] Details such as the naked idiot whom the doctor has failed to cure by blistering, the record of treatment for 'loin-bite', and the opium-addicted patient all repeat Kipling's description of the Dispensary of Boondi, which despite the latter's 'untouched Orientalism' is nonetheless, as Kipling grudgingly concedes, 'a good one, and must relieve a certain amount of human misery',[27] very unlike the Dispensary in Rhatore, which will clearly revert to chaos when Kate leaves at the end to marry Tarvin.

Chitor and its successors

There is always evil at Cold Lairs – above ground or below.[28]

That the states described in 'Letters of Marque', however peaceful in 1888, have formerly been 'dark places' is made plain in the summary of the violent history of Chitor, which takes up most of Letter X. Drawing, as often in the

'Letters of Marque',[29] on James Tod's *Annals and Antiquities of Rajasthan*, Kipling writes a grim tale of treacheries and massacres, not as a humorous, wry or even wondering 'Englishman', but as a story-teller who describes the first sacking in the fourteenth century when the Raja of Chitor had married the 'Rajput princess of Ceylon Pudmini, "And she was fairest of all flesh on earth" . . . and she became, in some sort, the Helen of Chitor, sought by Ala-ud-din the Pathan emperor.' Having trapped her husband by treachery, he attacked the city,' killed the flower of the Rajputs', and sacked it, prompting an appalling *sati*:

> When everything was hopeless and the very terrible Goddess, who lives in the bowels of Chitor, had spoken and claimed for death eleven out of the twelve Rana's sons, all who were young or fair women betook themselves to a great underground chamber, and the fires were lit and the entrance was walled up, and they died. The Rajputs opened the gates and fought until they could fight no more, and Ala-ud-din the victorious entered a wasted and desolate city. He wrecked everything except the palace of Pudmini and the old Jain tower . . . That was all he could do, for there were few men alive of the defenders of Chitor when the day was won, and the women were ashes underground.

This horror is followed by the second 'sacking' in 1535 when 'thirteen thousand were blown up in the magazine, or stabbed or poisoned, before the gates were opened'. The Third Sack in 1568 by Akbar emperor of Delhi 'was the most terrible of all, for he killed everything that had life upon the rock, and wrecked and overturned and spoiled . . . With the Third Sack the glory of Chitor departed, and . . . it was never again made the capital of Mewar. It stood, and rotted where it stood, until the enlightened monarch called in Executive Engineers to repair it.'[30] Recalling these massacres, the 'Englishman' visits the overgrown ruins:

> The death of Amber was as nothing to the death of Chitor – a body whence the life had been driven by riot and the sword . . . [There were] crazy stone stairways, held together, it seemed, by the marauding trees. In one bastion, a wind-sown peepul had wrenched a thick slab clear of the wall, but held it tight pressed in the crook of a branch, as a man holds down a fallen enemy under his elbow, shoulder and forearm. In another place, a strange uncanny wind sprung from nowhere, was singing all alone among the pillars of what may have been a Hall of Audience.[31]

It is as if the 'marauding' trees and the branch wrestling the stones apart were keeping alive the memory of violence mourned by the wind's inhuman song. The narrator experiences a direct confrontation with the horror of the past when he enters the shrine of the 'Cow's Mouth' or 'Gau-mukh':

> In a slabbed-in recess, water was pouring through a shapeless stone gargoyle into a trough; which trough again dripped into the tank. Almost under the little trickle of water, was the loathsome Emblem of Creation, and there were flowers and rice around it. Water was oozing from a score of places in the cut face of the hill; oozing between the edges of the steps and welling up between the stone slabs of the terrace. Trees sprouted in the sides of the tank and hid its surroundings. It seemed as though the descent had led the Englishman, firstly, two thousand years away from his own century, and secondly, into a trap, and that he would fall off the polished stones into the stinking tank, or that the Gau-Mukh would continue to pour water until the tank rose up and swamped him, or that some of the stone slabs would fall forward and crush him flat.[32]

This passage, which Kipling would re-work in a short story and a novel, is cited by Zohreh Sullivan as exemplifying colonial anxiety at a treacherously feminised landscape. Although I followed this reading in my own book *Rudyard Kipling*,[33] I now find the interpretation too simple since in its context within the 'Letters' the anxiety roused by what Kipling calls the 'Genius of the Place' isn't *only* panic at a highly sexualised alien landscape, though it is that too. It is also prompted by the dark history of Chitor and the legend that

> from the Gau-Mukh, a passage led to the subterranean chamber where the fair Pudmini and her handmaids had slain themselves. And . . . Tod had written, and the Stationmaster at Chitor had said, that some sort of devil, or ghoul, or Something, stood at the entrance of the approach. All of which was a nightmare bred in full day and folly to boot; but it was the fault of the Genius of the Place, who made the Englishman feel he had done a great wrong in trespassing into the very heart and soul of all Chitor.[34]

The terror lies as much in the vengeful ghosts of women burned to death as in the rock whose sliminess threatens the swallowing up of the 'broad daylight' by ancient night. Yet the 'unspeakable Gau-Mukh' and its 'peculiarly malevolent' chuckling spring do not prevent the narrator from returning to the ruined city by night, comically disturbing a 'living, breathing woman' who screams at him, and getting scratched by thorn-bushes; but the beauty of Chitor by moonlight, is, he flirtatiously tells his readers, more unspeakable still – a 'lovely, wild and unmatchable scene' too beautiful to describe.[35]

Kipling's fictions re-work this experience several times, first in the brief horror-story 'Bubbling Well Road', published three days before Letter X and presumably written at about the same time,[36] and more elaborately in *The Naulahka*. The narrator of 'Bubbling Well Road', losing his way inside a patch of jungle-grass he has rashly entered, hears an 'offensive' chuckle from a deep well in which a spring gurgles 'laughing to itself' over black corpses rotting in the depths into which he nearly slips and falls,[37] a trap for which he blames a sinister native priest. In *The Naulahka*, the European intruder likewise comes very near to sliding into the deadly pit, made deadlier still by its reptile guardians. The hero Tarvin, bent on stealing the jewel of the novel's title, a necklace worth nine 'lakhs' (4,500,000) rupees, which he believes is located in the 'Gau-Mukh' shrine of a forbidden ruined city, enters its wall through a gap where a tree 'writhed between the fissures and heaved the stonework apart',[38] like the peepul-tree that 'wrenched a thick slab . . . and held it tight' at Chitor. He passes down a street where 'tall-built palaces . . . revealed the horror of their emptiness', climbs a tower like that of Kumbha Rana, and descends, slipping on a rock 'worn . . . smoother than ice, by the naked feet of millions' to the sound of a 'malignant chuckle' from a deep pit, at the bottom of which is a 'square tank of water so stagnant that it has corrupted past corruption' holding a 'pillar carved with monstrous and obscene gods', fed by a drip from the 'rudely carved head of a cow'.[39] Unlike Kipling Tarvin dares to enter the subterranean chamber, despite a sinister 'sound like the shivering backward draw of a wave on a pebbly beach'. He shudders 'from head to foot' when his heel crashes through a skull, and a lighted match shows 'pale emerald eyes watching him fixedly . . . there was deep breathing in the place other than his own'. Rushing from the cave he notices 'a length of the mud-bank to his left' moving towards him. A 'welt of filth', with 'horny eyelids heavy with green slime', approaches as he scrambles up to safety and passes a crippled ancient leading a kid and calling '*Ao, Bhai*! Come, brother!' to 'the sacred crocodile of the Gau-Mukh . . . waiting for his morning meal'.[40]

Tarvin's adventure re-works Kipling's own numinous experience of flight from the 'Gau-mukh', leaving out the dead city's history and putting in a crocodile from the 'Jeypore Palace-Gardens' whose tank was 'swarming with *muggers*', one emerging with 'green slime thick upon his eyelids' when addressed as 'Brother' ('Bhai'), the usual greeting of those who feed him.[41] Kipling's apprehension of nightmare in broad daylight is thus actualised by the crocodile in the tank and the snake in the cave (in fact a nest of snakes, as Tarvin learns later from the wicked Queen). This highly coloured melodrama represents a half-way stage in the transformation of the dead city into the

'Cold Lairs' of 'Kaa's Hunting' and the cobra-guarded treasure-chamber of 'The King's Ankus'. Cold Lairs, remembered by its reptile 'Warden' as 'the great, the walled city – the city of a hundred elephants and twenty thousand horses, and cattle past counting – the city of the King of Twenty Kings',[42] is famously based on Amber and Chitor, which are directly recognisable in its overgrown ruins:

> Trees had grown into and out of the walls; the battlements were tumbled down and decayed, and wild creepers hung out of the windows of the towers in bushy hanging clumps.
> A great roofless palace crowned the hill, and the marble of the courtyards was split, and stained with red and green, and the very cobblestones in the yard where the king's elephants used to live had been thrust up and apart by grasses and young trees. From the palace you could see the rows and rows of roofless houses that made up the city looking like empty honeycombs filled with blackness.[43]

This description draws on several places Kipling visited in Rajasthan. The trees that split the cobblestones recall Chitor where the peepul tree wrenched slabs out of the wall and Amber where 'trees grow in and split . . . the walls', 'windows are choked with brushwood' and in empty houses 'the little grey squirrel sat and scratched its ears'. The 'ivory-studded doors' and the 'inlay and carved marble' of the women's quarters in Amber'[44] reappear even more splendidly in the cobra-infested ornamental summer-house 'built for queens dead a hundred years ago . . . of beautiful milk-white fretwork, set with agates and cornelians and jasper and lapis lazuli'. The ruined streets looking like 'empty honeycombs' sound like a dead version of Boondi where the 'gash' made by a stone staircase in the 'brown flank' of the Palace looked like 'a broken bees' comb' with a mass of grubs wriggling inside.[45] But since neither sacred places nor human ghosts mean anything to the 'Jungle People', there is no Gau-Mukh; the ancient reservoir of Cold Lairs actually becomes a refuge to Bagheera when endangered by a pursuing crowd of monkeys.

But Cold Lairs owes more to the Chitor of 'Letters of Marque' than its atmospheric ruins. Something very like the dark history related in Letter X is re-enacted at the end of the story, when Kaa massacres and devours monkeys by the hundred. This is an impossible feat; no python, even a huge one like Kaa, could eat more than one monkey at a sitting, let alone 'hundreds and hundreds'[46] followed by a panther and a bear, if Mowgli had not saved Bagheera and Baloo by pulling them away. The scale and cruelty of Kaa's off-stage feast ('Go and sleep, for . . . what follows it is well thou shouldst not see'[47]), is obscured for child readers by the excitement and satisfaction of Mowgli's rescue, his nursery punishment of 'half-a-dozen love-pats' from Bagheera, and the strong implication that the *Bandar-log* are only getting what they deserve. But though Kaa treats Mowgli gently and in later stories is his benign mentor, his performance as destroyer of the monkeys is chilling. Originally moved to join in the rescue by hunger and irritation at the memory of the *Bandar-log* calling him 'evil names', Kaa becomes enraged when Bagheera plays on the insult, infuriating the giant snake as skilfully as a courtier repeating slander to his monarch:

> 'Footless, yellow earth-worm,' said Bagheera under his whiskers, as though he were trying to remember something.
> 'Sssss! Have they ever called me *that*? said Kaa.
> 'Something of the kind it was that they shouted to us, but we never noticed them. They will say anything – even that thou hast lost all thy teeth, and wilt not face anything bigger than a kid, because (they are indeed shameless, those *Bandar-log*) – because thou art afraid of the he-goat's horns', said Bagheera sweetly. . . .
> Baloo and Bagheera could see the big swallowing-muscles on either side of Kaa's throat ripple and bulge.[48]

Throughout the hunt, the smooth-tongued panther continues embellishing his report of the monkeys' (possibly imaginary) insults:

> 'They called me – "yellow fish", was it?'
> 'Worm – worm – earth-worm', said Bagheera, 'as well as other things which I cannot now say for shame.'
> 'We must remind them to speak well of their master. Aah-sss! We must help their wandering memories.'[49]

In his fury over the monkeys' insolence, his resolve to 'help their wandering memories', and the cold, cruel greed of his eventual vengeance, Kaa has much in common with the bloody tyrant who in the Third Sack of Chitor destroyed 'everything that had life upon the rock'. In his dialogue with the hypnotised *Bandar-Log* he resembles a tyrant in an Elizabethan drama taunting his victims, like Marlowe's Tamburlaine saying to the doomed Virgins of Damascus: 'Behold my sword; what see you at the point?'; and when they reply 'Nothing but fear and fatal steel, my lord', mocking them: 'Your fearful minds are thick and misty then, / For there sits Death.'[50] Kaa likewise plays with the monkeys:

'The moon sets,' he said. 'Is there yet light to see?'

From the walls came a moan like the wind in the tree-tops: 'We see, O Kaa.'

'Good. Begins now the Dance – the Dance of the Hunger of Kaa.... *Bandar-log*, can ye stir hand or foot without my order? Speak!'

'Without thy order we cannot stir hand or foot, O Kaa!'

'Good! Come all one pace closer to me.'

The lines of the monkeys swayed forward helplessly.[51]

In 'The King's Ankus', greed and murder are associated with the lost treasury and its guardian cobra beneath Cold Lairs. This tale of the treasure which leads a succession of men to murder each other in order to possess it re-tells Chaucer's *Pardoner's Tale*, though Kipling privately disclaimed this ('I don't remember when I didn't know the tale. Got it I suppose as a fairy tale from my nurse in Bombay'[52]). It also re-tells Tarvin's treasure-hunt in *The Naulahka*, Mowgli's approach to the cave closely corresponding to Tarvin's journey to the 'Gau-Mukh', though not to its dénouement. Mowgli too passes through a boundary wall where a tree has 'forced out a solid stone', and once inside the cave, finds a human skull on the floor, although unlike Tarvin he is not scared by it, observing quietly that 'It is the bone of a man's head ... And here are two more'. Like the would-be plunderer meeting the guardian snake, Mowgli encounters the ancient 'Warden', though he is as immune to fear as to avarice; and whereas Tarvin finds only a snake's 'pale emerald eyes', Mowgli encounters unimaginable hoarded wealth, enumerated in one of Kipling's set-piece lists, two pages long, of deep drifts of gold and silver coins which had 'packed and settled as sand packs at low tide', of palanquins, candlesticks, 'images of forgotten gods, silver with jewelled eyes', of belts 'seven fingers broad' of jewels, and of locked wooden boxes fallen to powder, 'showing the rubies, diamonds, emeralds and garnets within'.[53]

Uniquely for an animal in the *Jungle Books*, the 'Warden of the King's Treasure', who is used to ceremonial feeding by 'the Brahmins my masters' like the sacred crocodile in *The Naulahka*, boasts of the history of the city and the genealogy of its founder: 'Salomdhi, son of Chandrabija, son of Viyeja, son of Yegasuri, made it in the days of Bappa Rawul'[54] though these forgotten names are unintelligible to the noble savage Mowgli. The treasure, then, is specifically Indian; its description is followed by sage remarks about the propensity of native princes to hoard their money rather than invest in

Government securities, and the one item Mowgli takes away is an exquisitely inlaid elephant-goad, a very Indian object. But the cobra's accurate prophecy that men 'will kill, and kill, and kill for its sake! . . . It is Death! It is Death!' would have been just as true for Englishmen or Australians. When Mowgli tells Bagheera to bury the ankus, Bagheera protests that object itself is innocent: 'The trouble is with the men',[55] and unlike the earlier episode in the *Second Jungle Book* when Messua is almost lynched by the villagers, we are not asked to decode this as 'The trouble is with the natives'. Both the echo of Chaucer and the Christian symbolism of the evil serpent, who at once embodies the sin of greed and 'fairly shook with evil delight'[56] at the prospect of destroying a greedy sinner, constitute an implied reminder that white men too would have killed to possess the stones. As often in the *Jungle Book*, the Jungle world to which Mowgli belongs (or thinks he belongs) defines by difference what it means to be human.

Boondi and *Kim*

The influence of Kipling's travels in Rajasthan on his later writings goes beyond the dark history of Chitor and its influence on Cold Lairs. Current tourist brochures for Bundi[57] aver that Kipling 'wrote a chapter of *Kim* while he stayed by the lake'; and although factually this is absurd, it has a grain of truth: Kipling's ten-day journey to this remote city where 'there were no Englishmen of any kind'[58] did deeply affect his greatest novel. Like Kim on the Grand Trunk Road encountering 'new sights at every turn of the approving eye'[59] he is from the start of the journey delighted by the experience of dawn on the road: 'It is good, good beyond expression, to see the sun rise upon a strange land and to know that you have only to go forward and possess that land – that it will dower you before the day is ended with a hundred new impressions and, perhaps, one idea.'[60] Once he gets to Boondi, where he has to show his *'purwana,* or written permit' to an uncooperative *munshi* (clerk), he is confronted by difference: no one else speaks English or uses his currency, so he has to change his money, which takes time although the courteous officials are picturesque: 'The faces of the accountants were of pale gold, for they were an untanned breed, and the face of the old man, their controller, was frosted silver.' In Boondi, Kipling encounters a way of living which he finds increasingly seductive. He is rueful about having to sleep in an improvised 'loosebox' made by twisting canvas around the pillars of a pavilion near the lake ('no door, but . . . unlimited windows'), irritated by the calls of animals and 'hundreds of water-birds keeping a hotel', and disconcerted that 'Englishmen are not encouraged in Boondi'. Yet he concedes that 'it is a mean thing to gird [mock] at a State which is not bound to do anything for intrusive Englishmen without any visible means of livelihood', and by the time he has been shown over part of the vast palace, hearing the wind sighing like a ghost around the pillars and looking down at the city spreading out below, he is embarrassed at himself:

> The Englishman began to realise first, that he had not been taken through one-tenth of the Palace; and secondly, that he would do well to measure its extent by acres, in preference to meaner measures. But what made him blush hotly, all alone among the tombs on the hillside, was the idea that he with his ridiculous demands for eggs, firewood and sweet drinking water should have clattered and chattered through any part of it all.
> He began to understand why Boondi does not encourage Englishmen.[61]

Unlike his earlier smug account of the agreeable freedom of Udaipur from 'the tourist who would have scratched his name on the Temple of Garuda and laughed horse-laughs upon the lake', Kipling now recognises his own demands as 'ridiculous'. Nighttime conversations with his minders the sepoys, swapping half-understood ghost stories as the 'stars came out and made a new firmament on the untroubled bosom of the lake',[62] tempt him to wish he could stay forever. He has not merely become attuned to the delight of free travel which Kim will feel so joyously on the Grand Trunk Road; he has also learned from those despised 'Orientals' an openness to unhurried enjoyment. Having 'fallen in love with "Boondi the beautiful [he] believed that he would never again see anything half so fair", promising if "you read Tod luxuriously on the bund of the Burra Talao" [the bank of the large lake], the spirit of the place will enter into you, and you will be happy'. Granted that this is a foreign visitor's daydream, the benign 'spirit of the place', like a redemptive version of the dreaded Gau-Mukh's 'Genius of the Place', allows him to feel pleasure, not anxiety, at the otherness of an Indian city. Returning, his carriage is delayed, but for once Kipling, still attuned to enjoyment, doesn't mind this. 'To enjoy life thoroughly, haste and bustle must be left behind. Ram Baksh has said that Englishmen are always bothering to go forward, and for this reason, although beyond doubt they pay well and readily, are not wise men.' The 'Englishman', chewing the 'sweet and purple' sugar-cane which Ram Baksh has pulled for him, discovers more as he lies for hours feeling the 'set of the day':

At a certain hour the impetus of the morning dies out, and all things, living and inanimate, turn their thoughts to the prophecy of the coming night. The little wandering breezes drop for a time, and when they blow afresh, bring the message . . . the unseen tides of air are falling. This moment of change can only be felt in the open and in touch with the earth, and once discovered, seems to place the finder in deep accord and fellowship with all things on earth.[63]

This brief moment in which Kipling learns from his Indian driver to loaf and invite his soul both prefigures and contributes to the moment at the end of *Kim* in which the boy, convalescing from exhaustion and breakdown, lies under a tree on a small hill – 'a look-out, as it were, above some new-ploughed level' – and like Kipling 'on the crest of a rolling upland' discovering a 'deep accord and fellowship with all things earth', is restored to well-being and to his lama's wisdom by Mother Earth who 'breathed through him to restore the poise he had lost lying so long on a cot cut off from her good currents'.[64]

There are of course differences as well as similarities between Kipling's brief holiday feeling of 'deep accord and fellowship with all things' and Kim's experience of oneness – not least the absence in the 'Letters' of any Indian mentors other than, for a brief moment, Kipling's driver 'Ram Baksh'. The uncharacteristic surrender to what Kipling would in another mood surely condemn as 'Oriental' laziness is followed in the next paragraph by the return to 'Deoli the desolate' where he finds the grave of a friend who had innocently prophesied 'We shall meet again'. The final 'Letter' emphasises the writer's own Anglo-Indian identity with its denunciations of the Native States for disallowing a 'free press' and over-taxing Indians, and of the British Government for its softness in not taxing them enough. Conversations with fellow Englishmen follow: first with a 'loafer' whose speaks longingly of the millions to be made 'if you just made these 'ere Injians understand that they had to pay an' make no bones about it', then with the Army (two soldiers bound for Peshawur), the Navy (two very young midshipmen on leave), and finally with an ignorant tourist who thinks Jeypore of 'the gas-jets and water-pipes' is 'purely Oriental'.[65] It seems that Kipling, having briefly succumbed to the seduction of Indian culture, promptly reacts against the temptation to 'go native all-together'[66] with racist revulsion and a renewed loyalty to the ideals of empire. Certainly his fictions composed shortly after the 'Letters' emphasise Indian darkness – in the chuckling pit of 'Bubbling Well Road', the description of Native States as 'the dark places of the earth' in 'The Man Who Would Be King' and the corrupt, backward Rhatore of *The Naulahka*. Harry Ricketts' suggestion that the 'existential panic' of Kipling's encounter with the Indian otherness of the 'Gau-Mukh' marked the point where he began to turn away from India[67] is also borne out by the hostility to 'natives' expressed in the sketches of Calcutta and Bengal which he wrote immediately after 'Letters of Marque' entitled 'The City of Dreadful Night'. These focus entirely on white men and are full of complaints of Indians' filthiness and of the 'Big Stink of Calcutta' that plagues the air indoors and out: 'And in spite of that stink, they allow, they even encourage, natives to look after the place!'[68] Yet though Kipling in 1888 repudiated 'natives' so fiercely, his immersion in the societies of Rajasthan had an enduring after-life in his greatest fictions of India.

Notes

1 Rudyard Kipling to Margaret Mackail, 15 January 1888, *The Letters of Rudyard Kipling, Volume 1: 1872–89*, ed. Thomas Pinney (London: Palgrave Macmillan, 1990), p. 150. Kipling is echoing God's sentence on Cain: 'A fugitive and a vagabond shalt thou be upon the earth' (Genesis 4:13).

2 See Zohreh Sullivan in *Narratives of Empire: the Fictions of Rudyard Kipling* (Cambridge University Press, 1993), pp. 19–20; Bart Moore-Gilbert, ' "Letters of Marque": Travel, Gender, and Imperialism', *Kipling Journal*, 281 (March 1997), pp. 12–22; Mary Condé, 'Constructing the Englishman in Kipling's *Letters of Marque*', *Yearbook of English Studies*, 24 (2004), pp. 230–9; Jan Montefiore, *Rudyard Kipling* (Horndon: Northcote House, 2007), pp. 28–9; David Sergeant, 'Whispering to the Converted: Narrative Communication in Rudyard Kipling's *Letters of Marque*', *Modern Language Review*, 104, no. 1 (2009), pp. 26–40; Howard J. Booth, 'Introduction', in Booth (ed.), *The Cambridge Companion to Rudyard Kipling* (Cambridge: Cambridge University Press, 2011), pp. 2–4.

3 Kipling, *Something of Myself and Other Autobiographical Writings*, ed. Thomas Pinney (Cambridge: Cambridge University Press, 1990), p. 26.

4 Kipling, 'Letters of Marque', *From Sea to Sea: Letters of Travel*, vol. 1 (London: Macmillan, 1899), Letter XV, p. 152.

5 Kipling, 'How the Whale Got His Throat', *Just-So Stories for Little Children* (London: Macmillan, 1902), p. 6.

6 Kipling, *From Sea to Sea*, vol. 1, Letter VIII, p. 72. The description of the panther alludes to 'The Prince of Darkness is a gentleman': Shakespeare, *King Lear*, Act III, scene 4, line 145. The King of Oudh was deposed after the 1857 Indian 'Mutiny', hence the sale of his goods.

7 Kipling, *From Sea to Sea*, vol. 1, Letter VI, p. 44.

8 *Ibid.*, Letter I, p. 2; Letter XV, p. 153.

9 *Ibid.*, Letter VI, p. 49.

10 Sergeant, 'Whispering to the Converted', pp. 28–34.

11 Rudyard Kipling to Margaret Mackail, in *Letters, Vol. 1*, p. 150.

12 Cf. 'clothed in purple and fine linen, and feasted sumptuously' (Luke 16:20); 'all sorts and conditions of men', from 'Prayers and thanksgivings upon several occasions' in the *Book of Common Prayer* (1662); Tennyson, *The Princess*, book viii, line 189, in Christopher Ricks (ed.), *The Poems of Alfred Tennyson* (London: Longmans 1969), p. 836.
13 Kipling, 'The Man Who Would Be King' (Allahabad, 1888), reprinted in *Wee Willie Winkie and Other Stories* (London: Macmillan, 1895), p. 203; letter in *Letters, Volume 1*, p. 153.
14 Kipling, 'Man Who Would Be King', *Wee Willie Winkie*, p. 205.
15 Kipling, *From Sea to Sea*, vol. 1, Letter XIX, p. 197; *Wee Willie Winkie*, p. 201.
16 Kipling, 'The Man Who Would Be King', *Wee Willie Winkie*, p. 205. Kipling's phraseology echoes Psalm 74:20: 'the dark places of the earth are full of the habitations of cruelty'.
17 Kipling, *From Sea to Sea*, Letter III, p. 20; Letter X, p. 91.
18 Bart Moore-Gilbert, 'Letters of Marque', pp. 18–19; Kipling, *From Sea to Sea*, Letter IV, pp. 27, 30–1; Letter XVI, p. 163; Letter V, pp. 34, 36, 29.
19 Kipling, *From Sea to Sea*, Letter XIII, pp. 128, 126.
20 *Ibid.*, Letter IV, p. 29.
21 *Ibid.*, Letter VII, p. 62; Letter XIII, p. 131.
22 Rudyard Kipling and Wolcott Balestier, *The Naulahka: A Story of West and East* (London: Macmillan, 1892), p. 79.
23 Kipling, *From Sea to Sea*, vol. 1, Letter XIV, p. 133.
24 Kipling and Balestier, *Naulahka*, p. 91.
25 *Ibid.*, p. 148.
26 *Ibid.*, pp. 130–1.
27 Kipling, *From Sea to Sea*, vol. 1, Letter XVI, pp. 163–4.
28 Kipling, 'The King's Ankus', *Second Jungle Book* (London: Macmillan, 1895), p. 164.
29 Kipling's 'Letters of Marque' frequently cite or allude to James Tod's *Annals and Antiquities of Rajasthan* (London: Smith and Elder, 1829). See *From Sea to Sea*, vol. 1, Letter II, p. 9; Letter VII, p. 56; Letter VIII, p. 68; Letter XI, p. 104; Letter XVIII, p. 191.
30 Kipling, *From Sea to Sea*, vol. 1, Letter X, pp. 85–6, 88, 89.
31 *Ibid.*, Letter XI, p. 96.
32 *Ibid.*, p. 100.
33 Zohreh Sullivan, *Narratives of Empire*, pp. 20–1; Jan Montefiore, *Rudyard Kipling*, pp. 28–30.
34 Kipling, *From Sea to Sea*, vol 1, Letter X, p. 101.
35 *Ibid.*, Letter XI, pp. 104, 105.
36 'Bubbling Well Road' first appeared in the *Civil and Military Gazette*, 14 January 1888, signed 'Traveller' and was collected in *Life's Handicap* (London: Macmillan, 1891). 'Letters of Marque' X, describing the Gau-Mukh, appeared in the *Pioneer* on 17 January 1888. For an excellent reading of the colonial implications of 'Bubbling Well Road', see Douglas Kerr, *Eastern Figures: Orient and Empire in British Writing* (Hong Kong: Hong Kong University Press, 2008), pp. 9–14.

37 Kipling, 'Bubbling Well Road', *Life's Handicap*, pp. 318–19.
38 Kipling and Balestier, *Naulahka*, p. 162.
39 *Ibid.*, pp. 162–7.
40 *Ibid.*, pp. 169–71.
41 Kipling, *From Sea to Sea*, vol. 1, Letter V, pp. 37–8.
42 Kipling, 'King's Ankus', p. 155.
43 Kipling, 'Kaa's Hunting', *The Jungle Book* (London: Macmillan, 1894), p. 67.
44 Kipling, *From Sea to Sea*, vol. I, Letter III, pp. 18, 20–1.
45 *Ibid.*, Letter XVII, p. 174.
46 Kipling, 'Kaa's Hunting', *Jungle Book*, p. 71.
47 *Ibid.*, pp. 79, 83.
48 *Ibid.*, pp. 61–2.
49 *Ibid.*, p. 64.
50 Christopher Marlowe, *Tamburlaine the great*, Act V, *Marlowe's Plays and Poems*, ed. T.R. Ridley (London: Dent, Everyman, 1967), p. 49.
51 Kipling, *Jungle Book*, p. 81.
52 Kipling, letter to Brander Matthews, 7 February 1905, *The Letters of Rudyard Kipling, Volume 3: 1900–10*, ed. Thomas Pinney (Basingstoke: Macmillan, 1996), p. 176.
53 Kipling, 'The King's Ankus', *The Second Jungle Book* (London: Macmillan, 1895), pp. 158–9.
54 *Ibid.*, p. 157. The legendary 'demi-god' Bappa Rawul, mentioned in Tod's *Annals and Antiquities of Rajasthan*, appears in 'Letters of Marque' as the first conqueror of Chitor. See Kipling, *From Sea to Sea*, vol. 1, Letter X, p. 83.
55 Kipling, *Second Jungle Book*, p. 174.
56 *Ibid.*, p. 161.
57 David Page, 'A visit to Bundi', *Kipling Journal* 343 (September 2011), p. 4.
58 Kipling, *From Sea to Sea*, vol. 1, Letter XV, p. 147.
59 Kipling, *Kim* (London: Macmillan, 1901), p. 103.
60 Kipling, *From Sea to Sea*, vol. 1, Letter XV, p. 146.
61 *Ibid.*, Letter XVII, p. 176; Letter XVI, pp. 158–9, 161–2; Letter XVII, p. 182.
62 *Ibid.*, Letter VII, p. 52; Letter XVIII, p. 188.
63 *Ibid.*, Letter XVIII, pp. 191–2.
64 Kipling, *Kim*, p. 404.
65 Kipling, *From Sea to Sea*, vol. 1, Letter XVIII, p. 193; Letter XIX, pp. 197–202.
66 Kipling, *Kim*, p. 177.
67 Harry Ricketts, *The Unforgiving Minute: A Life of Rudyard Kipling* (London: Chatto & Windus, 1999), p. 106.
68 Kipling, 'City of Dreadful Night, Jan–Feb 1888', in *From Sea to Sea: Letters of Travel*, vol. 2 (London: Macmillan, 1899), pp. 204–5.

12

Kipling's 'vernacular': what he knew of it – and what he made of it

HARISH TRIVEDI

> 'You don't speak my talk, do you, Councillor *Sahib*?'
> 'No, I'm sorry to say I do not,' said the Legal Member.
> 'Very well,' said Tods, 'I must *fink* in English.'
> (Kipling, 'Tod's Amendment')
>
> 'Then, why talk [in English] like an ape in a tree? . . . Talk Hindi and let us get to the yolk of the egg.' (Kipling, *Kim*).[1]

Kipling's literary reputation was made by writing about a very different country, India, with what struck his readers as exceptional insider knowledge and artistic inwardness. He could conceivably have done so without using a single word of an Indian language but he chose to infiltrate, inflect and hybridise his English with a large number of Indian words from a wide range of registers. His primary purpose in doing so was obviously to authenticate his depiction or representation of India, but a secondary function equally clearly seemed to have been to show (or show off) just how much he knew.

The 'vernacular' Kipling uses is thus not only the unseen yeast that leavens his literary bread, it is rather more the very visible and colourful icing on his fictional cake. His mastery of India and its languages is nothing without this knowingness; not only does he know but we must know too that he knows, and that he knows a lot more than most readers. The aesthetic principle here is not that of selection, economy and implication; it is, rather, that of abundance, exuberance, and copious and outright display. As an artist, Kipling in this respect walks a high tight-rope and his performance is both daring and spectacular. He goes further out than most comparable writers have done, and when at times he overreaches and takes a tumble it is part of the game he has chosen to play.

In this essay, I seek to address and explore a number of related questions concerning Kipling's knowledge of an Indian language. (With the singular exception of Sanskrit, the British in India referred to all Indian languages as 'vernaculars', which etymologically and historically, in the context of the Roman empire, meant the languages of the slaves or the conquered peoples; it may be more appropriate now to refer to them as independent languages with distinct names of their own.) Which Indian language did Kipling know? Was it 'Hindi', 'Urdu' or 'Hindustani', and what was it called by Kipling himself? In what circumstances did he acquire his knowledge of it, and just how well did he get to know it? Is his use of it significantly different in the successive phases of his literary career? If so, what is the trajectory of his progress? What were the artistic strategies through which he deployed his knowledge of an Indian language? What kind of a reader was he addressing in his Indian works, and how does the aesthetic effect produced on an English (or American) reader of his use of an Indian language compare with the effect produced on an Indian reader?

Hindi / Urdu / Hindustani

Was it 'Hindi' that Kipling knew or was it 'Urdu' or 'Hindustani'? The question has perhaps understandably been the source of wide confusion in Kipling scholarship, as for example in the simple bafflement expressed by William Dillingham when he explains that, in Kipling's short story 'The Son of his Father', 'the foreign tongue is perhaps Urdu, although A.W. Baldwin [Kipling's cousin] remarks that as a child Kipling was fluent in Hindustani'.[2] Even commentators with a native knowledge of one or more of these languages continue to speak of them without discrimination; for example Ambreen Hai, who was brought up in Karachi and went to high school there, refers to the language spoken in *Kim* initially as 'Hindi' but thereafter as either 'Hindi' or 'Urdu' as if the matter was of no consequence: 'Urdu/Hindi remains with him [Kim], resurfacing at crucial moments of crisis. There are times when Kim forgets that he is a "Sahib," when he has to switch consciously from Hindi or Urdu to English.'[3]

Nor does Kipling himself help matters. In *Kim* (according to a count I made), the language being spoken is termed by him eight times as 'Hindi', eleven times as 'Urdu', five times as 'Hindustani', and eighteen times as simply 'the vernacular'. What can only be called his blithe vagueness in the matter is aggravated by some glaring inconsistencies. At the beginning of the novel, the very first sentence spoken by the lama, who is new to Lahore and to India, is characterised by Kipling as being 'in very fair Urdu'. But a couple of pages later, the lama is said to speak to the curator, virtually his first interlocutor in the novel, in a 'bewildering mixture of Urdu and Tibetan',[4] which sounds rather more plausible. Even more intriguing is the fact that, in Kipling's description, the language that Kim speaks is almost always 'Hindi', while what nearly all the other characters, including the lama, Mahbub Ali, Creighton and Lurgan, speak to him in 'Urdu' or 'Hindustani'!

The fact of the matter is that Urdu and Hindi are related but distinct languages, with a significant overlap between them but with even more significant differences. Scholars and common speakers alike hold widely different views of the matter, which is not only far from settled but has been the subject of much public controversy and of momentous cultural and political consequence. To polarise the issue into two broad views, some people believe that 'Hindi' and 'Urdu' are substantially the same language, while others believe that the common ground between them is severely limited and even deceptive and that they must be regarded as two quite different languages. As for 'Hindustani', it is held to be a mixture of both Hindi and Urdu and thus precisely the ground, whether large or small, where they overlap. Whether this common ground is in fact large enough for 'Hindustani' to be called a language in its own right, or so small as to be only a desideratum rather than a functioning reality, has for long been vigorously debated.[5]

The matter is by all accounts complicated enough, but some basic information in this regard may help towards a better understanding of this aspect of Kipling's art. To start with, Hindi and Urdu are written in two quite different scripts, so that a person who can read one must still make a substantial effort to be able to read the other. Hindi is written in the *nagari* or *devanagari* script, in which Sanskrit and Marathi are also written, and which is very similar to the scripts of several other major Indian languages, such as Gujarati and Bengali. Urdu is written in what is basically the Arabic script as received in India through its modified form used for Persian, though the Urdu script differs from the Persian script too in some details, as for example in its transcription of retroflex sounds. The *nagari* script is written from left to right while the

Urdu / Persian / Arabic script is written from right to left. There are several Urdu sounds (such as those represented in roman by 'q' and 'z') which Hindi-speakers find it difficult to reproduce, while many Hindi 'compound consonants' or consonant clusters (such as 'dr' and 'tr') are pronounced by Urdu-speakers as two separate sounds (as 'dar' and 'tar').

On the other hand, the grammar and syntax of both Urdu and Hindi are nearly identical. So would the vocabulary of the two languages appear to be at first glance, at the level of ordinary street-level communication, though when it comes to, say, the radio or TV news bulletins, the level of mutual intelligibility drops substantially. At a 'higher' level of conversation, or in literary and discursive writing, the two languages diverge widely to become even more distinct and different, with an increasing preponderance of Sanskritic words in Hindi and of Arabic and Persian words in Urdu. There is hardly any literary work that is claimed by both the languages, and apparently not a single book has ever been written in Hindustani. In fact, the claim of Hindustani to represent the ground common to Urdu and Hindi has often led to absurd consequences. At the annual convention in 1936 of the Hindustani Academy, which had been set up in 1927 to promote the cause of this common language, in the lack of consensus, two different presidents were elected, Maulana Abdul Haque for the Urdu section and Pandit Ganganath Jha for the Hindi section. The foremost novelist Premchand, who had begun his career by writing in Urdu and then switched to Hindi in search of a wider readership, and now vigorously championed the cause of Hindustani, disarmingly confessed: 'if such a language already existed, where would be the need for an institution such as this Academy?' And another even greater advocate of Hindustani, Mahatma Gandhi, similarly admitted: 'But what is Hindustani? There is no such language apart from Urdu and Hindi.'[6]

Both 'Hindi' and 'Urdu' are by derivation Urdu / Persian / Arabic words, as is 'Hindustan' (for India) and 'Hindustani' for anything pertaining to the country, including its residents. But 'Hindustani' as the name of a language seems to have been an invention of the British colonial rulers, which they used from about 1800 onwards to refer to what they believed to be the *lingua franca* of the country, and which they themselves began to learn and propagate in order to be able to rule the country more efficiently.[7] To this end, in 1837, they proclaimed the language of lower administration to be Urdu – which they used virtually synonymously with 'Hindustani' – in several large provinces of North India where it was clearly a minority language while

Hindi was the majority language. In the face of sustained popular protest, this colonial policy had eventually to be reversed in these provinces in the period between 1880 and 1900 (the years during which Kipling wrote nearly all his Indian works); henceforth, both Urdu and Hindi in their respective scripts were granted equal official status. These developments set up Urdu and Hindi in a bitter adversarial relationship in which they competed for the same privileges in the same colonial space. Further, the two languages came increasingly to be associated with mutual religious hostility; Hindi, deriving mainly from Sanskrit, was widely seen to be a language of the Hindus while Urdu, with its preponderance of Arabic and Persian vocabulary, was seen as a Muslim language.

Some liberal historians of each language and literature have tended to play down these differences and to highlight the common ground between the two languages, while blaming the British for causing or at least widening the rift between them, as indeed between Hindus and Muslims generally, for their own devious imperialist ends, in accordance with their policy of 'divide and rule'. When the separate Muslim nation-state of Pakistan was created in 1947, its national language was declared to be Urdu, though only 7 per cent of the population knew the language and speakers of Bengali, Panjabi and Sindhi were in an overwhelming majority in the various far-flung areas constituting the new nation. The imposition of Urdu on such peoples was one of the more emotive factors behind the secession of Bengali-speaking East Pakistan in 1971 to form the independent nation of Bangladesh.

The *ayah*-effect: knowing and forgetting

This vexed linguistic history impinged on Kipling's experience of India in various ways. When he was a child growing up in Bombay between 1865 and 1871, his (unnamed) Christian *ayah* and his bearer Meeta must have spoken to him in a language that Kipling calls simply the 'vernacular'. This was almost certainly some form of basic Hindustani, if only because over much of colonial India the servants in British households spoke Hindustani, the only Indian language their masters could understand. These servants came from various regions of the country and often from different linguistic backgrounds, and Hindustani was often for them, as for Kipling's *ayah* (from Goa) and for Meeta (from Surat), probably not their mother-tongue (most likely Konkani and Gujarati, respectively) but an acquired language, of which they knew sometimes not very much more than their masters.

In his autobiography, *Something of Myself*, Kipling famously recalled his hybrid linguistic upbringing, in a passage routinely cited by biographers and critics. Before being put to bed, he recalled,

> We [he and his younger sister 'Trix'] were sent into the dining-room ... with the caution 'Speak English now to Papa and Mama.' So one spoke 'English,' haltingly translated out of the vernacular idiom that one thought and dreamed in.[8]

Apparently, then, 'the vernacular' was in effect Kipling's 'mother-tongue', if he habitually thought and dreamt in it and could speak in English only by translating with some difficulty out of the vernacular. This is just the kind of native contamination which the British in India sought to counteract by sending their children back home to England at the age of five or six, before they became too hybridised and lost their distinction as members of the master race.

Kipling created several child characters whom he endowed with a similar upbringing and bilingual ambidexterity, most notably Tods in 'Tods' Amendment' and the young Strickland in 'The Son of his Father'. In the latter short story, the seeming over-hybridisition of the child of Strickland, himself perhaps the most 'nativised' of all the adult English characters created by Kipling, becomes a major issue, resolved by the parents deciding that the son must not be corrupted any further but be sent to England. Apparently, such heartless banishment from their mothers to their official mother-tongue and back to the hitherto unseen 'home country' cured most Anglo-Indian children of their childish linguistic aberrations.[9] In another, less often cited passage in his autobiography, Kipling describes how this happened in his own case.

> So, at sixteen years and nine months ..., I found myself [back] at Bombay where I was born, moving among sights and smells that made me deliver in the vernacular sentences whose meaning I knew not.

Kipling evokes his subconscious processes here with an almost Proustian psychological sensitivity, as the familiar 'sights and smells' trigger memories of time past. Oddly enough, however, he does not mention sounds, for the buzz of the vernacular(s) too must have similarly surrounded him. Perhaps, the sounds made him conscious of a loss too poignant to name, for though he could still mechanically reproduce the sound of the vernacular, it was now mere sound, emptied of all sense; the poetic inversion in 'whose meaning I knew not' serves to underline the depth of his feeling. The fond sense of belonging to native India, which had made Kipling once address his own parents in translation, now lay shattered on his return to India and made him feel an uncomprehending stranger. There is clearly a tone of mitigatory defensiveness in the sentence that follows here: 'Other Indian-born boys have told me how the same thing happened to them.'[10]

This latter passage from Kipling's autobiography seems almost to cancel out the first; in any case, the first needs to be read not in isolation, as it too often has been, but in juxtaposition with the second. The wide gap in understanding was accounted for by Kipling with poignant imaginative engagement in his autobiographical short story 'Baa Baa Black Sheep'. This has been read mainly in terms of the oppression and cruelty that Kipling himself experienced as a little boy in England in what the 'House of Desolation',[11] but what is of interest in the present context is the beginning and end which frame the main narrative. The story begins as Punch, five, and Judy, three, are being put to bed by the *ayah*, Meeta, and a third servant, the *hamal* (a porter or palanquin-bearer), all participating in telling them a picturesque bedtime story, in the middle of which the *ayah* breaks to the children the news that they are to leave for '*Belait*' in a week's time. It is only at the port in Bombay that the children find out that the servants are not to travel with them. 'But Punch found a thousand fascinating things in the rope, block and steam-pipe line on the big P. & O. Steamer, long before Meeta and the *ayah* had dried their tears.' As the voyage proceeds, within a couple of days Punch 'nearly forgot the *ayah* and Meeta and the *hamal*, and with difficulty remembered a few words of the Hindustani, once his second-speech.' (That 'second-speech' may suggest that as Anglo-Indian children grew a little older, they acquired even before they left for England a greater competence in English than in the vernacular in which they might have earlier lisped.)

But Judy is even worse, for even before they reach Southampton, when her mother, 'Mamma,' speaks to her of their *ayah*, she says: '*Ayah*? What *ayah*?' This makes Mamma anxious that soon the children might forget her too. Which, of course, they have done when she returns five years later, whereupon she has to protest in anguish: 'I am your Mother – your own Mother!' Even the older Punch never quite remembers her from the days in India, not even when she uses for him the Hindi word 'pagal' in loving rebuke when he's been naughty. He does not know what it means ('a mad fellow'), or that it is a Hindi word, but her use of this single strange word serves to bring about a sort of reconciliation between mother and children.[12]

The unsentimental truth that the story underlines is that little children are not so much attached to the past as looking forward in keen excitement to each new experience to come. In their ready forgetfulness they can seem heartless, but of course they can't even remember what they have forgotten, in the sense that they cannot recall it even when they are reminded of it, not even when – as the story itself underlines – the trauma of loss is permanent. Such a pattern of knowing and forgetting contradicts the notionally beguiling but factually fallacious theory put forward by Ambreen Hai, under the rubric 'The Milk of Human Language', that Anglo-Indian children imbibed the local language effortlessly with their wet-nurses' milk.[13] Children are as a rule weaned some time before they begin to speak, a wet-nurse was often not the same person as the *ayah* who brought up the children, and, in any case, having had an Indian wet-nurse does not seem to have prevented Anglo-Indian children from promptly forgetting the native language, from whomsoever they might have learnt it, once they were back in Britain – or, as in the case of Punch and Judy (and, by inference, Rudyard and Trix), even before they landed there.

Learning again

So, when Kipling returned to India to work there for what he called 'seven years' hard', he had to learn his vernacular all afresh, virtually from scratch. There is no record of Kipling having employed a *munshi* or a *pandit* to teach him either Urdu or Hindi, as young British civil servants had traditionally done, for they had to pass successive examinations in an Indian language over a period of some years in order to earn increments in pay and promotions. In fact, all the evidence is that Kipling never properly learnt to read or write any Indian language. One example of Kipling signing his name in the Urdu/Arabic script was examined by a Pakistani scholar, Syed Sajjad Husain, who found 'the word "Kipling" hardly decipherable from the way the letters are formed' and a manuscript page on which Kipling tried several times to write his name in that script was said, by the Indian linguist S.S. Azfar Husain, to read, in Kipling's various attempts, as ' "Kinling," "Kiplig" or "Kipenling" '.[14]

Over the six and a half years of his journalistic career in India, Kipling lived successively in two cities, both in North India but over 700 miles apart, and quite distinct in their cultural ambience and linguistic mix as well. From October 1882 to November 1897, he stayed with his parents in Lahore, which was the capital of the state of Panjab (by the British spelt 'Punjab' and routinely mispronounced 'Poonjab') and the unrivalled centre of the

Panjabi language and culture. He was then transferred to Allahabad, the then capital of the North-West Provinces and Oudh, and one of the major cities of the vast central area of India that is sometimes called 'the Hindi heartland'. It was already as important a centre of nationalist politics as any other city in India and thus hosted the fourth annual session of the Indian National Congress in 1888, after the first three sessions had been held in the much larger metropolitan centres of Bombay, Calcutta and Madras. (Kipling wrote in his newspaper *The Pioneer* a blatantly hostile account of this three-day assembly which had consequences that hastened his departure from India, but that is another story.[15])

In Lahore and in Panjab generally, the natural language of communication among the rich and the poor alike was Panjabi. Placed socially above it and spoken by the urban educated class was Urdu, especially among the Muslims who constituted a little over half of the population of the province, and on top of course was English, which very few Indians in Panjab were by then proficient in. Allahabad, where the Hindus were a vast majority, was an ancient pilgrimage centre, regarded by devout Hindus as next in holiness only to Benares, which was eighty miles away. The common language here was Hindi, with Urdu far less important and prevalent than in the Punjab, and knowledge of English similarly confined to a very few. The University of the Punjab had been set up by the British at Lahore in 1882 and the University of Allahabad in September 1887, just two months before Kipling arrived in that city; these were, respectively, the fourth and the fifth Western-style universities to be established in India (after Calcutta, Bombay and Madras, all in 1857).

Though Kipling claimed to know the seamy side of Lahore as well as anybody, the language that he seems to have picked up there was not Panjabi but Urdu or more precisely its basic and watered down version, Hindustani. At the beginning of *Kim*, the policeman addresses Kim in Panjabi but Kim curtly tells him off, probably in Hindustani: 'thou art a buffalo.' During the train journey to Umballa (in Indian spelling, Ambala), the young Sikh soldier says 'jestingly' to Kim: 'Let thy hair grow and talk Panjabi ... That is all that makes a Sikh.' But this is not correct, for Panjabi is spoken equally by Hindus and Muslims, and this was even truer of the time that Kipling was writing about. When Kim is travelling with the lama on the Grand Trunk Road, he encounters and triumphs over another 'Punjabi constable' who knows apparently only one word of English: 'Halt!' The only other character in the novel to speak in Panjabi is the rough and unlettered Kamboh peasant wandering from one holy man to another seeking a cure for his sick child. In Benares as he approaches the lama, 'he bellowed in Punjabi: "O Holy One – O disciple of the Holy One . . .".' Kipling is here exploiting to broad comic effect the common view that Panjabi is a particularly harsh and loud language.[16]

Just as Kipling showed little knowledge of the most popular language of Panjab and in fact some prejudice against it, so he never seems to have taken any interest, while living in Allahabad, in Hindi, by far the most widely spoken Indian language, which was adopted as the official state language of India after independence. In Allahabad, his Hindustani did not acquire a Hindi colouring to modify its distinctly Urdu base, and he took no more interest in Hinduism than he had taken before. (His later choice of the lama, a Tibetan Buddhist, as the central 'Indian' character in *Kim*, represents an evasion of both India and its dominant religion, Hinduism.) He had set several of his short stories in Lahore and also his first unfinished novel, 'Mother Maturin,' and was later to set the opening chapter of *Kim* there, but he set no fiction of his even fleetingly in Allahabad, while his distaste for the English-educated Indian seems only to have hardened. In *Kim*, he takes pot-shots at 'students of the Punjab University who copy English customs' as well as at the letter-writer who describes his qualifications as 'Failed Entrance Allahabad University'.[17] One may surmise many reasons for such lack of interest and imaginative engagement on the part of Kipling. He was no longer a reporter covering a city but a features writer who was sometimes sent on long trips away from Allahabad and was in any case freer to contribute short stories and poems. He had soon after arrival become infatuated with Mrs Edmonia Hill, wife of an American professor at the local university, who attracted and absorbed a fair amount of his attention. Possibly, his first flush of enthusiasm for things Indian was over.

Nevertheless, shortly after arriving in Allahabad, Kipling was exposed to an India that he had not imagined to exist while he lived in Lahore. His new newspaper, *The Pioneer*, sent him off on two months of wandering around Rajputana (now Rajasthan) to various kingdoms big and small which were under paramount British protection but in most respects quite autonomous. Such local linguistic competence as Kipling had acquired in Lahore did not take him very far there, as he reported in 'Letters of Marque', published in the *Pioneer* 1887–8 and reprinted in *From Sea to Sea* (1899). Kipling found these states in a picturesque region of India often better run by their Hindu kings than the three-fifths of India which was under direct British rule, which in any case seemed so far away as to be unreal – for here was 'a planet within a planet, where nobody knows anything about the Collector's wife [or] the Colonel's dinner-party'.[18]

An Englishman was hardly looked upon here as the master or *sahib* by the sturdily independent natives; a camel-rider 'bore very patiently with the Englishman's absurd ignorance of his dialect'. The royal gardens in Jeypore (Jaipur) were 'finer than any in [British] India and fit to rank with the best in Paris' and the museum had arches on which were 'written, in Sanskrit and Hindi, texts from the great Hindu writers of old'. Kings here might not allow 'a free press' (which the British in the part of India they ruled did not either) but they would start weekly publications 'to encourage a taste for Sanskrit and high Hindi'. When 'the Englishman' (as Kipling described himself) was addressed at one place in 'Mewari', a local dialect of Hindi, he replied in his 'English-Urdu', aptly so called, and that was the end of the conversation. All the Indian fellow passengers in a *tonga* were called by honorifics such as '*Sahib* and *Hazoor*', except for 'the Englishman' who was a 'simple *tum* (thou)'; they soon prodded and pushed him with the handles of their swords and '[t]hen they slept upon him'.

In the remote and tiny but architecturally grand state of Boondi, he finds his very presence in the state closely interrogated by 'a one-eyed *munshi* (clerk)', and he discovers that only two men in the whole state can speak English. He must go and change his money, currency issued by the British government in 'India', into local currency issued by the Maharaja, in the Treasury situated in the stately 'Boondi-ki-Mahal', the Palace of Boondi (except that Kipling gets even this little phrase wrong; it should be 'Boondi-ka-mahal', in the masculine gender). He can't follow what anyone says and declares: 'They speak a pagan tongue in Boondi' which is 'quite unintelligible . . . It is the catching of a shadow of a meaning here and there, the hunting for directions cloaked in dialect that is annoying.'

In the perfectly picture-like Treasury with its row of accountants with 'pale gold' faces, Kipling feels the scene 'can without alteration be transferred to canvas', but he watches 'open-mouthed blaming himself because he could not catch the meaning of the orders given to the flying chaprassies, nor make anything of the hum on the verandah and the tumult on the stairs'. He finds that no one bothers to answer his literal little queries about the palace (e.g. 'When . . .' or 'How many . . .'), and ultimately 'blush[es] hotly' that he 'should have clattered and chattered through any part of it at all. He began to understand why Boondi does not encourage Englishmen.' He is so entranced and overpowered by this strange and leisurely land of pristine and silent beauty where he cannot follow almost anything that is said that he nevertheless wishes to stay on and live a long life there and then to die 'easily and pleasantly', without ever returning 'to the Commissioners and the Deputy Commissioners' of British India. The one person whose speech he has been able to follow is Ram Bakhsh, a tonga-driver from a neighbouring state, who is more than a match for Kipling, calls all the shots and does nearly all the talking, with Kipling barely able to get in a word edgeways. This was probably the most intense non-British experience of India that Kipling ever had, some of which he put to haunting fictional use (as in the Gau-mukh episode) in his other Indian novel *The Naulahka*. It was all a far cry from Simla, Lahore or even Allahabad; it was another world altogether in which Kipling was as enchanted as Alice in her wonderland and nearly as completely lost and bewildered.[19]

But it was of course no more than a passing interlude and the effect did not last; Kipling's reports from visits shortly afterwards to Calcutta, Jamalpur and Benares, all located solidly in British India, show him associating only with other Britishers and reverting to the common imperialist, racist attitudes.[20] Anyhow, Kipling was now a writer famous all over British India and had an eye fixed on the prospect of returning to England to try and make an impact on the metropolitan literary scene. He had, in his own opinion and that of some others, grown just too big for India. There seemed no need for him now to know and understand any more of India than he already did. Through his immensely popular and much applauded published works, he had effectively made good his claim that he knew his Anglo-India as no Britisher had done before.

All this while, like other Anglo-Indians, Kipling had hardly needed to speak in any form of an Indian language to anyone apart from the servants at home or club, drivers of vehicles, or the factotums in his office such as his versatile *daftary* (stationery-clerk). There is little evidence in Kipling's autobiography or the first volume of his *Letters* (covering the period 1872–89, from when he was about seven years old up to his final departure from India at the age of twenty-three) to suggest that he had a single Indian friend or even acquaintance of any standing; certainly, there are no letters to or from any Indian in this volume. Curiously, his Hindustani plays a more prominent and striking part in his poems and fiction than it seems to have done in his own life, for the world of his imaginative creation fairly resonates with it.

What Kipling knew

The effect of Kipling's use of Hindustani depends, of course, on just who is reading him and where. The eight early collections of his poetry and short fiction were not only written in India, on native ground, but also addressed to an Anglo-Indian readership. This vital circumstance changed when Kipling returned to England, so that he felt obliged to provide a glossary to his early Indian work *Departmental Ditties* (1886, enlarged 1890), when it was reprinted in England in 1891 for a metropolitan readership. This glossary with 131 items was long enough to be printed as a separate volume of 67 (nicely spaced) pages in the USA, where the need for a gloss might have been felt to be even greater.[21]

Meanwhile, in a Christmas letter in comic verse written in December 1883 to cousins in England, Kipling had vividly described his bilingual situation in India and also underlined the need to gloss and translate it for readers in England.

> Yet once more – by the *'chillag's'* light
> When *'wallahs'* wake you in the night
> With *'Hakim sahib ke ghar khan hai?*
> *Memsahib bemar'* – and you reply
> Half wakened *'Memsaheb bahut bemar?*
> *Tomara pahs ne hai sowar?'*
>
> This in a [*sic*] London city read
> Would prove the poet off his head
> But in an Anglo Indian Station
> It means – increase of population.[22]

Kipling glosses the italicised words on the right-hand side of the page as follows: 'chillag's' as 'wick in oil'; 'wallahs' as 'men'; 'Hakim sahib ke ghar khan hai? Memsahib bemar' as 'Where's the Doctor's House? The Memsahib is ill'; and 'Memsahib bahut bemar? Tomara pahs ne hai sowar?' as 'Is the lady very ill? Haven't you a mounted messenger to send?' Obviously, this is an impressive sample of what Kipling understands and can reproduce of the local speech, none of which without his gloss could be understood at all in London city. On the other hand, nearly all of it suffers from errors. *Chillag* should be *chirag*, which means simply lamp; *wallah* is a suffix which cannot be used by itself (though just possibly, this may be deliberate comic usage); *Hakim sahib ke ghar* should have the singular *ka* not the plural); *khan* should be *kahan* and *bemar* should be *beemar* (these are ungrammatical verbless fragments perhaps due to constraints of metre and rhyme); and the last line should be *Tumhare paas sawar nahin hai?* It would all have sounded exotic and wonderfully knowledgeable in London but comically incorrect in India.[23]

Nearly two decades later, Kipling similarly sought to provide explanations within the text for the Hindustani words that he used in *Kim* (1901), but his practice proved sporadic and erratic and he seems soon to have tired of it. In the opening chapter of *Kim*, for example, he wrote tautologically of 'the Ajaib Gher, the Wonder House' and on the same page explained within square brackets 'Khitai', 'Bhotiyal' and 'Bhotiya' as 'a Chinaman', 'Tibet' and 'Tibetan' respectively, but then did not gloss either 'lama' or 'guru' later in the same sentence. He explained 'a *chela* [disciple]' at the first occurrence of the word, its second occurrence two lines later is italicised too, but then at its third occurrence only a few pages later where it is printed in roman, he glossed it again, without any variation: 'my new chela [disciple].' By this point, in the new Penguin edition (2011), as many as 71 notes have already been provided by the editor.[24]

In general, editors and critics of Kipling's works have been exceptionally assiduous in annotating his Hindustani and discussing his use of it, with the kind of exegetical zeal that few modern writers have attracted except self-consciously obscure polyglot high modernists such as T.S. Eliot and James Joyce. In the first book-length study of Kipling's style, a PhD thesis submitted at the University of Lund by W. Leeb-Lundberg titled *Word-Formation in Kipling: A Stylistic-Philological Study* (1909), the author understandably kept clear of Indian words but he did declare that 'Kipling is a born Anglo-Indian, and that India with all its Oriental splendour of imagination runs in his blood'[25] – as if Kipling were a half-caste. An anonymous contributor published in an early issue (1927) of the *Kipling Journal* an extensive 'Glossary of Hindustani Words to be found in Rudyard Kipling's Works'; these are generally well glossed and follow without correction or comment Kipling's own erratic orthography, such as 'Khoota' for dog (in Hindi, *kutta*), or 'Kench', correctly explained as 'pull (imperative)' (in Hindi, *khainch*). Among other articles on the subject published in this flagship journal, Lieut. General Sir George MacMunn's 'Kipling's Hindustani' (1941) bore testimony to the author's own personal and at times arcane knowledge of the Indian languages, in conformity with his lukewarm verdict that 'This vocabulary is not always accurately rendered [by Kipling], but it will suffice and is interesting in its variety.' In contrast, Shamsul Islam's anachronistically titled essay 'Kipling's

Use of Indo-Pakistani Languages' (1969)[26] followed the common critical practice in praising Kipling's knowledge of Hindustani as being part of his 'superb craftsmanship' and contributing to his 'realistic effect', though Islam did not proceed to explain just how this effect is produced, for the somewhat patronising reason that 'The English reader does not need to know the vernacular words' to appreciate the overall effect.

But the most extensive and systematic study of Kipling's knowledge of 'Hindustani' (which term is used 'to include Urdu as well as Hindi') remains S.S. Azfar Husain's PhD thesis submitted at the University of London and later partially published as a book, *The Indianness of Rudyard Kipling: A Study in Stylistics* (1983). Husain argues with enthusiasm the case that 'the Indian elements in Kipling's language' as well as the fact that 'his language was deeply influenced by Indian languages' had not been studied and appreciated adequately by previous critics and then proceeds to fill the lack.[27] Husain's own method of study, which he characterises as 'Stylo-statistics' and which uses a large number of elaborate statistical tables, was mocked and roundly derided by both scholars of Kipling and of Urdu; G.H. Webb called the book 'ambitious and interesting but irritating', but spoke of 'the sludge of his statistics' and the 'mincing-machine of his analysis', and finally lamented that 'so numerate a study carries a sad air of antisepsis and sterility'. Christopher Shackle, professor of Urdu, refused to entertain Husain's main claim that Kipling was intimately acquainted with Hindustani, and declared that all the vast evidence Husain had marshalled only showed 'how badly Kipling knew Urdu'.[28] However, Husain's book cites more copiously from a wide range of Kipling's Indian works than any other critic, appending to his study an 'Overall Lexicon' of 483 Indian-language words used by Kipling. The 1927 glossary in the *Kipling Journal* had only 153 items – though, these, unsettlingly, include 30 items not in Husain's *Lexicon*, including for example 'arré', 'baja', 'boli' and 'budmash'.[29]

If we pick out (as Husain does not) a list of the ten Indian words that Kipling most frequently used, it is a surprise and even a bit of a disappointment to find that these are all names or collective nouns used as proper nouns: *Bagheera* (231 occurrences), *Baloo* (111), *Shere* (83), *mugger* (80), *chela* (73), *Hathi* (62), *Kala Nag* or *Nag* (56), *rukh* (55), *Gunga* (46) and *ayah* (35). It doesn't get any better later, for the eleventh is *Bandar-log* (33). There are only two human beings in this list, *chela* and *ayah* (though *Gunga* may sometimes refer not to the river but to Gunga Din); for the rest, it is all 'In the Rukh' (jungle) where neither Hindustani needs to be spoken nor

English. *Bagheera* actually means tiger; *Shere* is misleading as the Hindustani word is pronounced as in 'share'; and the word for 'bear' is *bhaloo* pronounced with the 'b' strongly aspirated.

Other frequently used words in Kipling's Hindustani lexicon are professional titles of Anglo-Indians' servants: *ayah* (above), *coachwan* (32 occurrences), *khansamah* (28), *darzee* (26), *khitmutgar* (19, correctly spelt *khidmatgar*), *chowkidar* (15) and *mehtar* (14, plus 4 of the feminine *mehtaranee*). Of the modes of transport, *ekka* occurs 29 times, *jhampani* 12, and *ticca-gharry* 10 times (though oddly, Husain does not mention *tonga*). Among caste-names, the most frequent are *Jat* (16), *bunnia* (15) and *chamar* (11), while the exotic casteless *faquir/fakir* occurs 30 times. Real words in Hindustani, such as *admi, afim* and *aram*, or *yogi, zoolum* and *zabberdusty*, are only rarely used by Kipling: Husain's list has 210 words used only once, and 81 more which he uses only twice.

There are of course more traditional and more literary ways of appraising Kipling's knowledge of Hindustani and the artistic effect that his use of it creates. Jan Montefiore in her *Rudyard Kipling* (2007) devotes a whole chapter to 'Imagining a Language: Kipling's Vernaculars' in which she considers in detail Kipling's use of the Indian 'vernaculars' with as much sensitivity and sympathy as perhaps any Western commentator has. She seems to think of 'Urdu' and 'Hindustani' as two different languages rather than of the latter as being an elementary basic-vocabulary version of the former and some-times a euphemism for it; she confuses Hindi with Hindustani, stating that 'modern Hindustani' is 'descended' from Sanskrit whereas modern Hindustani is all the Hindustani there is (for, as seen above, there are no references to this term before the British arrive in India), and it is descended no less from Arabic and Persian than from Sanskrit; and she is misled by Kipling's repeated assertion into believing that 'dewanee' means 'madness' while the Urdu/Hindustani word for that is *diwanagee*.

But Montefiore aptly cites and interprets a letter by Kipling in which he narrates at some length how he strategically motivated a native worker at his newspaper press by speaking to him in Hindustani and Panjabi, because, when spoken to in their own language, Kipling explains, 'they'll believe you and do things for you'.[30] (To appropriate here the anthropologist Bernard Cohn's formulation, one's command of a language helps one use it as a language of command.[31]) She picks out for analysis some early short stories in which Kipling confidently deploys a native character as the sole narrator, and she perceptively suggests that his use of archaisms such as 'thee' and 'thou' and 'ye' and 'bade' evokes 'a world of unlettered pre-industrial people' while it also contributes to a 'blurring' of different native registers. Perhaps the most useful insight Montefiore offers is her recognition that the Hindustani and the Hindustani-inflected English rendered by Kipling did not need to be accurate or even plausible to serve his purpose: 'Kipling has not so much "imagined a language" . . . as invented an artificial English equivalent to Indian language(s) . . . , inviting his readers to accept that artifice as reality.' The use of such a constructed rhetoric 'aestheticises' the misery and suffering of poor and starving Indians and distances and absolves the colonial ruler, so that the English reader can feel that he is 'an honorary citizen of this hidden Indian world, knowing its laws, customs and speech'. In a flourish of enthusiasm, she suggests that 'Kipling gives the illusion of undoing the curse of Babel, allowing his English readers to comprehend the strangeness of alien lives' and again, in conclusion, that *Kim* in particular 'appears to undo the curse of Babel by making its hero change languages as easily and as unrecognizably to the privileged reader, as he changes garments and identities'.[32] This is high approbation indeed.

What Kipling did not know

In contrast, the Indian post-colonial theorist and critic Gayatri Chakravorty Spivak has described Kipling's use of 'Hindusthani' as 'always infelicitous, almost always incorrect'.[33] Earlier, Jawaharlal Nehru, Indian nationalist leader who later became the first prime minister of India (and had as a boy read *The Jungle Books* and *Kim*),[34] had trenchantly characterised the nature and level of Hindustani that most Britishers in India as a rule acquired and used: 'It is astonishing how English people spend a life-time in India without taking the trouble to learn the language well. They have evolved, with the help of Khansamahs and ayahs, an extraordinary jargon, a kind of pidgin-Hindustani, which they imagine is the real article'.[35] And though Syed Sajjad Husain defends Kipling against Nehru by saying that he commanded a 'much wider vocabulary' in Hindustani than the pidgin-Hindustani of many other Anglo-Indians, he concludes his searching and thoroughgoing appraisal of Kipling's knowledge of India, which is as robustly post-colonial *avant la lettre* as any ever published, by observing that Kipling time and again says things about India which are 'so utterly ridiculous as to seem an insult to his own intelligence'.[36]

Spivak's outright dismissal of Kipling's Hindustani may seem too extreme to be just, and even most Indian readers of Kipling may be inclined to agree rather more with the (uncharacteristically) moderate assessment of the matter by Salman Rushdie instead. In his examination of two early volumes of short stories, *Soldiers Three* and *In Black and White*, he finds that though Kipling's use of 'a number of Hindi words and phrases' is kept 'at a pidgin *Hobson-Jobson* level', is often in the imperative mood as employed by English masters to their Indian servants, and is dumbly 'exclamatory' and predictably exotic even when Kipling puts his 'invented Indiaspeak' in the mouths of Indian characters, he gets 'much of it brilliantly right'.[37] On the other hand, it must be conceded that a close reading of Kipling's Indian texts turns up considerable *prima facie* evidence in support of Spivak's summary judgement.

It is seldom that Kipling uses a whole sentence of Hindustani, preferring to employ odd words here and there, but even his shortest sentences are not without error. In the poem 'For to Admire', admittedly spoken by an uneducated soldier, 'The Lascar sings, "Hum deckty hai!"' uses the incorrect gender and person as well as number, to say nothing of pronunciation; it should correctly be 'Ham dekhte hain', or, even better, 'Main dekh raha hoon'.[38] Even in 'Tods' Amendment', the short story in which Kipling famously makes the claim that a Hindustani-speaking English child like Tods (who seems modelled on the young Kipling himself), with his ear to the native ground, understands India far better and can do more good for the poor Indian than all the high and mighty Councillors of the Viceroy, the Hindustani that Tods uses is palpably incorrect. For example, he asks of the new Bill: 'Has it been *murummutted* yet . . . ?' and when the Councillor cannot understand even this elementary word, he proceeds to explain: '*Murrumatted* – mended – put *theek* . . .' But *murrammatted* (from *marammat*, though nouns are seldom used as verbs in Hindustani as in English) does not mean finalised or settled in draft, as Tods means here, but instead repaired, as with something used and broken, and cannot idiomatically be used of a piece of writing anyhow.

Nor is the word used comically here as a malapropism, for Tods' whole authority rests on his knowing his Hindustani. Indeed, he proceeds to patronise the Councillor Sahib by asking him 'with infinite compassion': 'You don't speak my talk, do you . . . ?' Again, it is not clear why Kipling uses two different words in this deliberately stilted translation when he could have more accurately said: 'You don't speak my speech' or 'talk my talk' – for the effect in Hindustani would arise from the verb and the noun being cognate: *boli bolna*. To point to a larger error which Kipling's fond valorisition of Tods' knowledge of Hindustani serves to obscure, Tods ends up advocating the interest not of the poor tiller of the land, as he thinks he is doing, but instead of the absentee landlords like 'Dita Mull, and Choga Lall, and Amir Nath' for even when Tods is said to be able to reach out, with his knowledge of Hindustani, to the common Indian, these rich traders in Shimla are the only Indians he gets to speak to, not the farmers in the faraway fields.³⁹

In his most mature Indian work, *Kim*, the name of the Hindu boy whom Kim shoos off the Zam-Zammah at the beginning of the novel is incorrect: it should be Chote (or Chhote) Lal, not Chota Lal. The very first Hindustani phrase that Kipling meant to put in Kim's mouth was grammatically incorrect: 'Hai mera ma' gets the gender wrong. In the manuscript, Kipling explains it within brackets as meaning 'O my mother', which is how it eventually appears in the published text, without the Hindustani. Kim continues to use throughout the novel, at five different places, what may be called a *murrammutted* version of the phrase, 'Hai mai', which means the same thing (except that this is an exclamation idiomatically used by one woman to another and not by a male).⁴⁰

What compounds these elementary errors is the fact that numerous Hindustani words as spelt by Kipling look and sound wrong even when they may be right. This begins with place-names, such as Amritzar, Umballa and Bikanir, which in the Indian mode of spelling them in roman are Amritsar, Ambala and Bikaner. A major change in orthographic convention that hasn't helped Kipling in this regard is that the sound that he and other contemporary Anglo-Indians represented by 'u' (as in Umballa) is now universally represented by 'a' – though it was sometimes so represented even then, as in Amritsar, where the initial vowel is pronounced exactly the same way as in Umballa. Another even more frequent source of confusion and error arises from the common British inability to aspirate, or a tendency wrongly to aspirate, some hard Indian consonants, such as b, k and t, which when aspirated form another distinct consonant altogether in Hindi/Hindustani: hence 'Baloo' for 'Bhaloo' and the misspelt title of *The Naulahka*, which should have been 'Naulakha', as in the name of the house in Vermont. Less glaring but even more grievous (or comical) is the misspelling of the old Queen's name: 'Sita Bhai' for Sita Bai. While 'bai' is a term of respect for women, 'bhai' means brother, so that 'Sita Bhai' is rather like saying 'Brother Elizabeth' or 'Elizabeth Esq.'.

Such errors are of course not Kipling's alone, nor peculiar to Anglo-India. The British colonial reinscription of Irish place-names seems eminently comparable here, especially as imaginatively depicted by Brian Friel in his play

Translations (1980), in which for example 'Bun na hAbhann,' which means literally 'the mouth of the river' is 'Anglicised' into English ordnance orthography as 'Burnfoot'.[41] The American anthropologist Franz Boas published in 1889 an article titled 'On Alternating Sounds' in which he argued that what was called 'sound-blindness' was in fact not deafness to foreign sounds but an inability to negotiate 'the differential threshold' because of a tendency towards 'involuntary assimilation' of foreign sounds into the phonetics of the listener's own language. Some related reasons for such assimilation of sounds from the Indian languages into English in colonial India must have been not only what Boas called 'the unphonetic character of English orthography'[42] but also the attitude of imperial superiority which probably prevented the British from even making an effort to get it right.

The uses of Hindustani – the comic and the ridiculous

Ultimately, the pleasure that most of Kipling's readers derive from his use of Hindustani is dependent not on how much of the language he knew or how well but just how he used it and what he made of it. Besides, his use of Hindustani is widely and systematically different in the exuberant early volumes written by 1889 while he was still in India and not yet twenty-four, and in his last and best work about India, *Kim*. In the former, the strategic sprinkling of Hindustani usually serves to produce or heighten a comic and ironic effect, while in the latter, it is not so much the openly displayed Hindustani elements themselves as the permeation of Kim's as well as the narrator's English syntax and usage by the invisible and subterraneous current of Hindustani, the translation between the two languages both in the linguistic and a wider cultural sense, and the constant switching to and fro of Kim between his two languages, that set up a deeper bilingual resonance.

It was astute strategy on Kipling's part to use his Hindustani in his early works in the service of all kinds of comic effects. As has been seen above, the general standard of British acquaintance with Hindustani was so deficient and defective as to be virtually a joke, and if no native-speaker dared laugh at it, this was plainly because, to invert the familiar Foucauldian–Saidian axiom, power was (a substitute for) knowledge – so that rather than being laughed at for their Hindustani, the British laughed at the defects of the Indian use of English instead. But Kipling, in his vantage position of a reporter-observer situated outside of and at an angle to the ruling British establishment of the army and the civil service, took it upon himself to call the bluff of the emperor's new linguistic garb. And he did not really have to be an expert in Hindustani to be able to do so; all he needed was to be just a step or two ahead of the Anglo-Indian pack, which couldn't have been difficult, and to have a sharp ear.

One little instance of such comic invention is 'Hitherao', as in '"*Hitherao!*" sez I, and he *hitheraoed* till I judged he was at a proper distance, an' thin I tuk him, fair an' square betune the eyes'.[43] The demotic vernacular of the brutish British soldier hitting an Indian is here reinforced by his equally illiterate use of the single Anglo-Hindustani word. 'Hitherao' would be two words in Hindustani, 'Idhar ao', meaning 'Come here,' but in the soldier's use, they are lumped into just the one word, with the cockney addition of an initial 'h', turning the Hindustani 'idhar' into the English 'hither', which by an apt verbal accident carries the same sense. The soldier's limited vocabulary and its tone of imperative command are both in evidence in his use of the same word again to describe the carrying out of his order: 'and he *hitheraoed*' (i.e. come-hered, so to say).

Kipling time and again achieved an inspired linguistic effect through his use of similarly hobbled and patently inadequate Hindustani (even without the help of an accidental pun as in 'hitherao' above), mainly by turning a woefully limited stock of Hindustani into a comic virtue. The following passage from *Plain Tales* may not have caught the attention of many Western commentators but all three of the Indian-born critics of Kipling cited above (Husain, Husain and Islam) were struck enough by it to have each quoted it in full. But they take the effect of the passage for granted without explaining just how it's achieved. This is the Irish soldier Mulvaney speaking in the short story 'The Three Musketeers':

> I purshued a *hekka*, an' I sez to the dhriver-divil, I sez, 'Ye black limb, there's a *Sahib* comin' for this *hekka*. He wants to go *jildi* to the Padsahi Jhil' – 'twas about tu moiles away – 'to shoot snipe – *chirria*. You dhrive *Jehannum ke marfik, mallum* – like Hell. 'Tis no manner of use *bukkin'* to the *Sahib*, bekaze he doesn't *samajao* your talk. Av he *bolos* anything, just you *choop* and *chel. Dekker?* Go *arsty* for the first *arder* mile from cantonmints. Thin *chel*, *Shaitan ke marfik*, and the *chooper* you *choops* and the *jildier* you *chels* the better *kooshy* will that *Sahib* be; an' here's a rupee for ye!'[44]

Originally written for the delectation of his fellow Anglo-Indians over a hundred and twenty years back in the hey-day of the Empire, this virtuoso passage now may not be readily intelligible to either the British or the (Hindustani-speaking) Indian reader. None of the twenty-seven Indian words printed in italics (by Kipling himself) has passed into common currency in English with the solitary exception of *Sahib*, and only a very few are followed by translation: for example 'snipe – *chirria*,' and '*Jehannum ke marfik* – like Hell'. Even an Indian may not be able readily to identify the Hindustani words, most of which are misspelt or misused in a characteristically Anglo-Indian manner, such as *hekka* (for *ekka*, a one-horse carriage), *jildi* (for *jaldi*, quickly), *marfik* (for *mafik*, like), *bukkin'* (for *bukking*, a hybrid formation for chattering, somewhat ineptly used here), *samjao* (wrongly used for *samjho*, the former meaning to make someone understand and the latter to understand oneself), *choop* (for *chup*, to keep quiet), *chel* (for *chal*, go), *arsty* (for *ahista*, slowly), and *arder* (for *adha*, half) and so on. The splendid climax of the speech, with all its grammatical deviations, may be translated literally into English as follows: 'If he says anything, just you quiet and go. Seen? [i.e. Got it?] Go slowly for the first half mile from cantonments. Then go, like the devil, and the quieter you quiet and the quicker you go, the better happy will that Sahib be'. The crowning phrase here perhaps, for its sheer helpless inventiveness, is 'the *chooper* you *choops*',[45] followed by 'the better *kooshy*' (wrongly used for *khush*, happy, for *khushi* would mean happiness), with the ubiquitous filler *mallum* (Do you understand?) providing another authenticating touch; the British used it whenever they suspected, with good reason, that their gibberish was not making any sense to their Indian interlocutors.

Repeatedly in these early works, Kipling enhanced his comic exploitation of such inadequate Anglo-Hindustani by giving it an ironical narratorial frame. It was spoken not by him as/or an omniscient narrator but instead by an uneducated soldier, almost as comically deviant in his use of English as of Hindustani, in his capacity either as a character in a story in the form of dialogue/monologue or as its framed or embedded participant-narrator. Much of the time, it was these other Anglo-Indians whose Hindustani Kipling was making fun of and not his own, except that he was caught out occasionally erring himself in his non-ironical narratives, as in 'Tods' Amendment'.

The uses of Hindustani: the subliminal and the sublime

In contrast, Kipling's far richer and more resourceful use of Hindustani in *Kim* has been textually analysed and theoretically categorised in widely varying ways, besides those already cited above. In his 'Orality in Kipling's *Kim*', David H. Stewart showcases 'the oral-aural elements' in this text by identifying 'four distinct languages' that in his view Kipling deploys in it. The first is the all-knowing narratorial voice as in 'almond-curd sweetmeats (*balushai* we call it)' – except that, incidentally, that example again suffers from the typical Anglo-Indian lack of aspiration; it should be *balushahi*. The second voice is the British English spoken by Creighton, the two army priests and the drummer-boy, while the third, in contrast with it, is the native English as spoken most notably by Hurree Babu. Stewart's 'fourth language in which over half the book is written', as he claims, is what he calls ' "actual" Urdu, often spoken with an accent' as for example in 'te-rain' or 'tikkut'.[46] But this is specious, for such modified pronunciation of English words is anything but ' "actual" Urdu', and obviously no part of the book is *written* in it. The most that can be claimed in this regard is that, in a large part of the book, a fair proportion of the dialogue that Kipling represents in English is supposed to be conducted in Hindustani.

Some other commentators on Kipling have offered broader theoretical formulations rather than dealing with actual examples of Kipling's use of language. Ian Adam in his essay on the 'Politics of Language Modes in Kim' begins with the sweeping post-modernist dis/avowal: 'Kipling's *Kim* both confirms and disconfirms Derrida's generalisations about Western thought', In Adam's scheme, this is so apparently for the fairly obvious reason that in this novel, the 'oral' is associated with 'the folk of India, the written with the British and their Indian allies, and the transcendent with the lama'.[47] This happens to be a categorisation broadly similar to the more recent one by Ambreen Hai, who (partly following Zohreh Sullivan who is following Lacan) distinguishes between three parts of the novel: Kim's early life of oral speech, his subsequent 'capture' and 'fall into writing', and finally the lama's spiritual 'map-making'[48] – though it seems a little reductive, in what is in other respects a highly sensitive and suggestive textual reading, to describe the lama's allegorical painting as cartography.

Viewed in whichever linguistic perspective, *Kim* is an extraordinary work, and certainly one of the most multi-lingually resonant novels ever written in the English language. It comprises characters who know and speak, to themselves if not also to others, Hindi, Urdu, Hindustani, Panjabi, Tibetan, Chinese, Pushtu and, off stage, presumably also Oriya, Pahari, French and Russian – not to mention several varieties of English, of course! – and yet all the various interlocutors seem to get by with whichever language they may use in any given situation, probably for the overriding reason that all these languages are ultimately subsumed into and rendered in Kipling's

English. It is anyhow a fitting culmination of the long history of Kipling's bilingual acquaintance with an Indian language personally from a tender age and his constant use of it in his works right from the beginning of his career in a whole range of imaginative contexts.

Kipling's competence in Hindustani is no better in *Kim* than in his earlier works and is in fact a little worse for it was a decade since he had left India. However, few editors or critics of Kipling have been so irreverent or churlish as to point out errors in his use of Hindustani; in fact, due perhaps to a lack of editorial confidence in emending even palpable errors of transcription or typing where Indian words are concerned, some glaring errors in the text of this classic had until recently gone uncorrected in edition after edition including the definitive Sussex and Burwash editions. These include 'Padma Samthora', which is an obvious error for 'Padma Sambhava', and the code-word repeatedly used by the agents of the Great Game, 'tarkeean',[49] which should correctly be 'tarkariyan' or at least (as somewhat waywardly spelt by Kipling in the manuscript) 'tarkarean', which is at least broadly intelligible. Both the words as traditionally printed are nonsense, which should have made the errors easier to detect. What is surprising is that Kipling himself, in the thirty-five years that he lived after the publication of *Kim*, should have allowed these errors to persist – if he ever re-read his book and noticed them.

But beyond these little errors, what is of much greater significance is the fact that Kipling set himself some new challenges in his use of language in this masterpiece of his. For one thing, there are no semi-literate British soldiers or haughty officials here merrily mispronouncing even elementary Hindustani words when using them in a bumbling and comically muddled manner. The main British characters, Creighton and Lurgan, are said to speak a superior and more competent form of an Indian language which can properly be called 'Urdu' or 'Hindi' (rather than the demotic Anglo-Hindustani) – and they use it for non-comic purposes, in a variety of normal semantic contexts. For another, Kipling chooses for his hero a boy who is said to have grown up with Hindustani as his first language, with only a rudimentary knowledge of English until the age of thirteen, when the novel begins. This 'not quite not white' boy was, unlike Tods or Adam Strickland, never sent 'home' to England; instead, he has been allowed to run almost completely native.

This was the severest test of his ability to render Hindustani that Kipling ever set himself and his achievement in this regard is therefore correspondingly greater. In representing Kim's speech, even when he is shown to be speaking in English, Kipling does indeed invent a new language which is not only peppered with some Hindustani words but often subliminally suffused and inflected by Urdu and Hindi, so that even when the words are all in English, the syntax, the collocation, and the cadence are unmistakably Indian.[50] This is an aspect of his work that needs detailed textual exposition and analysis in order to bring out the rare quality of his artistic achievement, and it might be illuminated further when compared with the representation of Indian languages by other major British novelists such as E.M. Forster, Edward Thompson and Salman Rushdie.

When Kipling achieved popularity and fame at the age of twenty with his very first (non-juvenile) book *Departmental Ditties* selling out within a month of publication and going into a bigger reprint, he had a shrewd idea of just why it had become an instant success: 'The Indian public like reading about what they know and do themselves.' As he put it to another correspondent: 'The little booklet just hit the taste of the Anglo-Indian public for it told them what they knew.'[51] In terms of his use of Hindustani in this book, which was a vital factor in its success, it seems to have been a case of what oft was said but ne'er so well expressed, for it was the ever so slightly exaggerated accuracy of his representation of Anglo-Indian speech that made the book sound deliciously right.

But in *Kim*, fifteen years later, Kipling produced a work of fiction which lay far beyond the ken of his fellow Anglo-Indians, for he set out to depict in it a world that existed only in his imagination and fantasy, and moreover a work in which he counterpointed the main plot of adventure relating to the Great Game, which could be called Anglo-Indian, with a sub-plot of spiritual pursuit of the sublimest of all states, *nibbana*, which all his readers would have recognised as Oriental (in the pre-Saidian sense). And not the least of the virtues of the novel is the creation of a multi-lingual ambience in which the colonial roles seem to be reversed in more ways than one. Taking the English language to places no Anglo-Indian may have taken it before, the intrepid Hurree Babu congratulates Kim on having acted effectively 'on the instantaneous spur of the moment . . . you take the bally bun, by Jove!', launches into another circumlocutory speech, and then pulls rank as a *sahib* might: 'You are subordinate to me departmentally at present.' Whereupon Kim decides to take him down a peg or two by shifting to native ground: 'Then why talk like an ape in a tree? . . . Talk Hindi and let us get to the yolk of the egg.'[52] It is the turn of the English language now to sound comic through its imitative misuse, and it is a British character who invites an Indian character to speak in an Indian language so that they can proceed without rigmarole or obfuscation to the heart of the matter. *Kim* is not only Kipling's masterpiece; it needs to be appreciated and acclaimed as one of the supreme examples of radical multi-lingual transactions in the whole of English literature.

Notes

1 Kipling, 'Tods' Amendment' (1887), *Plain Tales from the Hills*, ed. Kaori Nagai (London: Penguin Classics, 2011), p. 154; *Kim*, ed. Harish Trivedi (London: Penguin Classics, 2011), p. 222.
2 W. Dillingham, *Being Kipling* (New York: Palgrave Macmillan, 2008), p. 217, n. 5.
3 Ambreen Hai, *Making Words Matter: The Agency of Colonial and Postcolonial Literature* (Athens: Ohio University Press, 2009), p. 78.
4 Kipling, *Kim*, pp. 7, 10.
5 For a wide spectrum of views on these issues, see Amrit Rai, *A House Divided: The Origin and Development of Hindi/Hindavi* (Delhi: Oxford University Press, 1984); Christopher R. King, *One Language, Two Scripts: The Hindi Movement in Nineteenth Century North India* (Bombay: Oxford University Press, 1994); and Harish Trivedi, 'The progress of Hindi II: Hindi and the nation', in Sheldon Pollock (ed.), *Literary Cultures in History: Reconstructions from South Asia* (Berkeley: University of California Press, 2003), pp. 958–1022. For an account specifically of evolving British policy in this regard from 1785 to 1947, see David Lelyveld, 'Colonial Knowledge and Hindustani', *Comparative Studies in Society and History* 35, no. 4 (October 1993), pp. 665–82.
6 Trivedi, 'The progress of Hindi', pp. 979–80.
7 The *Oxford English Dictionary* defines 'Hindustani/Hindoostanee' as 'Of or pertaining to Hindustan (in the stricter sense), or its people or language, esp. the language', which in turn is defined as 'The language of the Muslim conquerors of Hindustan, being a form of Hindi with a large admixture of Arabic, Persian, and other foreign elements; also called *Urdū*.' This is correct in substance but inaccurate historically, for the successive waves of Muslim conquest of India and Muslim dynastic rule with Delhi as the capital had already begun in the late twelfth century, with the conquerors speaking a variety of Central Asian languages including Turkish and Persian, whereas the language recognisible as Urdu arose only in the eighteenth century. As the earliest use of the word, the *Oxford English Dictionary* cites a reference to the 'Grammar and Dictionary of the Hindustanee language, the universal colloquial language throughout India' from 1801, whereas the very titles of at least three publications held by the British Library in London predate this: *Abstracts of the Articles of War in English, Persian and Hindoostanee* published by the East India Company in 1796, and two far more widely circulated and influential works by the pioneering linguist John Gilchrist, *A Grammar of the Hindoostanee Language* (1796) and *The Antijargonist*

or a Short Introduction to the Hindoostanee Language . . . with an Extensive Vocabulary English and Hindoostanee (1800). (*Oxford English Dictionary*, online version, www.oed.com, accessed 20 June 2011.)
8 Kipling, *Something of Myself and Other Autobiographical Writings*, ed. Thomas Pinney (Cambridge: Cambridge University Press, 1990), p. 4.
9 Strickland reassures his wife, 'He'll grow out of it . . . I was sent home at seven, and they flicked it out of me with a wet towel at Harrow'; Kipling, 'The Son of his Father' (1893), reprinted in *Land and Sea Tales for Scouts and Guides* (London: Macmillan, 1923), p. 225.
10 Kipling, *Something of Myself*, p. 25.
11 Kipling, *Something of Myself*, p. 7.
12 Kipling, 'Baa Baa, Black Sheep', *Wee Willie Winkie* (London: Macmillan, 1895), pp. 272–5, 324.
13 Hai, *Making Words Matter*, pp. 32–8.
14 Syed Sajjad Husain, *Kipling and India: An Inquiry into the Nature and Extent of Kipling's Knowledge of the Indian Sub-Continent* ([Dacca,] East Pakistan: The University of Dacca, 1964), p. 138; S.S. Azfar Husain, *The Indianness of Rudyard Kipling: A Study in Stylistics* (London: Cosmic Press, 1983), p. 12.
15 Charles Allen, *Kipling Sahib: India and the Making of Rudyard Kipling* (London: Abacus, 2007), pp. 287–8.
16 Kipling, *Kim*, pp. 7, 35, 62, 190. This underlines the comic ineptness of the note on the 'Punjabi' language in Edward W. Said's edition: 'A softer dialect of Hindustani spoken particularly by Sikhs and hillmen' (*Kim* [London: Penguin Modern Classics, 1987], p. 341, n. 24). Punjabi is not softer than Hindustani, is not a dialect of Hindustani, and is spoken no less by Hindus and Muslims, while most hillmen have their own variety of language. Of all the critics of Kipling, only Shamsul Islam, himself an academic from Lahore, discusses Kipling's use of proverbs from Panjabi, which he with partisan pride describes as 'one of those rare languages in which almost every word is double-edged' (Shamsul Islam, *Kipling's Law: A Study of His Philosophy of Life* [London: Macmillan, 1975], pp. 18–19).
17 Kipling, *Kim*, pp. 17, 106.
18 Kipling, 'Letters of Marque' (1888), Letter IV, *From Sea to Sea*, vol. 1 (London: Macmillan, 1899), p. 25.
19 *Ibid.*, Letter IV, pp. 28, 30, 32; Letter XIX, p. 195; Letter VI, pp. 49, 50; Letter XVI, p. 156; Letter XVII, pp. 171, 174, 176, 180, 182–3; Letter XVIII, p. 186.
20 See the 1888 sketches in the series 'The City of Dreadful Night' and 'The Smith Administration', collected in Kipling, *From Sea to Sea*, vol. 2 (London: Macmillan, 1899), pp. 201–72 and 341–438.
21 Kipling, *Departmental Ditties*, 1st English edition (William Clowes, 1891), pp. 127–8. The glossary is unsigned but probably by Kipling. According to David Richards, some of its definitions are patently copied from Yule's *Hobson-Jobson*, which Kipling had reviewed in 1886 (see n. 23 below), but others which 'do not appear in Yule . . . exhibit a literary imagination' (David A. Richards, *Rudyard*

Kipling: A Bibliography [Newcastle, DE: Oak Knoll Press, 2010], p. 63). It was published separately as *Glossary to Accompany Departmental Ditties as Written by Rudyard Kipling* (New York: M.F. Mansfield and A. Wessels, 1899).

22 Kipling, 'A Cousin's Christmas Card', letter to Margaret and Philip Burne-Jones, *The Letters of Rudyard Kipling, Volume 1: 1872–89*, ed. Thomas Pinney (Basingstoke: Macmillan, 1990), p. 51. Collected in *Early Verse by Rudyard Kipling 1879–1889: Unpublished, Uncollected and Rarely Collected Poems*, ed. Andrew Rutherford (Oxford: Clarendon Press, 1986), pp. 204–5.

23 *Hobson-Jobson: A Glossary of Colloquial Anglo-Indian Words and Phrases, and of Kindred Terms, Etymological, Historical, Geographical and Discursive* (1886), by Col. Henry Yule and A.C. Burnell, was reviewed by Kipling in the *Civil and Military Gazette* (19 April 1886). He praised its 'eight hundred closely packed pages' as 'a glorified *olla podrida* [i.e. rich stew] of fact, fancy, note, sub-note, reference, cross-reference, and quotations innumerable', which will surely 'take its place among the standard works on the East' (Kipling: untitled review in *Kipling's India: Uncollected Sketches 1884–88*, ed. Thomas Pinney [London: Macmillan, 1986], pp. 158–60).

24 Kipling, *Kim*, pp. 7, 13, 17, 333–6.

25 Waldemar Leeb-Lundberg, *Word-Formation in Kipling: A Stylistic-Philological Study* (Lund: H. Ohlsson, 1909), p. 16.

26 Anonymous, 'Glossary of Hindustani words to be found in Rudyard Kipling's works', *Kipling Journal* 3 (1927), p. 29; Lt Gen. Sir George MacMunn, 'Kipling's Hindustani,' *Kipling Journal* 57 (1941), p. 6; Shamsul Islam, 'Kipling's use of Indo-Pakistani languages', *Kipling Journal* 171 (1969), pp. 15–19.

27 S.S.A. Husain, *The Indianness of Rudyard Kipling*, pp. 62, 17.

28 George Webb, untitled review of *The Indianness of Rudyard Kipling* by S.S. Azfar Husain, *Journal of the Royal Asiatic Society of Great Britain and Ireland* 1 (1987), pp. 146–8. (Webb's review copy, with several marginal comments, is now part of the Kipling Society Library at the City University, London.) See also Christopher Shackle, untitled review of Husain's *Indianness of Rudyard Kipling*, *Bulletin of the School of Oriental and African Studies* 48, no. 2 (1987), p. 386.

29 In contrast, perhaps the shortest such list is 'A Glossary for Kipling's *Kim*', comprising fourteen items, which the historian Eleanor Zelliot states she hands out to her students (Eleanor Zelliot, 'The dangers and pleasures of teaching Orientalist classic books: Kipling's *Kim* in the classroom', *ASIANetwork Exchange* (Fall 2000), pp. 24–5; I am grateful to John Walker for bringing this publication to my attention). While Zelliot is correct to point out that the Grand Trunk Road does not run to Bombay as shown in the maps provided in several editions of *Kim*, she makes errors of her own in stating that 'the Kyber [sc. Khyber] Pass runs from Peshawar on the Frontier to Kabul in Afghanistan', that 'bhang' is 'used in some rituals', and that 'being a merchant is about the only profession permitted' to a Jain (p. 25).

30 Jan Montefiore, *Rudyard Kipling* (Tavistock: Northcote House, 2007), pp. 32, 37, 34, 33.

31 Bernard S. Cohn, 'The command of language and the language of command', in his *Colonialism and its Forms of Knowledge: The British in India* (Princeton, NJ: Princeton University Press, 1996), p. 16.
32 Montefiore, *Rudyard Kipling*, pp. 35, 37, 36, 40, 41, 37, 46.
33 Gayatri Chakravorty Spivak, *Critique of Postcolonial Reason* (Cambridge, MA: Harvard University Press, 1999), p. 161. This summary judgement would have been even more damning had Spivak delivered it not as an *obiter dictum* but with some supporting evidence, and if she had not used the old Orientalist spelling of Hindustani, which is not her first Indian language. (This is, as Hurree Babu's and Grish Chunder De's was, Bengali.)
34 See my essay 'Reading Kipling in India', in Howard J. Booth (ed.), *The Cambridge Companion to Rudyard Kipling* (Cambridge: Cambridge University Press, 2011), pp. 187–99, in which I also look at Gandhi's response to Kipling and the comparisons made between Kipling and the Indian novelist R.K. Narayan.
35 Jawaharlal Nehru, *An Autobiography, with Musings on Recent Events in India* (1936; London: Bodley Head, 1989), p. 452.
36 S.S. Husain, *Kipling and India*, pp. 112, 156.
37 Salman Rushdie, 'Kipling', *Imaginary Homelands* (London: Granta, 1991), pp. 74–83, p. 77. This short essay, first published in 1990, has gone largely unnoticed in Kipling criticism and needs to be discussed in greater detail, especially in view of Rushdie's comparable use of Hindustani in his own fiction. (Rushdie himself was sent to school at Rugby when he was 13, later studied at Cambridge, and has thereafter never lived in India except for short visits.)
38 Kipling, 'For to Admire', *The Complete Barrack-Room Ballads of Rudyard Kipling* [1894], ed. Charles Carrington (London: Methuen, 1974), pp. 107–8; reprinted in *Works of Rudyard Kipling* (Ware: Wordsworth, 1994), p. 457. Kipling's own gloss to *Hum deckty hai* is 'I'm looking out', *Works*, p. 108.
39 Kipling, 'Tods' Amendment', *Plain Tales*, p. 154.
40 Kipling, *Kim*, pp. 15 (Kim ms. fol. 8), 61, 345.
41 Brian Friel, *Translations* in *Selected Plays* (London: Faber & Faber, 1984), pp. 409–10.
42 Franz Boas, 'On Alternating Sounds' [1889], in *A Franz Boas Reader: The Shaping of American Anthropology 1883–1911*, ed. George W. Stockling Jr (Chicago: University of Chicago Press, 1987), p. 73.
43 Kipling, 'The God from the Machine', *Soldiers Three and Other Stories* (London: Macmillan, 1895), p. 12. The same Anglo-Hindustani word 'Hitherao' is used by the soldier-speaker of 'Gunga Din' (Kipling, *Works*, p. 406).
44 Kipling, 'The Three Musketeers', *Plain Tales*, p. 58.
45 After pointing out some errors made by Husain in *The Indianness of Rudyard Kipling*, Shackle concludes his review with a withering use of this phrase: 'A case, perhaps, of "the chooper you choops..."' (meaning that the less Husain had said about these matters the better it would have been), p. 386.
46 David H. Stewart, 'Orality in Kipling's *Kim*', *The Journal of Narrative Technique* 13, no. 1 (Winter 1983), pp. 48, 52.

47 Ian Adam, 'Oral/literal/transcendent: the politics of language modes in *Kim*', *The Yearbook of English Studies* 27 (1997), p. 69.
48 Hai, *Making Words Matter*, pp. 73, 80.
49 See Kipling, *Kim* (London: Macmillan, 1901), pp. 17 ('Padma Samthora') and 261–2, 284 ('tarkeean'). These errors have been corrected in the 2011 Penguin Classics edition (p. 15, 'Padma Sambhava') and 185–6, 201 ('tarkarean').
50 For examples of Kipling's Hindustani usage in *Kim*, see notes to the text in the 2011 Penguin edition, pp. 332–77.
51 Kipling, letters to W.C. Crofts and Edith MacDonald, *Letters, Volume 1*, pp. 138, 139.
52 Kipling, *Kim*, p. 222.

13

Quotations and boundaries: *Stalky & Co.*

KAORI NAGAI

You ought always to verify your quotations.¹

In 'Slaves of the Lamp, Part II', the last story of *Stalky & Co.*, Stalky, aka Arthur Lionel Corkran, enters the stage as a cross-cultural agent, reminiscent of Kim, the hybrid boy *par excellence*. Now in India as an imperial officer, he commands the full confidence of his Sikh soldiers, who call him Koran Sahib and take him to be 'an invulnerable *Guru* of sorts'.² He speaks their language and acts as one of them, even taking them to pray at the Golden Temple at Amritzar, 'regularly as clockwork, when he can'. As his friend Tertius puts it, 'Stalky *is* a Sikh'. Stalky is also a favourite of the Pathan soldiers, who swear that he 'ought to have been born a Pathan'. When one of his Sikh soldiers starts a row with a Pathan, with his sword half drawn, Stalky intervenes by '[jabbering] Pushtu and Punjabi in alternate streaks', making puns in each language, and even quoting 'some woman's proverb or other, that [has] the effect of doublin' both men up with a grin'.³ His knowledge of native languages and customs is not limited to those of his allies. When Stalky and his men are besieged by two Afghan tribes, the Malôts and the Khye-Kheens, he successfully sets them against each other, acting on the knowledge that they are ancestral foes and do not trust each other. Stalky, an incomparable hero of the United Services College (USC), grows up to be 'a friend of all the world', who knows, and is befriended by, many different tribes in India.

Don Randall, in his *Kipling's Imperial Boy: Adolescence and Cultural Hybridity* (2000), famously characterises Kipling's adolescent heroes – Kim, Stalky and

Mowgli – as hybrid figures. Being in the 'in-between' period of transition from childhood to adulthood, these adolescent boys represent 'a liminal subjectivity situated on the in-betweens of cultures and cultural identities',[4] and therefore make ideal imperial agents who freely traverse cultural borders and negotiate cultural differences in the contact zones. These liminal figures of adolescence, Randall argues, should be read as hybrids, being 'marked by the trace of the colonial other'. The imperial boy thus emerges as an 'ambivalent' figure, constituting at once 'a site for the deployment of imperial power' and 'a potential site of resistance' against British imperialism.[5] In many ways, this reading is echoed by John McBratney's slightly later *Imperial Subjects, Imperial Space* (2002), which discusses Kipling's representation of the 'native-born' – a European born and raised in a colonial space – as the figure of cultural hybridity. Being 'racially "white" but culturally mixed',[6] the native-born with his 'dual cultural affiliations' makes 'the most resourceful, knowledgeable, and effective of imperial servants', while his hybrid identity opens up a 'felicitous space', in which the white boy can enjoy camaraderie with native people, free from racial differences and hierarchies.[7]

Randall convincingly argues that Stalky in India, though he is fully grown-up, should be seen as an 'adolescent' hero: his early training as a young boy in the USC remains with him and keeps him in touch with a 'textual process that writes the signs of colonial subjectivity upon the British schoolboy', and which 'registers – even as it disavows – the agency of the cultural other in the production of the hybridized imperial subject'. Randall thereby draws attention to the ways in which England and its colonial peripheries are 'intimately interconnected' and share the process of transculturation in the age of imperial globalisation. I would like to question, however, his key premise that intercultural encounters, through the liminal figure of the adolescent boy, inevitably result in textual hybridity, which secretly undermines the workings of the Empire by writing the signs of the Other on the coloniser's identity. For instance, Randall proposes the fact that Stalky is accepted as a member of the Sikh community as proof that 'Sikh culture has, at least partially, written itself upon Stalky'.[8] However, he does not take into account the fact that Sikhism is not the only culture which leaves its mark on him and claims his cultural affiliation. Despite Tertius' remark that 'Stalky *is* a Sikh', Pathans likewise consider Stalky as theirs, and nearly start a row when a Sikh officer asserts that 'Stalky [is] a Sikh'.[9] Significantly, Stalky's friendship with Sikhs, as I have shown in the opening paragraph of this article, does not oblige him to take their side; whenever Sikhs and Pathans start quarrelling, he chooses to pacify both parties by speaking in both languages. Stalky *might be* a Sikh, but is nevertheless free from the inter-tribal rivalry and enmity which indelibly marks native bodies with ethnic identities.

There is no denying the fact that the imperial boys, acting as mediators in the cross-cultural contact zone, can be read as 'hybrids', but it is necessary to take into account the ways in which Western hegemony and issues of race affect and shape their processes of acculturation. For instance, neither Randall nor McBratney accommodates differences between Kim's 'hybridity' and that of Hurree Babu – both are, in their framework, equally subversive due to their in-betweenness – despite the fact that it is Hurree, *not* Kim, who is explicitly named as hybrid in the text.[10] It is true that the various effects of intercultural encounter can all be described as 'hybridisation', but the ways in which East and West met to inscribe each other were – and still are – by no means symmetrical. While the colonised seek to become 'white' by erasing their outward signs as natives, such as accents and mannerisms, the coloniser, as he learns the syntax of the East, is not allowed to lose his markers as white, however partially, if he wishes to maintain his privileges as the White Man.

The coloniser did not merely submit himself, passively and unknowingly, to a 'textual process that writes the signs of colonial subjectivity'. Rather, he strategically sought to utilise, and counter the threat of, cultural inscriptions of his others. I propose to characterise the coloniser's encounter with non-Western cultures not as hybridisation, but as 'quotation' – the sampling of other cultures, while interdicting the effects of cultural hybridity. For instance, the Great Exhibition of 1851 was a symbol of imperial prosperity, in which countless samples 'quoted' from various cultures were displayed side by side, without intermingling with each other.

Quotation marks introduce different contexts into the main narrative, while clearly indicating the borders between them. In the same way, as Benton and Muth suggest, the 'cultural hybrid', which threatens the coloniser's absolute superiority, is always represented alongside the latter's desire to re-establish the essential border.[11] Another important aspect of quotations is the need to verify them and trace them to their sources. To recognise the colonised as 'hybrid' is then to know and identify the 'original' types of the native, uncontaminated by the effects of Westernisation, thus strengthening cultural dualism. It seems that Kipling's imperial boys are intended to be not 'hybrids', but masters of quotations, who are quick to identify cultural hybrids and safeguard the colonial borders. Interestingly, the Russian spy in *Kim*, after portraying Hurree as 'the monstrous hybridism of East and West', goes on to add 'It is *we* who can deal with Orientals':[12] the success of the Raj depends upon an ability to control the hybridity between East and West.

In *Stalky and Co.*, books and school lessons, 'odds and ends of speech – theatre, opera, and music-hall gags – from the great holiday world',[13] souvenirs and the first-hand account of travel by a naval uncle freshly back from Africa, various quotations from various sources constitute a medley of texts, from which the boys freely quote. The book delineates how the imperial boys, through the play of quotations, learn to perform scripts and to improvise roles and strategies. They transgress the school borders with books in their hands, and declare war against teachers and local inhabitants. Their acquired ability to quote from others' discourses will prove handy in their future dealings with the colonised, as when Stalky, by quoting some woman's proverb, prevents a row between Pathans and Sikhs. More importantly, quotations, which capture in a short phrase the essence of a nation – its historical and cultural contexts, its syntax of life and values – act as a kind of fetish which fixes the Other as a stereotype and contains the anxiety of hybridisation. In this context, it is important that *Stalky & Co.* is framed by, and palimpsested with, the *Arabian Nights*. The references to the *Nights* not only transform the school into the world of Aladdin, the Chinese Emperor, and the Slaves of the Lamp, and thereby into a training ground for colonial rule in the East, but also present the story as a fantasy in which quotations will work as magic words, with which the coloniser instantly establishes a master–slave relationship with the Oriental spirits.

Quotation and border crossing

'Slaves of the Lamp', Parts I and II, are the first two stories which Kipling wrote for the series (April–May 1897). Part I tells an episode from Stalky and Co.'s schooldays, and Part II is set years after their graduation from the USC, when the former students reunite at an old schoolmate's country estate, where they reminisce about the past and exchange news of Stalky's adventures in India. 'Slaves of the Lamp', which sets out to show the correspondence between the boys' schooldays and their future careers, provides the frame narrative of *Stalky & Co.*, to which Kipling thereafter added more stories. The first edition of *Stalky & Co.*, comprising nine stories, was published in 1899, and the final and extended edition with fourteen stories in total was published thirty years later under the title of *The Complete Stalky & Co.* (1929).

Stalky & Co. is the text of Kipling's which features the largest number of quotations. This is in large part due to the fact that Beetle, who is revealed at the end of the book to have been the story's narrator, is the fictionalisation of the author himself. What is recollected is the author's own 'vast and omnivorous'[14] reading experience. According to Beetle's comrade M'Turk, aka George Charles Beresford, the young Kipling's 'constant preoccupation was none the less books – "Books, books, books, books moving up and down again" – that is, down from a library's shelves and up again when read'.[15] In *Stalky & Co.*, the details of school life – mischief and adventures, exchanges with teachers, 'lickings' and bullying – are recalled with quotations from books, or as quotations themselves. Stalky & Co. – the three boy protagonists – spend most of their free time reading. Beetle is an admirer of Robert Browning, and M'Turk a disciple of Ruskin, and even Stalky, who, unlike the other two, does not appreciate high literature, raises battle-cries as he quotes from R.S. Surtees. Some books become the trio's guidebooks for action. For instance, when the students of the neighbouring House, orchestrated by its House-master King, start bullying Stalky & Co. and their housemates, saying that they do not wash and therefore stink, the former, inspired by Beetle's reading of Eugène Viollet-le-Duc's book on architecture, *Histoire d'une maison*, retaliate by putting a dead and stinking cat in the ceiling of King's House. Francis Galton's *The Art of Travel* is an inspiration behind their successful licking of two bullying senior boys, during which Stalky repeatedly and gleefully quotes from Galton – 'the bleatin' of the kid excites the tiger' – to terrorise his victims.[16] Margaret Oliphant's novel *A Beleaguered City* is also consulted to torment their House-master who has unjustly ordered the trio out of their study-room. They are firmly united in their low opinion of F.W. Farrar's bestsellers, *Eric, or Little by Little* and *St Winifred's, or The World of School*, famous for their priggish portrayal of school life, but they nevertheless have fun quoting from, and castigating, the books, when Stalky's aunt sends him both as birthday presents and the trio fail to sell them in town. The interweaving of texts and school life can most clearly be seen in 'The United Idolaters', in which Joel Chandler Harris's book *Uncle Remus*, which is 'full of quotations that one could hurl like javelins', is manically adopted by the boys as a model for their conversational style throughout the term. Such an outbreak of enthusiasm over a new and fashionable text is not an unusual occurrence in the USC, for, as the narrator informs us, Gilbert and Sullivan's operas *H.M.S. Pinafore* and *Patience*, likewise, had 'severely infected' the boys previously.[17]

That the boys' play of quotations is an important part of their colonial education can be seen in the fact that Stalky & Co. and their friends take pleasure in acting as primitive savages or racial others by adopting their supposed modes of speech. 'Where do they pick up these obscene noises?' complains King in '"In Ambush"', when he hears the boys gloating, in the manner of 'the primitive man's song of triumph', '[whirling] like a dancing dervish'. In 'The Satisfaction of a Gentleman', Dick Four, in his war against Stalky & Co, becomes the King of Ashantee and, with 'whistlings and quackings', speaks in Fantee phrases, learnt from his naval uncle who fought in the Ashantee War. Also in 'Slaves of the Lamp I', the boys play 'a small wooden West-African war-drum' to declare war against King; its 'devastating drone' transports the school into West Africa, the scene of ancient blood sacrifice, where 'the blare of... savage pursuing trumpets' is heard and 'the roar broke into short coughing howls such as the wounded gorilla throws in his native forest'.[18] The boys become natives or even animals so wholeheartedly that they appear, to the eyes of inexperienced onlookers, to show signs of monstrous hybridity. For instance, the boys' enthusiastic reception of *Uncle Remus*, a book about 'rabbits and foxes and turtles and niggers', horrifies a replacement teacher, who comes to believe that the boys are degenerating into what he calls 'the Animal Boy'.[19] Of course, the experienced USC teachers do not see any danger in the boys' quoting frenzy, and some even encourage it by quoting from the book themselves.

In *Stalky & Co.*, quoting and border-crossing go hand in hand. The boys transgress the school's bounds in search of quiet hide-outs in which to read books, and quotations from the books they read always hold the key to the success of their transgression. Conversely, their failed attempts to cross forbidden borders are punishable by 'lines' – the copying out of yet more quotations. In 'The Propagation of Knowledge', we learn that it is Beetle's 'custom of rainy afternoons to fabricate store of lines', which he can readily submit when the next punishment falls upon him: 'They covered such English verse as interested him at the moment and helped to fix the stuff in his memory'.[20]

The connection between quoting and border-crossing is well demonstrated in the opening story of the 1899 edition of *Stalky & Co.*, '"In Ambush"'. The boys 'ambush' their teachers, who are desperate to catch them red-handed, outside the bounds, and successfully trick them into the estate of the local landlord, in whose eyes and law the teachers turn into mere trespassers. Importantly, the title '"In Ambush"' is placed in inverted commas, as if it is itself a quotation. According to Ken Frazer, this is because the story is not about 'a real ambush involving real soldiers and real enemies', being merely 'a schoolboy prank'.[21] If this reading is correct, the quotation marks here indicate the co-existence of different contexts and space-times – past and future, school and frontiers, adulthood and childhood, the coloniser and native tribes – which overlap each other in the story. As Isabel Quigly argues, *Stalky & Co.* is 'the only school story which shows school as a *direct* preparation for life . . . as the first stage of a much larger game': 'the divisions between school and the world outside are less clearly defined than they are in most other school stories'.[22] Quotation marks point to these porous but still markedly drawn divisions, while keeping the reality of war in brackets, leaving the boys' world intact.

Moreover, the title ' "In Ambush" ' visibly demonstrates the story's theme – the border and its transgression – with its quotation marks signalling the moment of a cross-cultural encounter when an alien text invades the original narrative. Colonel Dabney, the local landlord, is made to play the role of a native tribe in the trio's mock battle, and firmly guards the border of his estate with notice boards, which read: 'Prosecuted with the utmost rigour of the Law'.[23] Stalky & Co. nonetheless trespass on his land, and nearly get killed by the keeper who fires barrels in their direction to shoot a fox. This apparent defeat unexpectedly turns into a golden opportunity to be given free access to the Colonel's estate, when M'Turk, enraged by the killing of foxes, goes straight to the Colonel to report the incident and consequently wins his trust. The key to M'Turk's success is his knowledge of the Colonel's 'tribal' language: he speaks to him, 'quoting confusedly from his father',[24] who is also a landlord in Ireland, and in the Irish brogue. As D.H. Stewart points out, M'Turk's choice of speech is 'class-specific':[25] by imitating his father and using his language, he speaks to the Colonel as a fellow landlord. Moreover, his Irish brogue – *his* tribal tongue, which Stalky and Beetle would not allow him to speak in the English school – works as a secret password to forge a connection with the Colonel, who turns out to be of Irish origin himself. Stalky, in turn, successfully befriends the Colonel's Lodge-keeper and his wife, using 'the broad Devon, which [is his] *langue de guerre*'. To speak in the Other's language is crucial to secure help from the local tribes and facilitate further operations. In contrast, the teachers, who do not have the same skill, are caught and reprimanded by the Colonel, and are chased away, utterly humiliated.

' "In Ambush" ' ends with the caning of the boys by the Head – the guarantor of school life and the whole system called imperialism – for their perfect outwitting of the teachers in the border war. Immediately after the punishment, the Head says:

> When you find a variation from the normal – this will be useful to you in later life – always meet him in an abnormal way. And that reminds me. There are a pile of paper-backs on that shelf. You can borrow them if you put them back. I don't think they'll take any harm from being read in the open.[26]

'When you find a variation from the normal ... always meet him in an abnormal way' – this maxim, taken together with the Head's reference to his paper-back collection, sounds like a quotation from a book. The Head here is demonstrating his skill in quoting to make aphorisms or maxims: an ability to improvise memorable phrases which encapsulate a general law or principle, out of his memories, past readings or experience, in order to meet unusual situations and impose himself upon them as the master of quotations. In any case, the moral is duly inscribed on the boys' bodies with the help of the cane, and the offer of free access to his library prompts the trio's further border-crossing, to read in their hide-outs.

It should also be noted that, by describing the boys' act of transgression as 'a variation from the normal', the Head cannily restores and consolidates 'the normal', namely the discipline of the USC: '[f]or there to be a transgression, the norm must be apparent',[27] as Todorov puts it in terms of literary genre. His language has a strong bearing on the contemporaneous racial discourses: a norm-deviation model of race sought to establish 'an absolute difference between the races', 'with the whites providing the norm from which all others were regarded as deviations'.[28] Moreover, the Head here urges boys to meet a deviation from the norm – in *our* language, 'hybridity' – 'in an abnormal way' – that is, in an equally or surpassingly 'hybrid' manner. According to Benton and Muth, the excellent performance of a 'cultural hybrid' is often represented as 'crafty'[29] – Bhabha also uses the adjective 'sly' to describe it[30] – and this curiously corresponds with the fact that Corkran's nickname 'Stalky' comes from the school vocabulary, which means 'clever, well-considered and wily'.[31] Stalky's wiliness is indispensable in dealing with, and outwitting, crafty hybrids. Stalky thus has much in common with Strickland, whose 'business in life is to overmatch [the natives] with their own weapons'.[32] And it needs plenty of 'stalkiness' to excel in the art of quoting.

The play of quotations not only prepares the boys for future cross-cultural encounters. It also creates for them secret passwords, with which they can identify and communicate with each other out in the colonies. If text is, by definition, 'a tissue of quotations drawn from the innumerable centres of culture'[33] and, after all, there is no single text which properly belongs to the coloniser, the school life, through shared education and reading experience, weaves a tissue of quotations which outsiders cannot recognise.

In 'Slaves of the Lamp', Parts I and II, we already see this privileged text emerging as the school production of *Aladdin*. In Part I, Stalky and his friends enter the scene as part of the 'Aladdin company at rehearsal'. They are performing H.J. Byron's pantomime 'Aladdin, or the Wonderful Scamp', but Byron's text, 'rewritten and filled with local allusions' and supplemented with recent music-hall tunes, is transformed into an original text, which the boys can claim as their own.[34] The school pantomime emerges as another space in which boys learn to act as 'the Other' by cross-dressing with quotes. It is interesting that the boys choose 'Arrah, Patsy, Mind the Baby' – a rewriting of a popular music-hall song by G.W. Moore, 'Patrick Mind the Baby' (1877) – as their theme-tune, marked with clear Irish ('Arrah', 'Patsy', 'ye') and feminine ('Mind the Baby') registers; this humorously introduces the subversive space of 'the Other' into the boys' school life.[35] In Part I, they are still in rehearsal, but the real performance suddenly starts in Part II, without any preliminary notice, on a battlefield in India. Stalky raises the curtain, when his former schoolmates, Dick Four and Tertius, unexpectedly stray into his fort, which is under siege by two hostile tribes, the Malôts and the Khye-Kheens. He promptly addresses them by their stage names: 'Hullo, Aladdin! Hullo, Emperor! . . . You're just in time for the performance'.[36] Even during the battle, Stalky sends signals to them by playing a tune from their version of *Aladdin*. The frequent references to Aladdin in Part II clearly indicate that Stalky's prime loyalty does not rest with his Sikh men, with whom he shares his fate, but with his school friends and fellow colonisers, with whom he shares this secret text. Later in the story, the quotation from *Aladdin* is used again by Stalky to seek help from his trusted friends in India: a native soldier, instructed to play the tune from *Aladdin*, turned out to be a messenger from Stalky, with a special request to Tertius and Dick Four to take care of new recruits. Through the texts they shared in boyhood, the game of quotations is being carried on in the colonies. Occasional exchanges of quotations from their shared cultural texts would prevent them from being hybridised by local contexts, and, moreover, guarantee them the continuation of the Game. In 'Slaves of the Lamp, Part II', the details of Stalky's heroic exploits are pieced together by the former members of the Aladdin Company, who have recently come back from India and are enjoying a get-together in

England. Their conversation, however, is frequently interrupted whenever *Aladdin* is mentioned, for they start singing tunes together – as if to ascertain whether the tunes in their memories are still true to the original.

It is symbolic that, in *Stalky & Co.*, quotations are staged in the theatrical space of the *Aladdin* play. Just like the stage costumes, the other's culture, adopted as quotations, can be easily changed. What has to be absolutely avoided is to be indelibly inscribed with the sign of the Other, for this would mean that the coloniser becomes hybridised and therefore loses his privilege. In 'Slaves of the Lamp, Part II', the failed cultural encounter for the coloniser is presented as a corpse: the body of Stalky's lieutenant, Everett, who is killed by the Malôts:

> Everett's body [was] lyin' in a foot o' drifted snow. It looked like a girl of fifteen – not a hair on the little fellow's face. He'd been shot through the temple, but the Malôts had left their mark on him. Stalky unbuttoned the tunic, and showed it to us – a rummy sickle-shaped cut on the chest. 'Member the snow all white on his eyebrows, Tertius? 'Member when Stalky moved the lamp and it looked as if he was alive?'

The body of Everett, who looks like 'a girl of fifteen', might remind us of the theme of homosexuality, so often associated with school stories. However, the more interesting point here is the fact that this body is presented as the corpse of a girl, rather than that of a boy – presenting a white, passive and 'feminine' surface, ready to be inscribed, and on which the Malôts leave their mark. The death of Everett presents the worst possible scenario in the coloniser's cross-cultural contact: when East and West meet, the beaten-down body of the West is violated by the sign of the East and turned into a grotesque hybrid. In such an encounter, the White Man is deprived of his privilege to disseminate his own sign. It is then no wonder that Stalky 'held a council of war up there over Everett's body',[37] which represents a violated and blurred border between East and West.

Stalky instantly 'quotes' the Malôt's mark left on Everett's body. He inscribes the corpse of a Khye-Kheen soldier with the same mark, and leaves it in a passage between the two tribes, thereby successfully breaking the truce barely maintained between these two ancestral foes. Stalky's friends immediately recognise that this is an improvised quotation from the scenario which he played as a boy in Part I, in which he cunningly set a local carter, 'Rabbits-Eggs', against King the house-master. Quoting from the original text woven in his boyhood in England allows him not only to counter-attack against the 'native' enemy, but also to reverse the effects of colonial hybridisation.

If modernist texts, by consciously losing quotation marks, blur the borders between texts and contexts, imperialism attempts to display an infinite inter-relation of quotations without losing the borders between them. The White Man emerges there as the master of quotations, and turns cultural and racial others into exotic and manipulable texts, trapped inside inverted commas. The politics of quotation is precisely that of the British Empire, which encouraged citation from, and appropriation of, other cultures, while strictly interdicting hybridisation. Furthermore, the play of quotations centres on the unique and privileged texts created 'at Home'. In *Stalky & Co.*, the 'Aladdin' text shared in the boys' schooldays becomes the norm, or even 'canonical', set in stone and endowed with authority; this provides protection from the endless proliferation of different voices which they expose themselves to and guards them from cultural hybridisation. The politics of quotation, then, necessarily entails the question of the archive, where such a text is safely stored.

The law of the USC: the commencement and the commandment

In 'Slaves of the Lamp, Part II', it is revealed that Beetle, who is now a writer, is the author of the stories collected in *Stalky & Co.*, and the story ends with his startling assertion that he is 'responsible for the whole thing',[38] including the colonial adventures of Stalky and other imperial agents. This remarkable ending adds to the structure of doubling in the book (childhood and adulthood, school and colonial battlegrounds, etc.) by splitting the figure of Beetle into a chronicler and his character. More importantly, Beetle the narrator *almost* supersedes the authority of 'the Head', who is supposed to be responsible for everything in the world of *Stalky & Co.*

The character of the headmaster Bates is based on Cormell Price (1835–1910), who was the headmaster of the USC when Kipling was a student, and the book was dedicated to him (*Stalky & Co.*, 1899), and later to his memory (*The Complete Stalky & Co.*, 1929). As a contemporaneous review puts it, '[r]everence for the head authority and contempt for all other authority' are underlying themes of the book, and the Head's 'penetrating influence throughout the school is most subtly indicated in every story'.[39] According to Steven Marcus, the Head represents 'an authority which can be believed in and trusted': 'he is a court of appeal to which one resorts with faith, and a source of justice whose verdicts one accepts with trust'.[40] Conversely, John Kucich, who explores forms of sadomasochism in British imperialism and rejects Marcus' sympathetic portrayal of the headmaster, argues that the Head's authority derives from his 'unjustness' or his 'boundless power to punish':[41] he embodies the abusive power, whose caning or 'execution' the boys willingly subject themselves to, thereby vicariously identifying themselves with his omnipotence. Nonetheless, Marcus and Kucich agree that the Head embodies the law to be obeyed, according to which the affairs of the USC, and of the Empire, are conducted.

I admire Kucich's reading which, by foregrounding recurring scenes of bullying and corporal punishment, draws attention to the brutal nature and ideological implications of imperial fantasy. However, it does not really do justice to the function of the USC as a house of learning, or explain why, for instance, the school chaplain, who never canes Stalky & Co., can command their full affection and trust. It seems to me that the Head's authority primarily comes from the fact that he knows and sees through everything, and his omniscience is best embodied, especially to Beetle's eyes, in his large and exquisite library. To be summoned to his office to be caned is to have a glimpse of his collection, and to have access to his books and, through them, to his power: in ' "In Ambush" ', Beetle, in the middle of receiving his punishment, is eyeing a copy of *Monte Cristo* on the lower shelf. Eventually, the Head gives Beetle 'the run of his brown-bound, tobacco-scented library', when he becomes the editor of the college paper. Beetle settles himself there in 'a fat armchair' and immerses himself in good literature, while the Head 'drifting in under pretence of playing censor to the paper, would read here a verse and here another of these poets; opening up avenues'.[42] If Beetle indeed partakes of the Head's authority to be 'responsible for the whole thing', he does so not by superseding him, but by having access to his library.

I suggest that the USC represents an imperial archive, of which Beetle becomes a 'librarian' and later a chronicler. This is somewhat different from what Thomas Richards, in his reading of *Kim*, calls 'the Imperial Archive' – the imperialist fantasy of ruling the Empire, by knowing, accumulating and controlling information[43] – although *Stalky & Co.* undoubtedly subscribes to such a fantasy. Stalky comments after the Khye-Kheen–Malôt expedition that Everett's grave, now marked with a forty-foot mound, 'should serve well as a base for future triangulations':[44] just like Kim the chain-man, Stalky contributes to the workings of the Indian Survey, which seeks to rule India by measuring it and turning it into a mass of information to be learned. Stalky's remarkable knowledge of various native cultures and languages is also part of this fantasy. In contrast, the archive entrusted to the narrator is a relatively limited one, confined to the Head's library and to the texts from his boyhood memories at the USC. Given that, as Jacques Derrida notes, 'archive' comes from the word *Arkhē*, which 'names at once the *commencement* and the *commandment*',[45] the USC is an archive in this double sense: the very place in which the boys' colonial adventures started and where the Head's unquestionable authority serves as the inviolable Law of the Empire. The Head embodies 'a guardian and a localization', both of which, according to Derrida, an archive needs to exist:

> the meaning of 'archive', its only meaning, comes to it from the Greek *arkheion*: initially a house, a domicile, an address, the residence of the super magistrates, the *archons*, those who commanded . . . The archons are first of all the documents' guardians. They do not only ensure the physical security of what is deposited and of the substrate. They are also accorded the hermeneutic right and competence. They have the power to interpret the archives. Entrusted to such archons, these documents in effect speak the law: they recall the law and call on or impose the law.[46]

The Head is the guardian of the memories of schooldays, whose authority and judgement the boys will always turn to for guidance, and his presence makes the USC the sacrosanct archive. This may explain why they detest so much the idea of having married House-masters (luckily for them, the USC has none), who would 'let their Houses alone'[47] to stay at their family homes. The houses multiplied by marriage beyond the school boundary would seriously undermine the Head's authority, which represents the oneness of the USC and of its law. Beetle, by turning into the third-person narrator, becomes part of the Head's archive as its chronicler, and is endowed with the same 'hermeneutic right and competence'. His first-hand knowledge of Stalky's incredible adventures gives his narrative a great deal of authenticity, even when he reports the teachers' conversations which he could not have heard himself. Yet his role is very different from that of the archon. Unlike the Head, who is tied to the USC, and therefore represents the boys' childhood, their past, Beetle, as a student, eventually has to leave the school, thereby representing their movement towards the future. As Derrida puts it, the question of the archive is *never* 'a question of the past', but of the future: 'the question of the future itself, the question of a response, of a promise and of a responsibility for tomorrow'.[48] By weaving stories out of the past to show how it became the solid foundation of future events, the narrator opens up the archive to its outside. This is beautifully encapsulated in a passage from the untitled poem which serves as an epigraph to *Stalky & Co.*:

> Wherefore praise we famous men
> From whose bays we borrow –
> They that put aside To-day –
> All the joys of their To-day –
> And with toil of their To-day
> Bought for us To-morrow![49]

As if to correspond with this opening poem, 'Slaves of the Lamp, Part II' ends with the narrator's boastful speech on the bright future of the Empire and his drawing attention to his own role as a writer in making such a vision possible: he makes himself answerable to the imperial archive, by taking up 'the question of a response, of a promise and of a responsibility for tomorrow', thereby becoming '*responsible* for the whole thing'.

The question of quotations is closely related to that of the archive, not only in that a quotation would not be possible without some kind of archive, but also in that it assumes authority by pointing to the location of its archive of origin. In order to sustain close correlations between childhood and adulthood, and thereby ensure the integrity and meaning of the imperial mission, the narrator constantly has to refer his friends' colonial adventures back to the USC, and ultimately to the Head's authority. Conversely, the authority and authenticity of a quotation come from its traceability to a source. As a chronicler of the imperial archive, Kipling's narrator has to be particularly attentive to his 'quotations': without his knowingness and vigilance, the myriad of voices from other cultures and contexts, which he famously captures in his text, would soon merge together to signify hybridity. Kipling's texts often demonstrate the obsession and fantasy of tracing a voice to its origin, from its accents or any other clues; for instance, Kim's name, 'Kim Rishti ke' turns out to indicate his Irish origin.[50] Many of the stories in *Stalky & Co.* follow the same pattern: those who know the sources of 'quotations' gain the upper hand and those who don't are easily fooled. Stalky specialises in attacking his ignorant enemies without being seen, in order to mislead them into believing the attacker is someone else. In the late story, 'The Propagation of Knowledge', King is overjoyed by the enthusiasm for and knowledge of English literature shown by the members of the Army Class, without knowing that Beetle is supplying them with information and all the quotes. King's gullibility is in sharp contrast to the quick perception of the chaplain, who immediately questions *where* the quotes are coming from, and identifies Beetle as the secret informant. The boys' admiration of, and affection for, the chaplain is due to his being a veteran player of the quoting game, as well as his reporting to the same authority: as Stalky says to the chaplain: 'You belong to the school – same as we do'[51], sharing, substantiating and watching over the same imperial archive.

(Mis)quotations: the fallibility of the imperial archive

In *Something of Myself*, Kipling recalls that he was instructed always to verify references while working as a sub-editor of the *Civil and Military Gazette* in India: 'the little that I ever acquired of accuracy, the habit of at least trying to verify references . . . I owed wholly to Stephen Wheeler', the chief editor.[52] Such training in working with newspapers, the centre where an imperial archive was daily produced and renewed, must have given basis to his narrator, whose 'knowingness' largely depends upon his ability to verify quotations. But however well equipped he is, this task of verifying quotations is inevitably accompanied by the fear of losing narrative control by not being able to do so; as Stalky exclaims to Beetle in 'The Propagation of Knowledge': 'You're sure it was Sammivel, not Binjimin? You *are* so dam' inaccurate!'[53] This is further exacerbated by the possibility that 'the archive' housed at the USC might at any time fail, due to its exposure to the passage of time and the rapidly changing world.

In this sense, it is important to note that Kipling added five more stories to the original *Stalky & Co.* (1899) and published it as *The Complete Stalky & Co.* in 1929. Four of the five added stories – 'Regulus' (1917), 'The United Idolaters' (1917), 'The Propagation of Knowledge' (1926) and 'The Satisfaction of a Gentleman' (1929) – were written and published during the gradual disintegration of the British Empire and in the devastating aftermath of the First World War. These stories, though upholding the same 'imperialist' framework, are more emphatically literary, laying bare the ways in which literature is translated into imperial ideologies, while drawing our attention to the moments in which the act of reading and quoting seems to fail as an effective strategy. For instance, 'Regulus', as Jan Montefiore argues, opens with the 'scene of (mis)translation': the students' struggle to translate Horace's ode under King's tutorship, far from successfully converting the Latin text into a political allegory of the British Empire, comically reveals many 'discrepancies' in the story as 'well-written right-wing propaganda'.[54] Moreover, in this story, reading texts, through which the imperial boys *should* learn freely to cross borders by acting different roles, is revealed to be dysfunctional by what Judith Plotz calls 'the schizophrenic behaviour' of Winton, Beetle's classmate, who, despite his ability to give a credible interpretation of the ode, becomes torn between the double roles of the boys 'as barbarians in need of mindless discipline and as Romans in need of sagacity'.[55]

'The Satisfaction of a Gentleman' (1929), written nearly half a century after Kipling graduated from the USC, also addresses the anxieties surrounding the imperial archive. In this story, Stalky & Co. are baffled by the punishment which they have received from the Head. Not only did he cane them for 'brewing', against which there is no school law, but also the ways in which he delivered his execution strike them as uncharacteristically noisy and hysterical. Moreover, they are troubled by his reference to 'the authorities' which they are purported to have offended, as he had 'never said a word about any authority except himself'. Unable to make sense of the Head's behaviour, the boys agree that 'for the first time in their knowledge of him, the Head must have been drunk. Nothing else explained his performance'. It is only years later that the Head confesses to one of the students, 'Pussy' Abanazar, what really happened: he was obliged to punish the boys in that way, in response to pressure from a member of the School Board, whom the boys had managed to upset, and who was intently listening behind the door while he was caning them. Pussy then sends Stalky, now in China, a coded telegraph to tell him about his conversation with the Head. But it has been mistranscribed and made almost unreadable by the time it arrives 'after two or three telegraphists of the Nearer and Farther Easts had had their flying shots at it'. At the end of the story, Stalky and Pussy, who also uncharacteristically fail to demonstrate their full mastery of the USC archive in this story, '[pass] the docket over to Beetle' and tell him to 'report and revenge', a challenge which Beetle eagerly takes up by writing this story.[56] It is significant that this story, which deals with the fallibility of the Head's authority and the corruptibility of a text coming from his archive, is the last story of *Stalky & Co.*, which 'completes' it. Sandra Kemp intriguingly identifies the discourses surrounding Kipling as 'the archive on which the sun never sets', which represents 'the location and repression of cultural anxieties'.[57] We may say that Kipling, in his extended and final collection, consciously acknowledged his imperial archive to be such a location.

Notes

An earlier and shorter version of this article was published in Japanese in Kazuhisa Takahashi and Makinori Hashimoto (eds), *Rudyard Kipling: Sakuhin to Hihyou* [Works and Criticisms] (Tokyo: Hakushosha, 2003), 309–28; an English version of this article was also given at the Kipling Conference, held at the University of Kent in 2007.

1 Kipling, 'The Dog Hervey', *A Diversity of Creatures* (London: Macmillan, 1917), p. 133.
2 Kipling *The Complete Stalky & Co.*, ed. Isabel Quigly (Oxford: The World's Classics, 1991), p. 285.
3 Kipling, *Complete Stalky*, pp. 283, 287, 288.
4 Don Randall, *Kipling's Imperial Boy: Adolescence and Cultural Hybridity* (Basingstoke: Palgrave, 2000), p. 16.
5 *Ibid.* pp. 167, 146–7.
6 John McBratney, *Imperial Subjects, Imperial Space: Rudyard Kipling's Fiction of the Native-Born* (Columbus: The Ohio State University Press, 2002), p. xiv.
7 *Ibid.* pp. xvii, xix.
8 Randall, *Kipling's Imperial Boy*, pp. 106, 90, 106.
9 Kipling, *Complete Stalky*, p. 287.
10 Kipling, *Kim* (London: Macmillan, 1901), p. 341.
11 Lauren Benton and John Muth, 'On cultural hybridity: interpreting colonial authority and performance', *Journal of Colonialism and Colonial History* 1, no. 1, paragraph 4. http://muse.jhu.edu/journals/journal_of_colonialism_and_colonial_history/v001/1.1benton.html (last accessed 28 February 2013).
12 Kipling, *Kim*, p. 341.
13 Kipling, 'The United Idolators', *Complete Stalky*, p. 143.
14 *Ibid.*, p. 223.
15 G.C. Beresford, *Schooldays with Kipling* (London: Victor Gollancz, 1936), p. 242.
16 Kipling, 'The Moral Reformers', *Complete Stalky*, p. 130. The phrase seems to be Stalky's 'misquotation' from, or misattribution to, Galton, and was very probably invented by Kipling himself.
17 Kipling, 'An Unsavoury Interlude', 'The United Idolaters', *Complete Stalky*, pp. 73, 144.
18 Kipling, ' "In Ambush" '; 'The Satisfaction of a Gentleman'; 'Slaves of the Lamp, Part I', *Complete Stalky*, pp. 38, 37, 243, 60, 64.
19 Kipling, 'The United Idolators', *Complete Stalky*, pp. 143, 152.
20 Kipling, 'The Propagation of Knowledge', *Complete Stalky*, p. 225.
21 Ken Frazer, in his e-mail posted on the Kipling's Society's mailbase, dated 16 June 2002, in response to the author's query about the quotation marks around ' "In Ambush" '. I am grateful to Lisa Lewis for kindly circulating my query on the mailbase.
22 Isabel Quigly, 'Introduction' to *Complete Stalky*, p. xv.
23 Kipling, ' "In Ambush" ', *Complete Stalky*, p. 32.
24 *Ibid.*, p. 41.
25 D.H. Stewart, 'Stalky and the Language of Education', *Children's Literature* 20 (1992): 39.
26 Kipling, *Complete Stalky*, pp. 42, 52.
27 Tzvetan Todorov, *The Fantastic: A Structural Approach to a Literary Genre*, trans. Richard Howard (Ithaca, NY: Cornell University Press, 1975), p. 8.
28 Robert J.C. Young, *Colonial Desire: Hybridity in Theory, Culture and Race* (London: and New York: Routledge, 1995), p. 125.
29 Benton and Muth, 'On Cultural Hybridity', paragraph 6.

30 Homi K. Bhabha, *The Location of Culture* (London: Routledge, 1994), Chapter 5, 'Sly Civility'.
31 Kipling, 'Stalky', *Complete Stalky*, p. 13.
32 Kipling, 'The Mark of the Beast', *Life's Handicap* (London: Macmillan, 1891), p. 198.
33 Roland Barthes, 'The Death of the Author', *Image: Music: Text*, trans. Stephen Heath (London: Fontana Press, 1977), p. 146.
34 Kipling, 'Slaves of the Lamp, Part I', *Complete Stalky*, p. 54.
35 For G.W. Moore's performance of his 'new ditty' 'Patrick, Mind the Baby' in St James's Hall, see for instance, 'The Moore and Burgess Minstrels', *The Era* (9 December 1877), p. 4. I would like to thank Jan Montefiore for pointing out to me the importance of Irish/feminine themes in this song.
36 Kipling, 'Slaves of the Lamp, Part II', *Complete Stalky*, p. 284.
37 *Ibid.*, pp. 284, 285.
38 *Ibid.*, pp. 296–7.
39 Anonymous review in the *Athenaeum*, No. 3755, 14 October 1899, collected in Roger Lancelyn Green, *Kipling: The Critical Heritage* (London: Routledge & Kegan Paul, 1971), pp. 226, 228.
40 Steven Marcus, '*Stalky & Co.*', in Elliott L. Gilbert (ed.), *Kipling and the Critics* (London: Owen, 1966), p. 157.
41 John Kucich, *Imperial Masochism: British Fiction, Fantasy, and Social Class* (Princeton, NJ: Princeton University Press, 2006), p. 143.
42 Kipling, '"In Ambush"', 'The Last Term', *Complete Stalky*, pp. 53, 259.
43 Thomas Richards, *The Imperial Archive: Knowledge and the Fantasy of Empire* (London and New York: Verso, 1993).
44 Kipling, 'Slaves of the Lamp, Part II', *Complete Stalky*, p. 293.
45 Jacques Derrida, *Archive Fever: A Freudian Impression*, trans. Eric Prenowitz (Chicago and London: The University of Chicago Press, 1995), p. 1.
46 *Ibid.*, p. 2.
47 Kipling, 'The Moral Reformers', *Complete Stalky*, p. 120.
48 Derrida, *Archive Fever*, p. 36.
49 Kipling, 'Let us now praise famous men', *Complete Stalky*, pp. 6–7.
50 Kipling, *Kim*, p. 121.
51 Kipling, 'The Moral Reformers', *Complete Stalky*, p. 120.
52 Kipling, *Something of Myself*, ed. Thomas Pinney (Cambridge: Cambridge University Press, 1990), p. 26.
53 Kipling, 'The Propagation of Knowledge', *Complete Stalky*, p. 227.
54 Jan Montefiore, 'Latin, arithmetic and mastery: a reading of two Kipling fictions', in Howard J. Booth and Nigel Rigby (eds), *Modernism and Empire* (Manchester: Manchester University Press, 2000), pp. 118–19.
55 Judith A. Plotz, 'Latin for Empire: Kipling's "Regulus" as a classics class for the ruling classes', *The Lion and the Unicorn* 17, no. 2 (December 1993), p. 162.
56 Kipling, 'The Satisfaction of a Gentleman', *Complete Stalky*, pp. 253, 252, 257, 258.
57 Sandra Kemp, 'The archive on which the sun never sets: Rudyard Kipling', *History of the Human Sciences* 11, no. 4 (1998): pp. 40–1.

14

Kipling, 'beastliness' and *Soldatenliebe*

HOWARD J. BOOTH

Any discussion of Kipling and sexuality soon comes up against Martin Seymour-Smith's 1989 biography. His central claim is that Kipling's life and writing take the form they do because he was in flight from his repressed homosexuality. Though Seymour-Smith sees Kipling as becoming more self-aware over time, whether or not Kipling acknowledged his desires to himself depends on what suits Seymour-Smith's argument at any given point. (In the psychoanalytic sense of the term, 'repression' can only be unconscious.[1]) Seymour-Smith positions himself as able to look through to a clear truth behind the ostensible record. Drawing on the biographical texts that were then available, by Lord Birkenhead and Charles Carrington, he claims to be able to correct their distortions (for which he blames Kipling's daughter, Elsie Bambridge). In seeking to demonstrate feelings for other men, Seymour-Smith downplays the intensity of Kipling's relationships with women – except, that is, with his mother. A whole set of assumptions about homosexuality are re-circulated: there is a fixed category of 'the homosexual' that has been established for all time by medicine and the law, a 'cause' can be adduced (a particular kind of relationship with the mother or misogyny) and a homosexual will act in certain ways (a wish to over-compensate for 'weakness', sadomasochism, and behaviour that is feminine yet also sometimes 'super-masculine').[2] Seymour-Smith's book, so easy to call into question, has limited and damaged subsequent discussions of Kipling and sexuality.

A queer studies approach to these issues would break with the reliance on the medical-legal category of 'the homosexual' and efforts to work back to Kipling's 'real' sexuality – where, of course, the very notion of 'a sexuality' is itself historically and geographically specific. Instead it would note that Kipling's life and career spanned the period when 'the homosexual' was defined and the associated sexual identities emerged. Concerns soon enter in that lie outside Seymour-Smith's compass. Kipling did not accept the newer position that there was a discrete section of the population disposed to specific sexual acts, who exhibit linked ways of thinking and acting. In Michel Foucault's well-known words, 'The sodomite had been a temporary aberration; the homosexual was now a species'.[3]

Looking at Kipling and same-sex passion expands the available set of textual responses to emergent sexological categories and related identities. Kipling held onto a position rooted in that of the church – which is not to say that Kipling had an orthodox faith – and maintained that same-sex acts were a wrong choice, where an initial false step could lead to a life of sin and then to ruin. Though some might be more susceptible than others, it was a route open to all, where Kipling's language is one of being sullied and indeed of contamination. Kipling's loyalty to the older model included his use of language; he preferred the word 'beastliness' to 'homosexuality'.[4] One response to this would be to say that Kipling's position was already becoming anachronistic, and that it can therefore simply be discounted in favour of a focus on the 'emergent' and soon-to-be 'dominant'. In discussions of sexuality, though, there is a need to go beyond an approach that envisions a single, straightforward line of development. As Ernst Bloch put it, 'Not all people exist in the same Now'; rather, there are overlapping temporalities.[5] Nor is it enough to look back on the past and simply to identify certain individuals or groups who can be viewed positively and said to anticipate later norms. Change occurs in an uneven and dynamic fashion, and even those positions that were already 'residual' were capable of acting upon and influencing others.[6]

Kipling did not identify with and adopt the new language of sexual categories and identities, where the position he held continued to inform the experience of sexuality in the first half of the twentieth century (and is still heard today in attenuated form, when it is claimed that the young are being led to adopt a gay 'lifestyle' they would not otherwise have taken up). In pre-1900 work he was drawn to depictions of a strong, active masculinity found especially in ordinary soldiers. Early proponents of society's acceptance of same-sex passion alighted upon his depictions of soldiers, misrecognising it as a homophile political strategy. Perhaps aware of this, Kipling retreated from the representational spaces he had used to depict and indeed celebrate masculinity and close relationships between men. A sense of constriction and indeed loss resulted.

Encroaching 'filth'

In later life, and in particular in published writing, Kipling maintained that his old school, the United Services College, had been particularly 'clean' – or, to use the language many were now using, that there had been little homosexual behaviour among the pupils. In 1917 Kipling wrote to his friend L.C. Dunsterville (on whom he had based Stalky in *Stalky & Co.* (1899)) after hearing, in Andrew Lycett's curiously opaque phrase, that Dunsterville's son had 'experienced it at his school',

> This is perfectly sickening. You can imagine what the old Coll. would have been with a system of cubicles instead of the old dormitories and the masters moving about at all hours through 'em – which was what saved us. I don't think that as the world is today the thing will count against him in the future as it would have done in our time. And yet – how many men do we know who have risen to all sorts of positions who when they were kids were – not found out! I always go in *deadly* fear of the cubicle system at any public school. They had it at Wellington and Eton, as we know is . . .

Lycett observes that then '[h]is words literally trailed off the page'.[7] Kipling's son John had been to Wellington and Oliver Baldwin, the son of his cousin Stanley, Eton. The sleeping arrangements matter because Kipling's believes that all are in peril; the system at the 'Coll.' is said to have 'saved' Kipling and Dunsterville (which implies of course that they, and perhaps all boys, need saving). While Kipling did tend to adopt heightened forms of expression in his letters, those on the topic of same-sex passion are particularly extreme and anxious. The language used here suggests that the news affects Kipling at a somatic level; it is 'perfectly sickening' and he goes in '*deadly* fear' of schools where boys do not sleep in dormitories. Kipling evokes a sense of pervasive danger – not only of doing certain things, but of being 'found out' – and all in a letter intended to reassure his friend.

The cubicle system was associated with the reforms at Uppingham School instituted by the Rev. Edward Thring (1821–87). Though Thring warned his boys of the (probably fatal) consequences of sexual 'vice', whether 'solitary' or 'dual' (to use the terms in the educational literature of the time),[8] he was also known for his commitment to what he called 'the Almighty wall'. Growth into what Thring called the 'true life' was facilitated by school architecture, living in small groups, individual rooms and the school 'machine' (that is, organisation).[9] Thring argued,

> Boys at school, also, should be protected by all their surroundings being framed – so as to shut off temptation. The whole structure and system should act as an unseen friend. There is much virtue, or vice, in a wall. Witness the one room. No words, no personal influence, no religion even, can do instead of the holy help of the wall, or overcome its evil, if evil. These words involve serious results in practice. They involve the teaching and training of every boy, with adequate machinery for doing it.[10]

This view of the child, then, stressed inner qualities that need to be brought on; for this to occur the boy has to be protected from those who might do him harm. Kipling, alternatively, stressed the unwatched child as being in peril. Boys need active and continuous monitoring.

In a letter of warning Kipling sent to his son when John was at Wellington, Kipling argued that boys needed to be guarded from the influence of some of their peers,

> What really bothered me most was not being able to have a last jaw with you. I wanted to tell you a lot of things about keeping clear of any chap who is even suspected of beastliness. There is no limit to the trouble possible if one goes about (however innocently) with swine of that type. Give them the widest of wide berths. Whatever their merits may be in the athletic line they are at heart only sweeps and scum and *all* friendship or acquaintance with them ends in sorrow and disgrace. More on this subject when we meet.[11]

Kipling shows his concern with contamination and with the damage that even the perception of 'beastliness' can do. As well as the suggestion of unrestrained animal 'beastliness' is a language around dirt and waste products ('swine', 'sweeps', 'scum').

The repeated return to schools and 'beastliness' in Kipling's letters differs from the position Kipling maintained in his published writing. In *Stalky and Co.* schoolboy friendships may be the royal road to a fully achieved masculinity, but, as Carolyn Oulton has pointed out, Kipling was very careful not to depict intense or sentimental schoolboy friendships. His characters reject what is called, in 'The Moral Reformers', 'beastly Erickin'. The reference here is to Dean Farrar's *Eric, or Little by Little*, first published in 1858, which saw friendships, extending to some physical intimacy, depicted between older and younger boys.[12] Such novels continued to be written well into the twentieth century, with the influence of nineteenth-century Hellenism brought to bear. An example is E.F. Benson's *David Blaize* of 1916, in which an intense friendship is seen as aiding 'normal' development. For all that this differs from Kipling's position, Benson too firmly rejects the sexual: both see boys as endangered by corruption. Benson also describes anything to do with male–male sex acts as 'filth' and 'beastliness'.[13]

In later work Kipling stressed that talk on such topics should be kept to a minimum. One of the Stalky stories published after the appearance of *Stalky & Co.*, 'The United Idolators' from 1924, questions a new master who proclaims the need to look into and address the school's moral state. Neil Cocks sees the story as arguing that it is important, in Foucault's terms, not to incite discourse about sex.[14] Kipling's memoir *Something of Myself* (1937) saw Kipling making his case in ways that idealised his old school and led him into saying things that simply were not true. Contradicting what we have seen in his earlier correspondence with Dunsterville, Kipling noted that his old school was 'clean with a cleanliness that I have never heard of in any other school'. He continued: 'I remember no cases of even suspected perversion, and am inclined to the theory that if masters did not suspect them, and show that they suspected, there would not be quite so many elsewhere.'[15] With the claim that there were 'no cases of even suspected perversion' at his old school, Kipling omits to mention his discovery, four years after leaving the school, that he had himself been suspected by his housemaster.[16]

Though sexological terms such as 'homosexual' are eschewed by Kipling in favour of a highly pejorative vocabulary, he did attempt to give his position the support of science. An extraordinary example of this is the letter – marked 'confidential' – that he wrote during the war to Sir Almroth Wright, a leading bacteriologist who served as a doctor in France during the conflict. Kipling did not know Wright personally, but he had been impressed by Wright's letter to *The Times* about the suffragette riots in 1912 and his *The Unexpurgated Case Against Woman Suffrage* of the following year. Wright argued that the suffrage movement should not be seen as a group of people with a cause, where the merits of their case could be debated. Rather the suffragettes' actions sprang from a 'mental disorder' rooted in the female body and specifically menstruation (the direct mention of which is what makes the book 'unexpurgated').[17]

Kipling, in his letter to Wright, sought to extend the argument to establish an organic basis for pacifism, which was no longer to be seen as a conscience-based objection to killing and war. The argument is that violence and war feeds its very opposite, it 'wakes, consciously or unconsciously, a certain perverted interest' from those inclined to take a passive role at a distance from conflict.[18] Kipling's effort to ground his argument in the body runs against the interest in mental functioning and its cultural basis. Ever-expanding in its scope, the effort to sustain a scientific thesis using a measured prose breaks down in the attempt to connect the 'unfailing beastliness' of the 'German character under stress', socialism and those who desire their own sex.[19] In the end one causal factor is accorded primary status,

> We in England persist in looking upon our pacifists as sports of nature developed by the play of 'politics' or as sincerely conscientious idiots. I think we make a bad mistake. It is not schools of thought we have to deal with, but temperaments whose roots go down to the dirt: brains with lesions unnoticeable or masked in time of peace, and every form of mental or physical impotence x-rayed as it were by the light and heat of war. . . . Here then, my case rests. Boiled and peeled, of course, it comes to this – that when the normal human being says, in his haste, of the Pacifists: – 'Oh! They are all b---s together!' he is nearer the scientific truth than he thinks.

Despite the claim that he is attempting to put his case on a scientific basis, Kipling ends up asserting that it is simply a matter of common knowledge that sodomy is at the root of the matter. Even as Kipling seeks to ground non-normative modes of behaviour in brain lesions he draws on his usual language of 'dirt'. He goes on to advocate 'kindly' and 'scientifically' conducted treatment of those affected in clinics for mental patients.[20] Those holding dissenting views should not be allowed to operate within society because they are physically damaged and not sane; if tolerated they will do serious harm to the war effort and the whole social fabric.

Kipling's belief that same-sex passion was threatening society and the coming generation grew in the 1920s. After the death of his son, Kipling became close to Oliver Baldwin. Andrew Lycett argues that it was early in 1924, at the very time that Kipling was coming to terms with the fact that his surviving child, Elsie, was to marry George Bambridge and leave home, that Kipling learned that Oliver had had affairs with other men and was living with a partner, Johnnie Boyle.[21] It was Oliver who had first introduced Bambridge to the Kiplings' house, Batemans; Kipling, writing his regimental history of the Irish Guards in the war, had been glad to have two former officers from John's regiment on hand. Whether Kipling heard the rumours about Bambridge's sexuality, which extended to a possible affair with Oliver, is not known, nor is there clear evidence concerning the extent of Elsie's awareness.[22] Even if Kipling's own knowledge stopped with the news about

Oliver and Johnnie Boyle, relations between Kipling and Oliver cooled markedly, with the latter's espousal of socialism a further factor. 'Beastliness' had come close to home: to Kipling's own family, the army and indeed the Irish Guards.

Such a sense of feeling beleaguered at a personal and societal level can be seen in the stand Kipling made in 1928 against Radclyffe Hall's *The Well of Loneliness*. He was summoned to appear for the prosecution at the trial in November and the appeal in December. On both occasions, though, the bench decided the book was obscene without hearing from expert witnesses.[23] Andrew Lycett finds it 'extraordinary' that Kipling should have strayed from his usual commitment to artistic freedom (the reason he cited for refusing honours from the state), which extended from support for Aubrey Beardsley in the 1890s to discussions about reburying Byron in Westminster Abbey in Poet's Corner in 1924.

Not only was Kipling in favour of Hall's text being banned, he may have helped provoke the action taken against the novel. He had opened a letter containing a flyer for *The Well of Loneliness* addressed to his daughter and sent from France. On 11 October 1928 he posted it on to the Home Secretary, some four days before Joynson-Hicks started to make public statements about Hall's novel.[24] The main body of his own letter, marked 'confidential', ran,

> I don't know whether anyone has sent you a sample like the enclosed. It came to me the other day from France addressed to Miss Kipling. There is no 'Miss Kipling' now, but I suspect that the trade is active among young girls, just the same as the smutty books of the old days used to be advertised from Belgium among the Public Schools. It seems to me pretty damnable, but I don't know if your powers stretch to bringing them up with a round turn. *Mem*. The whole point of the book is that people with that peculiar taste should be made much of and received into general society with their 'lovers'. Otherwise, as you know, there is no moral.[25]

The stress on the 'whole point' of the novel was perhaps influenced by the way Oliver Baldwin and Johnnie Boyle had set up home together. Wanting to have relationships with someone of the same sex is a 'peculiar taste', but Kipling's thrust is that a general vigilance is required. In a further letter of 25 October Kipling declared that he would be happy to provide evidence against *The Well of Loneliness*, writing 'What *I* object to is its being sent to unmarried women. That gives the whole game away.'[26] He believes that efforts are being made to ensnare those not yet firmly woven into the social fabric through marriage.

Kipling's belief in a general susceptibility can be seen in comments recorded by Hugh Walpole in his journal that same month: 'I asked [Kipling] at luncheon whether he approved of censorship (a propos of this tiresome stupid *Well of Loneliness*). No, he doesn't approve of the book. Too much of the abnormal in all of us to play about with it. Hates opening up reserves. All the same he'd had friends once and again he'd done more for than for any woman.'[27] Martin Seymour-Smith sees this passage as Kipling suddenly being direct and honest about his repressed homosexuality because of what he and Walpole shared: 'in those days of oppression homosexuals recognised and appreciated one another, even if they muted that recognition in deference to custom. By that time Kipling was probably "not homosexual", but if he was anything sexual at all, and it is hard not to be, then he would dwell emotionally in homosexual memories.'[28] A less contorted view of what Walpole records Kipling as saying is surely available: Kipling saw desire for the same sex as widespread, where he included himself in this; however, he believed it needed to be held firmly in check by self and society.

Kipling, London's homosexual sub-culture and soldiers

In his early career Kipling allowed himself to explore and hold up models of male–male intimacy that he regarded as positive and manly. Particularly important here was his stress on the ordinary soldier. With the new century he felt he had to forgo these imaginative possibilities, and not only because the old British soldier, the 'Tommy Atkins' figure, was disappearing with new forms of conflict. A powerful sense of loss remained, however.

The early years of Kipling's career in London came as the new homosexual identity was crystallising. He opposed the aesthetic or feminine to what he saw as the fully achieved masculinity of soldiers. The most often cited example of Kipling's response to London after his arrival to launch his career as a professional writer in 1889 is the poem 'In Partibus'.[29] Biographers look to it to ink in Kipling's response to the gloom of the capital and to its literary culture. The reaction to London is said to capture Kipling's fragile mental state.[30] Another line of response begins from noting that the poem was written to entertain and amuse an audience back in India. Charles Carrington saw it as borrowing from Lewis Carroll and, more recently, David Page has called for 'In Partibus' to be read as a comic poem rather than as verse that reveals Kipling's sense of alienation from his new home.[31] Though this second set of critics are surely right in terms of genre, readership and overall tone, there is more to say.

The opening stanza establishes a comic tone by introducing the pun on the title 'In Partibus' (short for 'in partibus infidelium', Latin for 'in the lands of the unbelievers') and the hope for a departing omnibus: 'The 'buses run to Battersea, / The 'buses run to Bow'. The city's pollution is described with humour, though the way it is personified and described suggests that London contaminates the body, 'I see the smut upon my cuff, / And feel him on my nose'. The wind too is a problem, 'Because he brings disgusting things, / And drops 'em on my "clo'es" '. The 'filth' of the capital of Empire is linked to its moral state, from which the upstanding man needs to protect his womenfolk,

> And when I take my nightly prowl,
>   'Tis passing good to meet
> The pious Briton lugging home
>   His wife and daughter sweet,
> Through four packed miles of seething vice,
>   Thrust out upon the street.

The 'vice' is not kept out of sight but rather '[t]hrust out' onto the public thoroughfare. In this it is worse than ports of North America and the Empire such as Sandy Hook and Port Said.

Kipling may also have been reacting to the visibility of a particular form of 'vice' – sex between men. Critics have not so far given attention to the fact that 'In Partibus' was written as rumours of 'The Cleveland Street Scandal' began to circulate in the press. It saw aristocratic men and telegraph boys linked with a male brothel at 19 Cleveland Street. The associated trials and media reporting continued into 1890. Directly implicated were Lord Arthur Somerset, a Major in the Royal Horse Guards and an equerry to the Prince of Wales, and Henry FitzRoy, Earl of Euston. However, rumours swirled about others, including Prince Albert Victor. Euston claimed that he had been given a card advertising *pose plastique* at the Cleveland Street establishment while walking through Piccadilly.[32] The area Kipling identified in 'In Partibus' as the 'four packed miles of seething vice', and which he described in the London sections of his novel *The Light That Failed* and in his late memoir *Something of Myself*, stretched from the Strand to Piccadilly – or, in Kipling's personal geography, from his lodgings in Villiers Street and 107 Piccadilly, which was then the home of the Savile Club. Matt Cook, in his *London and the Culture of Homosexuality, 1885–1914*, has seen a long-standing centre around the Strand – also a location for transsexual and heterosexual prostitution in its bars and music halls – being supplanted by the rapidly developing area around Piccadilly.[33]

Nature has become disordered in the London of 'In Partibus' because 'I cannot tell when dawn is near, / Or when the day is done'. The weak sunshine during the day and the gaslight at night are almost indistinguishable: 'I do not care / A cuss for either one'. After a rather laboured effort to connect the dirt of the city with the advertisements for soap – where the people of Bengal, it is said, are washed clean only by the sun – the I-voice contrasts the city's artists and soldiers,

> But I consort with long-haired things
>   In velvet collar-rolls,
> Who talk about the Aims of Art,
>   And 'theories' and 'goals',
> And moo and coo with women folk
>   About their blessed souls.
>
> But that they call 'psychology'
>   Is lack of liver-pill,
> And all that blights their tender souls
>   Is eating till they're ill,
> And their chief way of winning goals
>   Consists of sitting still.
>
> It's Oh to meet an Army man,
>   Set up, and trimmed and taut,
> Who does not spout hashed libraries
>   Or think the next man's thought,
> And walks as though he owned himself,
>   And hogs his bristles short.

What is wrong with the aesthetes, with their uncut hair, unregulated livers and lack of an active life, is that they are without control and discipline. On the other hand, the 'Army man' – his rank and status are ambiguous – is ordered, trimmed and balanced; soldiers provide a contrast with the dirt, gloom and vice of the city. The phrase 'as though he owned himself', however, suggests that all a man can do is take on a role and play it to the full, and in 'consorting' with the aesthetes the I-voice is closer to the women who are said to 'moo and coo' than to soldiers. Towards the end of the poem the I-voice appeals to Anglo-Indian readers, to 'kin beyond my ken', asking that if they have ever enjoyed his stories, 'For pity's sake send some one here / To bring me news of men!'. The final refrain again returns to the suburbs, where the departing buses from central London go, punning on 'Bus' as an interjection meaning 'enough' and 'finish' in Hindi.[34]

An opposition between aesthetes and soldiers would have been familiar to Kipling's early readers from the huge success of Gilbert and Sullivan's 1881 comic opera *Patience*. The officers of the Dragoon Guards 'fleshly men, of full habit', who were engaged to the maidens only 'a year ago', return to find themselves displaced in their affections by a single aesthete, Reginald Bunthorne.[35] As Angela puts it 'our tastes have been etherealized, our perceptions exalted'. The Colonel of Dragoons is shocked, singing of how, where women once yielded to 'a uniform handsome and chaste', now 'the peripatetics / Of long haired æsthetics, / Are very much more to their taste – / Which I never counted upon / When I first put this uniform on!'. 'In Partibus' picks up on the satire on the aesthetes, but the I-voice of that poem is not so much a manly soldier as, to adopt a phrase from Gilbert's lyrics, a 'melancholy literary man'.[36]

Carolyn Williams argues that, though *Patience* links aesthetes and sexlessness, 'by the late 1880s a popular association of *Patience* with male homosexuality had emerged'.[37] In *Patience* itself, however, the 'pure' nature of those who eschew the true red meat of a relationship with women is dwelt upon at such length it comes into question,

> Then a sentimental passion of a vegetable fashion must excite your languid spleen,
> An attachment *à la* Plato for a bashful young potato, or a not-too-French French bean!
> Though the Philistines may jostle, you will rank as an apostle in the high æsthetic band,
> If you walk down Piccadilly with a poppy or a lily in your mediæval hand.
>   And everyone will say,
>   As you walk your flowery way,
> 'If he's content with a vegetable love which would certainly not suit *me*,
> Why what a most particularly pure young man this pure young man must be!'[38]

The repeated stress on the purity of the love – and in metrical terms stresses abound here – suggests that it is in fact anything but 'pure'. Further, it is grounded in a dysfunctional body with a 'languid spleen'.

If Kipling was aware of the 'vice' near where he lived, he seems to have been unaware, or to have ignored, the role played by members of the military in London's sexual economy. Soldiers were not simply the embodiment of a conventional masculinity. The area around the Royal Parks and the nearby barracks had a marked reputation. As Cook observes,

> The notoriety of the central London parks was ongoing and Hyde Park was well known for the soldier prostitutes who picked up clients there. In 1903, in recognition of the problem, the army issued an order forbidding uniformed soldiers from 'loiter[ing] without lawful purpose in the parks after dusk'. Soldiers were nevertheless implicated in a number of gross indecency cases throughout the period and well into the new century, and they were figures of erotic fantasy for John Addington Symonds, Roger Casement, George Ives, the poet A.E. Housman and many others.[39]

Among the 'many others' are Gerard Manley Hopkins, with his 'The Bugler's First Communion', and D.H. Lawrence, author of the poem 'Guards'.[40] Among early homosexual writers, the American-born writer Edward Ireneaus Prime Stevenson often depicted the mutual affections of soldiers in his novels. In *White Cockades: An Incident of the 'Forty-Five'* (1887), set among post-Culloden Jacobites, Andrew Boyd establishes a close bond with Geoffry Armitage. A fugitive from the English, Armitage is eventually revealed as none other than Bonnie Prince Charlie himself. Stevenson's pornographic novel, *Imre: A Memorandum* (1906), published under the pseudonym Xavier Mayne, charts the establishment of a sexual relationship between two very masculine soldiers of the Austro-Hungarian Empire.[41]

Stories and verse such as Kipling's 'Follow Me 'Ome' and 'His Private Honour' seem to have led a number of early readers to assume that his intention, when depicting soldiers, was to offer coded references to same-sex passion.[42] A number of these responses surprise: the embezzler, author and colonial trader John Moray Stuart-Young, for example, fantasised that Kipling was a source of support and aid.[43] The response of others was more grounded in Kipling's texts, where an example would be John Addington Symonds, one of the main early homosexual apologists in Britain. Symonds knew of the link between soldiers and same-sex acts from personal experience. In his *Memoirs* there is an account of a visit to a male brothel 'near the Regent's Park barracks' in 1877, where he slept with a 'brawny young soldier'.[44]

Symonds wrote an essay on 'Soldier Love and Related Matter' for inclusion in *Sexual Inversion*, his collaboration with Havelock Ellis. It only appeared in the first, German, edition of the book published in 1896, three years after Symonds' death.[45] Symonds began to read German sexology relatively late in life, first engaging with the pamphlets of the earliest homosexual apologist Karl Heinrich Ulrichs in 1889; he soon sought out the elderly Ulrichs, then living near Aquila in Tuscany.[46] One of Ulrich's pamphlets *Ara Spei* (which means 'Altar to Hope'), the final note of which is dated 28 February 1864, had defended the interests of Urnings, as he called them, and 'our preference for soldiers', noting that 'It is a fact that in Germany it is doubtless predominant'.[47] In his essay, Symonds makes some attempt to explain the sexual interest in soldiers – he proposes the term 'hoplitomania' for what 'in Germany is known as *Soldatenliebe*' – in terms of the attractiveness of the uniform 'which emphasises their bodily shape' and their masculinity,[48] where '[t]hey exude a powerful male effluvium'. He links the attraction of soldiers to the broader significance of cross-class relationships, using cultural precedents from the Greeks to Pierre Loti to maintain that this is not a 'degraded' form of love but one that shows how society may be bound together by relationships across the classes.[49]

As Harry Ricketts has noted, Symonds alighted on Kipling as part of his search for art and artists who shared his sexuality and views.[50] Symonds' enthusiasm was sparked by Kipling's *Soldiers Three*, and he puzzled over the poem 'L'Envoi' which followed 'Black Jack' in early editions.[51] He felt a strong response to the lines 'Because I wrought them for Thy sake / And breathed in them mine agonies', noting that 'When I first read it I *felt* the lover in it'. However, he then 'got confused' and wondered whether the poet was not simply 'in a mysteriously religious mood', presumably as a result of the capital 't' in 'Thy'. Recognising in time that Kipling was not in sympathy with same-sex passion, Symonds started to question what he had read, and it was the depiction of soldiers on which he alighted. There was not enough 'Cru' – a strong, unmediated directness – about Kipling's soldiers, with Symonds noting, 'I fear that Kipling has dressed his soldiers up with more of literary buckram than they ought to have'.[52] Kipling himself thought Symonds a 'sugary gushing sort of a Johnnie'.[53] Nettled by reports of an attack on the accuracy of his portrayal of soldiers from among the 'long-haired literati of the Savile Club', Kipling naively asserted that he was 'naturally wrath' because 'not one of these critters has been within earshot of a barrack'.[54]

Writers, artists and more soldiers

While there are of course many Kipling stories and poems about ordinary soldiers,[55] *The Light That Failed* focuses on an artist-figure, Dick Heldar, who makes his reputation depicting fighting men. Kipling can thus be said to be making art out of art, and as self-reflexively considering his own practice as a writer who represented soldiers. The suggestion is that representing the military and war is the aim, reason and purpose of art. However, the situation is complex: *The Light That Failed* is also a text profoundly sceptical about whether artistic creation is an appropriate subject for fiction.

Discussion of same-sex feelings in the novel has focussed, as in Christopher Lane's reading, on Dick and Torpenhow.[56] However, the two bond alongside soldiers during colonial conflicts. Richard Le Gallienne noted the importance of fighting men to *The Light That Failed*. He observed in his 1900 book on Kipling that Dick is 'a war correspondent in love with soldiers'.[57] It is during the fighting in the campaign to retake the Sudan that Dick receives the wound that eventually causes his physical blindness, though what the novel regards as his 'blindness' to Maisie's unresponsiveness goes back to their childhoods, and the scene on the beach when she nearly shot him.

Dick's art and success are closely linked to the veracity of his representations; he is a champion of realism responding to modern warfare. That said, the novel is framed by references to Michelangelo, perhaps because of his monumental depictions of masculinity. In an example of the strange adjacency of Kipling to the sources of identification found by early male homosexual apologists, Michelangelo was being cast at this time as a major cultural figure from the past who was drawn to other men. (John Addington Symonds was the major figure in forming how late Victorians saw Michelangelo.[58]) Dick likens the skirmish that begins when the British troops are observed coming up by boat to a famous representation of nude soldiers bathing,

> A bugle blew furiously, and the men on the bank hurried to their arms and accoutrements.
> '"Pisan soldiery surprised while bathing,"' remarked Dick calmly. 'D'you remember the picture? It's by Michael Angelo; all beginners copy it. That scrub's alive with enemy.'[59]

Though Dick (and probably Kipling), have misremembered details of the Michelangelo, the cartoon does indeed represent naked soldiers hurriedly coming out of the water to engage their opponents.[60] Michelangelo is perhaps also silently evoked at very end of the novel. The way that Dick falls dead into Torpenhow's arms has been linked to a Pietà by Phillip Mallett (though he believes it to be 'probably unintended'). Michelangelo's sculpture at St Peter's in the Vatican is the best-known Pietà, but perhaps more apposite for *The Light That Failed* is his 'Florence *Pietà*', also known as *The Deposition*, in which the dead Jesus is held principally in a man's arms rather than Mary's.[61]

Most attention in *The Light That Failed* is given not to Renaissance precedents but to Dick's efforts to represent soldiers in ways that they themselves would see as accurate. He differs from Maisie, who throughout is fixated on exhibiting at the Paris salon, and the 'red-haired impressionist girl' she lives with,

> A small knot of people stood round a print-shop that Dick knew well. 'Some reproduction of my work inside', he said, with suppressed triumph. Never before had success tasted so sweet upon the tongue. 'You see the sort of things I paint. D'you like it?'
> Maisie looked at the wild whirling rush of a field-battery going into action under fire. Two artillerymen stood behind her in the crowd.
> 'They've chucked the off lead-'orse,' said one to the other, "E's tore up awful, but they're makin' good time with the others. That lead-driver drives better nor you, Tom. See 'ow cunnin' 'e's nursin' 'is 'orse.'
> 'Number Three'll be off the limber, next jolt,' was the answer.
> 'No, 'e won't. See 'ow 'is foot's braced against the iron? 'E's all right.'
> Dick watched Maisie's face and swelled with joy – fine, rank, vulgar triumph. She was more interested in the little crowd than in the picture. That was something that she could understand.
> 'And I wanted it so! Oh, I did want it so!' she said at last, under her breath.
> 'Me, – all me!' said Dick placidly. 'Look at their faces. It hits 'em. They don't know what makes their eyes and mouths open; but I know. And I know my work's right.'

When asked what she thinks of the picture, Maisie replies: 'I call it success'.[62] Later, though, she seems to find his range limited, asking 'Can you do anything except soldiers?'. The source of Dick's 'success', his realistic depiction of members of the armed forces, is eroded by the corrupting influence of London. Though at one point we are told of a footprint of a 'military model' in Dick's studio, his work starts to fall away both in terms of subject matter and the audience it attracts. The image of the soldier he has been working on using the model is considered too raw and unattractive for the market, so he produces an idealised and sentimental version more likely to appeal to wealthy purchasers.[63]

As in 'In Partibus', London is contrasted with the more straightforward and manly corruption of Port Said. Those in the art world are seen as 'a queer gang, – an amazingly queer gang!', where the word 'queer' was starting to mean those who desired their own sex in the 1890s.[64] Maisie and the red-haired girl are depicted as unable to act in a way that is considered natural for women. The latter – she is never accorded the dignity of a name – stays with Maisie yet is in love with Dick, though she never declares her love. Maisie's work is said to be doomed to fail; indeed, her very wish to become a successful artist is seen as evidence that she is neither wholly male nor female. Dick labels her art 'hermaphroditic futilities'. Much weight is given to Maisie's inability to care for and love others; she sees this as an attribute she simply does not possess. She says to Dick, 'I know what you want perfectly well, but I can't give it you, Dick. It isn't my fault; indeed it isn't. If I felt that I could care for any one – But I don't feel that I care. I simply don't understand what the feeling means.'[65] One of the faultlines of the novel is that while what she says here is not called into question she is still condemned for it as if it were a matter of individual choice.

Dick changes his subject matter when he takes on the challenge of painting his 'Melancolia'. (Maisie has been reading James Thomson's *The City of Dreadful Night*.) Torpenhow sees it as 'quite out of his regular line' and his advice is clear: 'You'd better stick to your soldiers, Dick, instead of maundering about heads and eyes and experiences.'[66] When Dick starts working on the painting, he begins to have problems with his eyes. (Initially, as in 'In Partibus', he thinks that liver pills might be the answer.[67]) An early reaction to his diagnosis and deteriorating sight is 'No more soldiers. I couldn't paint 'em.'[68] However, Torpenhow does get him into the Parks, where he responds to the Guards with 'Oh, my men! – my beautiful men!'.[69] It turns sour, though, when Dick recognises the music hall song played by the band; he remembers that its lyrics say that a true man who knows how to kiss will always find his love reciprocated. When Torpenhow goes to France to tell Maisie of Dick's blindness, her inability to respond is contrasted with the behaviour of the cook she sees kissing her lover, a French soldier. The red-haired girl is clear in the advice she gives to Maisie, 'Think! *I* should go back to London and see him, and I should kiss his eyes, and kiss them and kiss them until they got well again!'[70]

Kisses given and received are a running motif in *The Light That Failed*, and not only those between a man and a woman. When Dick realises he is wholly blind, Torpenhow accedes to Dick's request to hold his hand, eventually getting him to go sleep. Then 'Torpenhow withdrew his hand, and, stooping over Dick, kissed him lightly on the forehead, as men do sometimes kiss a wounded comrade in the hour of death, to ease his departure.' This is not sexual, but neither are the kisses between men and women. They seem more about a psychological need for the other in order to stave off loneliness.

Perhaps the nearest we get to sexual release is the description of Dick's journey on the armoured train near the end of the novel. It shows both Dick's infantile and sadistic view of conflict and his strong response to those who fight,

> 'Whitechapel – last train! Ah, I see yer kissin' in the first class there!' somebody shouted, just as Dick was clambering into the forward truck. . . .
> *Hrrmph!* said the machine-gun through all its five noses as the subaltern drew the lever home. The empty cartridges clashed on the floor and the smoke blew back through the truck. There was indiscriminate firing at the rear of the train, a return fire from the darkness without and unlimited howling. Dick stretched himself on the floor, wild with delight at the sounds and the smells.
> 'God is very good – I never thought I'd hear this again. Give 'em hell, men. Oh, give 'em hell!' he cried.[71]

Dick was allowed on the train as a result of an awkward conversation with an officer – a bond is established when both say that they are 'a public school man' – but he gets out of the camp and up towards the front line by speaking 'after the manner of a common soldier'. Dick receives his 'kindly bullet' and falls into Torpenhow's arms to create the novel's closing tableau.[72] Yet the dominant note is that he dies at one with soldiers in battle.

After 1900 Kipling's stories would still depict groups of men, including those set among soldiers past and present in the Masonic training lodge during and just after the war, but the form taken by the bonds has changed.[73] An exception, though an exemplar of true friendship in a book for children, is the story in *Puck of Pook's Hill* (1906) of two Roman soldiers, Parnesius and Pertinax, on the 'Great Wall' in the North.[74] It suggests that Kipling had come to see intense male–male companionship as something now lost and in the past. Though Puck makes fun of the 'Pious Parnesius on Friendship', Parnesius's statements are given weight: 'I know what goodness means; and my friend, though he was without hope, was ten thousand times better than I . . . He was that friend the Gods sent me.' He goes onto tell young Dan that 'your fate will turn on the first true friend you make'. Puck offers the following gloss: 'if you try to make yourself a decent chap when you're young, you'll make rather decent friends when you grow up. If you're a beast, you'll have beastly friends.'[75] There is a powerful sense of sadness and loss in the story because Parnesius and Pertinax are now parted. Puck brings only Parnesius to speak to Dan and Una, and at times memories of his friend come close to overwhelming the Roman. They decide to end their time in the army after the forces they commanded on the Wall are relieved by the soldiers of the new Emperor; we are not told what happens to them in later life. Dan, understandably enough, has a flurry of questions when Parnesius' tale breaks off, but it is at this point that old Hobden arrives and Puck and Parnesius disappear. Though the story of Parnesius and Pertinax is set in the distant past, the way it is told suggests, for all Puck's humour, that their closeness has been followed firstly by loss and then by an unshakeable, never-ending melancholy.

Notes

1 Sigmund Freud, 'Repression', *The Complete Psychological Works of Sigmund Freud*, vol. 14, ed. James Strachey et al. (London: The Hogarth Press and the Institute of Psycho-Analysis, 1959), pp. 146–58: 147.
2 Martin Seymour-Smith, *Rudyard Kipling* (New York: St Martin's Press, 1989), *passim*. Seymour-Smith added a 'Foreword to the Second Edition' to this American first edition in which he responded to a number of the book's initial reviews (pp. xi–xv). The book does have its virtues, often manifested when not driving forward its main thesis, especially the close readings of Kipling's texts that identify complexity and ambivalence. For a persuasive account of the problems of Seymour-Smith's argument, see Harry Ricketts' review in the *London Review of Books* 11.6 (16 March 1989): 13–14.
3 Michel Foucault, *The History of Sexuality, Volume One: An Introduction*, trans. Robert Hurley (1976; London: Penguin, 1990), p. 43.
4 It is striking that a writer who imagines human/animal interaction with such fantasy and complexity in the *Jungle Books* could have relied so much on the word 'beastliness' when describing human sexual behaviour of which he disapproved.
5 Ernst Bloch, *Heritage of Our Times*, trans. Neville and Stephen Plaice (1935, 1962; Cambridge: Polity Press, 1991), p. 97.
6 The terms 'dominant', 'emergent' and 'residual' are of course from Raymond Williams. See his *Marxism and Literature* (Oxford: Oxford University Press, 1977), pp. 121–7.
7 Kipling to Lionel Charles Dunsterville, 11 June 1917, cited in Andrew Lycett, *Rudyard Kipling* (London: Weidenfeld & Nicolson, 1999), p. 521. In a letter of 10 December 1912, Kipling had told Dunsterville, 'I wish you'd let me know where you are going to send him to his final school. The Modern School-life, tho' different from ours, has still a certain amount of roughness in it. But what impresses me most is the amount of beastliness – elaborate and organized – that seems to exist at some of those institutions.' Generally a schoolboy's life is no longer as hard: 'But Lord! how they are fed and warmed and cubicled and looked after in the modern house as compared to our day.' *The Letters of*

Rudyard Kipling, Volume 4: 1911–19, ed. Thomas Pinney (Basingstoke: Macmillan, 1999), p. 136.
8 Edward Thring, *Sermons Preached at Uppingham School*, 2 vols (Cambridge: Deighton, Bell, 1886), vol. 2, p. 15. On the Victorian public school and sexual morality see J.R. de S. Honey, *Tom Brown's Universe: The Development of the Victorian Public School* (London: Millington, 1977), pp. 167–96.
9 Donald Leinster-Mackay, *The Educational World of Edward Thring: A Centenary Study* (London: The Falmer Press, 1987), pp. 121–3.
10 George R. Parkin, *Edward Thring, Headmaster of Uppingham School: Life, Diary, Letters* (1898; London: Macmillan, 1900), pp. 276–7.
11 Kipling, *Letters, Volume 4*, p. 107.
12 Carolyn Oulton, '"ain't goin' to have any beastly Erickin'": the Problem of Male Friendship in *Stalky & Co.*', *The Kipling Journal* 82 (April 2008), pp. 56–61. Kipling, 'The Moral Reformers', *The Complete Stalky & Co.*, ed. Isabel Quigly (Oxford: Oxford University Press, 1987), p. 124. For a story that links Hellenism, schoolboy friendship, Oxford and soldiering see Walter Pater, 'Emerald Uthwart', *Miscellaneous Studies: A Series of Essays* (London: Macmillan, 1895), pp. 170–214.
13 David's development is aided by his friendship with an older boy, Maddox, who first recognises and then overcomes a desire to bring a sexual element into the friendship. Their 'boy-love' is as 'hot as fire and clean as the trickle of ice-water on a glacier'. Another boy who had once been a friend of David's, Hughes, is expelled for 'something beastly', though he later gets into Sandhurst, which leads David and Maddox to think that he 'must have become a decent chap again' (E.F. Benson, *David Blaize* (1916; London: Hogarth Press, 1989), pp. 201, 193, 292). Benson drew on his time at Marlborough in the 1870s, though the novel is set later. In the sequel, *David of King's*, the close phase of the friendship between David and Maddox dissolves at the end of their undergraduate days at Cambridge (E.F. Benson, *David at King's* (1924; Los Angeles: Viewforth, 2010), pp. 251–5, 271–2). Another old boy of Marlborough, T.C. Worsley, described teaching at Wellington, the school John Kipling had attended, in his 1967 memoir of the 1920s and early 1930s, *Flannelled Fool* (the title of course is taken from Kipling's 1902 poem 'The Islanders'). Worsley noted that in terms of sex and indeed generally '[t]he culture and *mores* at [Wellington] were a great deal harsher than at Marlborough – which was generally considered an exceptionally tough place itself'. Very differently from either Kipling or Benson, Worsley argued that he would have benefitted if, at an early age, 'someone loved, trusted and admired, could have broken down that false innocence of mine, and with gentleness and love taught me the uses of my body': T.C. Worsley, *Flannelled Fool: A Slice of Life in the Thirties* (1967; London: Hogarth Press, 1985), pp. 27, 180.
14 Kipling, 'The United Idolaters', *The Complete Stalky & Co.*, pp. 140–54; Neil Cocks, 'Hunting the animal boy', *The Yearbook of English Studies* 32 (2002), pp. 177–85.
15 Kipling, *Something of Myself and Other Autobiographical Writings*, ed. Thomas Pinney (Cambridge: Cambridge University Press, 1990), p. 16.

16 See Kipling's February 1886 letter to his former teacher, W.C. Crofts, the basis for King in the Stalky stories, reacting – indignantly and at length – to learning from his friend Dunsterville of the suspicions of another schoolmaster, M.H. Pugh, which had led Pugh to put Kipling in a room of his own. Pinney suggests that Kipling drew on Pugh in his depiction of Prout in 'The Impressionists' in *Stalky & Co.*: see *The Letters of Rudyard Kipling, Volume 1: 1872–89*, ed. Thomas Pinney (Basingstoke: Macmillan, 1990), pp. 117–23: 123 n. 1. In the story Prout does indeed get the wrong 'impression' time after time. When he asks 'Beetle' (based on Kipling himself) whether he has come across any 'soul corrupting influences', the boy replies, 'genuinely bewildered', 'Consequences of what, sir?'. He has retained his innocence, and the story that Prout fears is 'beastly' in the sexual sense turns out to have been a frightening ghost story. Kipling, 'The Impressionists', *Complete Stalky*, pp. 111, 114.

17 Wright's long initial letter to *The Times* appeared on 28 March 1912. He maintained that 'there is mixed up with the woman's movement much mental disorder; and [the doctor] cannot conceal from himself the physiological emergencies which lie behind'. The letter was reprinted as 'Letter on Militant Hysteria' in Almroth Wright, *The Unexpurgated Case Against Woman Suffrage* (London: Constable, 1913), pp. 167–87. See also, Michael Dunnill, *The Plato of Praed Street: The Life and Times of Almroth Wright* (London: The Royal Society of Medicine Press, 2000). For the wider context of how the campaign for women's suffrage was seen through the prism of science and medicine, see Lisa Carstens, 'Unbecoming Women: Sex Reversal in the Scientific Discourse on Female Deviance in Britain, 1880–1920', *Journal of the History of Sexuality* 20, no. 1 (January 2011), pp. 62–94.

18 Kipling, *Letters, Volume 4*, p. 420.
19 *Ibid.*, p. 419.
20 *Ibid.*, p. 421.
21 Lycett, *Kipling*, pp. 520–1.
22 Lycett believes that neither Carrie nor Elsie would have been told about Oliver's sexuality, as '[w]omen were not supposed to know about such things in the Kipling household' (*ibid.*, p. 521). Material included in Christopher J. Walker's 2003 biography of Oliver Baldwin, however, suggests that by the end of 1924 Elsie was either fully aware of how things stood – and accepting of the situation – or very naive indeed. In a letter written to Oliver Baldwin from Brussels in October, after their marriage, Elsie and George asked after Johnnie's health, further noting that they were attended by 'two very handsome footmen and a more handsome chauffeur'. Christopher J. Walker, *Oliver Baldwin: A Life of Dissent* (London: Arcadia, 2003), p. 124.
23 Diana Souhami, *The Trials of Radclyffe Hall* (London: Virago, 1999), pp. 201–18.
24 Lycett, *Kipling*, pp. 550–1.
25 Kipling, *The Letters of Rudyard Kipling, Volume 5: 1920–30*, ed. Thomas Pinney (Basingstoke: Palgrave Macmillan, 2004), p. 453.
26 Cited in Lycett, *Kipling*, p. 551.
27 Rupert Hart-Davis, *Hugh Walpole: A Biography* (London: Macmillan, 1952), p. 296.

28 Seymour-Smith, *Rudyard Kipling*, p. 121.
29 *Early Verse by Rudyard Kipling, 1879–1889: Unpublished, Uncollected, and Rarely Collected Poems*, ed. Andrew Rutherford (Oxford: Clarendon, 1986), pp. 470–2.
30 See for example Lycett, *Kipling*, pp. 188–9: 199 and Phillip Mallett, *Rudyard Kipling: A Literary Life* (Basingstoke: Palgrave Macmillan, 2003), p. 49. The poem is, however, discussed as part of the thoughtful consideration of Kipling and literary London in Harry Ricketts, *The Unforgiving Minute: A Life of Rudyard Kipling* (New York: Carroll & Graf, 2000), pp. 152–4.
31 Charles Carrington, *Rudyard Kipling: His Life and Work* (1955; London: Penguin, 1970), p. 186. David Page, in a note at the end of his review of the poem's reception for *The New Readers' Guide to the Works of Rudyard Kipling*, observes that 'One needs to remember that the poem was destined for Kipling's Anglo-Indian readers in the *Civil and Military Gazette*, who were well used to his entertainingly satirical light-hearted verse.' www.kipling.org.uk/rg_partibus1.htm (accessed 26 July 2011.)
32 See Morris B. Kaplan, *Sodom on the Thames: Sex, Love, and Scandal in Wilde Times* (Ithaca, NY: Cornell University Press, 2005), pp. 166–223.
33 Matt Cook, *London and the Culture of Homosexuality, 1885–1914* (Cambridge: Cambridge University Press, 2003), pp. 22–5.
34 See the notes on 'In Partibus' by David Page in the *New Readers' Guide*, www.kipling.org.uk/rg_partibus_notes.htm (accessed 26 July 2011).
35 W.S. Gilbert, *Patience; or, Bunthorne's Bride* (London: Chappell, 1881), p. 7.
36 *Ibid.*, pp. 8, 13, 10.
37 Carolyn Williams, *Gilbert and Sullivan: Gender, Genre, Parody* (New York: Columbia University Press, 2011), p. 171.
38 Gilbert, *Patience*, p. 15.
39 Cook, *London and the Culture of Homosexuality*, pp. 25–6. For the subsequent period see Matt Houlbrook, 'Soldier heroes and rent boys: homosex, masculinities, and Britishness in the Brigade of Guards, circa 1900–1960', *The Journal of British Studies* 42, no. 3 (July 2003), pp. 351–88. A consideration of writing, homosexuality and effeminacy from Symonds to J.R. Ackerley and Jocelyn Brooke can be found in the chapter ' "No sign of *effeminatio*"? Towards the military orchid', in Joseph Bristow, *Effeminate England: Homoerotic Writing after 1885* (Buckingham: Open University Press, 1995), pp. 127–65.
40 Gerard Manley Hopkins, 'The Bugler's First Communion', *The Poems of Gerard Manley Hopkins*, ed. W.H. Gardner and N.H. MacKenzie (Oxford: Oxford University Press, 1970), pp. 82–3; D.H. Lawrence, 'Guards', *The Complete Poems*, ed. Vivian de Sola Pinto and F. Warren Roberts (London: Penguin, 1977), pp. 66–7. The soldiers' marching is described in terms of a sexual act in an earlier version of Lawrence's poem entitled 'The Review of the Scots Guards', part of the 'Movements' sequence in an early Lawrence notebook held at the University of Nottingham, Manuscript E317, in Warren Roberts and Paul Poplawski (eds), *A Bibliography of D.H. Lawrence*, 3rd edn (Cambridge: Cambridge University Press, 2001).

41 Edward Irenæus Stevenson, *White Cockades: An Incident of the 'Forty-Five'* (London: John Slark, 1887). Xavier Mayne [Edward Irenaeus Prime Stevenson], *Imre: A Memorandum* (Naples: privately published by 'The English Book Press', 1906; ed. James Gifford, Peterborough, ON: Broadview, 2003).

42 In 'Follow me 'ome', the line 'Oh, passin' the love o' women' describes the feelings of the I-voice for his dead comrade. The source is of course David mourning Jonathan in the Bible, 2 Samuel 1:26. Kipling, *Rudyard Kipling's Verse: The Definitive Edition* (London: Hodder & Stoughton, 1940), p. 446. In 'His Private Honour' (1891), collected in *Many Inventions* (1893; London: Macmillan, 1911), pp. 136–62, the violence and aggression Ortheris feels after he is hit by the young officer Ouless, leading to a cathartic fight, can be read in sexual terms as desire, frustration and release.

43 John Moray Stuart-Young, the subject of a 2006 study by Stephanie Newell, was brought up in one of the poorest areas of Manchester. Working as a clerk he funded the lifestyle of a well-off aesthete by embezzling from his employer. He began to write to his literary heroes, among them Oscar Wilde, Edward Carpenter and Rudyard Kipling. In later memoirs he claimed that he was lifted out of Manchester by the intervention of 'Cousin Ruddy' – that is, Kipling – when in fact he was initially arrested and imprisoned. Leaving Britain to make his way in the colonies, Stuart-Young became a successful trader in Onitsha, Nigeria. The local people came to call him 'Odeziaku', which means arranger, manager or keeper of wealth. He contracted a series of 'boy marriages', of which there was a tradition in Ebo culture, where the elder man was responsible for setting up the child in adult life. Returning occasionally to England to oversee the publication of volumes of verse, autobiography and fiction, Stuart-Young dedicated a volume of poems about Africa to Kipling, and kept up a steady stream of often sub-Kiplingesque verse. See Stephanie Newell, *The Forger's Tale: The Search for Odeziaku* (Athens: Ohio University Press, 2006), pp. 25, 76, 126, 140, 153 and *passim*.

44 *The Memoirs of John Addington Symonds*, ed. Phyllis Grosskurth (London: Hutchinson, 1984), pp. 253–4. (There is also a brief reference to an earlier sexual encounter with a soldier in the Parks in a section of the *Memoirs* not included in Grosskurth's published version; see page 510 of the manuscript in the London Library. I am grateful to the London Library for letting me read the manuscript, and to Amber K. Regis for sharing her expert knowledge of the text.) In *A Problem in Modern Ethics*, Symonds asked whether 'a young man sleeping with a prostitute picked up in the Haymarket is cleaner than his brother sleeping with a soldier picked up in the Park'. Symonds, *A Problem in Modern Ethics: Being an Enquiry into the Phenomenon of Sexual Inversion, Addressed Especially to Medical Psychologists and Jurists* (1891; London: privately printed, 1896), p. 110.

45 J.A. Symonds, 'Soldatenliebe und Verwandtes' in Havelock Ellis and J.A. Symonds, *Das Konträre Geschlechtsgefühl* (Leipzig: Georg H. Wigand, 1896), pp. 285–304. It seems that the original English version of the text does not survive. The German text is translated into English as 'Soldier Love and Related Matter' and published

with contextual material in Symonds, *Soldier Love and Related Matter*, trans. and ed. Andrew Dakyns (Eastbourne: Andrew Dakyns, 2007), pp. 9–18.
46 Phyllis Grosskurth, *John Addington Symonds: A Biography* (London: Longmans, 1964), pp. 279–82, 292; Hubert Kennedy, *Ulrichs: The Life and Works of Karl Heinrich Ulrichs, Pioneer of the Modern Gay Movement* (Boston: Alyson, 1988), pp. 216–18.
47 Karl Heinrich Ulrichs, *Ara Spei*, cited in Kennedy, *Ulrichs*, p. 82.
48 Symonds, *Soldier Love and Related Matter*, p. 9.
49 *Ibid.*, pp. 10, 12.
50 Ricketts, *Unforgiving Minute*, pp. 150–1.
51 'L'Envoi', whose first line is 'And they were stronger hands than mine', does not appear in later editions of *Soldiers Three*. It appears in *Definitive Verse* as 'A Dedication', though the capital letters for 'Thy' and 'Thou' were changed to lower case (Kipling, *Definitive Verse*, p. 637).
52 *The Letters of John Addington Symonds, Volume 3: 1885–1893*, ed. Herbert M. Schueller and Robert L. Peters (Detroit, MI: Wayne State University Press, 1969), pp. 381, 423.
53 Kipling, *Letters, Volume 1*, p. 374.
54 *Ibid.*, p. 358.
55 A list of Kipling's soldier stories can be found on the Kipling Society webpage at www.kipling.org.uk/soldiers_fra.htm (accessed 26 July 2011.)
56 Christopher Lane, *The Ruling Passion: British Colonial Allegory and the Paradox of Homosexual Desire* (Durham, NC: Duke University Press, 1995), pp. 18–25. For an extended reading of *The Light That Failed* and masculinity see Robert Hampson, 'Kipling and the fin-de-siècle' in Howard J. Booth, ed., *The Cambridge Companion to Rudyard Kipling* (Cambridge: Cambridge University Press, 2011), pp. 7–22.
57 Richard Le Gallienne, *Rudyard Kipling: A Criticism* (London: John Lane, 1900), p. 148.
58 Aware of the 1863 Italian edition of Michelangelo's poetry that restored the male pronouns in a number of the sonnets – they had been changed by Michelangelo's great-nephew – Symonds began to translate all the sonnets into rhymed English. The initial published group was used by Walter Pater in his essay 'The poetry of Michelangelo', first published in the *Fortnightly Review* in 1871 and later included in his *Studies in the History of the Renaissance* (1873). Symonds' complete translation of the sonnets, the first in English, appeared in 1878, while his *Life of Michelangelo Buonarotti*, perhaps his greatest work, was published in the year of his death. Symonds, 'Twenty-three sonnets from Michael Angelo', *The Contemporary Review*, 20 (September 1872), pp. 505–15; Walter Pater, *The Renaissance*, ed. Adam Phillips (Oxford: Oxford University Press, 1986), pp. xix, 47–62; Symonds, trans., *The Sonnets of Michael Angelo Buonarotti and Tommaso Campanella* (London: Smith, Elder, 1878); Symonds, *The Life of Michelangelo Buonarotti* (2 vols. London: John C. Nimmo, 1893). Symonds prepared the ground for Wilde's use of Michelangelo's sonnets in *The Picture of Dorian Gray*. There the poems suggest a form for the relationship of Basil and Dorian: 'Was it not Buonarotti who had carved it in the

coloured marbles of a sonnet-sequence?' (Oscar Wilde, *The Picture of Dorian Gray*, ed. Isobel Murray (Oxford: Oxford University Press, 1981), p. 36.) Wilde included 'the sonnets of Michelangelo' among the precedents for the 'Love that dare not speak its name' in his famous speech at his first trial in April 1895, quoted in Richard Ellmann, *Oscar Wilde* (1987; London: Penguin, 1988), p. 435.
59 Kipling, *The Light That Failed* (1891; London: Macmillan, 1907), p. 23.
60 Michelangelo's lost *Battle of Cascina* – though copies were made, with that by Bastiano da Sangallo the best known – in fact depicted Florentine troops surprised by Pisan soldiers. The Florentines recovered to win the battle. Paul Fussell has shown that the way bathing soldiers were used to figure fragile male beauty in Uranian poetry was picked up and reworked in the verse of the First World War in *The Great War and Modern Memory* (1975; New York: Oxford University Press, 2000), pp. 299–309.
61 Mallett, *Rudyard Kipling*, p. 58; Linda Murray, *Michelangelo* (London: Thames and Hudson, 1980), p. 200. For Symonds' admiring account of this then rarely praised work see his *Life of Michelangelo*, vol. 2, pp. 198–203. In the 'Florence Pietà' Jesus is supported by the central figure of a man, believed to be Nicodemus (and modelled on Michelangelo himself), as well as by Mary Magdalene and Mary the mother of Jesus. It is this unfinished work that the elderly Michelangelo famously attacked and damaged. A recent critic links this to Michelangelo's sudden awareness that he had inserted male–male love into a Pietà: Leela Gandhi, *Affective Communities: Anticolonial Thought, Fin-de-Siècle Radicalism, and the Politics of Friendship* (Durham, NC: Duke University Press, 2006), pp. 44–6.
62 Kipling, *The Light That Failed*, pp. 72, 66, 67.
63 *Ibid.*, pp. 83, 46, 49.
64 *Ibid.*, p. 46. The Marquess of Queensbury referred to 'The Snob Queers like Roseberry' in a 1 November 1894 letter to Alfred Montgomery. Cited in Ellmann, *Oscar Wilde*, p. 402.
65 Kipling, *The Light That Failed*, pp. 152, 96.
66 *Ibid.*, pp. 182, 161.
67 *Ibid.*, p. 167.
68 *Ibid.*, p. 173.
69 *Ibid.*, p. 193.
70 *Ibid.*, p. 214.
71 *Ibid.*, pp. 188–9, 278–9. Dick's excitement can be compared to the earlier practical joke with the bellows in the novel (p. 142). Generally in Kipling's texts the release offered by practical jokes is only available to men in the company of men. See Phillip Mallett's 'Kipling and the Hoax' in his edited collection *Kipling Considered* (Basingstoke: Macmillan, 1989), pp. 98–114.
72 Kipling, *The Light That Failed*, pp. 276–7, 284, 289.
73 For a different view, which notes the homoerotic glances and bonds in 'The Janeites', both at the front and in the lodge, see Vincent Quinn, 'Jane Austen, queer theory and the return of the author', *Women: A Cultural Review* 18, no. 1 (2007): 57–83.

74 Both Symonds and Edward Carpenter claimed that accounts of relationships between soldiers in the classical period demonstrated that there were historical precedents for same-sex passion being seen as healthy and manly; their emphasis though was on ancient Greece. Symonds, *A Problem in Modern Ethics*, pp. 76–7; Edward Carpenter, *The Intermediate Sex: A Study of some Transitional Types of Men and Women* (London: George Allen and Unwin, 1908), pp. 41, 44–5.
75 Kipling, *Puck of Pook's Hill* (London: Macmillan, 1906), pp. 177, 176, 177.

15

'A race to leave alone': Kipling and the Jews

BRYAN CHEYETTE

> When first by Eden Tree
> The Four Great Rivers ran,
> To each was appointed a Man
> Her Prince and Ruler to be.
>
> But after this was ordained
> (The ancient legends tell),
> There came dark Israel,
> For whom no River remained.
> (Rudyard Kipling, 'Song of the Fifth River', 1906)

> Israel is a race to leave alone. It abets disorder. (Kipling, *Something of Myself*, 1937)

> Kipling knew something of the things which are underneath, and of the things which are beyond the frontier. (T.S. Eliot, 1941)[1]

Introduction: the first clue

It is not a coincidence, as Noel Annan has noted, that there were several influential and lasting reassessments of Rudyard Kipling written in the early years of the Second World War. The catalyst for many of these reassessments was T.S. Eliot's long introduction to his *Choice of Kipling's Verse* (1941) – 'meditating among the bombs in war-time London' – which was, as Annan implies, Eliot's editorial contribution to Britain's war effort.[2] Choosing to promote Kipling when Britain stood alone, after Dunkirk, was a clear indication of Eliot's cultural allegiances – English, conservative, anti-German and, in a verse anthology that included 'Gehazi' (1913) and 'The Waster' (1930), endorsing a seemingly acceptable form of domestic anti-Semitism.[3] This war-time context for critical discussion of Kipling still shapes our contemporary understanding, as can be seen in a number of recent collections and essays, but not always in an illuminating manner. The danger of reading Kipling back from the criticism of the 1940s – with an understandable focus as I will show on the question of fascism, anti-Semitism and the 'doctrine of racial superiority'[4] – is that it can lead to an overly teleological version of Kipling which gives the politics and context of the European continent in the late 1930s an undue prominence.[5]

But this is not a straightforward matter. A few years after Eliot's anthology was published, Hannah Arendt, a refugee from Nazi Germany, began work in the United States in 1944 on her monumental *The Origins of Totalitarianism* (1951). In this book she characterised Kipling as the very personification of 'The Imperialist Character' and proposed a connection between the Great Game of Empire and the 'game of totalitarianism':

> Lying under [the] nose [of The Imperialist Character] were many of the elements which gathered together could create totalitarian government on the basis of racism. 'Administrative massacres' were proposed by Indian bureaucrats while African officials declared that 'no ethical considerations such as the rights of man will be allowed to stand in the way' of white rule.[6]

The Origins of Totalitarianism was the first and best account of the links between the racism and dehumanisation of empire and of fascism, with Kipling, in the guise of The Imperialist Character, prefiguring these criss-crossing histories. It was in this spirit that Kipling's critics in the 1940s either characterised their subject as a 'fascist' or 'racist' or, with equal vehemence, denied these depictions. After all, both Arendt and Eliot regarded Kipling as 'The Imperialist Character'; only Eliot thought this was perfectly acceptable as Kipling was 'concerned with the problem of the soundness of the core of empire' which is 'something older, more natural and more permanent' and which speaks implicitly to the ability of Imperial Britain to survive the German onslaught. Kipling's vision was 'almost that of an idea of empire laid up in heaven' and, to this extent, the 'idea of empire' was akin to Eliot's *The Idea of a Christian Society* (1939) and equally removed from the brute realities of colonialism, racism and fascism. For this reason, Eliot could not 'find any justification for the charge that [Kipling] held a doctrine of racial superiority'.[7]

But it was not just Arendt, regarded as a rather marginal figure at the time, who could write about Kipling's imperialism in the 1940s under the sign of fascism. Edmund Wilson in *The Wound and the Bow* (1941) characterised Kipling as 'implacably opposed to every race and nation which has rebelled against or competed with the Empire'. Writing in a similar vein in 1941, H.E. Bates was to take the next step, comparing Kipling with Hitler.[8] In a 1943 essay in *The Nation*, Lionel Trilling, with more subtlety, responded explicitly to Eliot by arguing that 'Kipling is not properly to be called a fascist, but neither is his political temperament to be adequately described merely by reference to a [Tory] tradition . . . his Toryism often had in it a lower-middle-class snarl of defeated gentility, and it is this, rather than his love of authority and force, that might suggest an affinity with fascism.'[9] In this first version of his essay, which differs from that published in *The Liberal Imagination* (1950), Trilling also made the link between these 'affinities' and Kipling's anti-Semitism. He objected in particular to Eliot's inclusion of 'The Waster' (1930) in *A Choice of Kipling's Verse* on the grounds that the poem characterised a 'snippy, *persecuted* anti-Semitism of ironic good manners'. He argues that when Kipling writes 'etc.' in the poem the rhyme in two stanzas actually requires the word 'Jew':

> From the date that the doors of his prep-school close
>   On the lonely little son
> He is taught by precept, insult and blows
>   The Things That Are Never Done.
> Year after year, without favour or fear,
>   From seven to twenty-two,
> His keepers insist he shall learn the list
>   Of the things no fellow can do.
> (They are not so strict with the average Pict
>   And it isn't set to, etc.)

For Trilling, the 'gist' of 'The Waster' is that the English, because of their 'public-school code' are 'always being beaten by certain unscrupulous racial groups who do Things That Are Never Done to succeed'.[10] Eliot replied to Trilling's essay saying that 'I am not aware that [Kipling] cherished any particularly anti-Semitic feelings' and this blanket apologia has been reinforced by a good many contemporary critics.[11] Trilling, however, responded with telling effect:

> As anti-Semitism goes these days, I suppose Kipling is not – to use Mr Eliot's phrase – particularly anti-Semitic. I certainly should not think of isolating for discussion what anti-Semitism he has, but only of mentioning, as one aspect of a complex xenophobia, his queasy, resentful feelings about Jews.

Christopher Ricks rightly notes that 'not particularly anti-Semitic' were 'incautious words of Eliot's, not least in their measured air of caution'.[12] But the debate on Kipling's racism and fascism in the 1940s was not always reduced to either a conservative or radical position. As Trilling first noted, Orwell dismissed the 'liberal' critique as it resulted in 'contempt for *everything* that Kipling stood for'.[13] It was on these grounds that Orwell, who was probably aware of the Hitler comparison by Bates, was to challenge the accusation that Kipling was a 'Fascist': 'the "Fascist" charge has to be answered, because the first clue to any understanding of Kipling, morally or politically, is the fact that he was *not* a Fascist' (Orwell's emphasis).[14] As Kipling had spent most of his life warning of the 'German danger', Orwell writing in 1942 did not want to risk losing the legacy of this anti-fascist position by conflating Kipling with continental 'fascism'.

My essay will follow Orwell, resisting those who simply read Kipling back from the history of European fascism in the 1930s and 1940s. I take this position because, as I will argue, a teleological reading of Kipling flattens out the complexity of his use of what I shall call a Semitic racial discourse and reduces it to its most lethal 'fascist' form. But I also take seriously Hannah Arendt's 'boomerang effect' – that is, the ways in which European 'race-thinking' in the European colonies in Africa and South East Asia rebounded back on the continent of Europe in the form of German fascist anti-Semitism.[15] To this extent I agree with Trilling's argument that Kipling's feelings about Jews were a microcosm of much broader imperial concerns. These, rather than the history of European fascism, will be the focus of my essay, which is why I take a mainly historicist approach, contextualising Kipling's work in Victorian, Edwardian and inter-war Britain. As Boris Ford argued in 1942, no one with a sense of 'chronological exactitude' should simply dismiss Kipling as a 'fascist'.[16] But the problem with reading Kipling historically, in relation to British culture, is precisely that his imperial vision and use of racial discourse went far beyond national boundaries and democratic liberal constraints. I will now explore the tensions between contextualising Kipling, and reading him teleologically, in the section below.

Kipling and other teleologists

This essay is at pains not to conflate the Victorian, Edwardian and inter-war year contexts of Kipling's work with the most violent form of free-floating anti-Semitism in continental Europe in the 1940s – which would be, to say the least, a chronological inexactitude. There are those who assess images of 'the Jew' in the Victorian novel, for instance, with 'the memory of Nazi Germany still fresh'; but this form of 'back-shadowing', as I have argued elsewhere, leads to an ahistorical and rather crude version of literary anti-Semitism which lacks a defined context.[17] Yet there are limits to this historicist approach. For example, 'Gehazi' (1913) is described by Eliot rather misleadingly as 'passionate invective rising to real eloquence' and as an example of the 'important influence of Biblical imagery' in Kipling's fiction and poetry'.[18] The poem has been adopted in extreme anti-Semitic circles, well beyond its immediate context, although I discuss it here primarily with reference to the years leading up to the First World War, where the role of the public anti-Semite was initially considered beyond the pale.[19] Even 'The Waster', an inter-war poem which Trilling responded to in 1943 with the sensitivities of a Jewish American, looks back over a quarter of a century to 'The Army of a Dream' (1904), a didactic story about nation-wide military exercises to bolster the Empire after the debacle of the Boer War, written as part of the campaign for conscription which preoccupied Kipling from 1900 to 1913. The exercises were to include Jewish Voluntary Schools ('Jew-Boys') who, collectively in 'The Army of a Dream' or individually in 'The Waster', beat the 'English' students at their own game. A clarion call comes at the end of the long two-part story:

' *"To your Tents, O Israel! The Hebrew Schools stop the Mounted Troops"*. Pig, were you scuppered by Jew-boys? . . . By Jove, there'll have to be an inquiry into this regrettable incident!'[20]

Angus Wilson has described 'The Army of a Dream' as an example of Kipling's philo-Semitic 'respect for the Jewish contribution to Western civilization' which, if true, implies a low opinion of Kipling's 'respect' ('scuppered by Jew-boys'). Wilson argues that the use of 'Jew-boys' is slang common to the whole Victorian and Edwardian age but, as we will see, this term of abuse is quite specific to Kipling's self-consciously illiberal and racialised vocabulary and cannot be assimilated to the language of tolerant liberal reasoning, epitomised by the ideal of the 'Jewish contribution to Western civilization'.[21]

Nonetheless, if we compare 'The Army of a Dream' with, say, 'His Private Honour' (1891), we can see why Wilson regards the former story as philo-Semitic. 'His Private Honour', one of Kipling's more sadistic stories, concerns in part the persecution of a Jewish army recruit in the brutal overall context of the induction of new recruits. Private Anderson (renamed 'Samuelson' or 'the Jew') is bullied by Private Stanley Ortheris, a sympathetic figure who first appeared in *Plain Tales from the Hills* (1888). As John McClure has argued, the Cockney Ortheris was characterised in these early stories by the 'particular ferocity of [his] hatred' compared to the other 'musketeers' Privates Learoyd and Mulvaney.[22] This ferocity continues in 'His Private Honour' where the enraged Ortheris, after he is publically humiliated by Lieutenant Ouless, keeps the 'Jew monkey' or the 'pink-eyed Jew' in his place: 'If the Jew opened his mouth in the most casual remark, Ortheris would plunge down it with all arms and accoutrements'. The narrator's approval of Ortheris is assured, given his place in the pantheon of Kipling's earlier stories, and the retention of his 'honour' is clearly defined as a form of illiberal heroic masculinity: 'My rights! 'Strewth A'mighty! I'm a man.'[23]

But to read 'The Army of a Dream' as a 'philo-Semitic' version of an 'anti-Semitic' poem or story is to illustrate the limits of this vocabulary where the critic decides what is, or is not, 'anti-' or 'philo-'. My argument is that 'anti-Semitism' and 'philo-Semitism' are two relatively distinct aspects of a much broader history of differentiating Jews racially from other human beings, which is why I speak of a Semitic discourse.[24] The problem with a teleological perspective is that it tends to discount the ambivalence of a Semitic discourse where the boundaries between 'anti-' and 'philo-' are more blurred than is usually assumed. A teleological reading therefore flattens out the past in the name of our present post-Holocaust preoccupations. This problem of 'back-shadowing' is especially acute in the case of Kipling as he, crucially, was to reverse the so-called philo-Semitic figure of 'the Jew' in his stories and letters in the years leading up to the First World War.

A key instance of Kipling's refashioning of 'the Jew' teleologically can be found in a long letter to André Chevrillon which shows the extent to which he was eventually to reduce any ambivalence in his work concerning 'the Jew' to an unequivocal dread. Writing in October 1919, Kipling was to reassess the 'German danger' with the hindsight of nearly three decades. He argued that the 'sad new world' of 1919 began in 1896 with, in particular, the 'Kaiser's wire to Kruger' reinforcing the abject failure of the 1895 Jameson Raid. He related this defeat to the subsequent refusal of England to prepare itself militarily to halt Germany. By October 1919, a railway strike had just come to an end and Kipling was to read the 'German danger' back into the strike:

> Nominally, it is the Railway men and Trade Unions who are doing it. Actually it is the Hun, the Bolshevik and the Jew of Poland chiefly. In spite of their best efforts to speak and act like white men, one sees in the cruelty practised on the [abandoned] railway horses, the hand of the Hun.[25]

Such conspiracy theories were freely deployed by Kipling and intensified after the First World War. They were associated, as we will see, with the perceived loss of Empire (beginning with the failure of the Jameson Raid) which was related to the inability of 'the Jews' to act like 'white men'. In South Africa, at the turn of the century, Jews were deemed to have helped maintain the Empire, not unlike the idealised 'Man of the Future' who Kipling in 1899 hoped would shape the United States:

> Wait till the Anglo-American-German-Jew – the Man of the Future – is properly equipped. He'll have just the least little kink in his hair now and again; he'll carry the English lungs above the Teuton feet that can walk forever ... He'll be the finest writer, poet and dramatist, 'specially dramatist, that the world as it recollects itself has ever seen. By virtue of his Jew blood – just a little, little drop – he'll be a musician and a painter too.

While claims for Kipling's philo-Semitism have been made with regard to the 'Anglo-American-German-Jew' it is clear that this is a deeply racialised figure who is not quite 'white' with a 'little kink in his hair', 'Teuton feet' and a tiny drop of 'Jew blood'.[26] Much of this racialisation and conspiratorial thinking – significantly in a 'philo-Semitic' form – was present in Kipling's poetry, fiction and prose from the 1880s onwards, but this was not the same as the fascist version of 'the Jew'. As Craig Raine has noted, there is a dark double of the 'Man of the Future' in the first volume of *From Sea to Sea* who accounts for Kipling leaving the United States: 'I have met a lump of Chicago Jews and am afraid that I shall meet many more. The ship is full of Americans, but the American-German-Jew boy is the most awful of all'.[27] Kipling's earliest representations of 'the Jew' or 'Jew boy' thus veer between the supposed philo-Semitic 'Anglo-American-German-Jew' of the future and his supposed anti-Semitic mirror-image, the 'American-German-Jew boy'.[28] The advantage of contextualising Kipling's ambivalent racial discourse is that it recognises the historical contingencies of this discourse either within a British liberal cultural context or a more brute colonial context and not least, following Arendt, the mutually sustaining interconnections between both contexts.

Kipling's anti-Semitic philo-Semitism

As is well known, Kipling regularly visited South Africa from 1898 to 1908 and stayed in a house on the estate of Cecil Rhodes during the winter months. He could not have been further removed from the prevailing left-liberal malign representation of the conspiratorial 'Jewish financier' who was commonly blamed for instigating the Boer War.[29] Such pro-Boer conspiracy theories were countered by an imperial discourse where 'Jewish' money and power were supposedly aligned with Britain's imperial interests and could help shape the future.

Kipling was to confront pro-Boer public opinion in *Traffics and Discoveries* (1904) and, in particular, challenged the liberal or socialist version of 'the Jew'.[30] 'The Comprehension of Private Copper' (1902), for instance, associates pro-Boer politics with treachery and the decline of the Imperial Race. Private Alfred Copper's 'comprehension' is attained after he captures a 'renegid' Englishman who has been fighting for the Boers because his father had been betrayed as an 'Uitlander' (literally a 'foreigner') by a vacillating British government. The racial degeneration of the British colonialist is deemed by Kipling to be a consequence of an equivocating policy towards the Uitlanders which has deprived them of the benefits of the Empire for the previous eight years.[31] Private Copper thus begins to 'comprehend' the importance of Empire and of the Boer War in maintaining an English presence in Africa. In this context, he distances himself from the complaints of the 'renegid' with the help of the humourist McBride, who reads to him from 'Jerrold's Weekly',[32] a liberal pro-Boer newspaper:

> 'You're the aristocrat, Alf. Old Jerrold's givin' it you 'ot. You're the uneducated 'ireling of a callous aristocracy which 'as sold itself to the 'Ebrew financier. Meantime, Ducky' – he ran his finger down a column of assorted paragraphs – 'you're slakin' your brutal instincks in furious excesses. Shriekin' women an' desolated 'omesteads is what you enjoy, Alf... Halloa! What's a smokin' 'ektacomb?'[33]

Once the necessity of defending the integrity of the Imperial Race in Africa has been properly 'comprehended', Kipling is at pains to show the irrelevance to the ordinary soldiers of the ''Ebrew financier'. This maligned figure, ubiquitous within pro-Boer circles, was irrelevant to Kipling, who was at pains to utilise the power of the 'Jewish financier', following Benjamin Disraeli, John Buchan and Henry Rider Haggard, for the good of the Empire.[34] What is more, the 'Jewish financier' could also assume a philo-Semitic form, when aligned to Empire, in Kipling's stories of the period such as 'The Treasure and the Law'.

'The Treasure and the Law', the final story of *Puck of Pook's Hill* (1906), represents the climax of a sequence of tales in which other ethnicities (Roman, Anglo-Saxon, Norman, Viking) are formed into the myth of an organic

English history. The story's fabling is more abstract and quasi-allegorical than its predecessors, as spelled out in Puck's gloss 'The Sword gave the Treasure, and the Treasure gave the Law! It's as natural as an oak growing'; hence Kipling's reservation expressed in *Something of Myself* that it was 'too heavy for its frame'.[35] Published some nine months after the catastrophic – from Kipling's point of view – Liberal victory in the General Election of 1906, it contains a veiled reference to pro-Boer conspiracy theories of the time in the 'Song of the Fifth River' which accompanies it. In the poem, Kipling postulates a divine 'Jewish' connection to the 'Secret River of Gold' or the world's money supply:

> When first by Eden Tree
> The Four Great Rivers ran,
> To each was appointed a Man
> Her Prince and Ruler to be.
>
> But after this was ordained,
> (The ancient legends tell),
> There came dark Israel,
> For whom no River remained.
>
> Then He Whom the Rivers obey
> Said to him: 'Fling on the ground
> A handful of yellow clay,
> And a Fifth Great River shall run,
> Mightier than these Four,
> In secret the Earth around;
> And Her secret evermore
> Shall be shown to thee and thy Race.'

This God-given chosen relationship to the 'Secret River of Gold' has resulted in 'dark Israel' having the legendary capacity to anticipate both 'drought' and 'flood' and to 'turn [them] to his gain'. As a consequence, Jews are represented in the last stanza of the poem as having a mystical ability to follow the 'gold' throughout the ages:

> . . . the Fifth Great River keeps
> The secret of Her deeps
> For Israel alone,
> As it was ordered to be.

'The Treasure and the Law' illustrates the poem when Kadmiel tells how the Magna Carta was signed when King John needed to borrow money from 'us Jews' who, in return, 'sought Power – Power – Power! That is *our* God in our captivity. Power to use!' At this climactic moment in English history, Norman and Saxon, Jew and Christian, are subsumed under the Law with the power of 'we Jews' at the heart of this achievement:

> There can be no war without gold, and we Jews know how the earth's gold moves with the seasons, and the crops, and the winds; circling and looping and rising and sinking away like a river – a wonderful underground river. How should the foolish Kings know *that* while they fight and steal and kill?... [M]y Prince saw peace or war decided not once, but many times, by the fall of a coin spun between a Jew from Bury and a Jewess from Alexandria... Such power had we Jews among the Gentiles.

In this supposedly exemplary past, there is a 'natural' union between what is called 'the Sword', 'the Treasure' and 'the Law'.[36] The idealised partnership between 'Jewish' financial power ('the Treasure') and colonial Law – backed up by the imperial 'Sword' – is an implicit riposte to those pro-Boer conspiracy theorists who maintained that it was an unscrupulous Jewish plutocracy who promoted the Boer War. But, in opposing this contention, it is obvious that Kipling was still using a racially inflected 'philo-Semitism' which, not unlike its 'anti-Semitic' counterpart, constructed 'the Jews' as all-powerful and all-knowing financiers who, at the triumphant moment of a civilising Englishness, were able to align money, power and the law.

Kadmiel, who retells the story of the Magna Carta from the perspective of Moses in exile from the Promised Land, is explicitly identified with the romantic tradition of the omniscient, eternally Wandering Jew.[37] Even though he is embittered by persecution, he is an entirely sympathetic figure (*pace* H.R. Millar's illustrations, which make him seem fantastically sinister) as, most importantly, he pays a bribe of two hundred gold pieces to ensure that the drafting of Habeas Corpus applies universally. Kadmiel's timeless achievement was to dispose of his wealth in order to establish Law and Justice for the nascent English nation. In this way (as Hannah Arendt argued in relation to Benjamin Disraeli), the covenant of the biblical chosen people is passed on to the chosen imperial few who manage the present-day Empire. That is why, at the end of the story, the idealised Kadmiel, who harmonises law, money and power, is contrasted starkly not only with his contemporary 'Elias of Bury' but also with the modern pheasant-shooting 'Mr Meyer' who, by imitating the English gentry and disavowing his relationship to a God-given law, demonstrates the extent to which the biblically chosen have become degenerate. Although Kadmiel's 'Treasure gave the Law', leaving the English forever in his debt, the modern assimilated Jew remains suspect for Kipling.

Neither black nor white: Semitic ambivalence within the Empire

Salman Rushdie, in an essay on Kipling, highlights 'On the City Wall' (1888) as a key instance of Kipling's veracity with regard to pre-Independence India. Following Rushdie, Aamer Mufti has argued that 'On the City Wall' enacts the 'impossibility of the transition from colony to nation' following the exclusion of Muslims from the nation-state, unlike Lalun's 'eclectic' or cosmopolitan salon – a sanctuary from Indian political and religious strife situated on the borders of the city – with Lalun significantly not associated with any one religious or ethnic grouping.[38] As well as defining the limitations of Indian nationalism, 'On the City Wall' also speaks to a contemporaneous European nationalism where 'the Jews' like 'the Muslims' present what Mufti calls 'an insurmountable problem for narratives of national existence'.[39] These questions coincide in the figure of Wali Dad, a westernised Muslim, who has an extraordinary outburst when it comes to Jews frequenting Lalun's cosmopolitan salon. He is speaking to the English journalist who narrates the story:

> 'Outside of a Freemasons' Lodge I have never seen such [eclectic] gatherings. *There* I dined once with a Jew – a Yahoudi! . . . Though I have lost every belief in the world,' said he, 'and try to be proud of my losing, I cannot help hating a Jew. Lalun admits no Jews here.'[40]

In *Something of Myself*, Kipling remembers joining the Freemasons in 1885 in Lahore, three years before writing the story, where he met 'Muslims, Hindus, Sikhs, members of the Brahmo Samaj, and a Jew Tyler, who was priest and butcher in the city' commenting: 'So yet another world opened to me which I needed'.[41] But this version of cosmopolitan freemasonry is severely curtailed by the English-educated Wali Dad who, although poised like Kipling between Britain and India, needs viscerally to hate 'the Jew'. Such rampant Jew-hatred demonstrates the racial limitations of the westernised Muslim, illustrated later in the story when he turns savage: 'These swine of Hindus! We shall be gutting kine in their temples tonight'. Wali Dad, in a more civilised incarnation, had described Lalun's salon as 'Athenian',[42] which reinforces his identification with Hellenism rather than Hebraism, Aryan rather than Jew. But these remain European rather than Indian distinctions. That Jews fit uneasily unto the cosmopolitanism of Empire can be seen in the figure of the 'Jew Tyler' who is also limited by his role as a 'priest and butcher'. Such particularist limitations are writ large in 'Jews in Shushan' (1887) written a year before 'On the City Wall'.

The protagonist of 'Jews in Shushan' is 'Ephraim the Jew', also a butcher and would-be priest, whose Muslim servant, echoing Wali Dad, grinds his teeth with 'all the scorn he dare show his master'. Ephraim is introduced initially as a rather 'meek' child-like debt-collector who 'resembled an over-fed sheep', and who is utterly preoccupied with the desire to build a synagogue in Shushan by forming a prayer quorum of ten Jews: 'these eight of the Chosen People were [waiting for] their full congregation'. After his initial 'meek' appearance ('never was Jew more unlike his dread breed') Ephraim is, however, quickly transformed into a 'dread' example of the dangers of 'the Jew' outside of the Law. When the door which shuts Ephraim 'off from the world of the Gentile' is opened, he is seen as the 'butcher to our [Jewish] people', holding a 'half-maddened sheep':

> He was attired in strange raiment . . . and a knife was in his mouth. As he struggled with the animal between the walls, the breath came from him in thick sobs, and the nature of the man seemed changed. When the ordained slaughter was ended, he saw that the door was open and shut it hastily, his hand leaving a red mark on the timber . . . A glimpse of Ephraim busied in one of his religious capacities was no thing to be desired twice.

Ephraim's radical doubleness, not unlike that of Wali Dad, can be seen in the way in which he both resembled a sheep (associated with cowardice) and could savagely butcher a sheep in the name of a primitive religious ritual. Soon after this episode, Kipling's narrator comments rather po-facedly that the Jews of Sushan 'set at naught the sanitary regulations of a large, flourishing, and remarkably well-governed Empire'. Ephraim's quest to establish a synagogue in Shushan and become its 'priest', a constant refrain in the story, is here deemed a form of racial primitivism at odds with the wider cathedral of Empire. Thwarted by the deaths of his children and most of the other congregants, the consequences of Ephraim obeying his own savage Judaic laws – as opposed to 'the Law' of Empire – is severe punishment. His wife Miriam, driven insane by the death of their children, 'wander[s] over the country' looking for them but 'never came back'. Her suicide is deemed harshly by her co-religionists to be 'untrue to her race' and she becomes one of a number of suffering Jewish Miriams in Kipling's oeuvre.[43]

'Jews in Shushan' ends on a disparaging racial note when an unpleasant Subaltern whistles 'Ten Little Nigger Boys', which is described by the narrator as the 'dirge of the Jews of Shushan'. Kipling's primitive Jews are severely punished both for thinking that the synagogue could protect them from the 'sickness' that was decimating the city and for putting the needs of their own community ahead of the Empire. Most crucially, such racial primitivism could unleash dark forces – 'the nature of the man seemed changed' – which in another time and place would not be contained so easily. Next to the Anglo-Saxon chosen rulers of a well-governed Empire (who will eventually learn to reject the 'boastings' of the Gentiles), the outmoded 'Chosen People' of Shushan are reduced to 'Ten Little Nigger Boys'.

But not all Jewish blood in Kipling's stories of this time is racially primitive. 'His Chance in Life' (1887),[44] written in the same year as 'Jews in Shushan', offers a completely different reading of 'the Jew' in the domain of Empire. Set on the familiar racial 'borderline' where 'the last drop of White blood ends and the full Black tide sets in', 'His Chance in Life' concerns the 'very black' Michele D'Cruze, who has only 'seven-eighths native blood in his veins', his 'other blood being part 'Portuguese' and part 'black Jew of Cochin'. In the typically divided racial context of Kipling's Indian stories, D'Cruze finds himself confronted with a native riot and a local Police Inspector who regards him as a 'Sahib' because of the 'old race-instinct which recognises a drop of White blood as far as it can be diluted'. Kipling's narrator notes caustically that 'the man with the Cochin Jew and the menial uncle in his pedigree' was 'the only representative of English authority in the place'. By asserting his 'authority', and sending for the British Army to stem the riot, D'Cruze's heart becomes 'big and white in his breast'. But when faced with the authentic sign of 'Our Authority', in the guise of the young English officer who comes to take over, D'Cruze 'felt himself slipping back more and more into the native . . . It was the White drop of blood in his veins dying out'.[45]

What is clear from 'His Chance in Life' is that whether a 'Jew' was 'white' or 'black' depended ultimately on a wider relationship to British imperial 'authority'. As Stephen Arata notes, 'authority inheres in blood' but 'where blood is mixed' racial identity becomes 'fluid or problematic'.[46] 'Dark Israel' was problematic precisely because of its dangerous indeterminacy, which meant that it could be both 'white' and 'black', 'east' and 'west' at the same time. D'Cruze was to end up earning an imperial salary of sixty-six rupees, to pay for his fiancée's dowry, which contrasts markedly with Ephraim's loss of his family and friends for daring to engage in primitive Jewish rituals in the context of 'the Law' of Empire. Such were the stark options open to Kipling's Indian Jews situated awkwardly on the borderline between 'white' and 'black'.[47]

Neither white nor black: Jewish ambivalence outside the Empire

'For One Night Only' (1890), published a few years after Kipling's Indian stories, unleashes many of the dark, primitive forces (the 'Powers of Darkness') that have been characterised as 'the abyss' in Kipling's work.[48] It concerns a haunted theatre box which entraps its occupants and makes them face their worst fears. The story also refers back to the 'lump of Chicago Jews' on an Ocean-liner and 'the American-German-Jew boy . . . the most awful of all' in the first volume of *From Sea to Sea* discussed above. In 'For One Night Only' it is 'Geissler – the Chicago Jew' who is hated by Mrs Skittleworth: 'I hate Geissler. I could never send him anything at dinner without hoping that the fat, or the drumstick, or the stuffing would choke him, and then I would never send for the doctor.' As with Wali Dad, her Jew-hatred eventually explains her character, although this is not immediately obvious to the narrator, who first knew her 'On the Other Side of the World' [i.e. India]. But as England is regarded as 'the habitation of heathen the worse for being imperfectly converted' Mrs Skittleworth's unstoppable outbursts against 'the Jew' do finally connect her with the 'imperfectly converted' Wali Dad.

Mrs Skittleworth's all-consuming rage against Geissler ('the Israelite, whom I will never forgive') is occasioned when he obtains a cursed theatre box inexpensively, leading to the horrific evening. His purchase of the box is deemed to be a sign of his 'ineffable meanness' which, along with his gluttony – 'he is always hungry' – stereotypes the 'Chicago Jew'. Geissler's main characteristic, repeated throughout the story, is that he talks continually about 'founders' shares, whatever they may be. Things that grow up in a night out of nothing and are sold by telegraph.' And 'the worst of it is that he doesn't look like a Jew and he ought to'.[49] While his empty materialism ('Things that grow up in a night') is not racialised, it is contrasted with the very real night-terrors which Mrs Skittleworth and her party encounter in the theatre box: 'It was unspeakable. It was Chaos – raving, mad, howling Chaos!' The unexplained 'darkness of terror' affects those in the haunted theatre box in different ways. As Mrs Skittleworth observes, Geissler completely loses control and, after succumbing to the 'Powers of Darkness', finally looks like a 'Jew':

> All the Jew that ever cheated came out in Geissler's face . . . He was not looking at the stage, but into the darkness, and I was more than conscious that he must be staring fiendishly at the opposite box. Staring like a maniac . . . He looked hideous – as though being burned alive . . . He seemed to be in pain. Thinking of founders' shares possibly.

While those with a 'British education' can resist the worst of the darkness, Geissler is completely paralysed and limited to 'glaring into Tophet' or hell. Not unlike 'Ephraim the Jew', whose nature changes during his savage religious ritual, the 'hideous' or 'fiendish' Geissler is transformed by these dark forces. But, despite the outrageous stereotyping of the 'Chicago Jew' by Mrs Skittleworth, Geissler, along with the others in the box, is actually a victim not an instigator of a conspiracy. After the party flees the theatre box, it turns out that those outside were well aware of what they had confronted, which was why Geissler had been able to purchase the haunted box for a bargain price. Geissler is, then, as much a dupe as Mrs Skittleworth although he is blamed by her for the terrifying evening. In this early story, the superior forces of civilisation (which allowed Mrs Skittleworth's party to wait until the end of the first act of the play before leaving) enabled all but 'the Jew' to cope with the Powers of Darkness. The inferior Geissler, not unlike Mr Meyer in 'The Treasure and the Law', is merely vulgar and deluded, utterly unable to detach himself from the primitive forces unleashed in the theatre.[50]

Two widely divergent stories, 'Bread Upon the Waters' (1895) and 'The House Surgeon' (1909), also demonstrate the disturbing ambivalence of 'the Jew' who, like Geissler, represents both the modernising universalism of Capital – the 'dangerous solvent of society' as Noel Annan puts it – as well as the primitivism of the colonial subject.[51] In 'Bread Upon the Waters', a tale of revenge, Kipling recounts the adventure of McRimmon, a ship owner, who 'cuts the liver out o' Holdock, Steiner, Chase, and Company, Limited',[52] a supposedly unscrupulous rival firm of shippers who dismiss McPhee their chief engineer after twenty years of exemplary service because he refuses to run his ship, the *Breslau*, to a reduced time schedule. Throughout the tale, McPhee's traditional sea-faring values are juxtaposed with a ruthless modernity which he associates specifically with 'Young Steiner', the son of the firm's founder:

> The old Board would ne'er ha' done it. They trusted me. But the new Board was all for reorganisation. Young Steiner – Steiner's son – the Jew, was at the bottom of it, an' they did not think it worth their while to send me word.

While Steiner's father was acceptable to McPhee, it is 'Young Steiner' – one of the generation of British-Jews like Meyer who should have become more 'civilized' – who personifies a destructive financial efficiency and calculating disregard for the lives and customs of Britain's sailors. But, as with Mrs Skittleworth, there is a sense in which 'Young Steiner' is being blamed by McPhee for a materialism that is actually shared by everyone in the story. 'Bread Upon the Waters', in fact, is saturated with references to material wealth and the price of absolutely everything. We are told, for instance, that McPhee lives in a 'little twelve pound house' and the Holdocks, who are Methodists, live a mile away 'for they stayed by their money as their money stayed with them'. The story is framed by McPhee celebrating his £25,000 windfall and, as a result, his house is full of relatively modest new purchases such as curtains at 'forty-five shillings a pair'. McRimmon, who owns a rival firm and conspires with McPhee, is, we are repeatedly told, worth two million pounds. This wealth enabled McRimmon to attempt to 'break that Jew-firm'[53] after a wait of fourteen years (presumably because of Old Steiner). In fact, the whole dispute boils down to whether a ship can be repaired for less than £300 and whether it is worth more in unprofitable active service or as uninsured scrap.

'Young Steiner', at the very least, is part of a much broader materialistic context but McPhee's continued abuse of him – 'there's more discernment in a dog than a Jew' – leads to a form of scapegoating where spoken vulgarity is characterised as 'conversational Hebrew' and a rival shipping business as a 'Jerusalem firm'. McPhee, above all else, resents the challenge to his 'craftsmanship', which he characterises as his 'Shekinah' (from the Hebrew, 'divine presence'). The opposition in 'The Treasure and the Law' between Kadmiel and Meyer reappears in McPhee (taking the role of the divinely Chosen) against 'Young Steiner'. McPhee, that is, considers the prospect of bankrupting the 'Jew firm' to be one of 'those singular providences' that proves that 'we're in the hands of Higher Powers'.[54] But whereas 'The Secret River of Gold' works with the 'Higher Powers', 'Bread Upon the Waters' reflects upon the dire consequences of a supposed Jewish modernity – released from its sacred imperial obligations – whose potential power is utterly lawless. Yet given McPhee's prolonged if modest celebrations of his £25,000 windfall (including a £70 cruise with his wife at the end of the story) it is not at all certain whether McPhee can claim the role of the divinely Chosen or whether he is, after all, closer to the rough and ready materialism of 'Young Steiner'. Given that he tells the story to a narrator, who writes shipping pamphlets for money, a doubt remains whether the anti-Semitism of McPhee merely confounds the money-driven shipping business which shapes all of the characters in 'Bread Upon the Waters'.

By the time of 'The House Surgeon', a sophisticated reworking of 'For One Night Only', Kipling has produced a rather more benign version of a

'Jewish' materialism which typifies its main character, Maxwell M'Leod. Reminiscent of the Powers of Darkness in the earlier story, M'Leod's naïve and attractive materialism is juxtaposed throughout with the 'blasting gust of depression' which pervades Holmescroft, the large house which the M'Leod family have recently purchased and which is based on Kipling's 'unhappy' house in Torquay.[55] A superficially technical solution to the problem of combating evil is reflected in M'Leod's shallow methods of dealing with it:

> 'If I've spent a pound first and last, I must have spent five thousand. Electric light, new servants' wing, garden – all that sort of thing. A man and his family ought to be happy after so much expense, ain't it?' He looked at me through the bottom of his glass.

The attempt by M'Leod's 'moneyed innocence' to exclude the 'Horror of Great Darkness which is spoken of in the Bible', indicates, as John Coates has noted, the reason why Kipling constructed M'Leod as an assimilated Jew who has changed his name and married a Greek in a bid to deny his 'dark' racial heritage.[56] M'Leod, in this reading of the story, replaces biblical knowledge and morality (the 'Shekinah') with a facile materialism. Although he is rendered sympathetically, such assimilationism speaks especially to the degeneration of 'the Jews' as the Chosen People. His refusal to confront god-given timeless verities is signified by the 'fortifying blaze of electric light'[57] which envelops Holmescroft as well as the extra £1,000 which M'Leod has paid his lawyer to ensure that no death has occurred in the house since it was first built. The over-simple banishment of past suffering points above all, to the inadequacy of a liberal Arnoldian synthesis between Hebrew and Hellene as represented by M'Leod's marriage to a Greek woman. As with Wali Dad's championing of Athenian values, such liberal ideals do not lead to the painless progress of civilisation.

The 'Perseus' figure who narrates the story eventually discovers that a devout Calvinist had accidentally killed herself by falling out of a window at Holmescroft. Blaming her sister for committing suicide, Mary Moultrie had caused the guilt-ridden spirit of the dead to haunt Holmescroft. The skilful contrast between M'Leod's godlessness and Mary Moultrie's reprehensible presumption of God's purpose (like Ephraim's in 'Jews in Shushan') indicates the richly ambiguous perspective of the 'pagan Saviour' of Holmescroft.[58] Mary Moultrie is an avowed anti-Semite in the story – 'What ideas these Jews have of arranging furniture!' – but her anti-Semitism, unlike that of

Mrs Skittleworth or McPhee, is completely marginalised. Even the talk of 'South American railway stock' by Miss M'Leod's suitor is merely satirised by 'Perseus' as idle chit-chat: 'He told me at tea that these were days of financial specialisation.' Such phrases are laughably trivial next to the 'most terrible of all dreams' where, in trying to 'wipe [evil] out of our lives . . . we wake to the day we have earned'. Even the naïve materialism of M'Leod can lead potentially to the triumph of evil or 'the day we have earned'.

The narrator of Kipling's story articulates a richly divided voice, reinforced by the two poems that end 'The House Surgeon'. After 'Perseus' successfully banishes the Moultrie ghost, he and the M'Leod family riot through the house – parodying the biblical 'great darkness' by playing 'Blind Man's Buff' – and Miss M'Leod sings 'With Mirth, Thou Pretty Bird', which joyously asserts the acceptance of one's natural shortcomings (including such cheerful vulgarity as the M'Leods' gold grand piano). But this implicit celebration of the M'Leods' way of life is immediately undercut by 'The Rabbi's Song', an important coda, which stresses the need for a divinely 'spiritual' transcendence of one's present condition:

> Our lives, our tears, as water,
>   Are poured upon the ground;
> God giveth no man quarter,
>   Yet God a means hath found;
> Though faith and hope have vanished,
>   And even love grows dim,
> A means whereby His banished
>   Be not expelled from Him![59]

Echoing 'The Treasure and the Law', Kipling's poetic 'Rabbi' reiterates the sacred obligations of God's 'banished' people not to succumb (like Geissler) to what is called 'the desolation / and darkness of thy mind' caused by the rejection of Christ. Significantly, the stanza paraphrases an Old Testament text (II Samuel 14:14), referring back to biblical times when Jews, like Kadmiel, were chosen and could be on the side of the law. The possibility that the 'whispering ghosts' of 'the past' will dominate all those who have left their 'habitation' is echoed in M'Leod's inability to control the primeval forces which surfaced with a vengeance at Holmescroft. 'The Rabbi's Song', therefore, is at pains to emphasise that such 'darkness' must be replaced by the 'spirit' of god-given law. 'The Jews', long since 'expelled from Him', can be said to prefigure the danger, awaiting humanity as a whole, of those who replace a spiritual covenant with an empty materialism. But the immediate target of the poem is the 'desolation and darkness' of Mary Moultrie's Calvinist orthodoxy (lacking 'faith and hope') and, to this extent, the poem reinforces the philo-Semitism in the story with the Rabbi speaking Old Testament wisdom which Evangelicals brooding on damnation, such as Mary Moultrie, would do well to listen to.

In all three of these stories, Kipling was to displace the voice of the anti-Semite onto one of his characters. 'The House Surgeon', in fact, is explicitly concerned with the 'good Jew' such as 'The Rabbi'.[60] Four years after 'The House Surgeon', however, Kipling lost faith in the 'good Jew' and dissolved the distinction between good and bad, the biblically chosen and their modern-day degraded counterparts, with the voice of the anti-Semite no longer displaced. This loss of faith manifested itself in the poem 'Gehazi' (1913), where Kipling himself assumed the role of the Jew-hater.

'A leper white as snow': the end of ambivalence

Two years before leaving South Africa for good, when Kipling was 'sick and wearied of the state of things here [in the Rand]', he wrote to his long-standing friend H.A. Gwynne in March 1906 to agree with him that 'a certain type of Jew-financier – I have Albu in my eye – is most dangerous and should be hampered but the danger then is (since they all hang together) of weakening the others and so bringing on a bigger smash'.[61] When no longer imbued with 'the Law' of Empire, a powerful 'Jew-financier' (especially when 'they all hang together') was to prove a potentially devastating threat to the Empire ('a bigger smash'). Such was one of the 'lessons' of his South African years.

Kipling's loathing of the Liberal government of 1906–10, after South Africa was seceded, deepened on many fronts (such as Home Rule for Ireland, welfare reform, trade unionism, the Suffragettes and reform of the House of Lords). The so-called 'Marconi Scandal' (1911–14), a phrase coined by Cecil Chesterton, coincided with this 'decade of hating', in David Gilmour's pertinent phrase, and exemplified the supposedly corrupt nature of the British government in the years leading to the First World War.[62] It was the Imperial Conference of 1911 which approved plans for the building of state-owned Marconi radio stations throughout the Empire. As part of the armaments race with Germany, the Admiralty requested a way of communicating with the British navy, which Kipling thought was a particularly vulnerable wing of the armed forces. The Marconi tender was accepted in March 1912 by

Herbert Samuel, the Postmaster-General, with Godfrey Isaacs, brother of Attorney General Sir Rufus Isaacs, the managing director of the company. There was undoubtedly some insider dealing with American Marconi Company shares, which included the Chancellor of the Exchequer, Lloyd George and the Chief Whip, Alexander Murray.

A few months before writing 'Gehazi' Kipling, in a letter to Sir Max Aitken, comments on 'the Liberals' and Marconi: 'My insular mind hasn't got further than saying: "Thank God they ain't white". After all a Jew lawyer [Sir Rufus Isaacs] and a Welsh solicitor [Lloyd George] and Jack Johnston [an African-American boxer] and rabbits are much of a muchness.'[63] Such racial 'insularity' can be traced back through Kipling's letters especially with regard to those 'races' who were simply not 'white' enough.[64] 'Gehazi' was a response to the promotion of Sir Rufus Isaacs to Lord Chief Justice in October 1913. But what the poem accentuates, above all else, is the diseased nature of Jewish 'whiteness':

> Thou mirror of uprightness,
>   What ails thee at thy vows?
> What means the risen whiteness
>   Of the skin between thy brows?
> The boils that shine and burrow,
>   The sores that slough and bleed –
> The leprosy of Naaman
>   On thee and all thy seed?
>   Stand up, Stand up, Gehazi,
>   Draw close thy robe and go.
>   Gehazi, Judge in Israel,
>   A leper white as snow![65]

Whereas Kipling had hitherto compared contemporary Jews with divinely sanctioned biblical precedents, the biblical and contemporary are here elided ('all thy seed') and are eternally degenerate. 'Gehazi' marked a watershed and many apologists for Kipling's anti-Semitism, who argue that Isaacs is himself to blame for the poem (because of his 'insider dealing'), merely reinforce the logic of 'well-earned' anti-Semitism.[66]

'Gehazi' was a turning point for several reasons. Fearing the threat of libel, both Gwynne and Aitken refused to publish the poem, and when Aitken asked for it to be edited Kipling replied: 'I can't "garble" my "Gehazi". It's meant for the Jew boy on the Bench and one day – please the Lord – I may get it in.'[67] It was not published until 1919. But the 'Marconi Scandal' introduced Kipling to a programmatic anti-Semitism that was to become part of his *Weltanschauung*. Two main journals, completely disenchanted with parliamentary democracy and mainstream newspapers, promoted the 'Marconi Scandal'. The first was the *New Witness*, a mouthpiece of the Chesterbelloc grouping who saw the 'Marconi Scandal' as an extension of a conspiratorial 'Jewish financial' power into parliament, the press and even, significantly, the theatre and the music hall.[68] But the *New Witness*, made up of maverick liberals who were notably pro-Boer, would not have influenced Kipling directly. Leo Maxse's *National Review*, written from a conservative perspective but with a similar agenda to the *New Witness* with regard to the 'scandal', was a different story. As Gilmour has noted, Maxse, who Kipling knew quite well, 'had the ideal political credentials for close friendship with Kipling'. His *National Review* stressed the German-Jewish control of much of the British press and the power of 'cosmopolitan financiers domiciled in London' who were working in German interests.[69]

'The Village that Voted the Earth Was Flat' (dated 1913 but possibly completed in 1914) and 'As Easy as A.B.C.' (1912) were written at about the same time as 'Gehazi' and were to address implicitly this period of reassessment with regard to 'the Jew'. While the connexion with the 'Marconi Scandal' might seem far-fetched, Kipling was well aware of this context in a letter written in 1917:

> 'The village that voted' . . . is a sanguinary allegory of an iridescent 'civilization' . . . My own idea is that Bat Masquerier . . . was an Hebrew. Otherwise he wouldn't have been so vindictive about the beak's references to Jerusalem. Read 'The Village' in alternative strophes with 'As Easy as A.B.C.' (for they are both allegories) and you'll see how the music hall purveyors of mirth end up in both. You can't defeat the Jew – or the pimp.[70]

As this letter illustrates, Kipling was rethinking his earlier more desirable imperial constructions of 'the Jew' who now seemed utterly uncontrollable ('You can't defeat the Jew'). 'The Village that Voted the Earth Was Flat' is a story of revenge carried out by the narrator, his journalist friend Woodhouse, and the latter's young protégé Ollyett, who has a 'distant connection'[71] with Pallant, a Member of Parliament. Woodhouse, with Ollyett and Pallant in the car, is unjustly punished for speeding on the outskirts of the village of Huckley by its pompous magistrate, Sir Thomas Ingell. Ingell, a Radical Member of Parliament, is said to speak in a 'tone' that 'would have justified revolt throughout the empires'. The next case to be heard is that of Bat Masquerier, who drove without a licence, and who is described as a 'large, flaxen-haired man' with 'gun-metal-blue eyes'. All five meet after the hearings and agree to conspire to discredit Ingell and Huckley. Masquerier, a theatre impresario, is not enraged by Ingell's 'tone' but, as Kipling notes in his letter, by his anti-Semitism in asking Masquerier if 'he expected the police to go to his home address in Jerusalem' to find his driving licence. Such abuse, which is compared drily by the narrator to an 'established *auto-da-fé*'[72] is what motivates Masquerier to extract revenge.

As with Geissler, the blond, blue-eyed Masquerier does not 'look like a Jew' (he is the very personification of a masque or masquerade) but he is implicitly identified as 'an Hebrew' outside of his response to Ingell's anti-Semitism. He has both a 'magnetic' eye and a voice that was 'as magnetic as the look' and a Svengali-like hypnotic charm, not least because he is most famous for promoting the universally adored singer Vidal Benzaguen, who resembles Trilby in her appeal. Masquerier warns from the beginning that the discrediting of Ingell will be followed through to the 'dead finish' and it is his amoral pursuit of Ingell that differentiates him from his 'Anglo Saxon' co-conspirators. This is made clear in the story when even the hardened Ollyett states that he is afraid of him: 'He's the absolutely Amoral Soul. I've never met one yet' or 'I tell you I'm afraid of Bat. That man's the Personal Devil'.[73] After all, Masquerier's first name indicates a certain bat-like blindness to the 'Anglo Saxon' values of the other co-conspirators, who are supposedly on the side of morality.

What Masquerier and 'my people' (a constant refrain referring to his business networks) are able to do is unite the forces of popular culture – especially the music hall, cinema and the press – to disfigure parliamentary democracy. As J.M.S. Tompkins has noted, 'With these resources almost anything could be done, and almost anything, on so vast a scale, could get out of hand'.[74] The story demonstrates, with an uncanny understanding of the mechanics of marketing, just how it is possible to harness the 'psychology of crowds' to convince the world that Huckley is full of flat-earthers.[75] Once figures such as the Baron Reuter (a German-Jew and a particular target of Maxse) become involved –'it could have been none other' – then even Masquerier has to admit that his publicity machine is beyond his control:

> I'm glad I always believed in God and Providence and all those things. Else I should lose my nerve. We've put it over the whole world – the full extent of the geographical globe. We couldn't stop it if we wanted to now. It's got to burn itself out. I'm not in charge any more.

Masquerier's presumption of God's purpose, in the name of his business interests, is here contrasted with the sheer anarchy which has been unleashed globally ('we couldn't stop it if we wanted to now'). At the climax of the story the white-faced Woodhouse is repelled by the 'collective hysteria' that overcomes the House of Commons, especially the supposedly more primitive Irish MPs. While politicians are dismissed as leading a 'dog's life without a dog's decency' the fact that many are on 'all fours' by the end appals Woodhouse who, along with the narrator, is the only man who does not laugh hysterically at Ingell's humiliation. Although they have succeeded in transforming Ingell into a 'Gehazi' figure,[76] it is clear that the unbridled anarchy which concludes the story does not hit the right target. As Charles Carrington has noted, Woodhouse is reminiscent of the kind of individuals that Kipling knew well, such as Gwynne, who specialised in bringing 'moribund newspapers to life'.[77] During their time in South Africa, powerful Jews like Masquerier (who made a fortune out of discrediting Ingell) could be allied to the Great Game and could be opposed to (pro-Boer) radicals such as Ingell. But, in 'The Village that Voted the Earth Was Flat', Woodhouse is clearly reassessing his alliance, given the global level of disorder that Masquerier is able to unleash.

Disillusionment with both the press and parliamentary democracy certainly characterised the 'Marconi Scandal', but the alternative to such corrupt government was not always clear from Kipling's stories. 'As Easy as A.B.C.', for example, imagines a future world which, thanks to the 'Aerial Board of Control', is the epitome of sound world-wide government by a few good men. But this anaemic, risk-free world of 2065, with the shrinking of the world's population and the lack of the experience of death and emotional vitality, is by no means a technological utopia. The story is clear about the inequities of the past, namely the 'terror of crowds' or the 'disease' of democracy, described as the 'time of Crowds and Plague'.[78] Democracy in these terms is a form of primitivism with the 'old Voodoo-business of voting' and 'word-drunk people', and it is Jews in particular who are associated atavistically with such primitivism. As David Glover has noted, it is not a coincidence that Kipling regarded the 'Jewish science' of psychoanalysis as a form of 'voodoo and heathendom' best suited to a 'West African village'.[79]

'As Easy as A.B.C.' concerns the rescue of a group of anachronistic democrats in Chicago, with the A.B.C. imposing order from above, as the Chicago democrats are under attack by those who fear a return to the bad old days of 'Crowds and Plague'. The Chicago democrats end up on a London stage courtesy of the sceptical Vincent – an 'unbelieving Jew' – and Gerolstein, who specialises in a form of theatrical nostalgia, 'Cooking on coal-gas-stoves, lighting pipes with matches, and driving horses'. The impresario Vincent, however, believes in a nostalgia which will 'raise the Planet to loftier levels . . . a simple, old world life presented in its entirety to a deboshed [debauched] civilization'. He wants to stage a 'pageant to the world's beginnings' with, bathetically, Moshenthal 'do[ing] the music'. In an earlier corrupt age, the aerial controller would have 'played off Vincent against Gerolstein, and sold my captives [from Chicago] at enormous prices'. These democrats are full of 'bitter poison and unrest' and figures such as Vidal, Gerolstein and Mosenthal, echoing both their medieval forebears like Kadmiel but also the 'Man of the Future', are able to harness various plagues for their own ends.[80] To this extent, these Jewish impresarios provide an essential safety valve in preventing the return of repressed violence from getting out of hand. But, after the 'Marconi Scandal', Kipling's characterisation of democracy as a form of corruption meant that Gehazi-like Jews, at the heart of British liberal democracy and beyond its national boundaries, were perceived to have the power to unleash disease and disorder on a global scale.

Conclusion: 'A race that made the world Hell'

In a letter to André Chevrillon in November 1919, a month after Kipling wrote to him connecting the loss of South Africa in part to the 'the Jew of Poland', we have the 'Hebrew' Einstein both a 'Hun' and a 'Jew':

> But the phrase that sticks in my mind is that 'Space is warped'. When you come to reflect on a race that made the world Hell, you see how just and right it is that they should decide that space *is* warped, and should make their own souls the measure of Infinity . . . Einstein's pronouncement is only another little contribution to assisting the world towards flux and disintegration.[81]

After the First World War, Kipling came to believe in an anarchic 'Jewish World Conspiracy', bringing about 'flux and disintegration' even on an atomic level. A not untypical letter of November 1918 comments on the German capitulation at Sedan: 'We won't know for many years *why* the Hun was let off . . . on the West Front where we had him at our mercy. I suppose it was the Jews.' The Jewish propensity to assume God's purpose to destructive ends ('mak[ing] their own souls the measure of Infinity') made them a peculiar threat to Empire. A letter to his daughter Elsie in 1929, written in British-ruled Jerusalem, states that 'My dear, many races are vile but the Jew in bulk in his native heath is the Vilest of all'.[82]

Gwynne, who was particularly close to Kipling after the death of John, promoted such conspiracy theories as editor of the *Morning Post*, in the form of a series of articles, 'The Cause of the World Unrest', published in July 1920, which he partly authored with Ian Colvin. These articles argued that there was 'for centuries a hidden conspiracy, chiefly Jewish, whose objects have been and are . . . to arrive at the hegemony of the world by establishing some sort of despotic rule'. After being lobbied by Gwynne, Kipling came to believe that this conspiracy was 'absolutely in line with the work which the "international Jew" at his worst has accomplished and is accomplishing at the present moment'.[83] While Gwynne quoted Kipling as a supporter of such conspiratorial thinking, Kipling himself stressed that such views were not fit for publication and he was to largely confine such beliefs to his private letters and diaries.

In August 1923, Kipling corresponded with Rider Haggard about a proposed novel concerning 'the Jew upon whom the Doom has not begun to work', which was his definition of the '*good* Jew'.[84] The sketch of this novel located the 'Wandering Jew', reminiscent of Kadmiel, throughout history beginning with the 'dawn' of Christianity followed by the Crusades, the Black Death and the Inquisition and culminating in 'the painfully acquired wealth of the Wandering Jew which when attained worked only fresh horrors'.[85] The novel was never written, but two late stories, 'The Church that Was at Antioch' (1929) and 'The Manner of Men' (1930), have as their background 'the Jews' who have, from ancient times, endangered the very heart of the (Roman) empire. In 1918, Kipling characterised Edwin Montagu, Secretary of State for India, as a 'Yid' who patently did not want to 'save the British Empire': 'Racially, he does not care for it any more than Caiaphas [High Priest of the Jews] cared for Pilate: and psychologically he can't comprehend it.'[86] It was this psychological incomprehension, and disruptive racial character going back to the time of Caiaphas and the Roman Empire, that Kipling was to trace in these stories.

In 'The Church that Was at Antioch', Kipling is most concerned with Jews as colonials (like Ephraim the Jew) rather than as financiers (like Kadmiel). Much of the story is concerned with the 'food-differences between Greek and Hebrew Christians' in Antioch, which are being fermented by 'Synagogue Jews sent from Jerusalem'.[87] These food-differences threaten the livelihood of the 'little Jew shop-keepers' and 'Jew butchers' of Antioch and result in disputes not unlike the religious riots in 'On the City Wall'. But the contemporary context of the story is not the British Raj in its heyday but the troubled British Mandate period in Palestine in the 1920s. Centring on Valens, a Roman policeman, Kipling's version of the Middle East in the first century AD echoes his own perception of the contemporary mandate period: 'We've the unaccountable East to one side; the scum of the Mediterranean on the other; and all hellicat Judaea southward.'[88] From the Roman imperial perspective, Christianity in this period is made up of 'stiff-necked Hebrews', which troubles Valens ('their God had been born in the shape of a Jew') as national, racial and religious identity becomes fluid and indeterminate: 'the rumour in the city [was that] all Jews would be lumped together as Christians – members, that is, of a mere free-thinking sect instead of the very particular and troublesome "Nation of Jews" within the Empire'.[89] How can he keep order in rumour-ridden Antioch when he is not even sure of the difference between 'Hebrew' and 'Greek' Christians?

Such confusions are reflected in Kipling's description of the Jerusalem 'Arab-Jew-English police' during his 1929 visit.[90] In the contemporary period, of course, the option of converting Jews to Christianity was no longer a solution to the 'troublesome' Jewish nation. Kipling has the pagan Valens fatally wounded by a Cilician bandit pretending to be a 'Jew boy'; like Christ he forgives his enemy ('They don't know what they are doing'), and so embodies the very essence of Christianity. But this essence is racial, not religious, with Valens' authority deemed to be 'in the blood. The same with men as horses',[91] as his uncle states approvingly at the beginning of the story. The eternally unconverted and vile 'Nation of Jews within the Empire' imperils this racial authority. Not only are Jews no longer on the side of Empire as they once were in 'The Comprehension of Private Copper' and 'The Treasure and the Law', but they are now identified with the most unruly colonials ('hellicat Judaea'), like Muslims in South East Asia and Catholics in Ireland.[92]

By the time of 'The Manner of Men', Kipling's Christianity is the religion of suffering as can be seen by the figure of Paulus, travelling to Rome by ship, whose body has 'good, sound lictor's work and criss-cross Jew scourgings like gratings; and a stab or two; and besides those, old dry bites . . . That showed he must have dealt with the Beasts.' As this list of tortures indicates, 'the Beasts' refers to actual judicial punishments by the Romans but perhaps also, implicitly, 'some plot of the Jews', as an Edwardian commentator argued with reference to this passage of the Bible.[93] The shift in focus in Kipling's stories from the Old to the New Testament meant that he was less concerned with the new covenant (the English as the Israelites of Empire) than with those who suffer as a result of the failures of Empire.

While Paulus is called a 'Jew philosopher' in the story, Jews in general are described as 'circumcised apes', associated with other Semites such as the Phoenicians. Once again, it is not religious conversion but race and the law of Empire – 'if you will be obeying Caesar you will be obeying at least some sort of law' – that is endorsed by Kipling's Paulus. The primitivism of racialised Jews, no longer the chosen people of the covenant, leads in this sailors' story, as in 'Bread Upon the Waters', to their becoming universally hated ('jamming your Jew-bow into everybody's business'[94]). But, unlike 'The Church that Was at Antioch', the utterly primitive Jews in 'The Manner of Men' can evoke dark forces such as the Beasts which are unmediated by any religious or imperial form of civilisation. After all, in *Something of Myself*, Kipling is even afraid of the 'good little [Indian] Jew Tyler', the priest and butcher of the Jewish community in Lahore, who is spat at by his Muslim servant, a temptation which Kipling prudently resists: 'I swallowed my spittle at once. Israel is a race to leave alone. It abets disorder.'[95]

In 'The Church that Was at Antioch', the prefect of police warns Paulus that 'Jerusalem never forgives'.[96] Kipling took up this theme after a visit to Jerusalem in March, 1929 in a long unpublished poem, 'The Burden of Jerusalem' (1933):

> We do not know what God attends
> The Unloved Race in every place
> Where they amass their dividends
> From Riga to Jerusalem.
>
> But all the course of Time makes clear
> To everyone (except the Hun)
> It does not pay to interfere
> With Cohen from Jerusalem.
>
> For 'neath the Rabbi's curls and fur
> (Or scents and rings of movie kings)
> The aloof, unleavened blood of Ur,
> Broods steadfast on Jerusalem.[97]

Secret finance ('amass their dividends'), imperial disorder ('It does not pay to interfere / With Cohen from Jerusalem'), the cinema ('scents and rings of movie kings') and racial difference ('The aloof, unleavened blood of Ur') summarise Kipling's utterly irredeemable version of 'the Jew' in this period. He regards even the United States in *Something of Myself* as in danger of being overcome by the Powers of Darkness with its 'Semitic strain', made up of the 'wreckage of Eastern Europe', which has turned the country into a 'too-much-at-ease Zion'.[98] Kipling summarised this position as early as 1921 when the racial degeneration of Jewish immigrants were said to have 'Hebraized, internationalized, cosmopolitaned' the 'autochthonous' White Anglo-Saxon Protestant population of the United States.[99] Such is the seamless transition from the Rabbi's 'curls and fur' to Hollywood 'movie kings'.

At the end of the First World War, Kipling was the victim of a hoax when a forged poem purporting to be from his hand was published in *The Times* on 27 May 1918. The hoaxer crudely tried to implicate the Jewish writer Israel Zangwill in this deception by sending an obviously forged note from Zangwill to Kipling. Even after Sir Basil Thomson, Director of Intelligence at Scotland Yard, stated that Zangwill was not the culprit, Kipling continued to 'suspect more than a little' that a 'non-Aryan' hand or an 'un-European fist' was behind the hoax.[100]

By the 1920s and 1930s, 'the Jew' was to assume the role of Kipling's dark double (even adopting his identity as the hoaxer did) just as the 'Jewish World Conspiracy' was to embody the dark, repressed side of Empire: disorder, cosmopolitanism and a superficially theatrical rather than a timeless racial authority. At the end of *Something of Myself*, Kipling elaborates on the series of pens which he has used throughout the years to write with, the most recent being a 'smooth, black treasure . . . picked up in Jerusalem'. In this version of the treasure and the law, Kipling, who rejected the Jews of Jerusalem as the vilest of the vile, at the same time writes with a Jerusalem pen which, if he is not careful, might 'take charge'[101] and begin to write verse in the guise of a dark (Semitic) double. Such anxieties (associating him with the Hebraic, cosmopolitan or international) were clearly resolved after the First World War in the form of an extravagant and unambiguous use of a 'fascist' version of a Semitic discourse.

But Kipling's 'late' anti-Semitism should not be regarded as unchanging throughout his half-century of fiction-writing. In fact, the story of 'Kipling and the Jews' might well help us to understand the many other ways in which Kipling refashioned himself and his imaginative work throughout his lifetime.[102] Those who assume that Kipling's Jewish representations are typical of an inassimilable anti-modernist anti-Semitism of the 1920s and 1930s tend to flatten out his use of a Semitic discourse in a liberal, non-totalitarian (*pace* Arendt) context.[103] But, while Kipling was initially bounded by national culture, and a backward-looking form of Englishness, especially after his return from South Africa, his imperial vision meant that his version of 'the Jew' went far beyond the constraints of liberal culture. This was reinforced after the Balfour Declaration of 1917 where 'the Jews' were deemed by Kipling (and some of his close circle on the radical right such as Colvin and Gwynne) as an unruly national entity within the British Empire which matched their enduring role as global anarchists and financiers. To this extent, the figure of 'the Jew' was no different from other lawless colonials such as the Irish and Muslims – but, unlike these other colonials, Jews supposedly had the conspiratorial power to challenge the British Empire and promote a destructive communism in the East and denationalised capitalism in the West. At this point, but only at this point, Kipling's colonial racism took the form of a 'fascist' conspiratorial version of 'the Jew'.

Notes

I am grateful to Jan Montefiore for her incisive comments on an earlier version of the essay and for her exemplary editorial help.

1 Kipling, 'Song of the Fifth River', *Puck of Pook's Hill* (London: Macmillan, 1906), p. 281; *Something of Myself and Other Autobiographical Writings*, ed. Thomas Pinney (1937; Cambridge: Cambridge University Press, 1990), p. 130; Kipling, *A Choice of Kipling's Verse Made by T.S. Eliot with an Essay on Rudyard Kipling* (London: Faber & Faber, 1941), p. 20.
2 Noel Annan, 'Kipling's place in the history of ideas', in Andrew Rutherford (ed.), *Kipling's Mind and Art* (Edinburgh: Oliver & Boyd, 1964), p. 97. Annan gives a comprehensive account of war-time criticism on pp. 97–8.
3 Eliot's error in dating this poem 1915 (Eliot, *Choice*, p. 116) has been repeated by many critics including the 2006 online essay on 'Gehazi' by Julian Moore on the Kipling Society website (www.kipling.org.uk/rg_gehazi_moore.htm, accessed on 31 July 2011). For a recent account of Eliot's Semitic discourse see my 'T.S. Eliot and "race": Blacks, Jews and Irish', in David Chinitz (ed.), *A Companion to T.S. Eliot* (Oxford: Blackwell, 2009), pp. 335–50.
4 Eliot, *Choice*, p. 29.
5 For a recent example of the influence of 1940s criticism on contemporary accounts of Kipling, see the Introduction to Caroline Rooney and Kaori Nagai (eds), *Kipling and Beyond: Patriotism, Globalisation and Postcolonialism* (Basingstoke: Macmillan, 2010), pp. 1–17, which expands the teleological reading of Kipling from the Second World War to include the post–9/11 'war on terror' (pp. 6–7). I take issue with Benita Parry's otherwise admirable 'Kipling's unloved race: the tetreat from modernity', in *Kipling and Beyond*, pp. 18–36 precisely because the theories of anti-Semitism which she discusses refer mainly to the rise of European fascism.
6 Hannah Arendt, *The Origins of Totalitarianism* (1951; New York: Schocken Books, 2004), pp. 269, 282, 286.
7 Eliot, *Choice*, pp. 27, 29.

8. Edmund Wilson, 'The Kipling that nobody read' [1941], reprinted in Rutherford (ed.), *Kipling's Mind and Art*, p. 42; H.E. Bates cited in Norman Page, *A Kipling Companion* (London and Basingstoke: Macmillan, 1984), p. xiii.
9. Lionel Trilling, 'Kipling', in Rutherford (ed.), *Kipling's Mind and Art*, p. 91.
10. Trilling, letter in *The Nation* (1–16 October 1943 and 15 January 1944), cited in Christopher Ricks, *T.S. Eliot and Prejudice* (London: Faber & Faber, 1988), pp. 25, 28.
11. A representative apology for Kipling on the grounds that his anti-Semitism is merely 'metaphorical' can be found in Elliott L. Gilbert, *The Good Kipling: Studies in the Short Story* (Manchester: Manchester University Press, 1972), pp. 118–27.
12. Trilling and Ricks in Ricks, *T.S. Eliot and Prejudice*, p. 27.
13. Trilling, 'Kipling', p. 93.
14. See George Orwell, 'Rudyard Kipling' (1942), on p. 29 of this volume.
15. Arendt, *Origins of Totalitarianism*, p. 267.
16. Boris Ford, 'A Case for Kipling?', in Elliot L. Gilbert, *Kipling and the Critics* (London: Peter Owen, 1966), p. 62.
17. Anne Aresty Naman, *The Jew in the Victorian Novel: Some Relationships between Prejudice and Art* (New York: AMS Press, 1980), p. 49, discussed in Bryan Cheyette, *Constructions of 'the Jew' in English Literature and Society: Racial Representations, 1875–1945* (Cambridge: Cambridge University Press, 1995), pp. 1–12. For the dangers of 'back-shadowing' see Michael André Bernstein, *Foregone Conclusions: Against Apocalyptic History* (Berkeley, CA: Berkeley University Press, 1994).
18. Eliot, *Choice*, p. 16.
19. See Anthony Julius, *Trials of the Diaspora: A History of Anti-Semitism in England* (Oxford: Oxford University Press, 2010), p. 155. See also this essay below for the publishing history of 'Gehazi'.
20. Kipling, 'The Army of a Dream', Part II, *Traffics and Discoveries* (London: Macmillan, 1904), p. 299.
21. Angus Wilson, *The Strange Ride of Rudyard Kipling* (London: Secker and Warburg, 1977), pp. 241–2. Cheyette, *Constructions of 'the Jew'* finds 'the Jew' in widespread use in the Victorian and Edwardian periods, but not 'Jew-boy'.
22. John McClure, *Kipling and Conrad: The Colonial Fiction* (Cambridge, MA: Harvard University Press, 1981), p. 19. It is historically accurate that the cockney Ortheris should be characterised by his Jew-hatred, given that the East End of London was notoriously anti-Semitic.
23. Kipling, 'His Private Honour', *Many Inventions* (London: Macmillan, 1893), pp. 132, 130, 145, 153. This story's anti-Semitism is analysed in detail by Jan Montefiore in *Rudyard Kipling* (Horndon: Northcote House, 2007), pp. 72–5.
24. Bryan Cheyette (ed.), *Between 'Race' and Culture: Representations of 'the Jew' in English and American Literature* (Stanford, CA: Stanford University Press, 1996), pp. 1–15.
25. Kipling, *The Letters of Rudyard Kipling, Volume 4: 1911–19*, ed. Thomas Pinney (Basingstoke: Macmillan, 1999), p. 572.

26 Kipling 'From Sea to Sea', no. XXXIII (1889), collected in *From Sea to Sea: Letters of Travel* (London: Macmillan, 1899), vol. 2, p. 131. Craig Raine, in 'Kipling: controversial questions', *Kipling Journal* (September 2002), pp. 10–29, rightly argues that when it comes to 'the Jews', Kipling 'cannot be defended' (p. 25). The tiny drop of 'Jew blood' in Kipling's 'Man of the Future' is standard Victorian race theory, prefiguring George Du Maurier's *Trilby* (London: Osgood, McIlvaine & Co., 1894), where the figure of Little Billee is said to have an 'infinitesimal dose of the good old Oriental blood' which 'kept him straight' and loyal to Svengali (p. 227). Kipling's own 'His Chance in Life' (1887), discussed below, deploys a similar theory.
27 Kipling 'From Sea to Sea', no. VI, collected in *From Sea to Sea*, vol. 1, p. 262.
28 Raine, 'Controversial questions', pp. 25–6.
29 Claire Hirshfield, 'The British left and the "Jewish Conspiracy": a case study of modern antisemitism', *Jewish Social Studies* (Spring 1981), p. 95 and pp. 95–112.
30 Martin Van Wyk Smith, *Drummer Hodge: The Poetry of the Anglo-Boer War (1899–1902)* (Oxford: Oxford University Press, 1978), p. 105 and George Shepperson, 'Kipling and the Boer War', in John Gross (ed.), *Rudyard Kipling: The Man, His Work and His World* (London: Weidenfeld & Nicolson, 1972), p. 86.
31 C.A. Bodelson, *Aspects of Kipling's Art* (Manchester: Manchester, University Press, 1964), pp. 155–65.
32 'Jerrold's Weekly' was probably based on the notorious *Reynolds' Newspaper*, a popular Sunday weekly, which by 1899 was regularly promoting a 'Jewish world-conspiracy' (Hirshfield, 'The British left', pp. 111 and 100–1.)
33 Kipling, 'The Comprehension of Private Copper', *Traffics and Discoveries* (London: Macmillan, 1904), p. 170.
34 See my 'Neither black nor white: the figure of "the Jew" in imperial British literature', in Tamar Garb and Linda Nochlin (eds), *The Jew in the Text* (London: Thames and Hudson, 1995), pp. 31–41.
35 Kipling's 'The Treasure and the Law' was first published in the *Strand* magazine in October 1906; *Puck*, pp. 290–1, 293, 303. See also Kipling, *Something of Myself*, p. 110.
36 Kipling, 'The Treasure and the Law', pp. 281–2, 290, 303. Hugh Brogan, 'Kipling and history' (December 2007) on the Kipling Society website has an interesting reading of the story in these terms: www.kipling.org.uk/rg_history1.htm (accessed on 31 July 2011).
37 See also Kipling's 'The Wandering Jew', in *Life's Handicap* (London: Macmillan, 1891), which is not however connected with the mythical figure of Ahasuerus. Another non-mythic 'Wandering Jew', Ahasuerus Jenkins, can be found in 'The Army Head-Quarters' [1886], *Rudyard Kipling's Verse: The Definitive Edition* (London: Hodder and Stoughton, 1940), p. 5.
38 Salman Rushdie, 'Kipling', *Imaginary Homelands: Essays and Criticism, 1981–1991* (London: Granta, 1991), pp. 80, 74–80; Aamer Mufti, *Enlightenment in the Colony: The Jewish Question and the Crisis of Postcolonial Culture* (Princeton, NJ:

Princeton University Press, 2007), pp. 115–18; Kipling, 'On the City Wall', *Soldiers Three and Other Stories* (London: Macmillan, 1895), p. 329.

39 Mufti, *Enlightenment in the Colony*, p. 118.
40 Kipling, 'On the City Wall', p. 328.
41 Kipling, *Something of Myself*, p. 32.
42 Kipling, 'On the City Wall', pp. 343, 328.
43 Kipling, 'Jews in Shushan', *Life's Handicap*, pp. 291–6. Martin Seymour-Smith traces the 'Miriam' motif in Kipling's work from his poem 'The Prayer of Miriam Cohen' (1893) to 'They' (1904) and John of Burgos' Jewish mistress in 'The Eye of Allah' (1926), in *Rudyard Kipling* (London: Macdonald, 1989), pp. 114–15, 214–15 and 278–9, though not all Kipling's Jewish women are paragons of suffering. A passenger in *The Light That Failed* is described by Dick Heldar as 'a sort of Negroid-Jewess-Cuban, with morals to match' (p. 131). For a counter-example see the decidedly Gentile Miriam in 'The Brushwood Boy' (1898) discussed by Montefiore, *Rudyard Kipling*, pp. 68–71.
44 Kipling, 'His Chance in Life' (1887), collected in *Plain Tales from the Hills* (1888; London: Macmillan, 1890).
45 *Ibid.*, pp. 77, 79, 82, 76, 74, 73.
46 Stephen Arata, *Fictions of Loss in the Victorian Fin de Siècle: Identity and Empire* (Cambridge: Cambridge University Press, 1996), pp. 161–2.
47 For another example of a 'Black Jew' see 'The Rout of the White Hussars' (*Plain Tales*, p. 235). This argument contrasts with David Glover, 'Race, modernism and the question of late style in Kipling's racial narratives', in Len Platt (ed.), *Modernism and Race* (Cambridge: Cambridge University Press, 2011), pp. 97–115 who, in an otherwise exemplary essay, mistakenly argues that 'What stands unchanged across the very disparate social milieu that Kipling creates is the figure of the Jew, the degree zero of racial difference' (p. 113).
48 J.M.S. Tompkins, *The Art of Rudyard Kipling* (London: Methuen, 1964), pp. 185–221. Kipling's 'For One Night Only' (1890) appears in the Sussex edition of *The Works of Rudyard Kipling*, Volume XXIX, 'Uncollected Prose I' (London: Macmillan, 1938). Quotations that follow come from pp. 325–7.
49 Kipling, 'For One Night Only', pp. 325–6. Many of Kipling's most threatening Jews do not 'look Jewish'. Contrast this, for example, with 'A Naval Mutiny' (1931), which opens with a 'baby parrot' being compared to a crudely racialised 'little Jew baby', in *Limits and Renewals* (London: Macmillan, 1932), p. 183.
50 Kipling, 'For One Night Only', pp. 325–9.
51 Noel Annan, 'Kipling's Place', p. 114. It seems that Kipling, from the beginning, had a crude received view of Jews and money; in the autobiographical *Stalky & Co.* (London: Macmillan, 1899), 'Beetle' (Kipling) pretends to be charging interest and Stalky calls him a 'cold-blooded Jew' and says their House is a 'set of filthy Shylocks' ('The Moral Reformers', *Stalky*, pp. 107–11).
52 Kipling, 'Bread Upon the Waters', *The Day's Work* (London: Macmillan, 1899), p. 312.
53 *Ibid.*, pp. 287, 282–3, 314.

54 *Ibid.*, pp. 290, 295, 298, 291, 314–15.
55 Tompkins, *Art of Rudyard Kipling*, p. 130.
56 Kipling, 'The House Surgeon', *Actions and Reactions* (London: Macmillan, 1909), pp. 194, 201. For readings of this story, see John Coates, 'Religious cross currents in "The House Surgeon"', *The Day's Work: Kipling and the Idea of Sacrifice* (Madison, NJ: Fairleigh Dickinson University Press, 1997), pp. 76–9, and Daniel Karlin, 'Actions and reactions: Kipling's Edwardian summer' in this book. See also Hyam Maccoby, '"The Family Reunion" and Kipling's "The House Surgeon"', *Notes and Queries* (February 1968), pp. 48–50.
57 Kipling, 'The House Surgeon', p. 273.
58 Maccoby, 'Kipling's "The House Surgeon"', p. 50, and Coates, *The Day's Work*, pp. 76–82.
59 Kipling, 'The House Surgeon', pp. 295, 269, 273, 296, 298, 301.
60 *Ibid.*, p. 278.
61 Kipling, *The Letters of Rudyard Kipling, Volume 3: 1900–10*, ed. Thomas Pinney (Basingstoke: Macmillan, 1996), p. 210.
62 David Gilmour, *The Long Recessional: The Imperial Life of Rudyard Kipling* (London: John Murray, 2002), p. 212. See also Colin Holmes, *Anti-Semitism in British Society, 1876–1939* (London: Edward Arnold, 1979), p. 70.
63 Kipling, *Letters, Volume 4*, p. 181.
64 H.A. Gwynne (a 'good man') is described as 'white and of a large heart', and Sir Edward Strachey as 'a White Man all through' (Kipling, *Letters, Volume 3*), pp. 76, 22. Those 'races' who lacked whiteness included the Hun or Teuton, 'the nigger', 'the Jew' and even 'the Welsh', 'the Greek', 'the Pict' and 'the Celt'.
65 Kipling, 'Gehazi', *Definitive Verse*, p. 243.
66 Gilmour, *The Long Recessional*, pp. 232–4, and my 'Hilaire Belloc and the "Marconi Scandal" 1900–1914: A Reassessment of the Interactionist Model of Racial Hatred', *Immigrants and Minorities* (March 1989), pp. 131–42.
67 Kipling, *Letters, Volume 4*, p. 208.
68 Holmes, *Anti-Semitism in British Society*, pp. 72–9.
69 Gilmour, *The Long Recessional*, p. 210 and Holmes, *Anti-Semitism in British Society*, p. 80.
70 Kipling, *Letters, Volume 4*, p. 444.
71 Kipling, 'The Village that Voted the Earth Was Flat', *A Diversity of Creatures* (London: Macmillan, 1917), p. 161.
72 *Ibid.*, pp. 164–5.
73 *Ibid.*, pp. 167–8, 176, 185.
74 Tompkins, *Art of Rudyard Kipling*, p. 131.
75 *Ibid.*, p. 200.
76 Kipling, 'Village that Voted', pp. 200, 192, 207, 204, 213, 204.
77 Charles Carrington, *Rudyard Kipling: His Life and Work* (London: Macmillan, 1955), p. 405.
78 Kipling, 'As Easy as A.B.C.', *Diversity*, pp. 1, 6.

79 *Ibid.*, p. 23; Glover, 'Kipling's Racial Narratives', p. 109; Kipling, *The Letters of Rudyard Kipling, Volume 5: 1920–30*, ed. Thomas Pinney (Basingstoke: Macmillan, 2004), p. 48.
80 Kipling, 'As Easy as A.B.C.', pp. 37–8, 39–40. In 'The Treasure and the Law', Kadmiel infects a village with a harmless rash resembling bubonic plague (*Puck*, p. 298); in 'The Daughter of the Regiment' (1888), Mulvaney believed that 'the Wandherin' Jew takes the cholera wid him' (*Plain Tales*, p. 211); Kipling's part-Jewish 'Man of the Future' was 'especially a dramatist'.
81 Kipling, *Letters, Volume 4*, p. 592. Raine argues that these and similar remarks were merely the result of Kipling's traumatic loss of his son John: 'Kipling wasn't a racist . . . He was a father driven mad with grief' ('Controversial questions', p. 29). Harry Ricketts, *The Unforgiving Minute: A Life of Rudyard Kipling* (London: Chatto & Windus, 1999), p. 352, mistakenly argues on similar lines. For a useful counter to this orthodoxy see Glover, 'Race, modernism and the question of late style', on the 'lengthy arc of anti-Semitism that was so prominent in [Kipling's] Edwardian writings' (p. 109).
82 Kipling, *Letters, Volume 4*, p. 520; *Letters, Volume 5*, p. 481. Here Kipling followed Gwynne's Preface to the American edition of *The Cause of the World's Unrest* (1920), arguing that one should distinguish between 'those Jews who have adopted a single nationality and those to whom Jewish nationality is the only one that counts' (cited in Holmes, *Anti-Semitism in British Society*, p. 149).
83 Gwynne cited in Holmes, *Anti-Semitism in British Society*, p. 149 and letter to Gwynne from Kipling (25 October 1919), which was widely circulated by Gwynne. For this correspondence see Keith Wilson, 'The *Protocols of Zion* and the *Morning Post*, 1919–1920', *Patterns of Prejudice* 19, no. 3 (1985), p. 6.
84 Kipling, *Letters, Volume 5*, p. 149.
85 Morton Cohen (ed.), *Rudyard Kipling to Rider Haggard: The Record of a Friendship* (London: Hutchinson, 1965), pp. 116–17.
86 Kipling, *Letters, Volume 3*, p. 509.
87 Kipling, 'The Church that Was at Antioch', *Limits*, pp. 95, 92, 98.
88 *Ibid.*, p. 90. See also Kipling's comment on the 1917 Balfour Declaration where he notes the 'futility – not to mention the danger – of Balfour's messing himself up with things between Jews and Arabs', Kipling, *Letters, Volume 5*, p. 220.
89 Kipling 'The Church that Was at Antioch', p. 107.
90 Kipling, *Letters, Volume 5*, p. 405.
91 Kipling, 'The Church that Was at Antioch', pp. 111, 113, 90.
92 The contrast here is with Haggard and Buchan, who were both Zionists and thought that the 'Nation of Jews' within the Empire was a good thing. See my *Constructions of 'the Jew'* (chapter 5) for these figures in relation to Kipling and imperial discourse.
93 Kipling, 'The Manner of Men', *Limits*, p. 234; Dummelow (1909), quoted in Sandra Kemp, *Kipling's Hidden Narratives* (Oxford: Oxford University Press, 1988), p. 100.
94 Kipling, 'The Manner of Men', pp. 238, 226, 248, 227.

95 Kipling, *Something of Myself*, p. 130.
96 Kipling, 'The Church that Was at Antioch', p. 104.
97 Kipling, 'The Burden of Jerusalem', cited in Christopher Hitchens, *Blood, Class and Empire: The Enduring Anglo-American Relationship* (New York: Atlantic Books, 2004), pp. 86–8.
98 Kipling, *Something of Myself*, pp. 70, 78.
99 Kipling, *Letters, Volume* 5, p. 90.
100 Kipling, *Something of Myself*, pp. 131–2. This mistakenly puts the hoax forward a year to 1917, at the height of the 'life and death struggle'. See Gordon Phillips, 'The Literary hoax that fooled the Thunderer and did Kipling down', *The Times*, 1 August 1977.
101 Kipling, *Something of Myself*, pp. 133, 68.
102 Glover's subtle conjunction of 'race' and teleology in his 'Race, modernism and the question of late style' misses an opportunity to explore this question more fully in relation to 'the Jews', who remain 'unchanging' in this account.
103 Parry, 'Kipling's unloved race', pp. 22–8.

Select bibliography

Primary texts

Kipling major works

Plain Tales from the Hills Calcutta: Thacker, Spink & Co., 1888; 3rd edition London: Macmillan, 1890
Life's Handicap London: Macmillan, 1891
The Light That Failed London: Macmillan, 1891
The Naulahka: A Story of West and East (with Wolcott Balestier) London: Macmillan, 1892
Barrack Room Ballads and Other Verses London: Methuen, 1892
Many Inventions London: Macmillan, 1893
The Jungle Book London: Macmillan, 1894
The Second Jungle Book London: Macmillan, 1895
Wee Willie Winkie and Other Stories London: Macmillan, 1895
Soldiers Three and Other Stories London: Macmillan, 1895
The Day's Work London: Macmillan, 1898
From Sea to Sea and Other Sketches: Letters of Travel 2 vols, London: Macmillan, 1900
Kim London: Macmillan, 1900; Penguin Classics edition, ed. Harish Trivedi, London: Penguin, 2011
Just-So Stories for Little Children London: Macmillan, 1902
Traffics and Discoveries London: Macmillan, 1904
Puck of Pook's Hill London: Macmillan, 1906
Actions and Reactions London: Macmillan, 1910
A Diversity of Creatures London: Macmillan, 1917
The Years Between London: Methuen, 1919
Letters of Travel 1892–1913 London: Macmillan, 1920
Land and Sea Tales for Scouts and Guides London: Macmillan, 1923
A Book of Words: Selections from Speeches and Addresses Delivered Between 1906 and 1927 London: Macmillan, 1928
Limits and Renewals London: Macmillan, 1932

Kipling collections and editions

The Sussex Edition of the Complete Works in Prose and Verse of Rudyard Kipling London: Macmillan, 1937–39

Cohen, Morton (ed.), *Rudyard Kipling to Rider Haggard: The Record of a Friendship* London: Hutchinson, 1965

Eliot, T.S. (ed.), *A Choice of Kipling's Verse Made by T.S. Eliot with an essay on Rudyard Kipling* London: Faber & Faber, 1941

Kipling, Rudyard, *Rudyard Kipling's Verse: The Definitive Edition* London: Hodder and Stoughton, 1940

—— *Early Verse by Rudyard Kipling, 1879–1889: Unpublished, Uncollected and Rarely Collected Poems*, ed. Andrew Rutherford, Oxford: Clarendon Press, 1986

—— *Kipling's India: Uncollected Sketches 1884–6*, ed. Thomas Pinney, Basingstoke: Palgrave Macmillan, 1986

—— *Something of Myself and Other Autobiographical Writings*, ed. Thomas Pinney, Cambridge: Cambridge University Press, 1990

—— *The Letters of Rudyard Kipling*, ed. Thomas Pinney, 6 vols, Basingstoke: Palgrave Macmillan, 1990–2004

—— *The Complete Stalky & Co.*, ed. Isabel Quigly, Oxford: The World's Classics, 1991

—— *Works of Rudyard Kipling* Ware: Wordsworth, 1994 (reproduces text of the *Definitive Verse*)

Other primary texts

Arnold, Edwin, *The Light of Asia or: The Great Renunciation Being the Life of Gautama Told in Verse* London: Trubner, 1879

Benson, E.F., *David Blaize* [1916] London: Hogarth Press, 1989

Brooke, Rupert, *1914 and Other Poems* London: Sidgwick & Jackson, 1915

—— *Letters of Rupert Brooke*, ed. Geoffrey Keynes, London: Faber & Faber, 1968

Gilbert, W.S., *Patience; or, Bunthorne's Bride* London: Chappell, 1881

Gurney, Ivor, *Ivor Gurney: Severn & Somme and War's Embers*, ed. R.K.R. Thornton, Manchester: The Mid Northumberland Arts Group & Carcanet Press, 1997

—— *Ivor Gurney: 80 Poems or so*, ed. R.K.R. Thornton, Manchester: The Mid Northumberland Arts Group & Carcanet Press, 1997

Haig, David, *My Boy Jack* London: Nick Hern Books, 1997

Hibberd, Dominic, and John Onions (eds), *The Winter of the World: Poems of the Great War* London: Constable, 2007

Hopkins, Gerard Manley, *The Poems of Gerard Manley Hopkins*, ed. W.H. Gardner, Oxford: Oxford University Press, 1970

Jones, David, *In Parenthesis* London: Faber & Faber, 1936

Lawrence, D.H., *The Complete Poems*, ed. Vivian de Sola Pinto and F. Warren Roberts, London: Penguin, 1977

Murari Timeri, N., *The Imperial Agent: The Sequel to Rudyard Kipling's 'Kim'* London: New English Library, 1987

Sassoon, Siegfried, *Collected Poems 1908–1956* London: Faber & Faber, 1961

Symonds, J.A., *The Letters of John Addington Symonds, Volume III, 1885–1893*, ed. Herbert M. Schueller and Robert L. Peters, Detroit, MI: Wayne State University Press, 1969

Thomas, Edward, 'War Poetry', *Poetry and Drama, II* [1914], reprinted in *A Language Not to Be Betrayed: Selected Prose of Edward Thomas*, ed. Edna Longley, Manchester: Carcanet Press, 1981
—— *Edward Thomas: The Annotated Collected Poems*, ed. Edna Longley, Tarset: Bloodaxe Books, 2008
Wilde, Oscar, *The Picture of Dorian Gray* [1891], ed. Isobel Murray, Oxford: Oxford University Press, 1981

Secondary texts

Kipling

Allen, Charles, *Kipling Sahib: India and the Making of Rudyard Kipling* London: Little, Brown, 2007
Bayley, John, 'The puzzles of Kipling', in *The Uses of Division* London: Chatto & Windus, 1976
Beresford, George, *Schooldays with Kipling* London: Victor Gollancz, 1936
Bhaskar, K. Rao, *Rudyard Kipling's India* Norman: University of Oklahoma, 1967
Bodelsen, C.A., *Aspects of Kipling's Art* Manchester: Manchester University Press, 1964
Booth, Howard J. (ed.), *The Cambridge Companion to Rudyard Kipling*, Cambridge: Cambridge University Press, 2011
—— and Nigel Rigby (eds) *Modernism and Empire* Manchester: Manchester University Press, 2000
Carrington, Charles, *Rudyard Kipling: A Life* Basingstoke: Macmillan, 1955
Coates, John, *The Day's Work: Kipling and the Idea of Sacrifice* Madison, NJ: Fairleigh Dickinson University Press, 1997
Condé, Mary, 'Constructing the Englishman in Kipling's Letters of Marque', *Yearbook of English Studies* 24 (2004): 230–9
Crook, Nora, *Kipling's Myths of Love and Death*, Basingstoke: Palgrave Macmillan, 1990
Davie, Donald, 'Two of Browning's heirs', 'Thoughts on Kipling's "Recessional"', in *Essays in Dissent: Church, Chapel and the Unitarian Conspiracy*, Manchester: Carcanet, 1995, pp. 153–66, 215–25
Dillingham, William, *Being Kipling*, New York: Palgrave Macmillan, 2008
Gilbert, Elliott L. (ed.), *Kipling and the Critics* London: Peter Owen, 1966
—— *The Good Kipling: Studies in the Short Story*, Manchester: Manchester University Press, 1972
Gilmour, David, *The Long Recessional: The Imperial Life of Rudyard Kipling*, London: John Murray, 2002
Gross, John (ed.), *Rudyard Kipling: The Man, His Work and His World* London: Weidenfeld and Nicolson, 1972
Harbord, R.E. (ed.), *The Readers' Guide to Rudyard Kipling's Work*, 8 vols, Canterbury: privately printed, 1955–66

Holt, Toni and Valmai, *My Boy Jack: The Search for Kipling's Only Son* Barnsley: Leo Cooper, 1998
Husain, S.S. Azfar, *The Indianness of Rudyard Kipling: A Study in Stylistics* London: Cosmic Press, 1983
Husain, Syed Sajjad, *Kipling and India: An Inquiry into the Nature and Extent of Kipling's Knowledge of the Indian Sub-Continent* Dacca: The University of Dacca Press, 1964
Islam, Shamsul, *Kipling's Law: A Study of his Philosophy of Life* Basingstoke: Macmillan, 1975
Kemp, Sandra, *Kipling's Hidden Narratives* Oxford: Oxford University Press, 1988
—— 'The archive on which the sun never sets: Rudyard Kipling', *History of the Human Sciences* 11:4 (1998): 33–48
—— and Lisa Lewis (eds), *Rudyard Kipling: Writings on Writing* Cambridge: Cambridge University Press, 1996
Lancelyn Green, Roger, *Kipling and the Children* London: Elek Books, 1965
—— (ed.), *Kipling: The Critical Heritage*, London: Routledge and Kegan Paul, 1971
Laski, Marghanita, *From Palm to Pine: Rudyard Kipling Abroad and at Home*, London: Sidgwick and Jackson, 1987
Leeb-Lundberg, Waldemar, *Word-Formation in Kipling: A Stylistic-Philological Study* Lund: H. Ohlsson, 1909
Le Gallienne, Richard, *Rudyard Kipling: A Criticism* London: John Lane, 1900
Lewis, C.S., 'Kipling's world', in *They Asked for a Paper* London: Geoffrey Bles, 1961
Lycett, Andrew, *Rudyard Kipling* London: Weidenfeld and Nicolson, 1999
McBratney, John, *Imperial Subjects, Imperial Space: Rudyard Kipling's Fiction of the Native-Born* Columbus: Ohio State University Press, 2002
McClure, John, *Kipling and Conrad: The Colonial Fiction* Cambridge, MA: Harvard University Press, 1981
Maccoby, Hyam, ' "The Family Reunion" and Kipling's "The House Surgeon" ', *Notes and Queries* (February 1968): 48–50
Mallett Philip (ed.), *Kipling Considered* Basingstoke: Macmillan, 1989
—— *Rudyard Kipling: A Literary Life* Basingstoke: Macmillan, 2002
Montefiore Jan, 'Latin, arithmetic and mastery: a reading of two Kipling fictions', in Howard J. Booth and Nigel Rigby (eds), *Modernism and Empire* Manchester: Manchester University Press, 2000, pp. 112–36
—— *Rudyard Kipling* (Writers and their Work) Tavistock: Northcote House, 2007
Moore-Gilbert, Bart, *Kipling and 'Orientalism'* London: Croom Helm, 1986
—— 'Letters of Marque: travel, gender, and imperialism', *Kipling Journal* 281 (March 1997): 12–22
Oulton, Carolyn, ' "ain't goin' to have any beastly Erickin' ": the problem of male friendship in *Stalky & Co.*', *Kipling Journal* 326 (2008): 56–61
Page, Norman, *A Kipling Companion* Basingstoke: Macmillan, 1984
Parry, Ann, *The Poetry of Rudyard Kipling: Rousing the Nation* Bristol: Open University Press, 1992

Plotz, Judith A., 'Latin for Empire: Kipling's "Regulus" as a classics class for the ruling classes', *The Lion and the Unicorn* 17:2 (December 1993): 152–67

Quinn, Vincent, 'Jane Austen, queer theory and the return of the author', *Women: A Cultural Review* 18:1 (2007): 57–83

Raine, Craig, 'Kipling: controversial questions', *Kipling Journal* 304 (September 2002): 10–29

Randall, Don, *Kipling's Imperial Boy: Adolescence and Cultural Hybridity* Basingstoke: Palgrave Macmillan, 2000

Ricketts, Harry, *The Unforgiving Minute: A Life of Rudyard Kipling* London: Chatto & Windus, 1999

Rooney, Caroline and Kaori Nagai (eds), *Kipling and Beyond: Patriotism, Globalisation and Postcolonialism* Basingstoke: Palgrave Macmillan, 2010

Rutherford, Andrew (ed.), *Kipling's Mind and Art* Edinburgh: Oliver & Boyd, 1964

Said, Edward, 'The pleasures of imperialism', introduction to Kipling, *Kim* (Penguin Modern Classics) London: Penguin, 1987

—— *Culture and Imperialism*, London: Chatto & Windus, 1993

Sergeant, David, 'Whispering to the converted: narrative communication in Rudyard Kipling's Letters of Marque', *Modern Language Review* 104:1 (2009): 26–40

Seymour-Smith, Martin, *Rudyard Kipling* New York: St Martin's Press, 1989

Suleri, Sara, *The Rhetoric of British India* Chicago: Chicago University Press, 1992

Sullivan, Zohreh, *Narratives of Empire: The Fictions of Rudyard Kipling* Cambridge: Cambridge University Press, 1993

Tompkins, J.M.S., *The Art of Rudyard Kipling* [1959], 2nd edition, London: Methuen, 1964

Wilson, Angus, *The Strange Ride of Rudyard Kipling* London: Secker and Warburg, 1977

Wilson, Edmund, 'The Kipling that nobody read' [1941], in *The Wound and the Bow: Seven Studies in Literature* London: Methuen, 1962, pp. 94–161

Other criticism and history

Allen, Charles, *God's Terrorists: The Wahhabi Cult and the Roots of Modern Jihad* London: Little, Brown, 2006

Arendt, Hannah, *The Origins of Totalitarianism* [1951] New York: Schocken Books, 2004

Benton, Lauren and John Muth, 'On cultural hybridity: interpreting colonial authority and performance', *Journal of Colonialism and Colonial History* 1:1 (Fall 2000)

Bond, Brian, *The Pursuit of Victory: From Napoleon to Saddam Hussein* Oxford: Oxford University Press, 1996

Bristow, Joseph, *Empire Boys: Adventures in a Man's World* London: HarperCollins, 1991

—— *Effeminate England: Homoerotic Writing after 1885* Buckingham: Open University Press, 1995

Cheyette, Bryan, 'Hilaire Belloc and the "Marconi Scandal" 1900–1914: a reassessment of the interactionist model of racial hatred', *Immigrants and Minorities* 8:1–2 (March, 1989): 131–42

—— *Constructions of 'the Jew' in English Literature and Society: Racial Representations, 1875–1945* Cambridge: Cambridge University Press, 1995

—— 'Neither black nor white: the figure of "the Jew" in imperial British literature', in Tamar Garb and Linda Nochlin (eds), *The Jew in the Text* London: Thames and Hudson, 1995, pp. 31–41

—— (ed.), *Between 'Race' and Culture: Representations of 'the Jew' in English and American Literature* Stanford, CA: Stanford University Press, 1996

—— 'T.S. Eliot and "race": blacks, Jews and Irish', in David Chinitz (ed.), *The Blackwell Companion to T.S. Eliot* London: Blackwell, 2009, pp. 335–50

Cocks, Neil, 'Hunting the animal boy', *Yearbook of English Studies* 32 (2002): 177–85

Das, Sarat Chandra, *Religion and History of Tibet* Calcutta: Baptist Mission Press, 1891

Davids, T.W. Rhys, *Buddhism: Being a Sketch of the Life and Teachings of Gautama, the Buddha* London: SPCK, 1877

Derrida, Jacques, *Archive Fever: A Freudian Impression*, trans. Eric Prenowitz, Chicago and London: University of Chicago Press, 1995

Foucault, Michel, *The History of Sexuality Volume One: An Introduction*, trans. Robert Hurley [1976], London: Penguin, 1990

Fussell, Paul, *The Great War and Modern Memory* [1975] New York: Oxford University Press, 2000

Grosskurth, Phyllis, *John Addington Symonds: A Biography* London: Longmans, 1964

Hai, Ambreen, *Making Words Matter: The Agency of Colonial and Postcolonial Literature* Athens: Ohio University Press, 2009

Hitchens, Christopher, *Blood, Class and Empire: The Enduring Anglo-American Relationship* New York: Atlantic Books, 2004

Holmes, Colin, *Anti-Semitism in British Society, 1876–1939* London: Edward Arnold, 1979

Honey, J.R. de S., *Tom Brown's Universe: The Development of the Victorian Public School* London: Millington, 1977

Houlbrook, Matt, 'Soldier heroes and rent boys: homosex, masculinities, and Britishness in the Brigade of Guards, circa 1900–1960', *The Journal of British Studies* 42:3 (July 2003): 351–88

Howard, Michael, *The First World War: A Very Short Introduction* Oxford: Oxford University Press, 2002

Kaplan, Morris B., *Sodom on the Thames: Sex, Love, and Scandal in Wilde Times* Ithaca, NY: Cornell University Press, 2005

Kerr, Douglas, *Eastern Figures: Orient and Empire in British Writing* Hong Kong: Hong Kong University Press, 2000

Kucich, John, *Imperial Masochism: Fact, Fantasy and Social Class* Princeton, NJ: Princeton University Press, 2006

Lane, Christopher, *The Ruling Passion: British Colonial Allegory and the Paradox of Homosexual Desire* Durham, NC: Duke University Press, 1995

Lelyveld, David, 'Colonial knowledge and Hindustani', *Comparative Studies in Society and History* 35:4 (October 1993): 665–82

MacDonald, Lyn, *1914: The Days of Hope* London: Penguin, 1989

Mufti, Aamer, *Enlightenment in the Colony: The Jewish Question and the Crisis of Postcolonial Culture* Princeton, NJ: Princeton University Press, 2007
Nasson, Bill, *The South African War 1899–1902* London: Edward Arnold, 1999
Platt, Len (ed.), *Modernism and Race* Cambridge: Cambridge University Press, 2011
Pollock, Sheldon (ed.), *Literary Cultures in History: Reconstructions from South Asia* Berkeley: University of California Press, 2003
Priestley, J.B., *The Edwardians* London: Heinemann, 1970
Pykett, Lyn, *Engendering Fiction: The English Novel in the Early Twentieth Century* London: Edward Arnold, 1995
Richards, Thomas, *The Imperial Archive: Knowledge and the Fantasy of Empire* London: Verso, 1993
Ricks, Christopher, *T.S. Eliot and Prejudice* London: Faber & Faber, 1988
Rushdie, Salman, *Imaginary Homelands: Essays and Criticism 1981–1991* London: Granta, 1991
Said, Edward, *Orientalism* London: Routledge, 1978
Symonds, J.A., *A Problem in Modern Ethics: Being an Enquiry into the Phenomenon of Sexual Inversion, Addressed Especially to Medical Psychologists and Jurists* [1891] London: privately printed, 1896
—— 'Soldatenliebe und Verwandtes', in Havelock Ellis and J.A. Symonds, *Das konträre Geschlechtsgefühl* Leipzig: Georg H. Wigand, 1896, pp. 285–304
—— *Soldier Love and Related Matter*, trans. and ed. Andrew Dakyns, Eastbourne: Andrew Dakyns, 2007
Tod, Colonel James, *Annals and Antiquities of Rajasthan* London: Smith and Elder, 1829
Trotter, David, *The English Novel in History 1895–1920* London: Routledge, 1993
Waddell, L.A., *The Buddhism of Tibet or Lamaism* London: Allen & Co, 1895
Warren, Henry Clarke, *Buddhism in Translations* Boston, MA: Harvard University Press, 1896
Wilson, Trevor, *The Myriad Faces of War: Britain and the Great War 1914–1918* Cambridge: Polity Press, 1986
Winter, Jay, *Sites of Memory, Sites of Mourning: The Great War in European Cultural History* Cambridge: Cambridge University Press, 1995
Young, Robert J.C., *Colonial Desire: Hybridity in Theory, Culture and Race* London and New York: Routledge, 1995
Yule, Col. Henry and A.C. Burnell, *Hobson-Jobson: A Glossary of Colloquial Anglo-Indian Words and Phrases, and of Kindred Terms, Etymological, Historical, Geographical and Discursive* London: John Murray, 1886

Online sources

John Radcliffe (general editor), *New Reader's Guide to the Works of Rudyard Kipling*, www.kipling.org.uk
The *Oxford English Dictionary*, online version, www.oed.com
Journal of Colonialism and Colonial History, Project Muse, http://muse.jhu.edu/journals/journal_of_colonialism_and_colonial_history

Index

Note: author's main chapter entries are given in **bold**.

Adam, Ian 199
Albionism 12, 96–7
　see also Englishness
Allahabad (Prayag) 133–4, 138, 185–6
Allen, Charles 8, 13–14, 15, **142–58**
Amber, ruined city of 168
America, Kipling's response to 256, 276–7
　see also racism
Annan, Noel 250, 264
anti-Semitism 7, 10, 12, 17–18, 117, 250–284 *passim*
　see also fascism; Jews; T.S. Eliot; philo-Semitism; pro-Boer liberalism; primitivism
Arata, Stephen 262
archive, concept of
　see also imperialism 218–22
Arendt, Hannah 17, 251–3, 259, 277
Arnold, Edwin, *The Light of Asia* 13–14, 150–1, 153
artistry, Kipling's 1, 45–8, 55, 70, 115–20, 130–1, 160, 165
Auden, W.H. 7, 18, 82

Baldwin, Oliver 230–1, 244 n.22
Bambridge, Elsie (*née* Kipling) 225, 230–1, 244 n.22
'beastliness' 226, 228–31, 242 n.7, 244 n.16
　see also homosexuality
Benton, Lauren 209, 214

Bhabha, Homi 214
Bible 5, 29, 32, 98, 162, 174 n.1, 175 n.16, 254, 267, 275
biographers of Kipling 4–5
biographical criticism of Kipling 5–6, 9–10, 48–56, 113–14
Bloch, Ernst 226
Boas, Franz 196
Boers 24, 61, 65–7, 70
　Kipling's hatred of 24, 65–6, 68
Boondi (Bundi) 14, 163–4, 168, 171–2
Booth, Howard 3, 16–17, **225–49**
Brecht, Bertolt 6, 7
British Empire 24, 28–32, 35–6, 42, 63, 69, 99–101, 117, 149–50, 208, 217, 238, 241–2
　Jews in 257–9, 261–2, 273–8
　see also imperialism; masculinity
Brogan, Hugh 3, 5, 11, **73–90**
Brooke, Rupert 6, 11–12, 17, 79, 91, 98–103
Browning, Robert 5, 53, 102, 112, 115–16, 211
Buddhism, Kipling's interest in 13–14, 150–5, 186
Byron, Lord 43–4, 231

Calcutta 148, 174, 185, 188
Calvinism
　Kipling's dislike of 50, 119, 142
Carrington, Charles 4, 79, 153, 232, 249, 272

Carroll, Lewis 5, 232
  Alice in Wonderland 188
  Through the Looking-Glass 161
Chesterton, G.K. 1, 2, 5, 8–9, **22–7**
  'Chesterbelloc' 270
Cheyette, Bryan 6, 7, 10, 12, 17–18, **250–284**
Chitor, ruined city of 14, 160, 164–71
Christianity 119, 142–3, 154, 161, 171
  versus Judaism 267–8, 274–6
Civil and Military Gazette 143, 145, 159, 221
class antagonism 114
  Kipling's 32, 34, 114
Cocks, Neil 229
Conrad, Joseph, *Lord Jim* 146
conscription, Kipling lobbies for 70, 78
conservatism 39
  Kipling's adherence to 28–30, 39–40, 97, 101, 114, 269–70
Cook, Matt 233, 235–6

democracy
  Kipling satirises 116, 272
Derrida, Jacques 219
Dillingham, W. 178

Einstein, Albert, Kipling disapproves of 273
Eliot, T.S. 2, 18–19 n.7, 28, 32, 37, 68, 72 n.32, 94, 97, 250–1, 254
  see also anti-Semitism 250–2
Englishness 8, 9, 11–12, 25, 68, 70
  idealisation of 79, 94, 96–8, 112–13, 126
  see also Albionism

fables 132–3
  Kipling's 12–13, 45, 116, 130, 137–8

fascism 28–9, 39, 251–4, 278
  see also anti-Semitism
First World War
  Kipling's poetic response to 81–5, 93–4
  Kipling's political response to 5, 8, 10–12, 30, 54, 66, 69, 77–8, 80–3, 86–7, 93–4, 102, 268
  war poets influenced by Kipling 95–8, 103–6
Forster, E.M. 31, 73, 146
Foucault, Michel 226
Frazer, Ken 213
Freemasonry 147, 156 n.8, 162
Friel, Brian, *Translations* 196

Gau-Mukh shrine 14, 160, 166–8, 170, 174, 188
Germany 77–8, 80–2, 86–7
  Kipling's response to 7, 11, 29, 36, 65, 68, 77–87, 98, 253, 273
Gilbert, W.S. 211, 235
Gilmour, David 65, 268–70
Glover, David 272, 284 n.102
Green, Roger Lancelyn 131–2
Gurney, Ivor 6, 11–12, 91, 96–8

Haggard, Henry Rider 2, 143, 257, 274
Hai, Ambreen 178, 184, 199
Haig, David 5, 75–7, 88 n.7
Hall, Radclyffe 16, 231–2
Hibberd, Dominic 91, 94
Hindi language 178–81, 183, 186, 187, 201
  confused with Hindustani 181–2, 192
  relationship with Urdu 179–81
  see also Indian languages
Hinduism
  Kipling's dislike of 13, 144, 148, 150, 186

Hindustani language 15, 17–18, 178–81, 183, 185, 188–90, 193
  Kipling's comic misuse of 190, 196–98
  Kipling's errors in 191–6, 198, 200
  Kipling's knowledge of 188–193, 196–202
  see also Indian languages
Hobson-Jobson: A Glossary 194, 203–4 n.21, n.23
Holt, Tonie and Valmai 75
homosexuality 7, 16–17, 216, 225–49 *passim*
  as sexological category 226, 228–9
  Kipling's attitude to 225–31, 243 n.7, 244 n.16
  see also 'beastliness'; London; masculinity; school; soldiers
Housman, A.E. 73
Husain, S.S. Azfar 184, 191–2
Husain, Syed 184, 193
hybridity 15, 208–10, 214

imperialism 18–19 n.7, 30–1, 250, 218–22
  Kipling as spokesman for 7–9, 15, 24, 28–34, 42, 61–3, 69, 99–101, 138, 163, 173, 208–10, 217–21
  see also archive
Indian languages 15, 177–206 *passim*
  see also Hindi language; Hindustani language; Panjabi; Sanskrit; Urdu
Indian Mutiny ('First Indian Rebellion') 13, 134–7
Indian National Congress 4, 185
Indians
  Kipling's attitudes to 4, 30, 143–4, 161, 163–4, 172–4, 188
Islam (religion) 14, 144–8
Islam, Shamsul 190–1, 203 n.16

Jacobson, Dan 8, 10–11, **58–72**
James, William 42–3, 44, 53–4
Jarrell, Randall 1, 2, 3, 8–10, **42–57**

Jews
  Kipling's attitude to 7, 10, 17–18, 117, 119–21, 250–84 *passim*
  see also anti-Semitism
Jeypore (Jaipur) 163, 167, 187
Jones, David 6, 11–12, 91, 95, 97–8

Karlin, Daniel 6, 10, 12, 14, 17, **111–28**
Kipling, John 5, 63–4, 66, 75–7, 93
Kipling, John Lockwood 3, 131, 134, 147, 149, 150, 157 n.32
Kipling, Rudyard, books by
  Actions and Reactions 8, 12, 95, 96, 111–28
  Barrack Room Ballads 33, 103
  Departmental Ditties 105, 189, 201, 203–4 n.21
  From Sea to Sea 148, 159–74, 186, 256, 273
  History of the Irish Guards in the Great War 2, 87–8
  Jungle Books 2, 14, 41, 54, 116, 130, 137–8, 143, 149, 151, 160, 170–1, 191, 193
  Just-So Stories 62, 160
  Kim 2, 4, 14, 54, 62, 136–7, 143, 145, 148–55, 160, 171–3, 177–9, 190, 195–202, 209–10, 220
  The Light That Failed 16, 30, 237–41
  The Naulahka (co-authored with Wolcott Balestier) 14, 159, 163–4, 170, 173, 188, 194
  Plain Tales from the Hills 44, 122, 197
  Puck of Pook's Hill 2, 9, 11, 17, 62, 89 n.19, 96–7, 99, 126, 241–2
  Rewards and Fairies 96–7, 111, 126, 139–40
  Something of Myself 34, 45–54, 60–2, 98, 131–2, 143, 145–6, 182–3, 221, 260, 276–7
  Stalky & Co. 5, 7, 200, 207–24 *passim*
  The Years Between 92, 93–4, 105

Kipling, Rudyard, journalism of
  'The Bride's Progress' 148
  'The City of Dreadful Night' 174
  'Letters of Marque' 14, 159–74, 186, 256, 273
Kipling, Rudyard, letters of 4, 63, 66, 68, 85, 86, 109 n.56, 113, 144, 159, 161–2, 170, 230, 237, 242–3 n.7, 255, 268–70, 273–4
Kipling, Rudyard, poems by
  'Big Steamers' 77–8
  'The Burden of Jerusalem' 10, 18, 276–7
  'Cities and Thrones and Powers' 1, 99, 101, 126
  'Common Form' 5, 84, 93, 107 n.10
  'Dane-Geld' 36, 109 n.56
  'A Death-Bed' 84, 92
  'The Dykes' 11, 70–1
  'The 'Eathen' 15, 34, 104
  'Follow Me 'Ome' 33, 236
  'For All We Have And Are' 10, 81–3, 92–3, 102
  'Gehazi' 4, 10, 109 n.53, 251, 258, 268–70
  'Gunga Din' 37, 191
  'The Honoured Dead' 59–60
  'If–' 41, 99, 104, 158 n.58
  'In Partibus' 17, 232–5, 239
  'The Islanders' 9, 32, 61, 85
  'Justice' 84, 91, 237
  'My Boy Jack' 6, 63, 92, 106
  'Natural Theology' 85
  'The Outlaws' 83, 92
  'The Rabbi's Song' 267–8
  'Recessional' 29, 83, 98, 105, 143
  'The Return of the Children' 102, 104
  'Rhodes Memorial' 64
  'Road to Mandalay' 36, 37, 41
  'The Run of the Downs' 96
  'The Sergeant's Wedding' 33
  'A Song of the English' 64, 69, 143
  'Song of the Fifth River' 250, 258, 265
  'Tommy' 31, 80, 103
  'The Two-Headed Man' 154
  'The Waster' 10, 252–4
  'The White Man's Burden' 36–7
Kipling, Rudyard, stories by
  'The Army of a Dream' 254–5
  'As Easy as A.B.C.' 47, 272–3
  'Baa Baa, Black Sheep' 5, 183–4
  'Bread Upon the Waters' 264–6
  'Bubbling Well Road' 159, 166–7, 173, 175 n.36
  'The Captive' 109 n.56, 146–7
  'The Church That Was At Antioch' 274–5
  'The Comprehension of Private Copper' 257, 275
  'For One Night Only' 263–4, 265, 267, 271
  'Garm – A Hostage' 114, 116, 122–5
  'An Habitation Enforced' 12, 69, 111–14, 117–121
  'His Chance in Life' 262
  'His Private Honour' 236, 246 n.42, 254–5, 257 n.23
  'The House Surgeon' 10, 12, 14, 17, 117–21, 265–8
  'In Ambush' 212–14, 218
  'Jews in Shushan' 261–2, 264
  'Kaa's Hunting' 168–70
  'The King's Ankus' 164, 168, 170–1
  'Lispeth' 142, 152
  'Little Foxes' 117, 128 n.13
  'The Little House at Arrah' 135, 138
  'The Man Who Would Be King' 117, 128 n.13, 159, 162–3, 173
  'The Manner of Men' 274–6
  'Mary Postgate' 54, 86, 87
  'The Moral Reformers' 221, 244 n.16
  'The Mother Hive' 12, 13, 113, 115–16

Kipling, Rudyard, stories by (cont'd)
  'On the City Wall' 136, 260
  'The Propagation of Knowledge' 220–1
  'The Puzzler' 113, 118, 125
  'Regulus' 221
  'Rikki-Tikki-Tavi' 12–13, 59, 129–141
  'A Sahibs' War' 10, 40 n.11
  'Slaves of the Lamp Part I' 209, 210–11
  'Slaves of the Lamp Part II' 210–11, 215–17
  'The Son of his Father' 182, 200
  'Tods' Amendment' 177, 182, 194, 200, 203 n.9
  'The Treasure and the Law' 10, 17, 258–9, 264–5, 275, 283 n.80
  'The Undertakers' 13, 137–8
  'The United Idolaters' 211–12
  'The Village That Voted The Earth Was Flat' 5, 17, 46, 270–3
  'With the Night Mail' 5, 12, 114–16, 117
Kipling, Rudyard, war writing
  war poems 82–7, 93–4
  war reporting 33–5, 60–1, 87–8
Kipling Journal 75, 88 n.5, 190
Kiplingesque style 99–100
Kucich, John 7, 217–18

Lahore 133–4, 143, 145, 163, 184–6
Lawrence, D.H. 77, 101, 236
Lawrence, T.E. 146
Leeb-Lundberg, W. 190
Lewis, C.S. 8
Lewis, Lisa 8, 12–13, **129–41**
liberalism
  Kipling's dislike of 61, 78, 85, 258, 268–70
Liberal government
  Kipling attacks 78, 85, 268–70, 272–3

London 232–6
  Victorian sub-cultures in 233, 235–6
  see also homosexuality
Lycett, Andrew 4, 111, 126, 227, 230

McBratney, John 7, 15, 208–9
McLure, John 254–5
Mallett, Philip 238
'Marconi Affair' 17, 101, 109 n.53, 268–73
Marlowe, Christopher, *Tamburlaine* 169
masculinity
  Kipling's ideal of 98–100, 233–43, 255
  see also homosexuality; British Empire
Michelangelo 238, 247–8 n.58, 60, 61
militarism 23–4, 32, 70, 86–7
modernism 6, 26, 217
Montefiore, Jan **1–23**, 14, 107 n.10, 166, 192–3, 221–2, **159–76**, 279 n.53
Moore-Gilbert, Bart 163
Mufti, Aamer 260
Muth, John 209, 214
  see also Benton

Nagai, Kaori 3, 7–8, 15–16, **209–224**
  see also Rooney and Nagai

Onions, John 91
Orwell, George 1, 2, 8–10, 17, **28–41**, 253–4
Oudh 136, 160, 174 n.6, 185
Oulton, Carolyn 228

Panchatantra 132–3
Panjabi ('Punjabi') 185–6, 192, 203 n.16
  see also Indian languages
Parry, Ann 93, 107 n.7
Parry, Benita 278 n.5

patriotism
  Kipling's 24, 29–30, 32, 34, 69, 77, 81–3, 85, 114
philo-Semitism 7, 17, 254–7, 259, 268
  see also anti-Semitism
Pinney, Thomas L. 4
Pioneer newspaper 4, 133, 148, 150, 159, 167, 185–6
Plotz, Judith 221–2
poetry 37–8, 79, 82
  Kipling's 1–2, 11, 22, 36–40 ('good bad poet'), 61, 67, 70, 82–5, 96, 99
Primitivism 260, 263–4, 272, 276–7
pro-Boer liberalism 8, 257–9, 272
  see also anti-Semitism

Quigly, Isabel 213
quotations 5, 15–16, 207, 209–17, 220–2

racism 7, 10, 17–18, 28, 34, 61, 65–6, 145, 161, 164, 173–4, 250–84 *passim*
  see also America
Raine, Craig 256
Rajasthan 159–171, 186–8
Randall, Don 7, 15, 207–9
Rhodes, Cecil 32, 58, 62–5, 256
religion
  Kipling's views on 148–55
Richards, Thomas 218
Ricketts, Harry 4, 6, 10–11, 17, **91–110**, 174, 237
Ricks, Christopher 252
Rooney, Caroline and Nagai, Kaori 3, 278 n.5
Rosenberg, Isaac 91, 98
Roy, Arundhati 139
Rushdie, Salman 194, 204 n.7, 260
Rutherford, Andrew 3, 88

Said, Edward 7, 137, 139, 153, 196, 203 n.16

Sanskrit 178, 187, 192
  see also Indian languages
Sassoon, Siegfried 2, 6, 91, 94, 98–9, 100, 102–6
school 210–22, 227–9, 242–3 n.7, 244 n.16
  see also homosexuality
Second World War 38, 74, 81, 87
Sergeant, David 161
sexuality 148
  Kipling's 225–6, 231
Seymour-Smith, Martin 225–6, 232
soldiers 23–4, 32–6, 67, 98, 102–5, 122–4, 199–200, 234–9, 241–2
  see also homosexuality
South Africa 59–70 *passim*
South African war ('Boer War') 24, 60–2, 65–7, 257–9
Spivak, Gayatri Chakravorty 193
Stewart, David 198–9
Suleri, Sara 7, 137
Sullivan, Zohreh 3, 7, 137, 166, 199
Swinburne, A.C. 5, 70, 102
Symonds, J.A. 15, 236–8 n.58, 60, 61

Tennyson, Alfred Lord 1, 34, 36, 38, 102, 162
Thomas, Edward 11–12, 91, 94–6, 98, 102
Thring, Edward 228–9
Tod, Colonel James 165–6, 172, 175 n.29
Todorov, Tsvetan 214
Tompkins, J.M.S. 3, 271
Trilling, Lionel 252–4
Trivedi, Harish 8, 14–15, **177–206**
Twain, Mark 41, 62

Udaipur 160–1, 163, 172
Urdu 178–81, 191–2, 199, 200
  see also Indian languages

vernacular, Indian 47, 178, 181–4, 192
  see also Indian languages

vulgarity
  Kipling charged with 1, 31, 37

Waddell, L.A. 151
Wahhabi Islam 146–7
'Wandering Jew' 259, 274
war poetry 90–110
  Kipling's 81–5, 93–4, 102

Webb, G.H. 77, 191
Wilde, Oscar 1, 99
Wilson, Angus 254
Wilson, Edmund 35, 153, 251–2
Woolf, Virginia 2
Woolford, John 115–16

EU authorised representative for GPSR:
Easy Access System Europe, Mustamäe tee 50,
10621 Tallinn, Estonia
gpsr.requests@easproject.com

www.ingramcontent.com/pod-product-compliance
Ingram Content Group UK Ltd.
Pitfield, Milton Keynes, MK11 3LW, UK
UKHW021847140426
5217IPUK00022B/1638